THE DAILY DISCIPLE

BY CHARLES RICHARDSON

TRILOGY

The Daily Disciple

Trilogy Christian Publishers A Wholly Owned Subsidiary of Trinity Broadcasting Network

2442 Michelle Drive Tustin, CA 92780

Rights Department, 2442 Michelle Drive, Tustin, CA 92780.

Trilogy Christian Publishing/TBN and colophon are trademarks of Trinity Broadcasting Network.

Cover design by: Natalee Groves

For information about special discounts for bulk purchases, please contact Trilogy Christian Publishing.

Manufactured in the United States of America

10 9 8 7 6 5 4 3 2 1

Library of Congress Cataloging-in-Publication Data is available.

ISBN: 979-8-88738-245-6

E-ISBN: 979-8-88738-246-3

The Daily Disciple

Introduction

God has a plan for each of us who are destined to become His followers. The path we are on in this world allows us to choose the direction we take each day. We will either move closer to God with the things we do and the meditations of our hearts, or we will choose to take the path that will lead us away from Him. The purpose of this book is to plant some seeds from God's Word into your heart and mind, which will allow His truth to guide you with a daily message.

My mother had a little red box of "promises," which she kept by the kitchen table. Prior to our eating our breakfast as we began our day as children, we were to draw a card from the middle of the box and read the promise and the corresponding scripture as we sat around the table. We began each day with a message in our hearts from God's Word. After which, we prayed around the table to open our hearts further to listen for the soft whisper of the voice of God.

It is a treasure I hold in my heart today, so many years later, as I reflect on my childhood and my family. Not everyone is blessed with such an upbringing, and I know how fortunate I was to be raised by parents that shared such experiences with our family.

My prayer is that God will allow His Holy Spirit to flow through the words in this book daily with scriptures and thoughts which bring some light to the path for others who read it. The Holy Spirit is inside of each believer to serve as a Comforter and a Guide. Each day when I wrote in this book, I asked God to allow His Holy Spirit to guide me and to have His Word flow through me into the lives of those who read it. Be Blessed as you read God's Word each day.

A New Beginning

So it begins, another trip around the Sun. Each year commences with our hearts filled with hope for a new day. Some look forward to the coming of the new year with great anticipation. Others face the new year embracing fear and discouragement. We can decide to make our plans to gather our energy and improve upon that person we were before. Goals are established by many as they begin the year; some are geared to health and fitness, while others are dedicated to our business aspirations or to our spiritual growth.

We should truly embrace each day as such. Each day brings an opportunity for rebirth and rejuvenation. In the scripture we find in Philippians 3:13–14, the words read, *"Brethren, I count not myself to have apprehended: but this one thing I do, forgetting those things which are behind, and reaching forth to those things which are before, I press toward the mark for the prize of the high calling of God in Christ Jesus."* What a great way to focus our minds on that which is possible in our life's purpose. In the past, we may have come up short of things we wished to achieve, but it is not for us to dwell on that now. Rather, we press on toward the goal of possibilities of discovering God's calling for our lives.

We must embrace the fact that God has a plan for each of us. The Bible speaks about it many times over. We often lose focus on the quest for God's will and purpose for us as the whirlwind of life surrounds us. One of the greatest scriptures in the Bible is Matthew 6:33: *"But seek ye first the kingdom of God and His righteousness and all these things will be added unto you."* May this become a quest for our lives for the new year and beyond.

May this new day and new year rejuvenate you with hope, faith, and a sense of that which is important. May God be with you and bless you on this day.

January 2nd
Daily Disciplines and Focus—The Mind

We have the same twenty-four hours each day, and sometimes they seem to slip away into oblivion. I can recall many days on my journey in which I would come home exhausted from a day of work only to wonder what happened with the time and energy spent. There are so many things that occupy our thoughts and steal us away from that which is important.

Starting a new year, we can change that outcome, but we must do it by taking the year and reducing it to focusing on one day at a time. What is truly important, and are we making it the priority of our life? On this day, that which is important should be our faith journey, our family, our personal health, and finding God's purpose for our time on this earth. What is truly mission critical for today?

Focus on three dimensions of life: Mind, Body, and Spirit. What can we do today to develop and nourish each? Where is your mind taking you today? The Bible teaches us: *"We wrestle not with flesh and blood but against principalities, against powers, against the rulers of darkness of this world" (Ephesians 6:12).* The spiritual battle daily is waged inside of each of us. Ephesians 4:23–24 tells us to *"Be renewed in the spirit of your mind…put on the new man, which after God is created in righteousness and true holiness."* Recognize the battle for your mind is ongoing, and God is with you if you turn to Him on this day to win this battle. Renew your spiritual life each day through prayer and reading His Word.

May you focus on the most important aspects of your life and seek refuge in God's Word so your mind remains focused on God's will for your life on this day. Our spiritual growth and well-being are the most important things we should be devoted to each day.

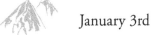

January 3rd

Daily Disciplines and Focus—The Body

Many new year's resolutions are dedicated to the idea of improving our lives by doing that which will allow us to improve our health through fitness and diet. This is another important aspect of who we are. In 1 Corinthians 6:19–20, *"Know ye not that your body is the temple of the Holy Ghost, which is in you, which ye have of God, and ye are not your own? For ye are bought with a price: therefore, glorify God in your body, and in your spirit, which are God's."*

Knowing my body serves as the "temple of the Holy Ghost," what am I doing to sanctify it today? We tend to fall into patterns of behavior that will either make our bodies healthier or bring down our health, which was a gift from God our Father. Exercise or lack thereof and the diet we choose contribute to our body's condition and well-being. In 1 Timothy 4:8, we are taught: *"Physical training is good, but training for godliness is much better, promising benefits in this life and the life to come" (NLT).* We are encouraged to physically train to improve our health but know that spiritual health requires much exercise and disciplines daily as well.

We are the sculptor of who we are along with God our Father, and it is up to each of us as to what we create in our lives, both spiritually and physically. Resolve on this day to be the best person and build the best "temple" you can for the Holy Spirit to live inside. May God Bless you as you choose the path you take today to do what is right for your health.

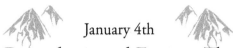

January 4th

Daily Disciplines and Focus—The Spirit

In the book of 1 Corinthians 15:40, the Bible reveals, *"There are also celestial bodies, and bodies terrestrial..."* and it goes on in the chapter to speak of the transformation from death into life with our spiritual body. The journey of life ends with death having no sting to those who have faith and believe in Jesus Christ as our Lord and savior.

What are we doing each day of our faith journey to develop our spiritual strength? As we dedicate ourselves to Matthew 6:33, which reads, *"Seek ye first the kingdom of God and His righteousness and all these things will be added unto you,"* we discover the blessings God has in store for us. In the chapter leading up to this passage, the people around Jesus were wondering what they would eat or drink or wear. I am sure they worried about all the cares of life as we do today. God's message to us is to turn our attention to our spiritual needs first, and those things will be taken care of as we walk with God in our life.

Instill the discipline to spend time with God first each day in your life as you apply this scripture to your daily walk. Devote time to discover the power of God's Word each day, and your journey with Him will become real and intimate. All else becomes secondary to your spiritual walk as you make this your daily discipline. How do you incorporate time with God in your daily journey? Praying is simply talking to God about your life, and those God has placed on your path for that day. May you find the time to bring the words of God into your life each day, and may you be blessed as you spend time in conversation with God all along the way today.

January 5th

Why Am I Here?

Did you ever pause to reflect on why God created mankind or, more specifically, why did he create me? It is not a coincidence that you or I were made to walk on the face of the earth and to interact with those we meet along the way. God has a purpose and a plan for each of us.

The creation of mankind is spoken of in the book of Genesis 1:27, which says that *"So God created man in His own image, in the image of God created He him; male and female created He them."* It is amazing and wonderful to realize we are each created in the image of God. As such, we can appreciate the value of each human life on the planet, which can and should embrace this. We may all be different, yet we are each cut out of the cloth God has chosen for us to wear.

Why, then, we may wonder why did he make us each so uniquely different and what is the purpose of my life? The question has been answered in the scripture in 1 Peter 4:10, which reads, *"As every man hath received the gift, even so minister the same one to another, as good stewards of the manifold grace of God."* The message in this verse is very powerful. We are not all blessed with the same talent. Rather, God has a plan for each of us to be used in serving those he brings to us along the way each day. To live the life filled with purpose that God intends for each of us, we must seek His will through prayer and meditation to embrace our own specific gift and then use it in His service.

May we each seek to discover what gift God has given to us and begin this day to find a way to use it in service to those He has given us on our journey.

January 6th

Talking with God and Listening to His Voice

We must seek God and commune with Him to have the time alone to hear His voice and learn of His will for our lives. Jesus taught us to pray in Matthew 6:6 when He says, *"When you pray, enter into thy closet, and when thou have shut thy door, pray to thy Father which is in secret; and thy Father which sees in secret shall reward thee openly."* So the first lesson of praying effectively is to be alone with God and to speak to him from your heart. It is a time of day which is like no other in the spiritual intimacy you achieve while spending time in prayer with God.

Jesus goes on to give us guidance in our prayer life in Matthew 6:9–13 when he says, *"After this manner therefore pray ye: 'Our Father which art in heaven, Hallowed be thy name. Thy kingdom come, thy will be done in earth, as it is in heaven. Give us this day our daily bread. And forgive us our debts, as we forgive our debtors. And lead us not into temptation but deliver us from evil; For thine is the kingdom; and the power, and the glory, forever. Amen."* This prayer is simple, but it asks God for what we need each day. We need to be forgiven for our own failures and learn to forgive those who have done us wrong along the way.

Praying to God is not limited to a few minutes in the morning or asking for a blessing prior to when you eat. In 1 Thessalonians 5:17, we are taught to *"Pray without ceasing."* The message is to continually speak to our Heavenly Father as we face the challenges and the opportunities of each day. As people are crossing your path and have needs, ask our Father in heaven to meet those needs as you lift them up in prayer as well. God will continue to bless you and reveal Himself to you as you do so.

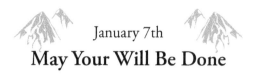

January 7th
May Your Will Be Done

As Jesus taught us to pray, He says, *"May your will be done on earth, as it is in heaven"* in Matthew 6:10. As we take time to pray, it is easy to seek a specific outcome for ourselves and others that we may lift in prayer. We do this based on our own understanding of what we feel would be for best. Our understanding is limited in the grand scheme of life. God's view is omnipotent and can see the picture of all that is to come.

When Jesus Christ faced his final moments and reflected on what was unfolding in the garden in his prayer to God recorded in Matthew 26:39, Jesus prayed: *"O my Father, if it be possible, let this cup pass from me: nevertheless, not as I will but as thou wilt."* We seldom know what is to come in our lives ahead. Jesus knew but also knew of the sacrifice to be made but prayed for God's will to be done regardless. It is a powerful example of how to face the darkest moments of the life we live on this earth.

As we journey, we look forward to mountaintop experiences filled with joy and exhilaration. Spiritually and physically, we have such moments along the way. The daily path we are on between those moments takes us through valleys and darker periods where we deal with sickness and death of loved ones and face personal challenges and adversity. In those moments in time, if we turn to God in prayer and seek His comfort and pray for His will to be done, we can take comfort in knowing He is in full control of our life always. In Matthew 28:20, Jesus said, *"I am with you always, even unto the end of the world."*

Let us take comfort in that promise and pray that God's will be done in our lives today as we walk with Jesus and His Holy Spirit on this day.

January 8th
Ask, and It Shall Be Given to You

Jesus encourages us to pray in His sermon on the mount. In Matthew 7:7–9, He speaks to the multitude, saying:

> *Ask and it will be given to you. Seek, and you will find. Knock and the door will be opened to you. For everyone who asks receives; the one who seeks, finds; and the one who knocks, the door will be opened. Which of you, if your son asks for bread, will give him a stone?*

This is a powerful message from Jesus about speaking to our Heavenly Father about that which we seek for our lives. As our Father in heaven, he wants what is best for our lives.

Be diligent in seeking His will in all that you do. Don't hesitate to reach out in your daily conversations with our Father in heaven to look for the needed guidance for your daily walk with Him. Jesus went on to say in Matthew 7:11, *"If you, then, though you are evil, know how to give good gifts to your children, how much more will your Father in heaven give good gifts to them who ask him."* God wants the best for all of us, and He wants to be there for those who diligently seek Him.

Today, be among those who spend time knocking on the door and seeking that which is a blessing and a gift from God. Know that if you seek Him, you will find and the door He directs you to, and once you knock on it, the door will be opened. It is a promise which Jesus shared with the multitude in His sermon on the mount, and He shares with us today. Be Blessed today on your journey as you seek the path God has for you today. As we are truly striving to find God's presence in our lives, we know He is waiting for us to come to Him with our Love and our requests. He will answer with the Love He has for us as our Heavenly Father.

January 9th

You Have Not Because You Ask Not

What is it that we seek from God in our daily prayer? Is our focus in those moments to ask God for earthly riches or success? What is our motivation in those moments alone with our Heavenly Father? Are we thinking of ways to grow closer in our walk with Him? Are we truly seeking for His will to be done in our lives? If we are devoted to seeking God's will and presence in our life, that is what we will find through dedication to prayer and the reading of His Word. We must understand all scriptures come from inspiration from God. Second Timothy 3:16–17 teaches us: *"All scripture is given by inspiration of God, and is profitable by doctrine, for reproof, for correction, for instruction in righteousness: That the man of God may be perfect, thoroughly furnished unto all good works."* If we seek God through His Word, we will find Him, and He will prepare us to do His work.

Each day of our lives, we begin a new journey that is directed by our Heavenly Father when we ask Him for that direction. We are never alone to discover our path when we ask our God to guide us. When we fail to ask for His guidance, our Father in heaven will let us choose our own path in the darkness of the world around us. Psalm 32:8 teaches us: *"I will instruct thee and teach thee in the way which thou shalt go: I will guide thee with mine eye."*

Let us not be driven by envy and selfish ambition in what we seek from our Heavenly Father on this day. Rather, let us continue to seek His will for us on our journey for this and every day. Be blessed today on your journey and seek His will in your life on this day.

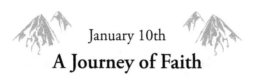

January 10th
A Journey of Faith

We are considering our spiritual life as a journey of faith. What does that mean? What truly is this faith that we speak of? In Hebrews 11:1, faith is described as: *"Now faith is the substance of things hoped for, the evidence of things not seen"* Faith is believing in God and His son Jesus Christ and is the path to finding the will of our Father God by believing on the resurrection of our Lord and Savior Jesus Christ. It is the pathway we take to our heavenly home.

If faith is so critical in our relationship with God, how is it possible to build our faith each day? In Romans 10:17, the Bible tells us that *"So Faith comes by hearing, and hearing by the word of God."* It goes to the essence again of seeking the truth and spending more time in the word of God, which builds our faith. In Hebrews 6:12, we are taught that through faith, we inherit the promises of God: *"But followers of them who through faith and patience inherit the promises."* The ultimate benefit of faith is our salvation. Second Timothy 3:15, *"and from childhood you have known the Holy Scriptures, which are to make you wise for salvation through faith which is in Jesus Christ."*

John 3:16 is the passage that best defines the Love of God and his gift of eternal life through Jesus Christ: *"For God so Loved the world that He gave His only begotten Son, that whosoever believes in Him should not perish but have everlasting life."* The faith journey asked of us by God is very simple. Believe in Jesus as the Son of God who gave His life for the sins of the world, and you will be given the gift of everlasting life. On this day, let us thank God for this gift and embrace the gift of eternal life with joy. Be Blessed on your faith journey on this and every day!

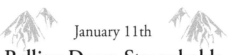# January 11th
Pulling Down Strongholds

We battle daily with the enemy of our soul as he tries to pull us from the path to righteousness. The temptations of the flesh are many, and the devil will try to entice us to seek after the lusts of the flesh and covet that which is not ours. In every life, the evil one will use something which we may desire to divert our thoughts away from the pursuit of God's will for our life.

It is our charge each day to shut out the voice of the evil one and attune our thoughts to the whisper of God. When we allow our thoughts to embrace subtle desires which pull us further from God, we are allowing Satan to create a space in our hearts in which he will try to build his strength and power over our soul. What we know is God is greater and stronger than the evil one, but it is up to each of us to turn our hearts toward God and seek His will!

In the book of 2 Corinthians 10:4, Paul writes a passage that speaks of these strongholds and how to deal with them. *"For the weapons of our warfare are not carnal but mighty in God for pulling down strongholds."* As Paul describes it, we are daily engaging in spiritual warfare. Be armed and ready for it and aligned with the mighty power of God in order to win the battle for your soul. Whatever the battle may be that you are facing today, keep turning your mind and heart to God and seek his will, and you will win the day today.

Romans 6:23 says, *"The wages of sin is death, but the gift of God is eternal life through Jesus Christ our Lord."* Be Blessed on your journey today and give the enemy no place in your heart or mind.

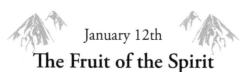

January 12th
The Fruit of the Spirit

The Bible uses the reference of the fruit of the tree as evidence of the spirit of the person. In the book of Matthew 7:15–20, Jesus taught us: *"Beware of false prophets, who come to you in sheep's clothing, but inwardly are ravenous wolves. You will know them by their fruit..."* There are many people who would try to bring influence into your life. Some take the position of leadership in both a spiritual and business position in our life. Are they to be trusted, and should you follow their guidance for you? Look at the fruit of their life and see for yourself if they are the spiritual leaders you would want to follow.

Seek to spend your life around those who demonstrate the qualities which you would want to emulate. The battle we face daily in our spiritual realm is one with the forces of good and evil struggling to win your heart and soul. Be able to recognize that which is coming from the spirit of God and turn your heart in that direction. The Bible teaches us in Galatians 5:22–23: *"But the Holy Spirit is Love, joy, peace, longsuffering, gentleness, goodness, faith, meekness, temperance; against which there is no law."* Jesus often taught us that we would know the tree by the fruit, and one possessing this fruit is of God's Holy Spirit.

When you find yourself behaving in a way that is outside the characteristics of the fruit of the spirit, it may be that we need to ask for God to renew His spirit within us. We should all strive to have the fruit of the spirit in evidence in all that we do each day. It is God's plan for each of us to be filled with His Spirit, and we should ask God for it to be manifest in our lives and as we seek it. Ask, and it shall be given, seek, and you will find it.

May the fruit of the spirit be made manifest in your heart and life on this day! May God Bless you in a special way today!

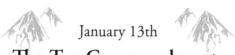

January 13th
The Ten Commandments

When Moses brought the children of Israel out of Egypt, he was guided by God daily as to where He would lead them, as described in Exodus 13:21, *"And the Lord went before them by day in the pillar of a cloud, to lead them the way; and by night in a pillar of fire, to give them light to go by day and night."* Can you imagine the magnificence of the journey with God's presence so real in your life as you walked in His path while focusing on His guiding light and cloud?

Moses was in daily communion with God to seek His direction and guidance. He was the leader God chose to bring His people out of bondage and slavery. During this journey, Moses would go to a private place to talk with God and seek His wisdom and direction. In Exodus 19:20, we are told: *"The Lord came down upon the top of Mount Sinai and called Moses to the top of the mountain, and Moses went up."* May we each be ready to climb to the top of the mountain to meet God when called? Moses lived, ready to always receive God's direction and guidance.

It was in this place, alone with God, that Moses was given the 10 Commandments for the people of God to follow. This was to become the law of those who follow God and seek His favor. God gives this to us in Exodus 20:2–17, in which He says, Have no other Gods before Him. You shall not make idols. Don't take the name of the Lord in vain. Remember the Sabbath Day and keep it holy. Honor your Father and Mother. You shall not murder. Don't commit adultery. Don't steal. Don't lie. Don't covet that which your neighbor has.

These are specific rules God has given us. Our lives should be lived consistent with these commandments every day. These commandments will live forever in our hearts as directives coming from God.

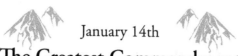

January 14th

The Greatest Commandment

In the book of Matthew 22:36–40, we are told about the Pharisees questioning Jesus about the commandments. One who was described as an expert in the law asked Jesus, *"Master, what is the great commandment in the law? Jesus said to him: Thou shalt Love the Lord your God with all thy heart and with all thy soul, and with all thy mind. This is the first and great commandment. And the second is like unto it. Thou shalt Love thy neighbor as thyself. On these two commandments hang all the law and the prophets."*

Jesus brings all the focus of His message on this to bring us into the spirit of loving one another. This is His powerful commandment for all to follow. In John 13:34–35, Jesus says, *"A new commandment I give you. That ye Love one another; as I have Loved you, that ye also Love one another. By this shall all men know that ye are one of my disciples, if ye have Love one to another."*

It is easy to Love those who are aligned with our way of thinking. Jesus teaches us to Love those who are completely different and who may oppose us and cause us harm. In Matthew 5:44–45, Jesus teaches us,

> But I say unto you, Love your enemies, bless them who curse you, do good to them who hate you, and pray for them who despitefully use you, and persecute you; That ye may be the children of your Father which is in heaven; for He makes His sun to rise on the evil and the good, and sends rain on the just and the unjust.

May we be seen by all as one of the disciples of Christ as we Love one another on this day. May we further be acting as the true children of our Father in heaven while Loving our enemies and praying for those who persecute us this day and every day. be blessed as you share love with all today!

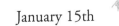

January 15th

May We Dwell in the Spirit of Love Today

We know that the greatest commandment, as clearly stated by Jesus Christ, is to *"Love the Lord your God with all your heart…your mind…and your soul…and…to Love your neighbor as yourself."* With that having been spoken clearly for us to embrace in our lives, what do we do with it? As we start each day, let us commit to refocus on this as our goal for each day.

In the book of Ephesians 5:2, we are told: *"And walk in Love, as Christ also has Loved us, and hath given Himself for us an offering and a sacrifice to God for a sweet-smelling savor."* What a wonderful objective we would have on this day to become a pleasing aroma to God as we walk in Love. Christ gave His entire life to teach us to Love and to teach us to seek the will of God in our lives. The idea of Loving all people we meet along the way is a difficult one for most to embrace. Yet, this is the direction we have been given by Jesus Christ to follow.

We see the directives of this throughout the New Testament of the Bible as the scriptures define the way of life for us. In 1 John 4:7–8, we are taught this: *"Beloved, let us Love one another: for Love is of God, and everyone that Loveth if born of God, and knows God. He that Loveth not knows not God."* That is a very powerful scripture to meditate on and embrace in our hearts. When we love one another, we are filled with the spirit of God. For God is Love. That is the spirit I want to fill my heart and soul on this and every day.

May God bless you and fill your heart with His Holy Spirit of love as you walk on the path God has given you for this day. Be Blessed today!

January 16th
The Great Commission

God has made it clear that we have a great commandment to follow as we make our way on our journey through this life we lead. What then is it that we are to do with this? In this turbulent world in which we live, what is our assignment, and what can we do that would be in God's will for our life.

In Mark 16: 15–16, we are given insight as to what Christ told His disciples just before He ascended into heaven: *"And He said unto them, Go ye into all the world and preach the gospel unto every creature. He that believeth and is baptized shall be saved; but he that believeth not shall be damned."* This was the last directive from Jesus to His closest followers. To extend that to those of us who follow Christ in the world today, we have the same commission. Share the Good News of Christ to those which God brings to the path we are on each day.

We are not all called to be preachers from a pulpit, but rather, our ministry will be the life God gives us to lead. God expects us to talk to others about our faith. In Romans 10:9, we are taught: *"That is thou shalt confess with thy mouth the Lord Jesus, and shalt believe in thine heart that God hath raised Him from the dead, thou shalt be saved."* I want the world to know that this is my belief. On this day and every day, this is the great commission for those of us who are followers of Christ. To tell others about Him in our own way and to demonstrate His Love in the life we live.

May God provide us on this day and every day the opportunity to live the life of Love and to witness our Lord Jesus Christ to others we meet along the way so that they can share this salvation message being given by God. Be Blessed today as you do so!

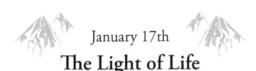

January 17th
The Light of Life

We are all here for a purpose. It is not an accident we were created in God's image and place on this earth. I believe God puts people on our path to help us to discover that purpose and to teach us His way. Correspondingly, the purpose of our life's journey is to assist those He has given to us in finding their place in God's plan as well. Life is not a spectator sport; it is a full contact experience of engagement. We are taught in James 2:20 that *"Faith without works is dead."*

The plan for each of our lives is to fulfill the great commission and to share the gospel of Jesus Christ, and His resurrection message to those God puts on our path. The greatest testimony is made manifest in living a life filled with the spirit of Love. If you walk around without Love in your heart and try to convince others with words alone, the message will carry no value. In John 8:12 (NLT), Jesus said: *"I am the light of the world. Anyone who follows Me will not walk in darkness. He will have the Light of life."* If we are sharing the light of the world with others, we are fulfilling the mission God has for us.

Living with a sense of purpose to bring the message of Christ to others is the highest calling of life. It doesn't mean we are "preaching" to one another as much as it is sharing the true meaning of life to those who God gives to us along the way. Ephesians 5:8 teaches us: *"For once you were darkness, but now you are light in the Lord. Walk as children of Light."* Don't worry about what to say and when to say it; if you truly want to be one who shares the "Light of life," God will give you the words in the moment of truth.

Be Blessed on this day and let the light of life shine through you.

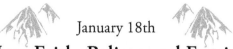

January 18th

Have Faith, Believe and Forgive

On the faith journey of our lives, we are told that all things are possible if we truly believe. Jesus spoke these words in Mark 11:22–26 (NLT):

Have faith in God. I tell you the truth, you can say to this mountain, may you be lifted up and thrown into the sea, and it will happen. But you must really believe it will happen and have no doubt in your heart. I tell you, you can pray for anything, and if you believe that you have received it, it will be yours. But when you are praying, first forgive anyone you are holding a grudge against, so your Father in heaven will forgive your sins, too.

The message is a powerful one on faith and believing. We face many apparent "mountains" in our life. Things that appear to be so big and difficult to overcome that we feel helpless as we deal with them. Jesus is telling us that there is nothing we can't overcome if we truly have faith and believe that God will remove that from our path. The key there is to believe it will be done with no doubt in your heart. The more we trust in God in our lives, the more we evidence the miracles unfold.

Jesus also made it clear that we are to forgive others against whom we hold a grudge in our hearts so the Father in heaven will forgive us of our sins. One of the interesting things about life is when we harbor something in our heart against another; it is our heart and soul which is suffering as a result. Don't dwell on the transgressions of others but free yourself of the burden of their sins. Forgive them and find your heart clear, so you are free to meet with God as you pray without this filter of negativity in your soul.

May we embrace this day with the power of faith and forgiveness, and may you move mountains that are on your path. Be Blessed on this day!

January 19th
The Unlimited Potential of Your Life

We sometimes wonder how we can live life to the fullest. Will our life become meaningful and have an impact of significance on the world in which we live? The enemy of your soul would like to fill your heart and mind with doubts about your ability to achieve such a positive result. Jesus taught us we could move mountains with our faith if we truly believe in that ability. Satan wants us to be limited by doubts.

One of the most empowering and inspiring scriptures in the Bible is found in Philippians 4:13, which says, *"I can do all things through Christ who strengthens me."* The scripture doesn't suggest I am able to do all things on my own, but rather, I can do all things through Christ, who brings me the strength to make that happen. What this tells me is we can all live a life filled with greatness if we choose to follow Christ and seek His will.

If we want a life that is great, we must seek what Jesus directs how that life is to be. In Matthew 20:26–28, He says, *"But it shall not be so among you; but whosoever will be great among you, let him be your minister; And whosoever will be chief among you, let him be your servant. Even so, as the Son of man came not to be ministered unto, but to minister, and to give His life a ransom for many."* It is clear in this message that we are here on earth to serve those who God puts on our path in ways He directs us to serve. We are here to be the light of the world and to spread the gospel of Jesus to others.

May we each find a way to be great in our service to others on this day, and may our light shine brightly with the Love of God in our hearts as we do so. Be Blessed today!

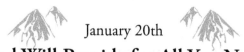

January 20th

God Will Provide for All You Need

The worries of this world will try to work into our hearts and minds. We face issues, trials, and tribulations as we go through life which cause us to fear what is next. Whether it be health, relationships, or money, there is much that occupies time in our minds as we concern ourselves for the future. When we dwell on these worries, our heart is drawn away from God as the devil intends. When your mind engages in such worries, draw close to God and trust in His Word.

We need to take comfort in the scriptures as God watches over us in our lives and guides us with His Holy Spirit. In 2 Corinthians 9:8, we are taught: *"And God is able to make all grace abound toward you; that ye, always having all sufficiency in all things, may abound to every good work."* It is clear in this text that God's plan for each of us is a life of abundance as we draw close to Him and serve others He puts on our path. Philippians 4:19 further states: *"But my God will supply all your need according to His riches in glory by Christ Jesus."* These words give us a wonderful promise of God's gifts which He intends for those who believe in Him and draw close to Him each day.

On this day of our journey and every day, let us live in the fullness of His promises and live the life of faith without fear or worry. We know that God is sufficient to provide for all we need and will do so according to His promises. Be Blessed on this day and be a blessing to those who you meet along the way.

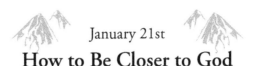

January 21st

How to Be Closer to God

As a believer in God and a disciple of Jesus Christ, we want to find the path that leads us closer to God in our life. All that we do and say should be with the objective of growing closer in our spiritual walk. In the book of James 4:8, the scripture tells us, *"Draw nigh to God, and He will draw nigh to you. Cleanse your hands, ye sinners, and purify your hearts, ye double minded."* It is clearly a battle for the spirit to be torn between the world around us and the God we seek to serve within us. The scripture clearly puts the idea of growing closer to God on us to take the action to move toward Him first. If we do so, He will come closer to us as a result.

What actions could we do today to make that step toward God? We know that the more we read His Word, the better our understanding of the path we must take for spiritual growth. We know that our opportunity to talk with God is there for us, and we should *"Pray without ceasing,"* as told to us in 1 Thessalonians 5:17. When we pray, the book of Psalm 100:4 gives insights into how to draw closer to God when it says, *"Enter His gates with thanksgiving; and into His courts with praise. Be thankful unto Him and bless His name."* The intimacy we seek is found when we take the time to praise God while we pray to Him.

May our hearts seek to be closer to God on this and every day. Today as we pray, may we enter his courts as we give Him thanks for all He has done for us, and as we praise His name, knowing He is worthy of our praise, we will continue to draw even closer to Him in all His majesty. Continue to draw closer to the God we serve each and every day!

January 22nd

What to Focus My Thoughts on Today

Every day brings a whirlwind of activity to occupy our thoughts and mind. We face family issues that can appear at times to be overwhelming at times. Problems come along, and we face the death of loved ones along the way. Life happens with moments of great sadness, wonderful happiness, and some may battle depression along the way. Some that you may know and love could be dealing with this without you knowing it today.

Where do we need to direct our thoughts so we can be on the path God would have for us today? In Philippians 4:8, we are taught: *"Finally brethren, whatsoever things are true, whatsoever things are honest, whatsoever things are just, whatsoever things are pure, whatsoever things are lovely, whatsoever things are of good report, if there be any virtue, and if there be any praise, think on these things."* Too often, we find our thoughts veering off this course to fixate on that which causes us to focus on someone or something that brings us anger and resentment in our hearts.

We sometimes will allow our minds to be unsettled with what we don't have as we long for more in our life. Philippians 4:11 deals with this by saying: *"Not that I speak in respect of want; for I have learned, in whatever state I am, therewith to be content."* It is great to have ambitions for growth in areas of life we can control, but as we work to achieve things for ourselves and our families, we need to be content with all the blessings God has provided for us already.

As we go through this day, God has given us, fix our thoughts on that which is excellent, and may we be content with what we have. Be Blessed on this day!

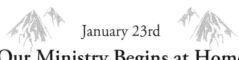

January 23rd

Our Ministry Begins at Home

We know that Christ commissioned us to share with others the gospel message in Mark 16: 15 when He said, *"Go ye into all the world, and preach the gospel to every creature."* The spreading of this gospel message begins with those God has given us in our home. In a home in which the father and mother are believers, it is incumbent upon each to bring the gospel message to the children and to teach them the path to righteousness.

One of the great scriptures in the Bible for parents is found in Proverbs 22:6, which says, *"Train up a child in the way he should go, and when he is old, he will not depart from it."* This was a teaching that was dear to the heart of my mother. I heard her recite it many times as a child. I was blessed in the respect of having God-fearing parents. On the path of my life, there were times when I chose to do and say things that were not consistent with the teachings of my parents, but God would put in my heart those messages which I had learned as a child to lead me back to the path to seek His will.

First Timothy 5:8 stresses the importance of the role of the parent in this responsibility when it says, *"But if any provide not for his own, and specially for those of his own house, he hath denied the faith, and is worse than an infidel."* The mission field of our life's ministry begins at home.

It is unfortunate that not all people were fortunate enough to grow up in a home with parents rooted in the word of God. Hence, the need to *"go out into all the world to preach the gospel"* to reach and teach those who are lost. God puts people on our path for such an opportunity. Let us embrace that opportunity when it comes along. May you be a blessing to your family today!

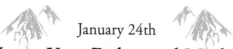

Honor Your Father and Mother

To honor your father and your mother is a commandment of God and is described in His Word as a law. This commandment is spoken of two times in the Old Testament and in five separate scriptures in the New Testament. Moses wrote of it in the books of Exodus and Deuteronomy. In both books, he wrote of a promise along with the commandment. In Deuteronomy 5:16, it says, *"Honor thy father and thy mother, as the lord thy God hath commanded thee. That thy days may be prolonged, and that it may go well with thee, in the land which thy Lord thy God giveth thee."* It is a beautiful promise for those who do so.

Paying honor to those who have brought you into this world and have guided your life through your childhood, and taught you lessons to enable you to be a man or a woman is easy for some. Having been raised in a family in which love was abundant, and the teaching of God's Word was a common practice, it has been easy to fulfill this commandment with joy in my heart. Others have not been as fortunate, and I understand the challenge you face if a parent or both were not among those who could freely share love and support you as you grew up. The scripture does not condition this commandment on whether the parents were good to you or not. It simply says to honor them in any case.

In Matthew 15:4 and Mark 7:10, the Bible speaks of a major consequence of disrespecting parents: *"For Moses said, Honor thy father and thy mother; and whoso curses father or mother, let him die the death."* That is a dire warning to maintain a spirit of honor for those who brought us into the world. We face the promise of a long, full life by obeying this commandment or the other consequences of death if we do not. Ephesians 6:2–3 says it clearly: *"Honor thy father and mother; which is the first commandment with a promise; that it may be well with thee, and that thou mayest live long on the earth."* Be Blessed today as we honor the parents, which were given to us on this earth.

January 25th
Walk with God Today

On this day, we have an opportunity to embrace the reality that God Loves us and wants to be close to us. It is up to each of us to take steps toward that reality and to spend our time drawing closer to the God we serve. It is His desire to walk with us and to talk with us if we are willing to do so as well. In the book of Micah 6:8, the prophet speaks to us, saying: *"He hath shewed thee, O man, what is good; and what doth the Lord require of thee, but to do justly, and to Love mercy, and to walk humbly with thy God."* In the words of the prophet, we are directed that God requires that we walk humbly with Him. In order to do so, we must humble our hearts to all dealings we have with those we meet each day.

Proverbs 20:7 teaches us that: *"The just man walketh in his integrity; his children are blessed after him."* Our walk with God is further discussed in Joshua 22:5, which says this: *"...Love the Lord your God, and to walk in all His ways, and to keep His commandments, and to cleave unto Him, and to serve Him with all your heart and with all your soul."* The directive is clearly given, we are to walk with integrity doing what is right, obeying His commands, being humble as we serve God with all our heart and soul. By doing so, we are walking with God at our side, and He will direct our paths toward righteousness.

It is a beautiful commitment to make in our spirit *each* day. Walking alongside God with His Holy Spirit in our heart as we approach each challenge we face. The opportunities which await us on such a journey are unlimited. May God give us the strength and desire to walk with Him on this day. Be Blessed today as you do so!

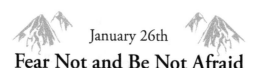

January 26th

Fear Not and Be Not Afraid

We face many fears in life as we go through the different stages. As children, we may fear the dark or the monsters under our beds as we lie alone in our rooms. In teenage years, we may have fears about relationships and acceptance of others. As adults, the fears may shift to those of money and security or health of ourselves and others whom we care about. As we age further, some fear the coming of the end of their time on earth, and death may afflict us.

When we dwell in the spirit of fear, we are not in a place God wants us to be. In Deuteronomy 31:6, the scripture reads: *"Be strong and of good courage, do not fear or be afraid of them; for the Lord your God, He is the one who goes with you. He will not leave you nor forsake you."* God does not give us the spirit of fear. It is the work of the enemy of our soul. In 2 Timothy 1:7, we are taught: *"For God has not given us a spirit of fear, but of power and of love and of a sound mind."* As we read the words of how God addresses fear, we see He has not put it in our mind. Those thoughts are attempts of the devil to take you away from God and away from the power of love and of a sound mind.

The only fear that is healthy is a respectful fear of the Lord. Proverbs 1:7 teach us: *"The fear of the Lord is the beginning of knowledge; but fools despise wisdom and instruction."* We are to "fear" the Lord out of respect and honor for His greatness and power over this universe in which we live. No other fear should occupy your heart, knowing God is with you on this day and every day. Be strong and of good courage as you walk on your path today. Be Blessed today!

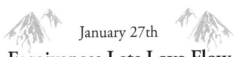

January 27th
Forgiveness Lets Love Flow

In life, we have many experiences with those we meet along the way, which result in anger and disappointment as a result of the way we are treated. As a result of the conflict, we carry in our hearts feeling of resentment and often want confirmation we are right in feeling the way we do. In doing so, we carry the burden of this experience within us, and it becomes a source of sorrow and pain. The interesting part of the experience is the person responsible for this is likely to be oblivious of the pain they have caused.

Rather than carry this burden inside, the scripture teaches us to release it through forgiveness. In the Lord's prayer, we are taught to ask for forgiveness of our sins as we forgive those who sin against us. That is a key lesson and a pray which we should have in our hearts every day. Ephesians 4:31–32 clearly says this: *"Let all bitterness, and wrath, and anger, and clamor, and evil speaking, be put away from you with all malice; And may you be kind to one another, tenderhearted, forgiving one another, even as God for Christ's sake hath forgiven you."* The beauty of forgiveness is that it clears our heart of the energy that produces such bitterness and anger, and it frees us up to embrace a tender heart for those who have sinned against us and replaces bitterness with Love.

Proverbs 17:9 (NLT) says, *"Love prospers when a fault is forgiven but dwelling on it separates close friends."* We can choose to carry this anger and hurt or be free from it in our heart. To allow Love to prosper and grow should always be our objective in the human relationships we have. Let us allow that to occur in all that we do on this day. The power of forgiveness enables love to prosper and our hearts to be free of burdens that separate us from those we are to love. Be Blessed today as you forgive those who have sinned against you.

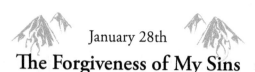

January 28th
The Forgiveness of My Sins

One thing is clear, and that is that mankind has a sinful nature. Temptation is part of the journey we are on, and even Jesus was tempted by the evil one in his lifetime. As a result, we have all yielded along the way to those temptations and have sinned. Romans 3:23 says it clearly: *"For all have sinned and come short of the glory of God."* This fact doesn't mean we are bad people; it simply means we are human. We face each day with a reality that the forces of evil will tempt us again to do that which is not in God's will for our lives.

The Bible teaches us to confess our sins to God, and He will forgive us. In 1 John 1:9, we are taught: *"If we confess our sins, He is faithful and just to forgive us our sins and to cleanse us from all unrighteousness."* We want to be free of the sins of our past, so we can walk on the path of righteousness with God each day. In Acts 3:19, the scripture also speaks about the power of confession and forgiveness when it says, *"Repent ye, therefore, and be converted, that your sins may be blotted out when the time of refreshing shall come from the presence of the Lord."* Anything that separates us from God is a sin. The evil one is alive and trying to do that every day in your life. God Loves us and wants us to be close to Him daily on our walk. When you pray, ask forgiveness for sins you have committed, and He will be just, and He will forgive you. It is written in His Word as a promise.

May this day be a day in which we ask for God's forgiveness of our sins and forgive those who have sinned against us. It will bring us closer to the presence of God as we do so. Be Blessed today!

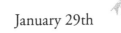

January 29th

The Search for Joy and Happiness

As we go through the daily struggles of our life, we seek ways to achieve joy and happiness through efforts of our own. There is a degree of happiness that comes from the things we accomplish and the homes in which we live or the possessions we acquire along the way. The things of life are clearly temporal and will lose their luster as we seek deeper experiences. True joy comes from our faith and relationship with God through Jesus Christ, our Lord and Savior. It is the only path to joy that is true and lasting.

First Peter 8:9 speaks to us about how joy comes to us through our faith and Love for Jesus: *"Whom, having not seen, ye Love; in whom, though now ye see him not, yet believing ye rejoice with joy unspeakable and full of glory. Receiving the end of your faith, even the salvation of your souls."* We have nothing that will take the place of our faith and Love for the one who gave His life for our sins when it comes to finding joy and happiness in life. Anything else will leave us wanting more.

There are times we face issues and need to find hope and joy to deal with the challenges of that moment in our life. Romans 15:13 gives us a path to reach that: *"Now the God of hope fill you with all joy and peace in believing, that ye may abound in hope through the power of the Holy Ghost."* May the power of the Holy Spirt bring you an abundant hope and fill you with joy and peace on this day, and may happiness fill your heart with songs of praise to God. Be Blessed today in all that you do!

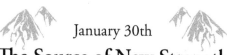

January 30th
The Source of New Strength

Each day we fight battles in our life that take a toll on our strength. The battles we face in business or school and the ones which result from interpersonal relationships, which become strained, cause us to grow weary and can take away our joy in those moments. If we try to work things out on our own, we can become overwrought and depleted of the energy needed to win such battles. Fortunately, for those who are believers, we have a source of strength to carry on victoriously in our life.

One of my favorite scriptures speaks to this in Isaiah 40:31, which says, *"But they who wait upon the Lord shall renew their strength; they shall mount up with wings of eagles, they shall run and not grow weary, and they shall walk and not faint."* The image of this verse is a beautiful message for our soul. Our God is the source of our strength and will carry us through all the darkest moments of our life. He will lift us up and give us the power to overcome any challenge we face. The key is to trust in the Lord for the strength we need to win our battles.

Isaiah 41:10 goes on to say: *"Fear thou not, for I am with thee: be not dismayed for I am thy God. I will strengthen thee, yea, I will help thee; yea, I will uphold thee with the right hand of my righteousness."* What an amazing promise coming from our God! If we have the faith in the God we serve, we will not fear anything that comes our way in life. He will fight our battles with us. May the power of His promise renew your strength and take away any fear you might have as you face this new day. Soar high on wings of eagles and be victorious in all you do today!

January 31st
May Peace Be in Your Heart

When the scripture describes the fruit of the spirit in Galatians 5:22: *"But the fruit of the Spirit is Love, joy, peace…"* Peace is among the first three attributes of the Holy Spirit mentioned. In this turbulent world of stress and conflict, peace is often a missing ingredient in our lives. Wars and rumors of war are always present on the evening news, and the evidence of the enemy surrounds us in the form of evil we witness on our journey through life.

One of the great blessings of those who believe in God and follow the path to righteousness is the gift of peace. We are taught in 1 Peter 3:11 to seek peace in all we do: *"Let him eschew evil, and do good; let him seek peace."* Finding peace in our world requires affirmative action on our part, even though it is a gift from God. Matthew 5:9 lets us know how important those who make peace are in God's eyes: *"Blessed are the peacemakers, for they shall be called the children of God."* When we are the ones who are making the peace in those situations where there is conflict, we are the ones God calls His children! Let us all strive to be among the ones God calls as such.

James 3:18 speaks to the harvest of those who sew seeds of peace: *"And the fruit of righteousness is sown in peace of them that make peace."* The yield is righteousness as the fruit of peace being sown is a wonderful promise for those who choose to bring peace to all relationships along the pathway of our lives. Hebrews 12:14 directs us further to seek peace with everyone: *"Follow peace with all men, and holiness, without which no man shall see the Lord."* May the peace that God gives us to fill your heart as you go through this and every day!

February 1st
Patience Is a Virtue of the Holy Spirit

When the Bible speaks to us about the fruit of the Holy Spirit, it lists love, joy, peace, and then forbearance. The definition of forbearance is having patient self–control and tolerance of others. The Bible teaches us we will know the tree by the fruit, and as such, we should strive to foster and develop these attributes of the Holy Spirit in our life. For many who have a "Type-A" personality like me or those who are simply driven to achieve much in their respective lives, being patient is not always an attribute that is easy to practice. I am challenged every day to establish and maintain this in my life. Whether it be driving or simply standing in line waiting for service in a restaurant or a store, our patience is being tested each and every day in some way.

Ephesians 4:2 guides us with these words: *"With lowliness and meekness, with longsuffering, forbearing one another in Love."* Live with the understanding that being humble and gentle and investing kindness into the lives of others yields a tremendous return on your investment. The enduring of the faults of others and making allowance which gives you the power to move past them results in a flow of love between you and others. It is the manifestation of God's Holy Spirit in your life.

As we are patient with others, we are also investing in doing that which is right as directed by God. First Corinthians 13:4 says it best with respect to patience as a byproduct of charity which is another word for Love: *"Charity suffereth long, and is kind; charity envieth not; charity vaunteth, not itself, is not puffed up."* The more we show evidence of our patience, the more we dwell in the spirit of Love which is where God resides. Don't get engulfed in the anxiety of the moment, and let the Holy Spirit guide you to a place of love, joy, peace, and patience on this and every day! Be blessed today as you allow His Holy Spirit to engulf you in all you do!

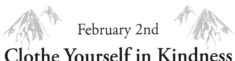

February 2nd

Clothe Yourself in Kindness

Another of the characteristics of the Holy Spirit, as described in Galatians 5:22, is the fruit of kindness which will be manifest in those who walk in this spirit. People all around us daily are experiencing fears and anxiety as a result of things happening in their world. Often those influences are not seen by us as we spend our time with them. The world is hungry for words of encouragement and gestures of kindness. As God calls us to be the light of the world, we need to embrace such opportunities to spread kindness to all we meet daily.

We are directed to 1 Colossians 3:12: *"Put on, therefore, as the elect of God, holy and beloved, bowels of mercies, kindness, humbleness of mind, meekness, long suffering."* Imagine the impact you will have on others who you meet with such a spirit in your heart. We live in a difficult time with a world filled with stress as the storms of life surround us each day. During it all, you are placed on a path by God to encounter those along the way who need a touch from the God we serve. A bit of compassion, kindness, humility, gentleness, and patience can change their life for a moment and plant the seeds of God's Love in their heart for this day. May God use us all in changing the heart of one who is oppressed today. In doing so, we change the world for better.

Job 6:14 teaches us that anyone who withholds kindness from a friend forsakes the fear of the almighty God we serve. We have a responsibility to be kind to others as God has been kind to us in giving us a path to salvation in Jesus Christ. If we are to be his people, we are to clothe our life in the spirit of kindness on this day. Be kind as you meet those on your journey today, and Be Blessed in doing so.

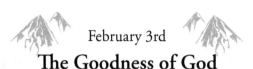

February 3rd
The Goodness of God

The Bible teaches us how God has blessed and protected us with His goodness throughout history. In Exodus 33:19, the word says, *"And He said, 'I will make all my goodness to pass in front of you, I will proclaim the name of the Lord before thee; and I will be gracious on whom I will be gracious, and I will show mercy on whom I will show mercy."* God journeyed with His chosen people then as He does today, as He has sent His Holy Spirit to be with us always. We need to embrace His presence and strive to achieve His will for our life as our own.

The goodness of God is manifest in His protection and His Love and mercy. In Psalm 23:6, David wrote: *"Surely goodness and mercy will follow me all the days of my life, and I will dwell in the house of the Lord forever."* David was a man after God's own heart, and his words were written as messages of Love to our Heavenly Father. We know God blessed him as he chose his lineage to be that in which Christ was born. May our hearts open to such an intimacy in our relationship with God in praise and worship.

In 2 Peter 1:5, we are directed to follow on this path to grow closer to God: *"Whereby we are given unto us exceeding great and precious promises: that by these ye might be partakers of the divine nature, having escaped the corruption that is in the world through lust. And besides this, giving all diligence, add to your faith virtue; add to your virtue knowledge; And to knowledge temperance; and to temperance patience; and to patience Godliness."* As we continue to strive to be the person God would have us to be on this day, we seek to bring goodness into all we do and to further add to our depth of knowledge in the reading of God's Word. As we do this, we will grow closer in our walk with God and be blessed accordingly. May this day be filled with goodness and Love in your heart for everyone you meet on your journey.

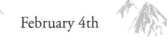

February 4th

May We Be Faithful as God Is Faithful to Us

One of the characteristics of the Holy Spirit being alive in our hearts, as described in Galatians 5:22, is faithfulness. In this context, we know that it means to be faithful to the God we serve in all things we do. One thing we can and should know is that God is faithful to us as His people. In 2 Timothy 2:13, the scripture reads: *"If we believe not, yet He abided faithful; He cannot deny Himself."* God Loves you and me, and He chose us to be His people. If we simply accept Jesus Christ as our savior, you and I are given the gift of salvation from our faithful God who has always Loved us. This is a gift from the one who created us and has always been faithful to us.

The Bible further speaks of God's faithfulness to us in 1 Corinthians 1:9 when it says, *"God is faithful, by whom ye were called unto the fellowship of His Son, Jesus Christ."* That is simply our calling in this life. To be in fellowship with Jesus Christ our Lord. The Bible further says in 2 Thessalonians 3:3: *"But the Lord is faithful, who shall establish you and keep you from the evil one."* God stands with us and will strengthen and protect us from the one who tries to steal our soul.

As God is faithful to us, so must we be each day in our walk with Him. 1 Corinthians 4:2 says, *"Moreover it is required in stewards that a man be found faithful."* Being faithful is simply remaining steadfast in your faith in God regardless of the circumstances you face in life. Know that God walks with you in every moment. At the end of our journey, when we pass through the veil of death, we want to hear those words spoken in Matthew 25:23: *"His lord said unto him, 'Well done, good and faithful servant; thou has been faithful over a few things, I will make thee ruler over many things; enter thou in to the joy of thy Lord."* May we journey on this day with a faithful spirit, and may God's will be done in our life this day and throughout all the days of our lives.

February 5th

God Wants Us to Be Happy

There are many times when happiness seems to be elusive in our life. We deal with many issues along the way which cause us stress and pain. Some of life is difficult to bear, whether it be the result of financial stress, human suffering from sickness, or perhaps the death of a loved one. Many things pull us from the happiness of life as we go from day to day. We have to lift those up in our prayers each day that God puts on our path as we know all will be dealing with some issues which may pull them down emotionally and/or physically as well.

In Psalm 144:15, the writer says, *"Happy is that people, whose God is the Lord."* So many people walk through life without a God present in their journey to strengthen them. It is easy to see how they become lonely and sad when troubles occur. For those of us who have chosen a path with God alongside, we should find happiness in everything that happens, knowing it will work together for good. Romans 8:28 is a marvelous scripture that teaches us: *"And we know that all things work together for good to them that Love God, to them who are called according to His purpose."* The beauty of the scripture tells us we know all things are working for our good. We don't just have to hope it is true.

Being confident in God's plan for you is a key to being happy in all that happens. The more we share Love with others as we go through this life, the happier we will become. The spirit of God is Love, and that is the spirit we must strive to be filled with as we live this life. 1 John 3:18 says, *"My little children, let us not Love in word, neither in tongue, but in deed and in truth."* The more we sincerely feel Love for one another and the more we take action to express that Love, the more happiness we will experience and realize joy on our daily journey in this life. That is God's ultimate plan for each of us. May you find true happiness and joy on this and every day! Be Blessed today!

February 6th

Choose Your Friends Wisely

It is God's plan for our life that we would have friends. In Proverbs 27:9, the scripture reads: *"Ointment and perfume rejoice the heart, so doth the sweetness of a man's friend.."* It will be good for your soul to be blessed with others who are there for you to bring such refreshment as you live your life. We are made for companionship and Love. As we read the Bible verses about friendship, we discover how our friends are there to bring Love, encouragement, and support in our most difficult times. They are with us to celebrate our victories and to lift us up in our times of defeat.

The Bible speaks of true friends and cautions us on those who might not be. Proverbs 18:24 says, *"A man that hath friends must show himself friendly; and there is a friend that sticketh closer than a brother."* Later in Proverbs 22:24–25, we are cautioned: *"Make no friends with an angry man; and with a furious man thou shalt not go; Lest thou learn his ways and get a snare to thy soul."* We take on characteristics of those we spend our time with. Proverbs 13:20 teaches us: *"He that walketh with wise men shall be wise; but a companion of fools shall be destroyed."* There are many scriptures guiding us on the choice of who we call our friends. The book of Proverbs, which was written by Solomon, who was known for his wisdom, speaks often about the influence of friends on your life.

True friends are treasures for us in our life. As the scripture says, they refresh our soul. Proverbs 17:17 says it this way: *"A friend Loveth at all times, and a brother is born for adversity."* God puts us together to help when needed and to share Love always with one another. We are here to support one another always. 1 Thessalonians 5:11 says, *"Wherefore comfort yourselves together, and edify one another, even as also ye do."* True friends are a great value in our life. May God Bless you with many true friends as you journey on this day.

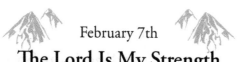

February 7th

The Lord Is My Strength

Every day we live, we face new challenges and opportunities. We are dealing with similar situations each day, but unexpected and difficult challenges come along in our life. It is easy to feel tired and overwhelmed when facing the stresses of life, whether they come in the form of sickness, either physical or emotional, financial stress, or that which comes from interpersonal relationships which are being tested. We want to always live on the mountaintop, but our journey includes much time walking through the valleys between those mountaintop experiences. Friends are often there to lift us up during such times. However, they are limited in what they can do to build us and restore us.

A great scripture that brings encouragement and strength is found in Psalm 28:7, which says, *"The Lord is my strength and my shield; my heart trusted in Him, and I am helped; therefore, my heart greatly rejoiceth, and with my song will I praise Him."* Take joy in the Lord, and He becomes your strength in whatever you might face in life. As you put your trust in God, you find the path to overcoming all obstacles you face in life. Turning to the scriptures gives you an understanding of how to increase that trust and faith. Isaiah 40:29 says, *"He giveth power to the faint; and to them who have no might he increaseth strength."* We may not always be strong in all that we do, but the God we serve is mighty, and His strength will carry us when we are weak.

Let us lift each other up with our prayer so that God gives strength to those we Love as well as to ourselves each day. Intercessory prayer for one another is a powerful way to keep those God has given you in a place of strength in their life. Ephesians 3:16 tells us, *"That He would grant you out of the riches of His glory, to be strengthened with might by His spirit in the inner man."* May you draw your strength from our Heavenly Father on this day and be Blessed!

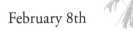

The Blessing of Finding Your Soulmate

The search for the spouse God has chosen for you is one of the most important missions we have in this world. God has intended for a man and woman to find happiness together in their time on earth. It is His perfect plan for many to have one to share the journey alongside. Others may find the life of solitude in service to our Lord and Savior Jesus Christ one which is fulfilling and complete. Seek God's will and purpose for your life as you choose the path for you.

In Matthew 19:5, we are taught: *"For this cause shall a man leave father and mother and cleave to his wife; and they twain shall be one flesh."* This unity, when blessed by God and abiding in His spirit, is one of the greatest experiences a man and woman can find on this earth. In Genesis 2:18, as part of the creation story, God says, *"And the Lord God said, 'It is not good for the man to be alone; I will make him a help meet for him."* God saw the need for this partnership and the value of what it would bring as man and woman were created in the beginning.

For this to be a blessed and uplifting relationship, we have responsibilities to one another. The relationship between husband and wife should be centered on Love. Ephesians 5:33 directs us: *"Nevertheless, let every one of you in particular so Love his wife even as himself, and the wife see that she reverences her husband."* Love is the key to success for both husband and wife to fulfill their marriage vows and to live a life filled with happiness. Proverbs 18:22 tells us this: *"Whoso findeth a wife findeth a good thing and findeth favor from the Lord."* I was among those who was able to find a wife who brought me favor from the Lord, and I have been blessed as a result. May your life be made complete in this way as God's plan unfolds for you.

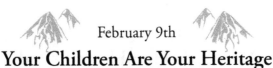

February 9th

Your Children Are Your Heritage

As you seek your purpose on this earth and determine the will of our Father in heaven, we may be chosen by God to have the blessing of children in our life. Not all receive this calling and/or blessing and their purpose in life is different according to the calling God has for them. If you receive the blessing of being a parent, know that it is a purpose like no other. God has placed the sacred trust of a young soul in your care, and it is your duty, above all else, to nurture it and raise it to become a man or woman rooted and grounded in the faith.

Psalm 127:3 describes children as: *"Lo, children are a heritage of the Lord, and the fruit of the womb is His reward."* As a parent, it is our duty to teach our children the commandments and directives of our God. In Deuteronomy 6:6–7, we are told: *"And these words I command thee this day shall be in your hearts. And thou shalt teach them diligently unto thy children and shall talk of them as thou sittest in thine house, and when thou walkest by thy way, and when thou liest down, and when thou risest up."* The message is clear as a parent, present God's Word and the teaching of Christ to our children always. Proverbs 23:24 speaks to the reward of raising a child who embraces his faith: *"The father of the righteous shall greatly rejoice; and he that begetteth a wise child shall have great joy of him."* Fulfill the duties as a parent, and the reward of great joy will come from the child you raise. Your heritage is what will pass on to future generations.

May God bless you with a loving and deep-rooted relationship with the children He gives you. May each day bring you opportunities to express your Love for those children and to strengthen your bond in Christ. Be Blessed today in those relationships.

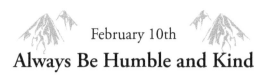

Always Be Humble and Kind

There is a great song by Tim McGraw with this title, and the words of the song carry a powerful message about life. If you have not heard it, I recommend that you do so. Possessing and demonstrating these virtues of humility and kindness brings us closer to being God's people. In Colossians 3:12, the scripture reads: *"Put on therefore, as the elect of God, holy and beloved, bowels of mercies, kindness, humbleness of mind, meekness, longsuffering."* The spirit of God's chosen people is to embrace the world in such a way we are caring and loving those with whom we come in contact in our lives.

As we deal with human relationships, we have many occasions in which people have sinned against us or treated us in a way that appears to be unkind or wrong. In those moments, we are tested. The human instinct is to struggle and attempt to prove we are right and the other is wrong. The Bible directs us in 1 Peter 4:8: *"Above all have fervent charity among yourselves; for charity shall cover a multitude of sins."* The attributes of Love or charity are written about in 1 Corinthians 13:4 as it shares with us: *"Charity suffereth long, and is kind; charity envieth not; charity vaunteth not itself, is not puffed up."* The human mind and spirit tell us to win when we face these moments; the Holy Spirit teaches us to let Love flow and move past them while Loving each other always.

The spirit of humility in our life is desired by God. For us to grow closer to being called God's people, we should always be humble and kind. In Psalm 14:4, the Word teaches us: *"For the Lord takes pleasure in His people; He will beautify the meek with salvation."* May your walk today be one that is both humble and kind to those who God puts on your path, and God will take pleasure in you!

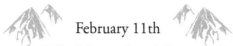

February 11th
The People We Meet Are Not an Accident

God puts us in a place each day to minister to one another. People are directed to us as teachers and spiritual guides, and some are brought to us for us to serve in a way that furthers the message of Christ. We are given opportunities to tell others about the story of Christ and how we can live eternal life if we embrace the moment and do so. First and foremost, our life is to be an example of how the spirit of Love is alive in all that we do.

In Hebrews 12:1, the Bible describes our life this way: *"Wherefore seeing we also are compassed about with so great a cloud of witnesses, let us lay aside every weight, and the sin which doth so easily beset us, and let us run with patience the race that is set before us."* In our daily life, many people observe what we do and say. We have been chosen by God to be a part of the lives of those He places on our path, and they have been chosen to be a part of our life. When we keep our mind and heart focused on the life and teaching of Jesus, we can have a significant impact on those around us each day as we minister to them along the way.

Further in the book of Hebrews 13:1–2, we are told: *"Let brotherly Love continue. Be not forgetful to entertain strangers; for thereby some have entertained angels unawares."* Imagine the power of that thought. God may have directed an angel into your life this day to see how you will deal with him. The cloud of witnesses which surround us each day each has a unique gift from God and a particular need. We should be living with a spirit of Love, and a desire to be of service to those God gives to us each day. We may be hosting an angel or two along the way without knowing it. Be Blessed today as you Love one another on your journey!

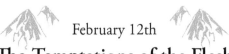

February 12th

The Temptations of the Flesh

The mind, body, and spirit are the components of life that make us who we are. We may spend more time thinking about those things which pertain to our body as we face afflictions or deal with personal insecurities or strive to improve our appearance and good health. The mind will focus on what we determine to be important, and we must continually tune it in to that which we decide is the path we want for our life's development. There are many things alluring us, trying to take us away from the path to a deeper relationship with God in our spirit.

Anything which separates us from God is a temptation that leads to sin. In the book of James 1:14–15, we are taught: *"But every man is tempted when he is drawn away by his own lusts and enticed. Then when lust hath conceived, it bringeth forth sin, and sin, when it is finished, bringeth forth death."* We wrestle daily with desires and thoughts which are not designed to take us closer to God. Whether it be in business or some other aspect of our life, we are enticed away from the path we should follow. The path to return to God is through prayer to enable you to overcome this temptation as it happens.

When you face trials and temptations, you are given a chance to overcome those and to grow in your faith journey. In James 1:2–3, it says, *"My brethren, count it all joy when ye fall into diverse temptations; Knowing this, that the trying of your faith worketh patience."* James goes on to write about this in verse 12, in which he says, *"Blessed is the man who endureth temptation, for when he is tried, he will receive the crown of life, which the Lord hath promised to them that Love Him."* We will all be tested along the way of our life daily. That test will give you the chance to overcome temptations as Jesus did when he was tempted by Satan. When you overcome temptations, the blessing of God is upon you. Be Blessed on this day!

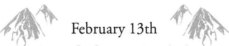 February 13th

Salvation Is a Gift from God through Faith

We are all sinful by nature, and as such, we are separated from God as a result of that sin as it takes place in our heart. The scripture teaches us in Romans 3:23, *"For all have sinned and come short of the glory of God."* God knows and understands the frailty of our human nature. He Loves the world He created and sent His only Son to die for the sins of the world so that we, who believe in Him, can and will have life eternal with our Heavenly Father. One of the greatest scriptures in the Bible clearly tells us this in John 3:16, which says, *"For God so Loved the world, that He gave His only begotten Son, that whosoever believeth in Him should not perish, but have everlasting life."* Believing in Him is the way to salvation; it is the truth, and life eternal is the gift from God for all who believe.

All that God is asking from us in order to accept this gift of salvation for our souls is to have faith in His Son, who died on the cross for us. It seems simple enough to follow this plan for salvation. What exactly is faith? Hebrews 11:1 defines it as: *"Now faith is the substance of things hoped for, the evidence of things not seen."* In Hebrews 11:6, it goes on to say: *"But without faith it is impossible to please Him; for he that cometh to God must believe that He is, and that He is a rewarder of them that diligently seek Him."* The journey to God is founded on faith. Let us all diligently seek our Heavenly Father always.

With faith being so critical in our relationship with God, how do we increase it? In Romans 10:17, we are taught: *"So then faith cometh by hearing, and hearing by the word of God."* It is for this reason we are to read scriptures daily and seek to listen to the teaching of others through services at a church or through Bible studies in groups. There are teachers God has planned for us, but we must seek if we are to find the message to build our faith. May your faith journey lead you to the gift of salvation, and may you grow your faith every day.

February 14th

A Day to Celebrate Our Love

This is a day we celebrate Love throughout the world. Pope Gelasius declared February 14th to be St Valentine's Day around the end of the 5th century. Over the centuries to follow, Valentine's greetings were popular, but the first known written Valentine's Day message, which remains today, was a poem by Charles, Duke of Orleans, to his wife while he was imprisoned in the Tower of London. This began the tradition of messages and cards being sent to those we Love, which we continue to practice today. The joy of pausing to reflect and share thoughts with those we Love is a wonderful tradition to enjoy.

One tradition we should add to our day of celebration of Love is the reading of the chapter in the Bible, which is called the Love chapter. First Corinthians 13 is the chapter that speaks about Love in a beautiful way. First Corinthians 13:4–8 talks that "Love is patient, Love is kind, it does not envy. It does not boast; it is not proud. It is not rude. It is not self-seeking; it is not easily angered. It keeps no record of wrongs. Love does not delight in evil but rejoices with the truth. It always protects, always trusts, always hopes, always perseveres. Love never fails." The chapter concludes with this truth in verse 13, saying, "And now these three remain: faith, hope, and Love. But the greatest of these is Love." We celebrate the greatest gift of all from God on this day which is Love.

Love is not limited to the day of celebration but rather a daily quest of our life with God in our heart. First Corinthians 16:14 tells us, *"Let all your things be done with charity."* Be blessed in your relationships and seek the Love God has chosen for you. In Proverbs 18:22, we are told: *"Whoso findeth a wife findeth a good thing, and obtaineth favor from the Lord."* May the blessing of finding the one who gives you Love be a cause for celebration in your heart on this day. May Love flow freely through your heart and soul each day of your life. Happy Valentine's Day!

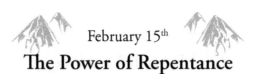

February 15th

The Power of Repentance

We are called upon by God to repent and ask forgiveness for our sins. It demonstrates to God our desire to turn away from our sinful nature and to seek a life which is pleasing to Him. When we truly repent and ask such forgiveness of our sins, God is faithful to forgive us of those sins as it is told to us in Acts 3:19: *"Repent ye, therefore, and be converted, that your sins may be blotted out, when the times of refreshing shall come from the presence of the Lord."* The Lord has promised to blot out those sins from which we have asked for His forgiveness, and we live a life refreshed and free from our sins. We start over as a new creature in our spiritual walk when we repent of our sins to our God.

There is joy in heaven when a sinner asks God for forgiveness and repents his sins before God. Luke 15:7 tells it this way: *"I say unto you, that likewise joy shall be in heaven over one sinner that repenteth, more than the ninety and nine just persons, which need no repentance."* God cares for every soul and wants us all to turn toward Him and His salvation. A repentant man brings joy to the angels of God as described in Luke 15:10 which says this: *"Likewise, I say unto you, there is joy in the presence of the angels of God over one sinner that repenteth."* The pathway to the kingdom of heaven starts with this one act of repenting of our sins. From there, we build on our faith in God and draw closer to Him for our walk each day. When we are living in sin, we cannot get close to God for sin separates us from Him. When Jesus began to preach, his message was built on repentance of sins. Matthew 4:17 tells us this: *"From that time Jesus began to preach, and to say, 'Repent, for the kingdom of heaven is at hand."* Essentially, the message being now is the time to repent and find God in your life.

The alternative to repentance is spiritual death. Luke 13:3 says this plainly: *"I tell you, Nay; but, except ye repent, ye shall all likewise perish."* Ask God for forgiveness of sins and believe in Jesus as His Son and accept the gift of salvation.

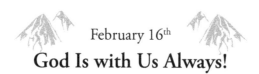

February 16th

God Is with Us Always!

Life has many moments in which we are dealing with difficulties and disappointments which can cause us to be discouraged. Those times often result in feelings of despair, and we can feel alone. The Holy Spirit is always with us and is there to provide us with comfort and guidance in all that we will face in this lifetime. Jesus promised us this when He departed from the earth and ascended into heaven. In John 14:16-17 Jesus told his disciples: *"And I will ask the Father, and He will give you another helper to be with you forever, even the Spirit of truth, whom the world cannot receive, because it neither sees him nor knows him. You know him for he dwells with you and will be in you."*

We have no moments when we are alone and without the Holy Spirt of God in our hearts and lives. There is great comfort to all who believe in Jesus Christ as the son of God to embrace this spirit in our lives. We have nothing to fear and there is nothing we face that we cannot overcome with the power of God working through His Holy Spirit in our lives. There will be times we need to overcome the enemy who will try to discourage us and to defeat us, but with the power of the Holy Spirit, we will conquer the enemy every day of our lives.

While the devil will try to lie to us and to cause us to embrace fear and defeat, we have no reason to fear or to accept anything less than complete victory in the challenges of life we face each day. Know this, God is with you always and He will be there in your darkest moments to bring you the light you need to guide you through the darkness. Be Blessed today as you embrace this beautiful truth!

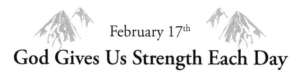

February 17th

God Gives Us Strength Each Day

As we journey through the world around us, we find many obstacles we must cross and there are burdens we encounter in our lives. We don't face these challenges of life without a source of strength to overcome them each day. God has the power and the grace to help us deal with all that we face and will be there to strengthen us as we seek His holy presence in our life. Psalms 28:7 says this plainly: *"The Lord is my strength and my shield; my heart trusted in Him, and I am helped: therefore, my heart greatly rejoiceth; and with my song will I praise Him."* We have the ability to trust in God and sing praises to His holy name as we draw our strength from Him each day. We never walk alone on this path of life.

The enemy of our souls wants to crowd our thoughts with fear and doubt as we face the challenges in our life. He will invade our hearts and raise doubts about our ability to deal with issues related to our health or the health of a loved one. He will drive questions into our minds about financial challenges we might face along the way. Fear is a weapon he will use to cloud our hearts and minds. God intends for us to be delivered from such thoughts of doubt and fear. Second Timothy 1:7 says this: *"For God hath not given us the spirit of fear; but of power, and of Love, and of a sound mind."* We know these thoughts of fear are not from God, we can take comfort in His power and Love whatever we may face.

The great power which God gives to us is without limit. Philippians 4:13 speaks boldly about it as it tells us: *"I can do all things through Christ which strengtheneth me."* Walk confidently with God at your side and the Holy Spirit living within you on this and every day. Draw your strength from the power of God and be blessed as you do so!

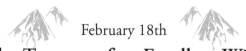

February 18th

The Treasure of an Excellent Wife

Our spouse and family are treasures for us in life. God has ordained the sanctification of the relationship between a man and woman in marriage. In the union, the value of a wife to a man is spoken of many times in the scriptures. In Proverbs 12:4, the Bible says, *"A virtuous woman is a crown to her husband."* For those of us who have found such a woman, we know with certainty that these words are true, and such a wife is a blessing always in our life. Proverbs 31:10 goes on to speak of this valued relationship by describing it as: *"Who can find a virtuous woman? For her price is far above rubies."* The author of Proverbs, King Solomon, sees the excellent wife as a great treasure in the life of the man.

The Bible is very clear on the significance of maintaining fidelity in the relationship between man and wife. In Malachi 2:15, the words of the prophet tell us: *"Take heed to your spirit and let none deal treacherously with the wife of his youth."* Trust in the relationship of your marriage is such a critical piece for your Love to endure and grow. To have a marriage that prospers, we must commit to the fidelity of the relationship forever on both sides. Hebrews 13:4 speaks to this as well when it says, *"Marriage is honorable in all, and the bed undefiled: but whoremongers and adulterers God will judge."* The blessings of the marriage relationship depend on your faithfulness to one another. God commands it of us.

As we embrace the coming of each new day, may we renew our vows of marriage to the one we have been given as a gift from God. The beauty of this relationship is a treasure in our life if we honor it and are true to it. Be blessed today as you let your Love flow through this spiritual partnership in your life.

February 19th

As a Christian, Have No Fear of Death

One of the greatest fears many people have in life is the ultimate destiny of facing death at the end of our journey. The dark veil through which we must all pass is one which brings doubts and fears into the minds of many. The Bible tells us clearly it is a part of our passage to where we are going. In Hebrews 9:27, the scripture reads: *"And it is appointed unto men once to die, but after this the judgement."* We know we are going through this experience as a child of God. We also know that Jesus died for our sins, and our faith will give us life eternal.

In the book of Hebrews 2:13–15, we are given this message:

And again, I will put my trust in Him. And again, I and the children which God hath given me. Forasmuch as the children are partakers of flesh and blood, He also Himself likewise took part of the same; that through death He might destroy him that had the power of death, that is the devil; and deliver them who through the fear of death were all their lifetime subject to bondage.

We no longer are in bondage to the fear of death. As one who walks in the faith of Jesus and his resurrection, we have nothing to fear with the passing of life from this world into the next. Jesus overcame death and the grave, and so will we all.

We serve a living savior who sits at the right hand of God. He has made atonement for our sins and is able to help each of us deal with the temptations of life. Be Blessed today and every day in knowing you should have no fear of death and take victory over any such thoughts all the days of your life. First Corinthians 15:55 speaks confidently of our victory over death when it says this: *"O death, where is thy sting? O grave, where is thy victory?"* Through Christ, we have won the victory over death and the grave as God has rewarded our faith with eternal life through Jesus our Savior. Be Blessed in this knowledge and have no fear!

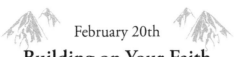

February 20th
Building on Your Faith

As a believer, you will be surrounded by people who may not share your faith in Jesus. The scripture tells us in Jude 19–22: *"These be they who separate themselves; sensual, having not the Spirit. But ye, beloved, building up yourselves on your most Holy faith, praying in the Holy Ghost, keeping yourselves in the Love of God, looking for the mercy of our Lord Jesus Christ unto eternal life. And of some, have compassion, making a difference."* We know there are people who God places on our path who are not believers. As they justify in their own minds their lack of faith, they attempt to bring you into alignment with their own understanding. The scripture tells us to build ourselves up as we pray in the Holy Spirit and to be merciful to those who doubt. As we show compassion to non–believers, we will make a difference in the lives of some.

The importance of dedicating time daily to reading God's Word and to praying in the Holy Spirit to have communion with God is the critical piece to growth and being able to sustain our faith journey. Every day of my life, I dedicate the first hour of the day to this purpose. Once done, I am ready for what God calls for me to do each day. My prayer asks for God to help me become the best man that I can be that day, as well as the best husband and father that I can become. If that is the desire of your heart, God will grant it to you as you earnestly seek it. As Matthew 7:7 clearly says, *"Ask and it shall be given to you; seek and you will find; knock and the door will be opened to you."*

The more we dedicate time to the reading of God's Word and to listening to those who are teachers of His holy Word, and the more time we spend talking with God in prayer, the stronger our faith journey becomes. We don't shy away from the people who lack faith; rather, as Jesus did when He walked on His journey in this world, we embrace those moments as opportunities to share the message of the gospel with others. May your faith grow on this day and always!

February 21st
Support in Times of Grief

In the experience of life, we go through all emotions and face times of tragedy and sadness along with happy times of joy. When we suffer through difficult times, our hearts mourn for those we Love who are sick or who may pass on through the veil of death to their life beyond. In such times, we reach out to those we Love to lift their spirits and console them. In Romans 12:15, we are told to: *"Rejoice with them who do rejoice and weep with them who weep."* To pray with those who need comfort is a great source of comfort and support we can give, along with guiding them to do the same at such a time.

We need to ask for God to direct us in the comforting of those who need this support. Second Corinthians 1:3–4 teaches us: *"Blessed be God, even the Father of our Lord Jesus Christ, the Father of mercies, and the God of all comfort; who comforteth us in all tribulation, that we may be able to comfort them which are in any trouble, by the comfort by which we ourselves are comforted of God."* To follow Christ in our lives, we must act in times like these to be there for others. Demonstrate your Love in ways that bring support when those who are hurting need comfort.

One thing is for certain in all times—God is with us. In Deuteronomy 31:8, we are promised: *"Be strong and of good courage, fear not, nor be afraid of them, for the Lord thy God, He it is that doth go with thee, He will not fail thee, nor forsake thee."* Knowing this, we have a source of strength and comfort regardless of what we face. Matthew 5:4 tells us, *"Blessed are they who mourn, for they shall be comforted."* We know those moments will arise in our life when we will be in mourning for others. Let us seek God's presence during those times, and let us each be there for those who need our support during those times in their lives. May this day be a day filled with joy in your heart, and may you be a blessing to others you meet along the way and give comfort to those who need it.

February 22nd

Take Victory over Temptations and Sin

We live in a world filled with sin and temptation. As you look at the headlines or read the news of the world around you every day, you see the manifestation of evil and sin abounding in this world. We need not fear the world or the power of sin if we are aligned in our heart and soul with God. With respect to the temptations you will face, 1 Corinthians 10:13 teaches us: *"There hath no temptation taken you but such as is common to man; but God is faithful, who will not suffer you to be tempted above that which you are able; but will with the temptation also make a way to escape, that ye may be able to bear it."* We know that God is always with us, and He will be there for us but do not expect to live a life without temptation.

The evil of this world is not to be feared. We have victory through the blood of Jesus on the cross to overcome the enemy in this world. First John 5:4 teaches us: *"For whatsoever is born of God overcometh the world: and this is the victory that overcometh the world, even our faith."* We are incapable of doing battle against the forces of evil on our own. However, through the power of the Holy Spirit and walking in faith, we have the power of God to do battle and be victorious in all that we do. Ephesians 6:10 encourages us: *"Finally, my brethren be strong in the Lord, and in the power of His might."* We don't do battle alone in our life. We have God with us, and he is mighty. Deuteronomy 20:4 tells us, *"For the Lord your God is He that goeth with you to fight for you against your enemies, to save you."*

Our journey of faith on this earth is not without spiritual battles, which we will face along the way each day. We know this, God goes with us into each of those battles, and with Him, we will be victorious. May you live a life of victory on this and every day!

February 23rd

Put on the Full Armor of God

As we watch the world around us, we find the news of wars and rumors of wars that were prophesized in the Bible as evidence of the end of time nearing. We find the true battles we face daily going beyond that of flesh and blood, but rather of the forces of good and evil which compete for our soul. In Ephesians 6:12, we are told: *"For our struggle is not against flesh and blood, but against principalities, against powers, against the rulers of the darkness of this world, against spiritual wickedness in high places."* The evidence of evil is everywhere in this world, and yet the battle of good versus evil is one which is being won daily by Christians everywhere who are empowered by God.

To face this battle and win it daily, we are to put on the full armor of God as taught to us further in the book of Ephesians 6:13–18, when the word reads:

> *Wherefore, take unto you, the full armor of God, that ye may be able to withstand in the evil day, and having done all, to stand. Stand therefore, with your loins girt all about with truth, and having on the breastplate of righteousness; And your feet shod with the preparation of the gospel of peace; Above all, taking the shield of faith, wherewith ye will be able to quench the fiery darts of the wicked. And take the helmet of salvation, and sword of the Spirit, which is the word of God; Praying always with prayer and supplication in the Spirit.*

We face our individual battles each day, as do those who God has put on our path for us to support. We are to lift in prayer all of the Lord's people as directed in this scripture. We need not fear the battles we will face each day. As 1 Corinthians 15:57 clearly states: *"But thanks be to God who giveth us the victory through our Lord Jesus Christ."* Be Blessed and victorious in your walk today as you wear the full armor of God in all your battles!

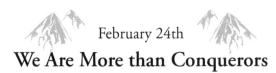

February 24th

We Are More than Conquerors

We face battles daily in life and deal with hardships brought on by the world around us. The enemy of our soul wants us to lose sight of the goal of finding the path daily to walk closer to God. However, the battle has been won for us by our Lord Jesus Christ, and we only must maintain our focus on Him and what He has taught us to win each battle we face. A beautiful scripture that affirms this is Romans 8:37, which says, *"In all these things, we are more than conquerors through Him who Loved us."* The power described in the scripture is that we are not in this alone, but God who Loved us is with us as we deal with all things in our life.

We are called upon to spread the word of God to others in our world to bring the message to those God has put on our path each day. Second Corinthians 2:14 says, *"Now thanks be unto God, which always causes us to triumph in Christ, and maketh manifest the savor of His knowledge by us in every place."* What a glorious calling for each of us to spread such a fragrance throughout our world. We are not here to be defeated by any enemy, nor are those who live in our world around us. In order for our friends and family to live in victory, they must turn to God in all things and let God lead them each step along the way.

First John 5:4 says this: *"Because everyone born of God overcomes the world. And this is the victory that has overcome the world; our faith."* Through your faith in Jesus, you are given the power to overcome the forces of evil in this world. Share the message with those God gives you. Today and every day, know that we are more than conquerors in this world. Be triumphant today in all that you do!

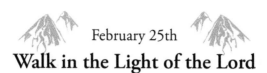

February 25th

Walk in the Light of the Lord

We face each day as the sun rises, surrounded by world which lives in darkness. The spiritual darkness is the result of sin and separation from God. It is God's plan for each of us to walk in His light each day as we move closer to Him in our hearts and minds. Psalm 89:15 speaks to the blessing of walking in His light when it says, *"Blessed is the people who know the joyful sound; they shall walk, O Lord, in the light of thy countenance."* The idea of walking in His light is certainly what we want to accomplish. How do we find this path for this day? 1 John 1:4–7 teaches us to live in joy as we walk in the light of God:

> *We write this to make our joy complete. God is light; in Him there is no darkness at all. But if we claim to have fellowship with Him and we walk in darkness, we lie and do not live out the truth. But if we walk in the light, as He is in the light, we have fellowship with one another, and the blood of Jesus, His Son, purifies us from all sin.*

The scripture speaks of fellowship with one another as a key component of this walk in the light. As you read the first epistle of John further, you can see more clearly what this walk in the light must entail. First John 2: 9–10 clearly states: *"He that saith he is in the light, and hateth his brother, is in darkness even unto now. He that Loveth his brother abideth in the light, and there is none occasion of stumbling in him."* What a powerful message this scripture brings to us. We live in a world with people who are all around us who are different than us in many ways. We have political differences, ethnic differences, basic faith differences, and attitudes that are wildly different as well. If we choose to walk in the light, we will have Love in our hearts in meeting with each of these as we go through the day regardless of these differences without prejudice in our hearts.

May you have the Love of God in your heart, and may the light of God illuminate your path as you walk on this day and every day!

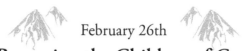

February 26th
Becoming the Children of God

Our quest in life is to live a life in all we do that will bring us into a relationship with God as a child of our Heavenly Father. What a beautiful thought it is to be considered a child of God. First John 3:1–2 speaks to that directly when it says, *"Behold, what manner of Love the Father hath bestowed upon us, that we should be called the sons of God; therefore, the world knowest us not, because it knew Him not. Beloved, now we are the sons of God, and it doth not yet appear what we shall be: but we know that, when He shall appear, we shall be like Him; for we shall see Him as He is."* It is an amazing thought to hold in your heart that we have the privilege of being known as a child of God. His Love for us is what makes this possible.

As a child of God, we turn away from sin. Sin is what separates us from God, and as such, if we walk as a child of God, we seek to sin no more. First John 3:3–6 tells us, *"And every man that has this hope in him purifieth himself, even as He is pure. Whosoever committeth sin transgresseth also the law; for sin is the transgression of the law. And ye know that He was manifested to take away our sins; and in Him is no sin. Whosoever abideth in Him sinneth not; whoever sinneth hath not seen Him, neither known Him."* As a child of God, we seek to purify our life from the sinful nature of this world. When sin occurs in our life, we seek God's forgiveness, and He is faithful and just to forgive us of our sin. We are not perfect, but we are forgiven, and we strive to sin no more.

How do we know if we are a child of God? First John 3:10 says it clearly: *"In this the children of God are manifest, and the children of the devil: whosoever doeth not righteousness is not of God, neither he that Loveth not his brother."* If we continually strive to do that which is right and we Love our brother and sister, we are walking through this world as a child of God. May that be the path we choose to take this day and every day!

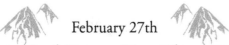

February 27th

Praising God Draws You Closer to Him

It is important to always be thankful for the things God has done for us in our life. We should do so daily. As we speak to God and thank Him for His goodness, it brings us closer to Him in our hearts and in our minds. When we want to grow in our intimacy with Him, we should add praise and worship to our communications with God. Psalm 100:4 teaches us this as it says, *"Enter His gates with thanksgiving and into His courts with praise; be thankful unto Him and bless His name."* The author of the Psalm was David, who was joyful in His praise of God all his life. It was out of his lineage that Christ was born, so it is clear how God favored this man who praised Him continually.

First and foremost, God is worthy of our praise. When the scripture speaks of entering his courts, it talks about His inner sanctum. The place in which He inhabits. That is where we can grow closest to God in our relationship. David spoke of singing the praises to God often in his writings; in Psalm 34:1, he says, *"I will bless the Lord at all times; His praise shall continually be in my mouth."* What a wonderful way to dwell in the house of the Lord forever in our hearts. Create a spirit of praise in our hearts that is continually on our lips. That will keep us closer to God regardless of what we face in this world. Hebrews 13:15 tells us to continually offer praise as it says, *"By Him, therefore, let us offer the sacrifice of praise to God continually, that is, the fruit of our lips giving thanks to His name."*

Whatever the world brings to us each day, there is nothing that is more powerful or important than God's presence in our life. God is our source of strength in all we face. May we draw ever closer to Him in all we do as we praise Him continually each day. Be Blessed today as you praise the Lord our God!

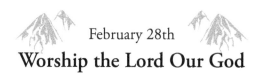

February 28th
Worship the Lord Our God

We talk about the significance of being thankful to God for His many blessings to us in our lives, and we know this is important as we tune in to Him. We know we can grow closer to God as we praise Him for who He is. Each day we seek to add to the way we can express our Love for the Father as we build on our relationship with Him. The Bible speaks to us of worship in 254 scripture verses from Genesis to Revelation. Worship is defined as the "feeling or expression of reverence or adoration for God." When we take time to worship our God, we have a time that gives us pause to reflect on His majesty as the creator of all that is and all that is to be.

When Jesus was tempted by the devil during His time on earth, the devil offered to give Him dominion over all. He would see if He would worship the evil one. Matthew 4:9–10 describes this exchange as it says, *"And saith unto Him, All these things will I give thee, if thou will fall down and worship me. Then saith Jesus unto him, 'Get thee hence Satan, for it is written, Thou shalt worship the Lord thy God, and Him only shalt thou serve."* Even Satan recognizes the power of worshipping and tries to lure our Lord and Savior Jesus Christ into the worship, which is only reserved for God the Father.

When Jesus ascended into heaven, Luke 24:50–53 describes the moment this way: *"And He led them out as far as to Bethany, and He lifted up His hands, and blessed them. And it came to pass, while He blessed them, He was parted up from them, and was carried up into heaven. And they worshipped Him and returned to Jerusalem with great joy. And were continually in the temple praising and blessing God."* As we worship and praise God, great joy will fill us each day. Let us seek ways on this day to find worship and praise in our heart and soul continually. Be Blessed today as you worship the Lord our God!

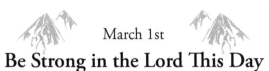

March 1st

Be Strong in the Lord This Day

Each day of our life, we face challenges in this world. Some are financial, some of the challenges pertain to our health or the health of those we Love. We face times when we grow weary and need support to meet the issues we are dealing with in our lives. We may find ourselves working through emotional stresses which come from relationships and difficulties with work or school. There are so many factors in life that bring us to vulnerable moments in our spiritual, mental, and physical journey. What we know is that God is always there for us whenever we turn to Him.

A beautiful scripture to lean on during such times is found in Psalm 28:7, which says, *"The Lord is my strength and my shield; my heart trusted in Him, and I am helped; therefore, my hear greatly rejoiceth; and with my song will I praise Him."* The author, David, was one who called upon the Lord with songs of joy and praise continually. As a result, his heart was filled with the joy of the Lord as he faced any battle. When we learn to do the same, we will never feel defeated. Isaiah 41:10 gives us this promise: *"Fear thou not, for I am with thee; be not dismayed; for I am thy God: I will strengthen thee; yea, I will help thee; yea, I will uphold thee with the right hand of my righteousness."* It is amazing comfort and feeling of power to know that God has promised to uphold us with His mighty and righteous right hand. Fear has no place in our hearts when we embrace this truth.

Whatever the challenge you might face in this world, we know we will overcome it with victory in our hearts with God in control. Keep your thoughts tuned into the mighty power God has given you. Ephesians 6:10 tells us, *"Finally, my brethren, be strong in the Lord and the power of His might."* May the mighty power of our God be your source of strength as you face challenges along the path on this day. God is with you and will deliver you. Be Blessed today!

March 2nd
Be Joyful in Your Walk Today

The daily walk of one who believes in Jesus Christ and has asked for the forgiveness of his sins should be a joyful experience each day. We are given the gift of eternal life and victory over the grave. With enthusiasm, we should be rejoicing and sharing the good news with others as they witness our journey through this world. Too often, people take refuge in sorrow rather than joy. That is not the spirit God intends for us to embrace. Psalm 68:3 says quite clearly: *"But let the righteous be glad; let them rejoice before God; yea, let them exceedingly rejoice."* If you walk with God and know He is present in your life, why would you want to dwell on any emotion other than joy and happiness?

God's Love for us has opened the door for eternal salvation as His gift to us. Whatever temporary issues we face that try to steal our joy are unable to do so when we focus on His Love and know He is there with us. Colossians 1:12 tells it this way: *"Giving thanks unto the Father, which hath made us meet to be partakers of the inheritance of the saints in light."* We are given an inheritance to share as His holy people, which is a cause for unmitigated joy if we embrace that thought as we travel through this world. Ecclesiastes 9:7 expresses that we should take joy in this passage: *"Go thy way, eat thy bread with joy, and drink thy wine with a merry heart, for God now accepteth thy works."*

Take joy in your heart as you embrace the life you are living. Share that joy with others each day. Roman 12:12 teaches us: *"Rejoicing in hope, patient in tribulation, continuing instant in prayer."* When others see you living this way, they will want to know what gives you such joy. It then will open the door for you to tell them of your faith journey and invite them to embrace Jesus Christ as well. If joy is missing in your life, they will not want to follow the path you are on. Be joyful on this day and share the Love of God with others God places on your path.

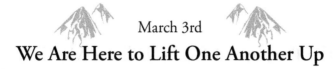

March 3rd

We Are Here to Lift One Another Up

We are brothers and sisters in Christ. We belong to one another, and God has a purpose for bringing us together on our journey in life. We share many joys and sorrows together as we go through this time on earth. When one of us is dealing with difficulties, we are here to help them through it with support. The scripture is clear about this in Galatians 6:2 when it says, *"Bear ye one another's burdens, and so fulfill the law of Christ."* The message doesn't suggest it as an option but rather directs it as being the "law of Christ."

One great illustration of God's people lifting one another up is found in Exodus 17:9–13, which details a battle in which Joshua was leading God's people against the Amalekites as the scripture reads:

> *Go out and fight the Amalekites. Tomorrow I will stand at the top of the hill with the rod of God in my hands. So, Joshua did as Moses had said to him, and fought with Amalek: and Moses, Aaron and Hur went up to the top of the hill. And it came to pass, when Moses held up his hand, that Israel prevailed, and when he let his hand down, Amalek prevailed. But Moses hands were heavy, and they took a stone and put it under him, and he sat thereon. Aaron and Hur stayed up his hands, one on one side, one on the other—so that his hands remained steady until the going down of the sun. So, Joshua overcame the Amalekite army with the sword.*

We may not face an army to overcome, but by lifting each other up, we are victorious together.

Finding those around us who need us to serve is God's plan for our life. God will put those people on your path who need your help and support. First John 3:17–18 teaches us: *"But whoso hath this world's good, and seeth his brother in need, and shutteth up his bowels of compassion from him, how dwellleth the Love of God in him? My little children, let us not Love in word, neither in tongue; but in deed and in truth."* May we find ways to support one another through Love on our journey today. The victory is ours when we do.

March 4th

The Purpose of God's Will for Me Today

When I pray to God each morning after I read my scriptures, I include the Lord's prayer our Savior Jesus Christ taught us to pray. Matthew 6:9–12 is where Christ teaches us:

After this manner therefore pray ye: Our Father which art in heaven, hallowed be your name, Thy kingdom come, Thy will be done, in earth as it is in heaven. Give us this day our daily bread and forgive us our debts as we forgive our debtors.

As we start each day, are we talking with God? If we do, are we making petitions, or are we listening for His Holy voice?

The first thing Christ teaches us in our prayer is to recognize the holiness of our Father in heaven. We are to praise and worship God, and as we do, He will inhabit our prayer with His Love for us as His children. Next, we are to seek His will for our life. When we seek God's purpose in our life, we often think in terms of the entirety of our journey. The reality is we need to break it down to what it means for each day. In the prayer, Christ says to ask for our "daily bread." What this speaks to goes beyond the food we eat but speaks to the purpose God has for us for that day. Ephesians 1:11 tells us, *"In whom also we have obtained an inheritance, being predestined according to the purpose of Him who worketh all things after the counsel of His own will."* We were chosen to fulfill a purpose of God's plan for our life. It is up to each of us to seek that purpose for each day.

Second Corinthians 5:5 (NIV) says it this way: *"Now the one who has fashioned us for this very purpose is God, who has given us the Spirit as a deposit, guaranteeing what is to come."* Not only is our life with a specific purpose made by God, but we have been given the Holy Spirit to empower us to achieve the result God has for us to fulfill. Seek each day God's will and purpose for your life in prayerful conversation with our Heavenly Father. As you do, the joy of Love will flow through your life to others you meet along the way each day.

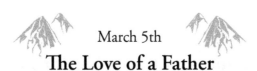

March 5th

The Love of a Father

I was not blessed with children until I was fifty years old. In today's standards, that is considered late in life to start a family. It was at this time when God unveiled a deep spirit of Love in my life that I had not experienced before. I have two beautiful sons who have enriched my life in ways I could not have imagined until I got to experience the joy of being a parent. Not all will be chosen to have this role in their lives, and God has a plan for some, which is to live without children. We are each blessed in different ways and called to a ministry that is unique to the gifts we are given. I feel fortunate God gave me this role in my life.

We are the children of a Heavenly Father who Loves us greatly. First John 3:1 tells us, *"Behold, what manner of Love the Father hath bestowed upon us, that we should be called the sons of God: therefore, the world knoweth us not, because it knew Him not."* God has loved us from the beginning of time with a powerful Love like no other. In John 3:16, His love for us is the reason He gave His Son to die for us: *"For God so Loved the world that He gave His only begotten Son, that whosoever believeth in Him should not perish, but have everlasting life."* God's plan for this world is to offer the gift of eternal life to those who believe in the Son, Jesus Christ, who died for our sins.

We need to approach our Heavenly Father with our thoughts and prayers daily. As we commune with God, He will give us all we need for each day of our lives. Matthew 7:9–11 teaches us: *"Or what man is there of you, whom if his son ask bread, will give him a stone? Or if he ask a fish, will he give him a serpent? If ye the, being evil, know how to give good gifts unto your children, how much more then will your Father, which is in heaven give good things to them that ask Him?"* Embrace God's Love as that of your Father in heaven. He is there for us today and every day to answer our prayers with His holy gifts to enrich our lives.

March 6th

Perseverance Is a Key to Spiritual Growth

As we begin each day of our journey, we never know what trials we may find along the way that day. We learn to overcome obstacles, trials, and tribulations as we experience life on earth to achieve victory in Christ. These challenges make us stronger and build our character as we overcome them. Romans 5:3 teaches us: *"Not only so, but we glory in tribulations also, knowing that tribulation worketh patience."* The harder life comes at us at times results in our mind, body, and spirit building strength through perseverance.

Hebrews 12:1 describes our life as a race we are running with a destiny we will fulfill when it says, *"Wherefore seeing we also are compassed about with so great a cloud of witnesses, let us lay aside every weight, and the sin which doth so easily beset us, and let us run with patience the race that is set before us."* This scripture talks about a cloud of witnesses that surrounds us. Are these simply the people which God puts on our path who are watching our lives as we pass by, or is the cloud of witnesses, including angels, He assigns to watch over us? I believe it is both each day. For us to grow, we need to throw off that which hinders us and avoid the sin which entangles us so easily. Those challenges each day might be something different than what it was the day before.

James 1:4 tells us, *"But let patience have her perfect work, that ye may be perfect and entire, wanting nothing."* Perseverance is a powerful attribute in business and in life. Continuing to finish the work you are given regardless of the challenges you might face. Find comfort in the fact God has given you the strength to carry on and reach the finish line of any race He has given you to run. Second Thessalonians 3:5 tells us, *"And the Lord direct your hearts into the Love of God and into the patient waiting for Christ."* Press on to the prize which is before on this day living in God's Love and Christ's perseverance.

March 7th
The Conversion of the Brothers of Jesus

The Bible teaches us that Jesus had four brothers who lived with Him as he grew into a man. They didn't believe in Him when He began His ministry, as we learn in Mark 6:3–6, which says,

> *Is not this the carpenter, the son of Mary, the brother of James and Joses, and of Juda and Simon? And are not His sisters here with us? And they were offended at Him. But Jesus said unto them, 'A prophet is not without honor, but in his own country, and among his own kin, and in his own house. And He could there do no mighty work, save that He laid His hands upon a few sick folk and healed them. And He marveled in their unbelief. And he went round about the villages.*

It must have been very sad for Jesus to experience this lack of faith from His own family during His ministry.

When He returned to Nazareth and declared He was the Messiah, His former friends and neighbors became angry and tried to throw Him off a cliff. John 7:5 tells us, *"For neither did His brethren believe in Him."* When He hung on the cross, none of His brothers were there with His mother. John 19:26–27 tells us, *"When Jesus therefore saw His mother, and the disciple standing by, whom He Loved, He saith unto His mother, 'Woman, behold thy son.' Then saith He to the disciple, 'Behold thy mother!' And from that hour that disciple took her into his home."*

Following His resurrection, Jesus appeared to over 500 men, including His brothers, as described in 1 Corinthians 15:6–7: *"After that, He was seen of above 500 brethren at once; of whom the greater part remain unto the present, but some are fallen asleep. After that He was seen of James, then to all the apostles."* Christ's appearance to James had a profound impact on his life. He became a fervent believer and leader of the early church. Both he and Christ's brother Judas (Jude) wrote books that are in our Bible. The resurrection power awakened their faith and transformed them as it will each of us today.

March 8th
The Power of the Resurrection

The power of the resurrection of our Lord and Savior Jesus Christ is immense. We can do all things through Christ, who strengthens us when we have faith in Him. The early church leaders faced intense resistance from the established Jewish church leaders, and many true believers were put to death for their beliefs. Yet, they pressed on as faithful servants spreading the gospel since many were eyewitnesses to Jesus's resurrection. Jesus told us of this power in Acts 1:8 when He said: *"But ye shall receive power, after that the Holy Ghost is come upon you: and ye shall be witnesses unto me both in Jerusalem and Judaea, and in Samaria, and to the uttermost parts of the earth."*

Acts 4:33 tells us how the apostles testified of the resurrection with great power when it tells us, *"And with great power gave the apostles witness of the resurrection of the Lord Jesus; and great grace was upon them all."* These were men who saw firsthand Christ the risen savior. As we journey today, it should be our quest to seek and find this power in our lives. We are told to ask, and it will be given unto us. Philippians 3:10 teaches us: *"That I may know Him, and the power of His resurrection, and the fellowship of His sufferings, being made comfortable unto His death."* To know Christ truly is to know of the power of His resurrection from death into life eternal.

The book of Revelation speaks of the end of time on earth and tells us in Revelation 20:6: *"Blessed and holy is he that hath part in the first resurrection. On such the second death hath no power but shall be the priests of God and of Christ and shall reign with Him for a thousand years."* What an amazing end of the time on this earth is coming. We are here to seek His will for our life each day to find how to best embrace the power of His resurrection in our life. May that power flow through you with the Holy Spirit on this day!

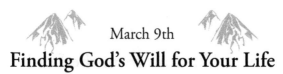

March 9th
Finding God's Will for Your Life

It is God's will for each of us to find salvation and live a life of purpose. It is through His scriptures that we discover His meaning and direction, and through prayers, we grow closer to Him to better understand His will for each of our lives. When you spend time with God, He will begin to reveal His plan for you as you grow in the spirit. Jeremiah 29:11 reveals to us: *"For I know the thoughts that I think toward you, saith the Lord, thoughts of peace and not of evil, to give you an expected end."* It is an incredibly powerful thought to embrace that the God of the universe has a specific plan for each of us. To do the will of the Father is the highest possible calling in this world today.

What is God's will for each of us? In 1 Thessalonians 4:3, we are taught: *"For this is the will of God, even your sanctification, that ye should abstain from fornication."* To be sanctified is to be set apart and free from sin. God calls His people to live a life with the highest moral standards. Ephesians 5:17–20 tells us,

> *Wherefore, be ye not unwise, but understanding what the will of the Lord is. And be not drunk with wine, wherein is excess, but be filled with the Spirit; Speaking to yourselves in psalms and hymns and spiritual songs, singing and making melody in your heart to the Lord. Giving thanks always for all good things unto God the Father in the name of our Lord Jesus Christ.*

God is calling us to be joyful in His Spirit and lift each other with positive thoughts concerning the gifts which come from the Holy Spirit of God.

The result of seeking God's will is live an eternal life in Jesus Christ. Hebrews 10:36 speaks to this when it says, *"For you have need of patience, that, after ye have done the will of God, ye might receive the promise."* The promise of God is waiting for us as we seek and do His will in our lives, and you discover His purpose. May you take steps toward this every day to grow closer to God the Father as you seek His will for your life. Be Blessed as you do so!

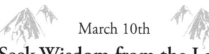

March 10th

Seek Wisdom from the Lord

We spend much of our lives trying to figure out what is the best path we should take. The answers are not always clear to us as we try to do what is best for ourselves and our families. Proverbs 3:5–6 teaches us: *"Trust in the Lord with all thine heart and lean not unto thine own understanding; in all thy ways acknowledge Him, and He shall direct your paths."* When we seek guidance from the Lord and ask for His direction, we know He is there to guide us.

Wisdom is something we are told that comes with age and experience. Some people have both and lack wisdom as they attempt to live a life without the benefit of God's direction. Wisdom is a virtue we should seek from God. James 1:5 teaches us: *"If any of you lacks wisdom, let him ask of God, who giveth to all men liberally without finding fault, and it shall be given him."* Once again, this is another beautiful promise from God of His benevolent Spirit. The more time you spend in the scripture, the more you gain wisdom that God is freely giving us. Psalm 119:105 says to us: *"Thy word is a lamp unto my feet, and a light unto my path."* We live in a world of darkness, but Jesus is the light of the world and will illuminate the path we should be on. Proverbs 9:11 (NIV) promises this: *"For through wisdom, your days will be many, and years will be added to your life."*

There are 208 scriptures in the Bible speaking of wisdom. The one which gives us a clear understanding of the wisdom which comes from God is James 3:17, which says, *"But the wisdom that is from above is first pure, then peaceable, gentle, and easy to be intreated, full of mercy and good fruit, without partiality, and without hypocrisy."* If we ask for God to give us wisdom, He will do so. As we gain this wisdom, our path becomes brighter, and days will be added to our life. Seek God's wisdom for your life today in your thoughts and prayers. His wisdom adds quality and value to each day of your life.

March 11th

Pray for Others God Has Given to You

The idea of praying to God continually in our hearts and minds is one we need to embrace. The Bible teaches us to pray without ceasing in 1 Thessalonians 5:16–18, which says, *"Rejoice evermore, pray without ceasing, in every good thing give thanks, for this is the will of God in Christ Jesus concerning you."* All we face in life is in the will of God for us. That is true for those we share this journey of life alongside. Our prayers for them should be uplifting and supportive but also ask God to draw them closer as they deal with the trials of their life.

The prophet Samuel prayed for the people and their king who had turned away from God as was written in 1 Samuel 12:23, which says, *"Moreover, as for me, God forbid that I should sin against the Lord in ceasing to pray for you, but I will teach you the good and the right way."* Samuel saw it as a sin in his life if he failed to pray for those who were falling away from God. Daily my mother taught me to lift up by name all of those in my family and to ask God to draw them closer and protect them and keep this in His will. I petition the Lord for that which is good for their lives each day. My mother said, if I don't do that, who will?

What kind of prayers are answered by God? Ephesians 6:18 teaches us: *"Praying always with all prayer and supplication in the Spirit, and watching thereunto with all perseverance and supplication for all saints."* I don't think there is any matter too small or too large for our God who created every one of us. Prayer is a conversation you have with God. Pray for those who lead our world. Second Timothy 2:1–2 guides us with this: *"I exhort therefore, that, first of all, supplications, prayers, intercessions, and giving of thanks, be made for all men; For kings, and all those in authority; that we may lead a quiet and peaceful life in all godliness and honesty."* In this troubled world, we need to petition God for peace and the well-being of all we meet along the path. God answers prayer! Be Blessed today as you talk to our Heavenly Father in your time with Him.

March 12th

God Favors the Humble Man

There are many references in the Bible to meekness and humility, and in every case, the word of God teaches us to be humble before the Lord in all that we do. One of God's greatest chosen leaders on earth was Moses. Number 12:3 tells us this about Moses: *"Now the man Moses was very meek, above all men on the face of the earth."* God chose this man to stand before Pharoah and demand the release of His people from Egypt. Psalm 25:9 tells us, *"The meek will He guide in judgement, and the meek will He teach His way."* If you are one who lives continually with great pride in your heart, it is difficult to humble yourself before God and to learn of His ways.

In Psalm 149:4, we are told: *"For the Lord taketh pleasure in His people, He will beautify the meek with salvation."* The victories of life are always the result of our God giving them to us. As we remain humble in His sight, we are prone to find victory in all that we do. Matthew 23:12 and Luke 14:11 both say: *"And whosoever shall exalt himself will be abased; and he that shall humble himself will be exalted."* To find favor from our God, we must maintain a humble nature while understanding all our gifts come from our Father in heaven. In our dealings with one another, Ephesians 4:2 teaches us: *"With all lowliness and meekness, with longsuffering, forbearing one another in Love."* In our interpersonal relationships, our egos often stand in the way of this as we strive to be the one who is right in any dispute we might encounter. God wants us to take the approach of humility, gentleness, and patience in our dealings with one another.

With the understanding that God will lift you up if you are humble in all you do, 1 Peter 5:5 says it well: *"Likewise, ye younger, submit yourselves unto the elder. Ye, all of you be subject one to another, and be clothed in humility: for God resisteth the proud and giveth grace to the humble."* Knowing this is how God feels, let us all "clothe ourselves in humility" in all we do each day.

 March 13th

Trust in the Lord with All Your Heart

Trust is not something that is easily given in today's world. We become skeptics of those around us as we are far too often disappointed with the way people violate our trust. Trust is something that must be earned. One thing is for certain. God is worthy of our trust and faith. A walk of faith requires that we step out believing in some moments prior to realizing we will secure a validation of that faith. The scripture teaches us in Proverbs 3: 5–6 to: *"Trust in the Lord with all thine heart and do not lean on thine own understanding. In all thy ways acknowledge Him, and He shall direct thy paths."* This is a powerful message and lesson for us all but a difficult one to embrace. Our minds and our egos want us to be in control of all things we face. We realize that God is in control, and through faith, we must humbly trust Him and acknowledge Him as such.

If we live by faith, we are pleasing to God. Hebrews 11:6 says plainly: *"But without faith, it is impossible to please Him, for he that cometh to God must believe that He is, and He is a rewarder of them who diligently seek Him."* There is joy and peace in your heart and mind that comes from believing as it is described in Romans 15:13, which says, *"Now the God of hope fill you with all joy and peace in believing, that ye may abound in hope, through the power of the Holy Ghost."* The life that is filled with joy, peace, and hope, filled by the power of the Holy Spirit, is the kind of life we should all strive to achieve. Having faith in God is the starting point to create that kind of life for each of us.

We must allow our faith in God to produce the trust that He is in control and will give us the strength each day to face whatever comes our way. Psalm 28:7 says it this way: *"The Lord is my strength and my shield; my heart trusted in Him, and I am helped; therefore, my heart greatly rejoiceth; and in my song will I praise Him."* May our song give thanks and praise to the Lord as we trust Him in all we do today!

March 14th

Let's Build Each Other Up Today

As we journey through life each day, we are in constant contact with others who are dealing with multiple issues in their own lives. We often know of the challenges they face, but many times may be unaware of the difficulties in their life. God puts us there for a purpose, and He puts them there to offer Love and support for us. To share the Love of God with one another is the highest possible calling we will have on this and every day of our life. First Thessalonians 5:11 was written to direct the church to do this when it says, *"Therefore, comfort yourselves together, and edify one another, just as also ye do."* When those we meet with each day tell us of their conflicts and difficulties, we need to be mindful of how we can direct their thoughts to what God would have them to be.

It is easy at times to validate negativity that comes out of the mouth of those around us or is coming from our own hearts and minds concerning others. The world is filled with negative energy in human relations, which stems from spirits that would pull our souls from the path God intended for us. We don't have to choose to travel on that path and are directed away from it in the scripture. Ephesians 4:29 teaches us: *"Let no corrupt communication proceed out of your mouth, but that which is good to the use of edifying, that it may minister grace unto the hearers."* It is easy to join in the indignation of others as they speak of shortcomings of other people in their lives. It is much more powerful to lift them up as we guide them to thoughts God would have for those moments to bring grace into the minds of all.

I Love the scripture written in Hebrews 10:24–25, which says it this way: *"And let us consider one another to provoke unto Love and to good works, not forsaking the assembling of ourselves together, as the manner of some is, but exhorting one another, and so much more as you see the Day approaching."* Let us take the initiative today to stir up one another to Love and good works.

March 15th
God Is Our Refuge in Times of Trouble

All people face times of trouble in various phases of their lives. There is any number of things that cause us to feel overwhelmed by what we might face on any day of our life. Whether it is sickness or financial stress, or the burden of caring for another without all the resources we feel we need to do so, we may face times of anxiety which bring sadness and feelings of helplessness to our hearts and minds. God wants us to turn to Him at all such times as well as those times when we are healthy, happy and experiencing a Love of the life we live.

In the book of Psalms, David continually calls upon the Lord as his refuge and his strength. In Psalm 34:8, he says, *"O Taste and see that the Lord is good; blessed is the one who trusteth in Him."* When we turn to God during times of need, we are strengthened by His power and His holy presence in our life. Psalm 46:1–2 tells us, *"God is our refuge and strength, an ever-present help in trouble. Therefore, we will not fear, though the earth be removed and the mountains be carried out into the midst of the sea."* When God is with us, we have nothing to fear in this world and beyond. Second Corinthians 4:16–17 teaches us this: *"Therefore, we do not lose heart. Though outwardly we are wasting away, yet inwardly we are being renewed day by day. For our light and momentary troubles are achieving for us an eternal glory that far outweighs them all."* Take courage and have no fear in the face of trouble. It is only for a moment, and we will pass through it with God at our side.

We know to take courage in the face of whatever adversity we might encounter. When you face times of difficulties or burdens you feel are too heavy, turn to God and know He is with you. Deuteronomy 31:6 affirms this for us as it says, *"Be strong and of good courage; fear not, nor be afraid of them. For the Lord thy God, He it is that doth go with thee; He will not fail thee, nor forsake thee."* Take great comfort in knowing you are never alone as God is with you.

The Righteous Will Live by Faith

There are many questions we face which remain mysteries during our life's journey. We may wonder why bad things happen to those who are good. Why do some who are living good lives face death earlier than others who appear not to be? We are not able to see all that God has the perspective of seeing, and we must believe His will is being done even when we can't understand it all. A journey of faith is sometimes a difficult one to comprehend from the human mind. That being said, a righteous man trusts in God the Father and accepts life each day as it comes. Romans 1:17 tells us, *"For therein is the righteousness of God revealed from faith to faith; as it is written; The just shall live by faith."*

The more you spend time in the gospel message, the more you see the words unveil the Spirit of God and His righteousness. Ephesians 3:17–19 offers this about the power that comes through faith: *"That Christ may dwell in your hearts by faith; that ye, being rooted and grounded in Love, may be able to comprehend with all saints what is the breadth, and length, and depth, and height; and to know the Love of Christ, which passeth knowledge, that ye may be filled with all the fullness of God."* The power of faith can take us to a place where we experience the fullness of God in our souls. That is a place every heart, mind, and soul should aspire to be.

Finding righteousness by our own works is not in God's plan for us. We can only find it through our faith in Jesus Christ. Philippians 3:9 teaches us: *"And be found in Him, not having my own righteousness, which is of the law, but that which is through faith in Christ—the righteousness that comes from God on the basis of faith."* Let us continue our faith journey, ever growing closer to God and His righteousness as we strengthen our faith in Jesus Christ each day!

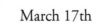

March 17th

The Powerful Combination of Faith, Hope, and Love

As we face each day and start anew, we should embrace the opportunities that life gives us with enthusiasm for building upon the faith, hope, and Love which come from believing in the God who created us. The scriptures are filled with reference to these key Christian attributes and share with us the meaning and power of each. Faith is described as an access point for us to God's grace in Romans 5:2 which says, *"By whom we have gained access by faith into His grace in which we now stand; and rejoice in the hope of the glory of God."* We see the value of these forces working together again in 1 Thessalonians 5:8 describes how these work together as our protection each day as it says, *"But let us, who are of the day, be sober, putting on the breastplate of faith and Love, and the hope of salvation as a helmet."* God is with us when faith, hope, and Love are abundant in our heart and soul. We stray from Him when they are not in our hearts.

As we continue to walk with God each day, we have work that He has called us to do. As we engage in His work our faith, hope and Love are the keys to having it yield fruit. First Thessalonians 1:3 speaks to it this way: *"Remember without ceasing your work of faith, and labor of Love, and patience of hope in our Lord Jesus Christ, in the sight of God and our Father."* Paul was writing to this early church, and his message was speaking to how their faith, hope, and Love were making a difference in the lives of others they were reaching with the gospel.

In our Christian life, the believer is enabled by these powerful spiritual characteristics. In all we do today, may our hearts be filled with the power of all of these. First Corinthians 13:13 sums it up this way: *"And now these three remain: faith, hope and Love. But the greatest of these is Love."* May each of these flow through our lives into the hearts and minds of those we meet today.

March 18th
Fear the Lord Your God

Throughout the scriptures, we are told to fear the Lord your God. In those passages, we are being taught to hold God in high reverence as a warning to be aware of His divine authority over all that exists in this world and universe He created. In Deuteronomy 10:12, we are taught: *"And now Israel, what does the Lord your God require of thee but to fear the Lord thy God, to walk in all His ways, and to Love Him, to serve the Lord your God with all thy heart and with all thy soul."* In this passage, Israel represents the people of God, which as a believer in Christ, we have become. Joshua 4:24 teaches us: *"He did this so that the people of the earth might know that the hand of the Lord is powerful and that you might always fear the Lord your God."*

What does it truly mean to fear the Lord? Proverbs 8:13 teaches us this: *"The fear the Lord is to hate evil; pride and arrogancy, and the evil way and the forward mouth do I hate."* The forces of evil and good are on the battlefield of life, and we are to hate that which is evil and fear the Lord by doing so. Psalm 34:9 tells us, *"O Fear the Lord, ye His saints, there is no want in them that fear Him."* God's holiness must be reverenced in our hearts. His power and Love for His people are absolute. Essentially, if we Love God our Father, we will reverence Him and follow His commandments.

Proverbs 2:1–5 sums it up this way: *"My son, if thou wilt receive my words and hide my commandments with thee, so that thou incline thy ear unto wisdom, and apply thine heart to understanding; Yea, if thou criest after knowledge, and lifest up thy voice for understanding; if thou sleekest her as silver, and searchest for her as for hidden treasures; then thou shalt understand the fear of the Lord, and find the knowledge of God."* God is with us as our Heavenly Father and has Love for us. He is to be honored and feared as we see Him as the ultimate ruler of our universe. Be Blessed as you do so today!

March 19th

Be Anxious for Nothing and Find Peace

We live in a war-torn world with people being displaced from their homes and killed for reasons we cannot explain. The rumors of wars will always be with us, and battles will wage around us throughout our lives. Amidst it all, we are blessed with a God who will smile upon us and give us peace. We are promised in Numbers 6:24–26 this blessing: *"The Lord bless thee and keep thee; the Lord make His face to shine upon thee and be gracious unto thee; the Lord lift up His countenance upon thee and give thee peace."* We are provided with the strength to carry on in every situation we will face in life if we are able to turn our hearts and minds to the one who is control of it all and who will give us peace.

If we approach all we do knowing the Lord is near and there to support us, it changes our spirit. In Philippians 4:7–8, we find a powerful text saying this:

> *And the peace of God which passeth all understanding, will keep your hearts and your minds through Christ Jesus. Finally, brethren, whatsoever things are honest, whatsoever things are just, whatsoever things are pure, whatsoever things are lovely, whatsoever things are of good report, if there be any virtue, and if there be any praise, think on these things.*

Turning your thoughts toward that which is positive and away from the negative things happening can bring you peace that transcends all understanding. A positive mindset like this lead to a positive life with God.

We can't always control our circumstances, but we can always steer our thoughts to that which is good. God will be with us and give us the power to do so. Your gentleness, which will be evident to all around you, will bring peace to others as well as the Lord blesses those around you through you. May you be blessed with a peaceful spirit blessed by the Lord on this day!

May the Holy Spirit Be with Us on This Day!

When Christ was with us on earth and His time had come for His ascension into heaven, He told us in John 14:18 that we would not be alone when He left as He said: *"I will not leave you comfortless; I will come to you."* Jesus knew that God's plan included sending His Holy Spirit to comfort and interceded on behalf of the believers. In John 14:16–17, Jesus says, *"And I will pray the Father, and He will give you another Comforter, that He may abide with you forever. Even the Spirit of truth, whom the world cannot receive, because it seeth Him not, neither knoweth Him; but ye know Him; for He dwelleth with you, and shall be in you."* The Holy Spirit is alive in each believer to support us in all we need to deal with the issues of life.

The Holy Spirit is there to bring righteousness, peace, and joy to the believer. Romans 14:17 speaks to this when it says, *"For the kingdom of God is not a meat and drink, but of righteousness, peace and joy in the Holy Ghost."* There is no substitute for the power and the presence of the Holy Spirit in your life. He is to be our Spirit of truth as defined in John 16:13–14, which says, *"Howbeit, when He, the Spirit of truth is come, He will guide you into all truth, for He shall not speak of Himself, but whatsoever He shall hear, that will He speak and He will show you things to come. He shall glorify me, for He shall receive of mine, and shall show it unto you."*

The Holy Spirit is alive in the heart of believers. He is here to comfort and guide us. May He guide our path and speak to us that which Jesus has made known to Him for us. Be empowered and blessed as His Spirit flows through you today!

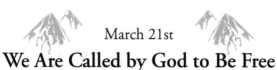

March 21st
We Are Called by God to Be Free

We celebrate our freedom in this country and in places around the world at various times. The ability to make our own choices and live in a place where we are not slaves to any man is a blessing from God. It is God's plan for our lives that we enjoy such freedoms from oppression and sin. Galatians 5:13–14 specifically tells us this as it says, *"My brethren, you have been called unto liberty; only use not liberty for an occasion of the flesh, but by Love serve one another. For all the law is serve in one word, even in this; Thou shalt Love thy neighbor as thyself."* We know the sacrifice many have made in our world for freedom to exist. In the spiritual sense, Jesus Christ made that sacrifice for each of us for us to enjoy freedom from the bondage of sin.

John 8:36 says it very clearly: *"If the Son therefor shall make you free, you are free indeed."* Jesus paid the ultimate price for us when He laid down His life for the sins of the world. This freedom is not something we have earned by obedience to the law but rather the result of the price that Christ paid for us on the cross. Acts 13:38–39 tells us, *"Be it known unto you therefore, men and brethren, that through this man is preached unto you the forgiveness of sins; And by Him all that believe are justified from all things, from which ye could not be justified by the law of Moses."* Such freedom from sin is a gift from God and one to be treasured.

With each day of our journey, we need to celebrate this joyous freedom by serving one another humbly in Love as the scripture directs us to do. First Peter 2:16 offers us this perspective as freedom when it says, *"As free, do not use your liberty as a cloke of maliciousness, but as the servants of God."* Enjoy your spiritual freedom on this day and serve those you meet along the way with Love as we are commanded to do. Be Blessed as you do so!

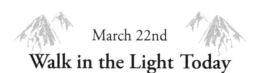

March 22nd

Walk in the Light Today

As a believer, the scripture often describes His people as having been called to come out of the darkness of the world and to walk in the light of His truth. First Peter 2:9 says it this way: *"But you are a chosen generation, a royal priesthood, a holy nation, a peculiar people; that ye may show forth the praises of Him who called you out of darkness into His marvelous light."* We are to be humbled by such a calling of God in our lives. As a priest in His holy nation, we are called to declare His praises to those He gives us who we meet along the way. Jesus uses us to bring others into His holy light as we do.

The scriptures speak to the role of the believer to share this light of the world in Acts 26:17–18 when it says, *"Delivering thee from the people, and from the Gentiles, unto whom now I send thee; To open their eyes, and to turn them from darkness to light, and from the power of Satan unto God, that they may receive forgiveness of sins, and inheritance among them who are sanctified by faith that is in me."* We are called to serve one another in Love. What could be greater in service to our fellow man than to help them turn from darkness to light in receiving forgiveness of sins and a place among those who are believers in Christ?

Seek God's direction as to what role He has for you in this journey of light on this day. We are all given different gifts to use in the service of God. We do know that when we walk in the light, it is witnessed by others. John 3:21 tells us, *"But he that doeth truth cometh to the light, that his deeds may be made manifest, that they are wrought in God."* Let your life be your testimony as to the truth of the light of God. Your ministry of Love and service to your neighbor will bring the light of God into your world on this day. Be Blessed as you do this!

March 23rd

Listen to God's Word for You Today

How do we find that place to hear the word that God has for us each day? In the Old Testament, God spoke to His people often through the voice of prophets to whom He gave His messages for His people. When Christ came to walk among the people, the message was spoken directly to us as people who were lost and now are redeemed through Christ as a result of His crucifixion and resurrection. Those words are recorded for us to receive in His holy book. The more time we spend in the scripture, the more often we can hear God's Word as it speaks to our hearts.

Prayer is the key to having communion and communication directly with God. As we spend our time having these conversations with our Heavenly Father and as we open our hearts and minds to Him, we will receive His messages more clearly. Jeremiah 33:3 tells us how God calls for us to speak to Him when it says, *"Call unto me and I will answer thee, and show ye great and mighty things, which thou knowest not."* What majestic access it is to have a direct connection to the Holy One, who is the creator of all things!

As we read God's Word and meditate on the message it contains and seek through prayer a better understanding of how it pertains to our life, we will receive His wisdom and understanding of what it means for us today. Proverbs 2:1–5 tells us, *"My son, if thou wilt receive my words, and hide my commandments with thee; so that thou incline thine ear unto wisdom, and apply thine heart to understanding;... If thou seek her as silver, and search for her as hidden treasures, Then shalt thou understand the fear of the Lord, and find the knowledge of God."* The scripture teaches us to seek God's insights and understanding and to treasure it in our hearts. As we do so, we find the knowledge of God in our life. Read His Word and pray for His wisdom and understanding on this day.

March 24th
How to Find Happiness on This Day

We live our lives in search of happiness and joy. There are many times we face issues that try to steal this treasure from us. How can we find the path to happiness each day along the way? The scripture guides us to happiness as we read in Ecclesiastes 2:26, which tells us, *"God giveth to a man who is good in His sight, wisdom, and knowledge, and joy…"* To please God will bring us happiness, and in order to do so, we must follow His path, seek His will, and Love one another as He has commanded us to do so.

The more we obey God, keep His commandments, Love one another, and live a humble and unselfish life, the more true happiness we experience. Proverbs 29:18 tells us, *"Where there is no vision, the people perish; but he that keepeth the law, happy is he."* We discover His truth through hearing the Word of God and discovering His laws for our life. The more we abide within the framework of His commandments, the happier our life on this earth will be. There is no substitute for obedience to the word of God. The more time we spend in our life doing good things for others, the more we will rejoice and find happiness in doing so. Ecclesiastes 3:12 tells us, *"…but for a man to rejoice, and to do good in his life."* The more our minds turn to do something which is good for another, the more happiness and joy we get to experience each day. The more good we do for one another, the more happiness God gives us in our hearts and souls to share with others as well.

May God fill your heart with happiness on this and every day of your journey in this world. There may be someone on your path today that needs a special message from you to help them understand how God is there for them as well. Share the Love in your heart and carry the message of God's Word and let happiness flow through you like a river of life. Be Blessed as you do!

March 25th

Finding Contentment in Christ

The Bible is filled with verses that speak to us about finding contentment with the place we find ourselves in the place God has put us. Our lives become a series of experiences that allow us to grow ever closer to God if we endeavor to do so. The story of Job is about a man who faced incredible personal losses and afflictions as he was tempted to turn from God. Rather, he determined to allow his faith to build in the face of much adversity and moments which would lead to sadness. Job 36:11 teaches us: *"If they obey and serve Him, they shall spend their days in prosperity and their years in pleasures."* As Job remained faithful and devoted to God, that is exactly what happened in his life.

The apostle Paul lived a life in which he was persecuted and thrown in prison and seemingly always under attack by the Jewish church leaders who felt threatened by his ministry as he taught the message of Jesus Christ and His resurrection to the early Christian church. Through all his persecution, he continued to share the message and brought many to Christ, and his words written in the Bible continue to do so. In Philippians 4:11–13, Paul writes these words: *"Not that I speak in respect of want; for I have learned, in whatever state I am in, therewith to be content. I know how to be abased, and I know how to abound; everywhere and in all things, I am instructed both to be full and to be hungry, both to abound and to suffer need. I can do all things through Christ who strengtheneth me."*

One of the greatest scriptures in the Bible is Romans 8:28, which is a great comfort when you are going through challenges in your life which says, *"And we know that all things work together for good to them that Love God, to them who are the called according to His purpose."* Knowing this to be a great promise gives us the ability to embrace contentment is all we face each day. May we all embrace being content in any and every situation we face on this day!

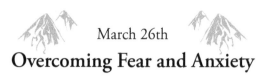

March 26th

Overcoming Fear and Anxiety

As humans, we face many fears along the way. As children, we may fear that which does not exist, such as the monster under the bed. As adults, our fears turn to things we often don't control and, in many cases, anxiety about things that never will happen while we worry about the future as it relates to finances or jobs, or potential health issues. Often fears are manifested in concerns about Loved ones who might face difficult times as it brings stress and worries into our hearts. First Peter 5:7 teaches us: *"Casting all your care upon Him, because He careth for you."* Be assured that God wants us to turn to Him in these times of need. His Love for us is absolute. He does not want us to walk alone in such moments of our lives as His Holy Spirit lives within us.

In Matthew 6:25–26, Jesus spoke these words when dealing with worry and fear:

> *Therefore I say unto you, Take no thought for your life, what ye shall eat, or what ye shall drink; nor yet for your body, what ye shall put on. Is not life more than meat, and the body than raiment? Behold the fowls of the air; for they sow not, neither do they reap, nor gather into barns; yet your heavenly Father feedeth them. Are ye not much better than they?*

That puts a pretty good perspective on why we should not worry about the things we face in life. Jesus goes on to teach us not to worry about the future in Matthew 6:34 when He says, *"Take therefore no thought for the morrow; for the morrow will take thought for the things of itself. Sufficient unto the day is the evil thereof."* Live in the moment God has given you. Each day is a treasure unto itself.

God speaks to us in Isaiah 41:13, in which He says, *"For I the Lord thy God will hold thy right hand, saying unto thee; Fear not, I will help thee."* If God is for us, then nothing can stand against us. Be strong and courageous in all you face on this and every day. Live without fear or worry.

March 27th

Finding Rest in This Troubled World

The world is filled with many influences in our lives which give us reasons to allow stresses and concerns to enter our thoughts. As they invade our minds, we may find the must needed rest being stolen from us when we try to get the required sleep needed to restore our strength. The Bible specifically teaches us to rest each week with the commandment of keeping the Sabbath day holy and not trying to work seven days a week. Hebrews 4:9–10 guides us to this rest when it says, *"There remaineth therefore a rest to the people of God. For he is entered into his own rest, he also has ceased from his own works, as God did from His."* It is God's plan for each of us to find rest as we live our lives for Him. Too often, I have heard people proudly say they work seven days a week as though it were a badge of honor. It is simply an ego-driven attempt to try to do more than others which directly contradicts God's plan for our lives.

When we are following this plan with a day of rest each week and still have the trouble of falling asleep at night due to the mind-raising concerns of the world around us, God is our refuge and will give us rest if we seek Him. Jesus tells us to come to Him when we are feeling burdened in Matthew 11:28 when He says, "Come unto me, all ye that labor and are heavy laden, and I will give you rest." The idea of turning all our burdens over to Jesus and having Him give us rest should be comforting to every believer. Have a prayerful conversation with God the Father and ask for this rest for your soul, which was promised by our Lord and Savior Jesus Christ. Praying at night when you lie down to go to sleep is a way to bring peace to your soul and allow rest to enter in.

Psalm 127:2 speaks to the gift of sleep God gives us amidst all we do: *"It is vain for you to rise up early, to sit up late, to eat the bread of sorrows; for so He giveth His beloved sleep."* Sleep is a treasure and a gift from God, and a necessary weapon in the battles we face in life. May you find rest in God today.

March 28th

Those Called Blessed by Jesus

There are wonderful teachings of Jesus in the book of Matthew, which take place when He spoke to the great multitude of people who had gathered in what is called the sermon on the mount. In this message, we are taught what we call the Beatitudes, which are blessings spoken of by Christ. The first of these which Jesus spoke to the people about was found in Matthew 5:3 when Jesus says, *"Blessed are the poor in spirit, for theirs is the kingdom of heaven."* What did Jesus mean by this? If we substitute the word "humble" for "poor," we can see a clear picture of His message. Those who approach God with a humble spirit and recognize our emptiness of spiritual life without God, then we can be open to the blessing of His presence in our heart, mind, and soul.

If we walk with pride and feel we have no need for God in our life, we are separated from Him and all He can and will do for us. Often, the richer we are in the things on the earth, the poorer we are in our spiritual life as our pride steers us into thinking we can take care of ourselves. James 4:6 teaches us: *"But He giveth more grace. Wherefore He sayeth, God resisteth the proud, but giveth grace to the humble."* We must not find ourselves to be self-satisfied or proud in our hearts, or we will be deficient in the longing to have God in control of our lives. The Lord's prayer teaches us to seek His Will in all we do each day.

In Matthew 5:5, Jesus goes on to say in his sermon on the mount: *"Blessed are the meek, for they shall inherit the earth."* The words of Jesus are very clear about being humble and meek before God and man. Those who are He calls "blessed," and the reward is to inherit the earth and receive entry into the kingdom of God. May we find this spirit of humility and meekness in our life each day before God and man and receive His blessings as we do.

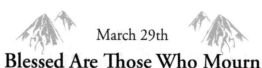

March 29th

Blessed Are Those Who Mourn

In the sermon on the mount, Jesus called others being "blessed by God." In Matthew 5:4, Jesus says, *"Blessed are they that mourn, for they shall be comforted."* We will all have times in our lives when we mourn and need to be comforted. Jesus Himself mourned and wept when Lazarus died, and He saw the grief of Mary, his sister, and the others who came with her when she came to meet Jesus. John 11:35 says, *"Jesus wept."* Personal grief is going to happen to us as we go through life's journey. There are and will be tragedies in each life as we go through our human experiences. God is there to comfort us, as Jesus promised in this sermon. Third Corinthians 1:3–4 tells us, *"Blessed be God, even the Father of our Lord Jesus Christ, the Father of mercies, and the God of all comfort. Who comforteth us in all our tribulation, that we may be able to comfort them which are in any trouble, by the comfort wherewith we ourselves are comforted of God."*

One of the most difficult times we will face in our lives is that time when we have a Loved one pass away. It is particularly sad when they are younger and seemingly have so much more life than they should be living. We turn to the word of God and find messages to comfort us at such times. First Thessalonians 4:13–14 tells us, *"But I would not have you be ignorant, brethren, concerning them which are asleep, that ye sorrow not, even as others which have no hope. For if we believe that Jesus died and rose again, even so them also which sleep in Jesus will God bring with Him."* As difficult as it is during the times of such loss for the human mind to embrace, the spiritual truth of death is a mere portal through which we travel, it is our faith and our hope in God that we leave this place to be with our Lord Jesus Christ forevermore.

Therefore, we know that God will bring comfort to those who mourn, and as Jesus said, we will be blessed by God as we go through this time.

March 30th

Blessed Are Those Seeking Righteousness

As Jesus spoke about those considered to be blessed by God in His sermon on the mount, He spoke about those who seek righteousness in their life. Matthew 5:6 when Jesus said: *"Blessed are they which do hunger and thirst after righteousness, for they shalll be filled."* The words chosen to describe the search for righteousness by Jesus was to "hunger and thirst" for it. When we hunger or thirst for the fulfillment of a need, we earnestly seek it with all we do. What is righteousness? In the scriptures, we can find the definition in Deuteronomy 6:25, which says, *"And it shall be our righteousness, if we observe to do all these commandments before the Lord our God, as He commanded us."* Certainly, a righteous man is one who lives his life within the law given to us by God in His Ten Commandments.

The Bible goes on to define righteousness as a man who lives his life with faith in Jesus Christ. In Romans 1:17, the scripture teaches us this about righteousness: *"For therein is the righteousness of God revealed from faith to faith; as it is written, They shall live by faith."* The scripture goes on to talk about righteousness through faith in Romans 3:22 which says, *"Even the righteousness of God which is by faith of Jesus Christ unto all and upon all of them that believe."* We are all one in the Spirit as we follow Jesus and believe in Him. If we "hunger and thirst" as we seek the word of God through Christ Jesus and His teachings, we will be filled with His righteousness as God has promised.

The great promise of life everlasting comes through believing in Christ as we know. In Romans 8:10, the scripture speaks to this in reference to the righteousness of that faith when it says, *"And if Christ be in you, the body is dead because of sin, but the Spirit gives life because of righteousness."* Be blessed as you hunger and thirst for righteousness today!

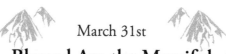

March 31st

Blessed Are the Merciful

As Jesus continued to speak about those blessed by God, He identified those who are merciful as being blessed in Matthew 5:7, which says, *"Blessed are the merciful, for they will obtain mercy."* He is telling us we will be receiving God's blessing of being shown mercy as a result of our showing it to others. We are called to be merciful and not judgmental of others in our lives. Luke 6:36–37 speaks to this by saying: *"Be ye therefore merciful, as your Father also is merciful. Judge not, and ye shall not be judged. Condemn not, and ye will not be condemned. Forgive, and ye shall be forgiven."*

The human mind is far too quick to form opinions and to pass judgment on the behavior of others. Something might be said or done which is not consistent with how we feel it should be said or done, and we pass judgment on the person involved. God directs us to be merciful and Loving in those situations. We, too, have misguided moments in our lives which need forgiveness from others. James 2:13 teaches us: *"Because judgment without mercy will be shown to anyone who has not been merciful. Mercy triumphs over judgment."* We are not here to pass judgment on others; rather, we are here to share Love with all we meet.

If we walk humbly with God, we are called to be merciful to others. Micah 6:8 says it clearly: *"He has shown thee, O man, what is good. And what doth the Lord require of you? But to do justly and to Love mercy and to walk humbly with your God."* As we follow this simple directive, our God will show us mercy in all we do, and His Love can flow through us into the lives of all we meet. Blessed are the merciful, and may we be among those who are so on this day.

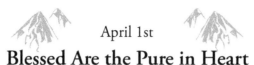

April 1st

Blessed Are the Pure in Heart

As Jesus continued to speak about those who are blessed, He talks about the "pure in heart" in Matthew 5:8 when He says, *"Blessed are the pure in heart, for they will see God."* What a wonderful promise to those who are pure in their hearts. God looks upon us and sees what is in our hearts each day. First Samuel 16:7 tells us, *"The Lord seeth not as a man seeth; for the man looketh on the outward appearance, but the Lord looketh on the heart."* It is difficult as a human not to prejudge someone based on their outward appearance. We have first impressions which are made each day formed by what a person might wear or how they style their appearance. What we can't see is what is in their heart.

David knew that God was looking into a man's heart as he wrote in Psalm 51:10 as he petitions God to renew his spirit as he writes: *"Create in me a clean heart, O God, and renew a right spirit within me."* That is a prayer that is one we can all use to petition our God to renew our spirit daily. The more time we spend reading God's Word and the more time we spend seeking God's will for our life, the more our heart is made pure by God. To achieve a pure heart, we must put away the desires of the flesh as described in Colossians 3:5, which says, *"Put to death, therefore, whatever belongs to your earthly nature: sexual immorality, impurity, lust, evil desires and greed, which is idolatry."* To be able to find purity in our hearts, we must turn away from these things which compete for our spirit.

May we diligently seek a heart that is pure in all that we do on this day. In our prayers with God, may our conversation with God seek His will, and may we ask Him to create a pure heart in our lives. He will renew our spirit as we seek His presence. The beautiful blessing Jesus told us for those who are pure in heart is they will see God. May that be our hope on this day. Be Blessed today, and may your heart be pure!

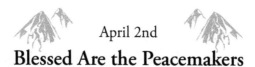

April 2nd
Blessed Are the Peacemakers

The teaching of Jesus on those who are called "Blessed" by God goes on in the sermon on the mount in Matthew 5:9 when Jesus teaches us: *"Blessed are the peacemakers, for they will be called the children of God."* We all know those who are around us who bring peace to disputes when they occur in the world around us. When arguments break out, they are there to defuse the anger and try to bring reason to the combatants. Our egos try to win out in such battles with others as we attempt to prove we are right. As we do so, God is not pleased with our efforts. To be a child of God, we seek to bring peace to all such situations. Showing Love to one another is not done by conquering them in thought or deed. Rather, it is submitting the ego and will of man and humbly striving to let the Love of the Father flow through us.

We are taught in the scriptures to seek peace in 1 Peter 3:11, which tells us, *"Let him eschew evil and do good; let him seek peace and pursue it."* There is no question that God is directing us in our relationships with those around us to be encouraging rather than finding cause to confront one another. In 2 Corinthians 13:11, the Bible says, *"Finally, brethren, farewell. Be perfect, be of good comfort, be of one mind, live in peace; and the God of Love and peace shall be with you."* The power of this message is evident in that we should reconcile with those we disagree with and bring Love and peace back into all relationships. As we do so, God is with us.

Second Thessalonians 3:16 shares this with us: *"Now may the Lord of peace Himself give you peace always by all means. The Lord be with all of you."* As we endeavor to find God's presence, He wants peace for all His people. Blessed are the peacemakers, for they will be called the children of God. Let us each make peace in all we do on this day!

April 3rd

Those Who Are Persecuted for Righteousness

As Jesus concluded His message on those who He called "Blessed" in the sermon on the mount, He spoke of those who face persecution for their faith when He said in Matthew 5:10–11: *"Blessed are those who are persecuted for righteousness' sake, for theirs is the kingdom of heaven. Blessed are ye when men shall revile you, and persecute you and say all manner of evil against you falsely for my sake."* In the days of the early church, the kind of persecution believers in Jesus Christ would experience included all manner of punishment, imprisonment, and death. We see many stories in the Bible about how Paul was persecuted for his beliefs and his ministry to others about Christ. In many parts of the world today, religious persecution is widespread and evil forces attempt to block the message of Jesus.

In our world in America, we are blessed with religious freedom, and the early pilgrims who came to this country had that as one of the key goals for moving here. However, persecution takes place here now in ways that are less evident. It is often the unbeliever who tries to mock and belittle the faith of those who walk with Jesus in their hearts in this world today. Second Timothy 3:12 tells us, *"Yea, and all that will live Godly in Jesus Christ shall suffer persecution."* It is easier at times to conform to the world than to be separated from it. We are not here to conform to the hearts of those who live without faith. In John 15:20–21, Jesus taught us: *"A servant is not greater than his Lord. If they have persecuted me, they will also persecute you. If they have kept my saying, they will keep yours also. But all these things will they do unto you for my name's sake, because they know not Him who sent me."*

Stand steadfast in your faith as you go through each day of your journey. We are promised a life everlasting with God and Jesus in heaven as a reward. Be strong in your faith, and Love those who persecute you along the way today!

April 4th
Let Your Light Shine Today

As Jesus continued to teach during His sermon on the mount, He spoke to the people about having the responsibility to light up the world in which we live. In Matthew 5:14–16, Jesus teaches us: *"Ye are the light of the world. A city that is built on a hill cannot be hid. Neither do men light a candle and put it under a bushel, but on a candlestick; and it giveth light unto the whole house. Let your light shine before men, that they may see your good works."* This teaching is clear that we are given His light to share with others. As a believer, we are ambassadors of Jesus Christ in the world of darkness around us. In John 8:12, Jesus told his followers: *"I am the light of the world; he that followeth me shall not walk in darkness but shall have the light of life."* We know our world is surrounded by darkness and uncertainty. The path to the blessings of God is made clear as we walk in the light that Jesus gave us to share with this world.

Jesus spoke to us about not hiding our light under a bowl, but rather to put it on a stand to share with everyone in the house. Those in our "house" are those God puts on our path each day. Until we began to embrace the teachings of Jesus and gave our heart to Him, we walked in darkness in this world. Ephesians 5:8 says it this way: *"For ye were sometimes in darkness, but now are ye light in the Lord; walk as children in the light."* We all know people in our lives who walk in darkness on this day. It may well be God has put you on the path with them to shine your light for them to see. It is our calling to do so and to illuminate the world we are given around us each day.

Romans 13:12 describes the light of the gospel as an armor we put on to protect us from the darkness of this world when it says, *"The night is far spent, the day is at hand; therefore let us cast off the works of darkness and put on the full armor of light."* May the light of Jesus Christ shine through us this day.

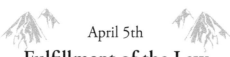

April 5th
Fulfillment of the Law

Jesus went on to teach us in His sermon on the mount about how He came not to abolish the law but rather to fulfill it. God gave His people the Ten Commandments of the Law in the book of Exodus 20:1–17. His words were established to guide us away from evil in our lives and in our hearts. Jesus elaborated on this when He says in Matthew 5:17–19:

> *Think not that I am come to destroy the law, or the prophets, I am not come to destroy but to fulfill. For verily I say unto you, Till heaven and earth pass, one jot or one tittle shall in no wise pass from the law, till all be fulfilled. Whosoever therefore shall break one of these least commandments, and shall teach men so, he shall be called least in the kingdom of heaven; but whosoever shall do and teach them, the same shall be called great in the kingdom of heaven.*

These commands which God has given us are everlasting on the earth, and we can see how to conduct our lives by following them each day.

All of Christ's teachings are consistent with the Law God gives us. He lived His life honoring all and teaching those who He met accordingly. In John 14:15, Jesus tells us, *"If you Love me, keep my commandments."* From the beginning, the Bible teaches us to follow God's commandments if you Love God. Deuteronomy 11:1 says, *"Thou shalt Love the Lord thy God and keep His charge, and His statutes, and His judgements, and His commandments always."* The guardrails of His commandments will keep you on the roadway to heaven and the path to finding God's favor. They are simple, and they are pure and will lead us to righteousness in our life.

Second John 1:6 says it very beautifully: *"And this is Love: that we walk after His commandments. That, as you have heard from the beginning, ye should walk in it."* May our lives be lived in fulfillment of the Law on this day, and may we walk in Love with our God by our side as we live while keeping His commandments.

April 6th
I Saw God Today

There is a beautiful song by George Strait in which he sings of seeing God as he goes through his day. The lyric of the song describes how he sees God in the flower growing in the middle of the sidewalk, pushing up through the concrete. He sees God in the flashing of the lights in the shadow of the hospital and in the older couple holding hands. He saw God in the beauty of the sunset and on the face of his newly born baby girl. The essence of the song tells us that God's fingerprint is everywhere if we just pause to see what beauty is found in life all around us. I see the magnificence of God's creation whenever I pause to witness the spectacular beauty of the masterpiece He creates in sunset of a summer sky. God's beauty is evident as the orchid unfolds its blossoms to adorn our world.

The scriptures speak of such beauty in Matthew 6:28–29, which says, *"And why take ye thought for raiment? Consider the lilies of the field, how they grow; they toil not, neither do they spin; Yet I say unto you that not even Solomon in all his glory was arrayed like one of these."* The message from Jesus in this passage was about how much more we concern ourselves with the outward appearance as a measure of beauty. True beauty in the eyes of God is not based on outward appearances. He says in Ecclesiastes 3:11: *"He hath made everything beautiful in His time; also, He hath set the world in their heart, so that no man can find out the work that God maketh from the beginning to the end."* All that is in its moment of beauty on earth will pass away. Isaiah 40:8 says this: *"The grass withers and the flower fades, but the word of our God will stand forever."*

The message of the song by George Strait is a powerful one. See God in all that is around you each day. Know that the magnificent beauty of a sunset or a flower is passing quickly by us. The true beauty of this world in the eyes of God comes from within us. May the beauty in your heart bless those who you meet along the way today so they can see God in you!

April 7th

May Our Trust in God Grow Each Day

Trust is something that is difficult to do in human relationships. Trust is something that must be earned rather than given. Too often in our lives, we may have trusted in someone who let us down or disappointed us by not honoring our trust in them. As a result, we are often skeptical and reluctant to trust those until they have proven to be worthy of such trust. The walk of faith requires us to trust in our God for the salvation, strength, and support we need in our human experience. As we learn to trust in Him, we find our joy and peace growing and the power of the Holy Spirit becoming more alive within us. This is talked about in Romans 15:13: *"Now the God of hope fill you with all joy and peace in believing, that ye may abound in hope by the power of the Holy Ghost."* To grow in your faith, you must allow your Spirit to embrace the idea of growing in your trust in our Heavenly Father.

Throughout the book of Psalm, David extols the virtue of having put his trust in God and the rewards he has received by doing so. Psalm 62:7–8 says it this way: *"In God is my salvation and my glory: the rock of my strength, and my refuge, is in my God. Trust in Him at all times; ye people, pour out your heart before Him; God is a refuge for us."* David was the most powerful man on earth during his time here. David speaking again of his trust in God as his shelter from the storms of life in Psalm 91:1–2, which says, *"He that dwelleth in the secret place of the most high shall abide under the shadow of the Almighty. I will say of the Lord, He is my refuge and my fortress: my God, in Him will I trust."*

Throughout the book of Psalms and throughout all of the Bible, the message of trust in God and the refuge He offers us is empowering to all of us as His people. As we build our trust in Him, God pours out His blessings on all who place their trust in Him. May our faith and trust in God grow each day as we seek Him in all that we do. Be Blessed today as you do so!

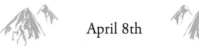

April 8th

Easter Story—The Journey to Jerusalem

As Jesus and His disciples were returning to Jerusalem for the final time and as He approached the time of His destiny to die for the sins of the world, He made it clear to His disciples that which was about to unfold. Matthew 20:17–19 tells us this:

> *And Jesus going up to Jerusalem, took the twelve disciples apart in the way, and said unto them, Behold, we go up to Jerusalem, and the Son of man shall be betrayed unto the chief priests and the scribes, and they shall condemn Him to death. And they shall deliver Him to the Gentiles to mock and to scourge, and to crucify Him: and the third day He shall rise again.*

Jesus was fully aware of all that was about to happen on His journey.

As they came close to the city, Jesus sent two of His disciples into the city and told them they would find an ass and a colt for Him to ride into town on. The people celebrated His entry into the city as though He was a conquering hero, as described in Matthew: 21:9, which says, *"And the multitudes that went before, and that followed, cried, saying, Hosanna to the Son of David, Blessed is He that cometh in the name of the Lord, Hosanna in the highest."* The celebration of Jesus was significant in the city, and all the people were made aware of His entry. There was joy in the hearts of those who followed Him as they saw Him be a man who came with the power of God.

When Jesus entered the city, He went to the temple He took charge. Matthew 21:12–14 teaches us:

> *And Jesus went into the temple of God, and cast out all of them that sold and bought in the temple, and overthrew the tables of the moneychangers, and the seats of them who sold doves, And said to them, It is written, My house shall be called a house of prayer; but ye have made it a den of thieves. The blind and lame came to Him at the temple, and he healed them.*

May we reflect on the significance of God's message to the world through Jesus on this day. May we make His house, which is our life, a house of prayer today!

April 9th

Easter Story—His Teachings in Jerusalem

The next day in Jerusalem, Jesus taught the people with parables. He spoke of the parable of the householder who demanded fruit from his vineyard and sent his son to collect it. Matthew 21:38 tells us, *"But when the husbandmen saw the son, they said among themselves, This is the heir, come let us kill him and let us seize on his inheritance."* Jesus was telling those around Him about His coming death as He told the story. He told the parable of the marriage feast and then had leaders of the temple debate Him on various issues.

As He debated the Pharisees, He concluded with scripture that carries great power in Matthew 22:36–40, which says, *"Master, which is the great commandment of the law? Jesus said unto him, Thou shalt Love the Lord your God with all thy heart, and with all thy soul, and with all thy mind. This is the first and great commandment. And the second is like unto it. Thou shalt Love thy neighbor as thyself. On these two commandments hang all the law and the prophets."* What a great message from Jesus as He spoke to those who He knew sought to kill Him. His heart was filled with Love for all men, and He continued to deliver the message to those who were looking for ways to bring Him down.

Jesus then spoke to the multitudes and to His disciples, and He told of the woe of the Pharisees and the teachers of the law. In Matthew 23:13, Jesus said: *"But woe unto you, scribes and Pharisees, hypocrites! For ye shut up the kingdom of heaven against men; for ye neither go in yourselves, neither suffer ye them who are entering to go in."* Jesus made it very clear that He understood the spiritual battle He faced with the leaders of the church at that time. His teaching was to guide us to the path to righteousness, and they did all they could to prevent it for fear of losing their power over the people. The path to God is through our faith and belief in Jesus Christ. There is no other way. May our faith in Jesus grow this Easter season!

April 10th

Easter Story—Jesus Prepares the Disciples

Jesus took the disciples up to the Mount of Olives and spoke to them about the end of time and His return in the last days. At the end of which, He once again told them of His upcoming death in Matthew 26:1–2, which says, *"And it came to pass, when Jesus had finished all these sayings, He said unto His disciples, Ye know that after two days is the feast of the Passover, and the Son of man is betrayed to be crucified."* Jesus had not only told them this was coming, but He was also now telling them exactly when it would happen.

As the last supper was held, Jesus foretold to the disciples that one would betray Him, and Judas went to do so with the chief priests. After the supper, they went back to the Mount of Olives, and Jesus told them of His resurrection and where He would then meet them again after they scattered; Matthew 26:31–32 tells us, *"Then saith Jesus unto them, All ye shall be offended because of me this night, for it is written, I will smite the shepherd and the sheep of the flock shall be scattered abroad. But after I am risen again, I will go before you into Galilee."* The difficult moment for Jesus was at hand, and He knew the journey which He was on would be one He faced alone. After all this time with His disciples as they observed Him and His miracles, they were about to run from the danger of those who sought to kill Him.

We face no such danger in our world today, but we sometimes run from the blessings of the Master when we turn away from Him. He has taught us through His words, and the story of His miracles should be deeply held in our hearts and souls. His plan for our lives is for Him to walk with us daily. May we learn from the story of Easter to stay close to God and our Lord and Savior Jesus Christ always. We know there is death, but we also know that resurrection follows. Be Blessed today as you think about these things.

April 11th

Easter Story—The Prayers in the Garden

For there to be a resurrection, the death of Christ had to occur. It was God's plan for it to happen, and Christ was given as a sacrifice for the sins of the world. As Jesus faced His destiny, three times He prayed in the Garden of Gethsemane as reported in Matthew 26:41–44: *"Watch and pray, that ye enter not into temptation; the spirit indeed is willing, but the flesh is weak. He went away again the second time and prayed saying, O Father, if this is cup may not pass away from me, except I drink it, thy will be done. And He came and found them asleep again; for their eyes were very heavy, And He left them and went away again, and prayed the third time, saying the same words."* The moment of the betrayal and the events to follow had arrived. Jesus knew it was unfolding, and He could have called for angels to come to His rescue. Rather, He prayed for the will of the Father to be done in His life. He called on His disciples to "watch and pray," but they slept through these moments as He knew they would.

Our destiny is unfolding each day. As it does so, we need to heed the words of Jesus as He directs us to "watch and pray," and as we do so, seek the will of the Father. He cautions us that the spirit is willing, but the flesh is weak. Our strength comes from the Father, and we cannot fight our battles alone. Isaiah 40:29 tells us, *"He giveth power to the faint, and to them that hath no might He increases strength."* God is the One who will deliver us *through* the battles we face, and it is His strength we draw from. Philippians 4:13 says, *"I can do all things through Christ who strengtheneth me."* There is nothing that can stop you from achieving God's plan for your life if you drink from the cup He has given to you and seek His will in all that you do.

May God's blessing pour out on you this Easter season as you seek His will for your life. May the prayer on our lips be to Him, "May your will be done." Be Blessed today as you seek His will for this day and always.

April 12th

Easter Story—The Death and Resurrection

The Easter message brings a culmination of the life of Jesus with His sacrifice on the cross for the sins of the world. His death was necessary as such, but the glorious resurrection which follows gives us hope in our faith in the power of God over death. When Jesus hung on the cross and breathed His last breath, the world grew dark, as described in Luke 23:44–45, which tells us, *"And it was about the sixth hour, and there was a darkness over all the earth until the ninth hour. And the sun was darkened, and the veil of the temple was rent in the midst."* In Matthew 27:54, we are told of a great earthquake as He died and the response of those watching: *"Now when the centurion, and they that were with him, watching Jesus, saw the earthquake, and those things that were done, they feared greatly saying, Truly this was the Son of God."*

Fortunately for all mankind, the story does not end there. The message of Easter is a story of the cross for certain, but the power of the empty tomb is what makes it all real for those of us who believe. In the book of Matthew, it tells of Mary Magdalene and Mary, the mother of Jesus, going to the tomb early on the first day of the week. Matthew 28:5–10 says,

> *And the angel answered and said unto the women, Fear not ye; for I know ye seek Jesus, who was crucified. He is not here: for He is risen, as He said. Come, see the place where the Lord lay. And go quickly and tell the disciples that He is risen from the dead, and behold, He goeth before you into Galilee; there shall ye see Him, Lo, I have told you. And they departed quickly from the sepulcher with fear and great joy; and did run to bring His disciples word. And as they went to tell the disciples, behold, Jesus met them, saying, All hail. And they came and held Him by the feet and worshipped Him. Then Jesus said unto them, 'Be not afraid, go tell my brethren, that they go into Galilee, and there they shall see me.*

The power of the resurrection brings eternal life to all believers today!

April 13th

Easter Story—Jesus Meets with the Disciples

The disciples had scattered in fear when Jesus was taken in the Garden of Gethsemane. Peter had denied Jesus three times as Jesus had said He would during the time of Jesus' arrest and prosecution. It was a very difficult time for each of them spiritually to have been alone and away from Him. The message of His resurrection came from Mary Magdalene and Mary, the mother of Jesus. I can only imagine how they must have had doubts and fears during this time despite having been eyewitnesses to the miracles and teaching of Jesus during His life on earth. They were told to go to Galilee and that He would go ahead and meet them there.

The book of Mark 16:10–16 describes the events as they unfolded:

And she went and told them that had been with Him, as they mourned and wept. And they, when they heard that He was alive, and had been seen of her, believed not. After that, He appeared in another form to two of them, as they walked, and went into the country. And they went and told it to the residue; neither believed they them. Afterward He appeared to the eleven as they sat at meat and unbraided them with their unbelief and hardness of heart, because they believed not them which had seen Him after He was risen. And He said unto them, Go ye into all the world, and preach the gospel to every creature. He that believeth and is baptized shall be saved; but he that believeth not shall be damned.

Mark 16:19 tells us, *"So then after the Lord had spoken to them, he was received up into heaven, and sat on the right hand of God."* The resurrection of Jesus and the message He gave to His disciples just prior to His ascension into heaven is called the great commission. It is His directive to all His followers. If you believe, it is what He wants from each of us. Boldly carry the message in your heart to others God places on your path each day that Jesus Christ lives today!

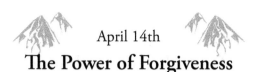

April 14th

The Power of Forgiveness

We can find ourselves in relationships that are abusive, whether physically or emotionally, and the best possible outcome is to remove ourselves from these as soon as possible. There exists evil in the hearts of some people, and they often unveil that in hostile and abusive ways. I was told of one such relationship by a friend involving one of his daughters this week, which resulted in a terrible situation from which she miraculously and fortunately escaped. It is easy to imagine how much anger and feeling of animosity or even hatred could invade our heart for such a person who would do such a thing to a family member or to you personally.

When we walk away from such a relationship, the power over us can continue as the spirit of anger, and all that it entails remains in our heart. The enemy of our soul will justify the feelings and try to isolate us from the power of forgiveness. The enemy of our soul is around us every day, seeking to destroy the faith walk we are on. His approach is to create isolation, his method is lying to us in our heart, and the goal of Satan is to lead us to death spiritually. First Peter 5:8–9 teaches us: *"Be sober, be vigilant; because your adversary, the devil, as a roaring lion, walketh about, seeking whom he may devour; Whom resist steadfast in the faith, knowing that the same afflictions are accomplished in your brethren that are in the world."*

When we harbor thoughts of resentment and anger, they are infecting us and not the ones who caused such feelings to occur. Ephesians 4:31–32 tells us, *"Let all bitterness, and wrath, and anger, and clamor, and evil speaking, be put away from you, with all malice: And be ye kind one to another, tenderhearted, forgiving one another, even as God for Christ's sake has forgiven you."* As we do this, our life becomes free of such negativity and opens the door for Love to enter. Fill your heart with Love and forgive on this day!

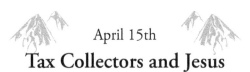

April 15th
Tax Collectors and Jesus

April 15th in America is a day of significance in that we have our income taxes due to the government on this day. In the days in which Jesus walked in his time, there was a "temple tax" which was charged to the people of that society. This was talked about in Matthew 17:24, which tells us, *"And when they came to Capernaum, those that received tribute money came to Peter, and said, 'Doth not your master pay tribute?'"* When Jesus questioned Peter about this practice, He concluded they didn't collect from their own children but only from strangers. Jesus lived His life in a way that honored the customs and responsibilities of a good citizen of the land in which He lived. He sent Peter to the sea to catch a fish and in its mouth were the coins needed for the tax due for Peter and Jesus, and it was paid, as we find out in verses 25–27 of Matthew 17.

Tax collectors of the time were considered very low in the social sector. Jesus chose one to be one of His 12 disciples as Matthew was one when Jesus called him in Matthew 9:9: *"As Jesus passed on from thence, He saw a man named Matthew, sitting at the receipt of custom; and He saith unto him, 'Follow me,' and he arose and followed Him."* The power of Jesus was immense to be able to speak to these chosen disciples and have them immediately leave their life's work to walk with Him as followers. The church leaders of that time criticized Jesus for socializing with tax collector and sinners as described in Matthew 9:11: *"When the Pharisees saw this they asked, 'Why does your master eat with publicans and sinners?"* In their evil hearts, they sought to disparage Jesus for affiliating with those of the lower social sector. Jesus saw His time on earth to be better spent with those who needed His teaching to find their path to heaven.

May God bless us today as we pay the taxes which we have due, and may we embrace all social requirements as citizens and as children of God every day!

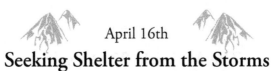

April 16th

Seeking Shelter from the Storms

The journey of life is one in which we are often surrounded by the storms of life. They symbolically appear in many forms but appear to be turbulent as they become manifest around us. The storms may take shape as financial or physical stresses or emotional in nature as they become a force with which we wrestle in our world. Too often, our minds get caught up in the turbulence of the moment as we try to bring order to the chaos that appears. The disciples experienced such a storm literally when crossing a lake on a boat with Jesus asleep below deck. Luke 8:23–25 tells us what happened:

> *But as they sailed, He fell asleep: and there came down a storm of wind on the lake; and they were filled with water and in jeopardy. And they came to Him, and awoke Him saying, Master, master, we perish. Then He arose and rebuked the wind and the raging of the water; and they ceased and there was a calm. And He said unto them, "Where is thy faith?" And they being afraid wondered, saying to one another, What manner of man is this! For He commandeth even the winds and the water and they obey Him.*

The power of having Jesus with you in moments of your life when storms rage around you is truly amazing and will protect you in all you face.

The words of David written in Psalm 107:28–30 foretold of Jesus calming the storm many generations prior to this event with the disciples when it says, *"Then they cry unto the Lord in their trouble, and He brought them out of their distresses. He maketh the storm a calm, so that the waves thereof are still. Then are they glad because they be quiet; so He bringeth them unto their desired haven."* God is in control of our lives as we face the most turbulent situations on our journey. When they occur, our faith is being measured and tested.

We need to build our faith and know that God is with us always. Nahum 1:7 says this: *"The Lord is good, a refuge in times of trouble. He cares for those who trust in Him."* May our trust in Him grow and our faith be made stronger!

April 17th
The Majestic 23rd Psalm

One of the most majestic and beautiful passages in the Bible was written by David in the 23rd Psalm. David was chosen by God to lead His people as king. He was a man who was a shepherd and lived modestly. He became a mighty warrior who slew the giant Goliath. His words resonate today as a tribute to the greatness of God as our shepherd. The Psalm reads:

The Lord is my shepherd; I shall not want. He maketh me to lie down in green pastures, He leadeth me beside still waters, He restoreth my soul; He leadeth me in the paths of righteousness for His name's sake. Yea, though I walk through the valley of the shadow of death, I will fear no evil; for thou are with me; thy rod and thy staff they comfort me. Thou preparest a table before me in the presence of mine enemies; thou annointest my head with oil; my cup runneth over. Surely goodness and mercy shall follow me all the days of my life; and I will dwell in the house of the Lord, forever.

The messages contained in this Psalm carry great hope and trust in the Lord our God. The book of Psalms is filled with such messages about David's faith and trust, which he uses to praise our Heavenly Father. As our shepherd, He is guiding us to a path that will lead us to righteousness in our life on earth and, further, to a place in heaven in which we will eternally find peace and joy. He will provide us with the nourishment we need on our journey to take care of the physical and spiritual needs we have daily if we embrace God's Love with trust and faith. His rod and staff are used as a shepherd to guide us away from harm and danger as we walk through the darkest valleys we face on our journey. There is nothing to fear as we walk through those times in our life.

I find great comfort as I read this Psalm and reflect on it often in my life. There is peace that comes from knowing we are not alone on our journey and that God watches over us as we go along. May the power of this passage fill your heart with Love and peace as you journey today!

Surrounded by the Family of God

There is no greater treasure for me in the world in which I live than the family which God has given me. I am blessed with those who share Love with me daily and who surround me in my world. I pray continually for their lives and for those who God has put on my path. 1 Timothy 5:8 speaks about the importance of the family when it says, *"But for any provide not for his own, and especially for those of his own house, he hath denied the faith, and is worse than an infidel."* God has intended for us to minister in all ways to the earthly family He has given to us. The most important part of that ministry is to give Love in abundance to all those God has given us as our earthly family and ensure they are on the path to righteousness in God's plan.

The family of God goes beyond the earthly family to others who have faith in Jesus and our Heavenly Father. Mark 3:35 teaches us that: *"For whosoever shall do the will of God, the same is my brother, and my sister, and mother."* To be surrounded by such people emboldens our faith and lifts us up in times of difficulty. Proverbs 17:17 teaches us: *"A friend Loveth at all times, and a brother is born for a time of adversity."* We know who we can count on when our backs are against the proverbial wall in life. We all have friends who may lack the faith and need to learn of power of a walk with Jesus. We demonstrate that in our daily life. However, it is critical we ask them about their faith, walk along the way and tell them of Jesus. In John 1:41, Andrew did exactly that: *"He first findeth his own brother, Simon, and saith unto him, We have found the Messiah, which is, being interpreted, the Christ."* Allow God to use you in this way with those He has given you in your life. Ask for His guidance on how to be make this happen.

Our blessing of our family is a gift from God. We are surrounded by those God has chosen for us. Build brothers and sisters in the faith to walk alongside you. May God bless the lives of others as you minister to them on this day.

April 19th

Learning to Plant Seeds of Faith

Every person is given gifts from God to use in His service. Some are blessed with great speaking abilities, and others are given hearts of gold which willingly give unto others quietly in support during times of need. There are those chosen to be preachers, and others minister behind the scenes. Each is equally important in delivering the message of God's Word. Galatians 6:9 tells us to use the gift God has given us in doing good: *"And let us not be weary of doing well, for in due season we shall reap, if we faint not."* Doing good is simply giving of ourselves in service to others. The more we share the good news of God to others, the greater the harvest of souls of those we care for becomes. Second Corinthians 9:6 says, *"But this I say, He which soweth sparingly shall reap also sparingly, and he which soweth bountifully shall reap also bountifully."* The harvest of souls is ultimate objective of any believer's life as we help others find God.

When we are giving of ourselves to others, we are receiving the blessing of God. Doing good and planting seeds is simply sharing the word of God with others along the way. Luke 8:11 tells us about the parable of the sowing of seeds this way: *"Now the parable is this: the seed is the word of God."* The way God has for you to spread this word is what you need to diligently seek in prayer with God. How can you be used each day? Matthew 9:37–38 says, *"Then saith He unto His disciples: The harvest truly is plenteous, but the laborers are few; pray ye therefore the Lord of the harvest, that He will send out laborers into the harvest."* May we each join as laborers in this harvest of lives each day.

The planting of a seed may be as simple as asking one, "How is your faith walk?" Open the door to a conversation about whether they have a relationship with God. In doing so, you may discover a want and need from one who is ready to listen to the story of our Lord. Let God guide you and empower you as you do. We plant seeds, and God will then nourish them through us if we let Him.

April 20th

The Lord Will Guide You on Your Journey

Our lives have many moments of uncertainty as we face crossroads along the way. Should I take this new job or move from where I am to a new home or location? What career path is going to be best for me? What subjects should I concentrate on with my studies in school? There are many building blocks that form the foundation of the life we live, which must come into place along the way. When we consider whether it is time to retire and live out our life beyond the structure of business, how will we know the time is right? We have a God who is there with us each step along the way to guide us if we allow Him to do so. Psalm 32:8 says it clearly: *"I will instruct thee and teach thee in the way which thou shalt go. I will guide thee with mine eye."* It gives me great comfort to know that when I seek God's will for my life, He will be there with me and for me to guide me through these times of decision.

As we journey, there will be times of setbacks, and no journey is without adversity. Know that you are not alone during these times and at those moments in your life. Psalm 37:23–24 assures us of this: *"The steps of a good man are ordered by the Lord; and he delighteth in His way. Though he fall, he shall not be utterly cast down; for the Lord upholdeth him with His hand."* The great assurance that God will not let us fall as we seek His will and walk on the path to which He has directed us should bring us comfort in the face of life's challenges. We are part of God's plan as we turn over our life to Him. Jeremiah 29:11 tells us this: *"For I know the thoughts that I think toward you, saith the Lord, thoughts of peace and not of evil, to give you an expected end."* We are truly blessed as the children of God to have the master of the universe in control of the plan for our life. Earnestly seek His will, and it will be so in your life today.

Take great joy and comfort in knowing our path will be illuminated by God as we travel on life's highways. Pray to Him for guidance and direction daily.

April 21st

The Sins That Separate Us from God

We live in a world that is sinful in nature. The temptations of the flesh surround us each step along the way. As humans, we have a "sinful nature" as described in Romans 7:18, which says, *"For I know that in me (that is in my flesh) dwelleth no good thing: for to will is present with me; but how to perform that which is good I find not."* We are not able to overcome that sinful nature on our own, but God will deliver us from it as was written in Romans 7:25, which says, *"I thank God through Jesus Christ our Lord! So then with the mind I myself serve the law of God; but with the flesh the law of sin."* Fundamentally, we wrestle daily in the world against this in our spirit. Satan will attempt to separate us from God through sin.

We may stumble, through sin, as we journey through life and feel unworthy of God's grace. First John 1:9 lets us know: *"If we confess our sins, He is faithful and just to forgive us our sins, and cleanse us from all unrighteousness."* We have a God who Loves us and understands the imperfection of human nature. We know others sin against us as we go through life. Matthew 6:14–15 teaches us to forgive them as they do: *"For if you forgive men their trespasses, your heavenly Father will also forgive you. But if you forgive not men their trespasses, neither will your Father forgive your trespasses."* The scriptures teach us to Love one another, and as we do, forgiving one another of transgressions is a way to Love them for who they are. It is spiritually unhealthy to harbor thoughts of such sins of others, and it only damages us when we do.

A human life is not lived without sin. Only one came to earth and lived such a life, and that is Jesus Christ. He came into this world to die on the cross for the sins of the world. First Corinthians 15:3 says, *"For I delivered unto you the first of all that which I received, how that Christ died for our sins according to the scriptures."* The price has been paid for our sins, and we are forgiven!

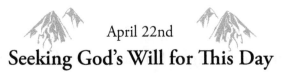

April 22nd

Seeking God's Will for This Day

If we begin each day with the Lord's prayer in our hearts and on our lips, we ask that God's will be done in our lives. That should be the perpetual reminder of our purpose in this world, and we should seek it earnestly. What is God's will for us for this day in which we now live? First Timothy 2:3–4 teaches us: *"For this is good and acceptable in the sight of God our Savior; Who will have all men to be saved, and to come into the knowledge of the truth."* God wants salvation for all His people, which is a gift to us through the death and resurrection of our Lord Jesus Christ. If we believe in Him, we will be saved. The knowledge of the truth comes from reading and seeking the truth in His Word daily. Setting aside time to meditate on His Word will enlighten us to His truth.

We face circumstances and adversity in life which challenge us and may make us question why these things happen to us. God walks with us through all these moments. First Thessalonians 5:18 tells us to give thanks in the face of such times in our lives: *"In everything give thanks, for this is the will of God in Jesus Christ concerning you."* If we accept this and walk with confidence, knowing it is God's will for us, we can give thanks to God for His presence as He walks alongside us through these moments as well. Hebrews 13:20–21 says,

> *Now the God of peace, that brought again from the dead our Lord Jesus, that great shepherd of the sheep, through the blood of the everlasting covenant; Make you perfect in every good work to do His will, working in you that which is well pleasing in His sight, through Jesus Christ; to whom be the glory forever and ever.*

God will equip us with what we need to do His will on this day. We need to be thankful for whatever we face each day as God prepares us for the work He has for us to do. To Love our God with all our heart and soul and to Love one another keeps us on the path He has chosen for us. May God's will be done in our lives on this day!

April 23rd

May Your Light Shine in the Darkness

The scriptures make many references throughout about how we live in a world of darkness and that Jesus came to be the light of the world. It also speaks to the role of the believer as that of one in which we are the light of the world as well. Being such a light is to be sharing the truth of God's Word with those who have yet to discover His truth. Ephesians 5:8 talks about how we were once in the darkness and now walk in the light as it says, *"For ye were sometimes in darkness, but now are ye light in the Lord, walk as children in the light."* As we seek God's plan and guidance, He will illuminate the path on which we are to travel. Psalm 119:105 says, *"Thy word in a lamp unto my feet and a light unto my path."* The more time we spend in God's Word, the more clearly our path becomes illuminated.

The purpose of the life of a believer is to let the light of God's Word shine through us into the lives of others we meet on our journey. Second Corinthians 4:6 tells us, *"For God, who commanded the light to shine out of darkness, hath shined in our hearts, to give the light of the knowledge of the glory of God in the face of Jesus Christ."* It is a beautiful truth that we were put here with a purpose to share this magnificent light in the world of darkness and to help others see it through our lives. First Peter 2:9 proclaims: *"But you are a chosen generation, a royal priesthood, an holy nation, a peculiar people; that ye should show forth the praises of Him who called you out of darkness into His marvelous light."* It is a powerful thought to accept that God called each of us out of darkness into His marvelous light, to be the light of the world in which we live daily.

May God use each of us on this day to share His light with those who are brought to our path. May His will be done in our life as we do so. May the blessing of God be upon you as you walk in His light today!

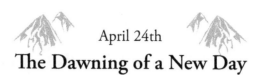

April 24th
The Dawning of a New Day

As we celebrate the resurrection of Jesus and face a world in which we live without the fear of death, we carry with us the message of His life and the words He gave us to guide us in our journey. We understand the passage of time goes very quickly, and the time is soon coming when we will walk with Jesus in heaven if we believe in Him. While on earth, we have a purpose and a plan for our life which is what we need to seek. It is called the "will of God" for our life, and it starts out as a mystery and becomes revealed as we spend time in meditation on the word of God through His scriptures and prayer. Devoting time each day to these steps will lead us to that understanding.

One thing about life, we can't go back to redo those things that have happened before. Nor can we transport ourselves into the future to take care of moments that have not yet arrived. We live in the moments which God has given us for today. When we ask God to forgive us for our sins of yesterday, we need not walk back in our minds to those transgressions. They have been forgiven. Romans 12:2 teaches us: *"And be not conformed to this world, but be transformed by the renewing of your mind, that ye may prove what is that good and acceptable, and perfect will of God."* God's plan for each of us is that we do that which is good for one another and that we share Love as we pass through the time we have together. In doing so, we fulfill the great commandment as taught to us by Jesus.

God will guide us on our path if we seek His will and direction. Psalm 16:11 tells us this: *"Thou wilt show me the path of life, in thy presence is fullness of joy; at thy right hand there are pleasures for evermore."* Jesus lived to teach us the way, the truth, and the life as He said in John 14:6, if we live by His teachings, we are on the path which leads to God's blessings and a life of doing His Will.

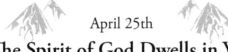

April 25th

The Spirit of God Dwells in You

When Jesus spoke to His disciples about His death, He told them He would not leave them alone, but rather the Holy Spirit would come to comfort them and give them guidance and strength. He said to them in Acts 1:8: *"But ye shall receive power, after the Holy Ghost is come upon you; and ye shall be witnesses unto me both in Jerusalem, and in all Judea, and in Samaria, and unto the uttermost part of the earth."* The power of what to say and when to say it, as far as speaking to others about Jesus, is something that comes from the Holy Spirit, which is sent to those of us who believe. We must seek His spirit, and it will be given to us.

There are many references to the Spirit of God, which lives within us in the Bible. Romans 8:9 tells us as believers: *"But ye are not in the flesh, but in the Spirit, if so be that the Spirit of God dwells in you. Now if any man have not the Spirit of Christ, he is none of His."* We are destined to have this Spirit in our hearts and lives as we turn our life over to Jesus and His teachings. In Ezekiel 36:27, we are promised: *"And I will put my Spirit within you and cause you to walk in my statutes and ye shall keep my judgements and do them."* God does not want us to live in sin, separated from His plan for our lives. He wants to pour out His glory upon us as we seek His will. The Holy Spirit is here now to give us hope, joy, and peace as described in Romans 15:13, which says, *"Now the God of hope fill you with all joy and peace in believing, that ye may abound in hope, through the power of the Holy Ghost."*

When you experience the joy, peace, and hope of the Spirit of God in your life, you can face any challenge that awaits you on this or any other day. You can spread the message of the power of God's Love to others as you meet them along the way. In doing so, their life is also able to be filled with this joy, peace, and hope. May God Bless you richly today on your journey as you embrace His Spirit.

April 26th

May His Truth Set You Free

The world in which we live is filled with sin and evil, which can ensnare you. The enemy of our souls seeks to destroy us each day. The refuge we have is in the Spirit of God, which lives within us and has the power to free us from the sinful nature that exists. In the book of John 14:6, we are taught: *"Jesus saith unto him, 'I am the way, and the truth, and the life. No man cometh unto the Father, but by me.'"* The way to the path to God the Father is through faith and belief in His Son, Jesus Christ. There is no other way.

When Jesus spoke to those who walked with Him and became His believers, Jesus spoke about how they would be free in their lives in John 8:31–32: *"Then said Jesus to those Jews which believed on Him, If ye continue in my word, then ye are my disciples indeed; And ye shall know the truth, and the truth shall set you free."* The freedom which Jesus spoke about was the freedom from sin, and the spiritual oppression sin brings to your soul. Our desire should be to draw near to God in our hearts each day. Psalm 145:18 tells us how to do so: *"The Lord is nigh to all who call upon Him, to all who call upon Him in truth."* As we walk with God each day in seeking His will for our life for that day, the Spirit guides us and shields us, and draws us near to God.

If you earnestly seek the path that God has planned for you each day, He will be there to direct your steps. In Psalm 25:5, David spoke of this when he said: *"Lead me in thy truth, and teach me, for thou are the God of my salvation; on thee do I wait all day."* May our hearts be as devout in seeking God to take us where He wants us to go this day. Be Blessed as you seek His direction for your life today.

April 27th

There Will Be Times of Trouble

In all lives, we will face times of trouble. There will be heartache and disappointments. We all will face times of sickness and experience the loss of a loved one. The Bible tells us we have those moments, but it says God will be with us in such times. Psalm 91:14–16 tells us, *"Because He hath set His Love upon me, therefore will I deliver him, I will set him on high because he hath known my name. He shall call upon me and I will answer him; I will be with him in trouble, I will deliver him, and honor him. With long life, I will satisfy him, and show him my salvation."* The scripture clearly says we will face times of trouble, but it is also clear that God will be with us and protect us when we call upon His name.

Why do we face trouble in our lives is a question we cannot answer easily? We know we can gain strength when we face and overcome adversity in our lives. God enables us with the power to overcome any obstacle on our path. Romans 8:37–39 says, *"Nay, we are more than conquerors through Him that Loved us. For I am persuaded, that neither death, nor life, nor angels, nor principalities, nor powers, nor things present, nor things to come, nor height, nor depth, nor any other creature, shall be able to separate us from the Love of God, which is in Jesus Christ our Lord."* Regardless of the troubles of life we may face, our destiny is to be victorious through God, who is with us each step along the way.

Whatever it is we will face, we have God with us, and we will overcome. John 16:33 confirms this: *"These things I have spoken unto you, that in me ye might have peace. In the world, ye shall have tribulation, but be of good cheer; I have overcome the world."* Our journey is not alone. God will be with us in all times of trouble we face along the way, and we will prevail through Christ.

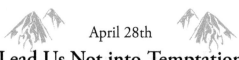

April 28th

Lead Us Not into Temptation

When we pray the Lord's prayer, we ask God to keep us from temptation. What does that mean? The definition of temptation is being enticed by something that appears to be appealing, but we know that it is wrong. As a human, we may be eating a lot more sugar and calories than we know to be healthy. It is possible our temptations are health-related or sexual in nature or that we desire riches, power, or control. The temptations of life take many forms. Anything which separates us from God is a sin. What keeps your heart and soul separate from the God we serve?

Where does temptation come from in our lives? The scripture teaches us that we are tempted by our own sinful nature and evil desires in James 1:13–14: *"Let no man say when he is tempted, I am tempted of God; for God cannot be tempted with evil, neither tempteth he any man. But every man is tempted, when he is drawn away of his own lust, and enticed."* Our Lord Jesus Christ was tempted by the devil after he had been fasting and praying in the wilderness for 40 days, as described in Matthew 4. Jesus was hungry, and the devil attempted to get Him to turn the stones into bread. Jesus rebuked him in verse 4: *"But He answered and said, 'It is written, Man cannot live by bread alone, but by every word that proceedeth out of the mouth of God.'"* The devil went on to tempt our Lord to prove He was the Son of God and offered to give Him authority over the entire world if He would worship the devil. Verse 10: *"Then saith Jesus unto him, Get thee hence, Satan, for it is written, Thou shalt worship the Lord thy God, and Him only shalt thou serve."* When Jesus spoke these words, Satan left Him, and the angels came and attended to Him.

We have authority through the sacrifice that Jesus made on the cross over sin and temptation. We cannot overcome it without turning to Him when temptations come our way. Through Jesus, we have the power to overcome.

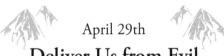

April 29th
Deliver Us from Evil

We can see the evidence of the evil one in this world every day. It comes across on the evening news as we witness the spirit of wickedness as it works in the lives of those who allow it. God gives us the power to overcome it if we seek His spirit in our hearts. The devil plants the seeds of evil in the hearts of those who will allow it to have a place. In Mark 7:21–23, Jesus was talking to His disciples about the evil which is planted by the devil in the hearts of man: *"For from within, out of the heart of men, proceed evil thoughts; adulteries, fornications, murders, thefts, covetousness, wickedness, deceit, lasciviousness, an evil eye, blasphemy, pride, foolishness: all these evil things come from within, and defile the man ."* When we allow the devil to have any place in our hearts and thoughts, he will put such evil in place.

For our hearts to be pure of such evil, we must seek that time alone with God daily to occupy that place for good. James 4:7 teaches us: *"Submit yourselves therefore to God. Resist the devil, and he will flee from you."* Each of us knows the trappings of the evil one. Christ spoke of the things in His message to His disciples. When such thoughts are in your heart, the devil has put them there. We will face trials, and the devil will seek to bring evil into the hearts of the believers. When he does, we must resist him and turn to God for deliverance. Second Timothy 4:18 promises that He will deliver us: *"And the Lord shall deliver me from every evil work and will preserve me unto His heavenly kingdom: to whom be the glory for ever and ever."*

As you walk with God daily, your spirit is strengthened to overcome the temptations that come your way, and your heart turns away from the snares of the evil one. The more you resist the devil, the more he will flee from your heart. As we pray the Lord's prayer, may we seek the deliverance from evil in our life. Be Blessed today as you do so.

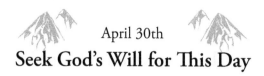

April 30th
Seek God's Will for This Day

As we pray the Lord's prayer, we ask that His Will be done on earth as it is in heaven. What does it mean to seek and find God's will for our life each day? We know the great commandment is to Love God first and foremost in all that we do. Matthew 22:37–40 is quite clear on this: *"Jesus said unto him, Thou shalt Love the Lord thy God with all thy heart, and with all thy soul, and with all thy mind. This is the first and great commandment. And the second is like unto it, Thou shalt Love thy neighbor as thyself. On these two commandments lie all the law and the prophets."* As Jesus directed us, this is what is God's will for our lives. Each day of our lives, we are to be seeking ways to express our Love for God and for those we meet as we go through each day. That is clearly God's will.

God's will extends into aspects of our life in decisions we make, which determine where we live and what we do. If we are truly seeking to serve God as His children, we will come to crossroads and forks in our path, which require prayerful consideration as to which way to go. God has a plan for us if we are faithful to seek it daily. Romans 12:2 teaches us: *"And be not conformed to this world, but be transformed by the renewing of your mind, that ye may prove what is that good and acceptable, and perfect, will of God."* As I pray for people God has given to me in my life, I ask Him for His will to be done in their lives as they face decisions that can change their direction. Such prayers are heard by God, and He will deliver them to the place He wants for them when you pray accordingly.

We know God wants us to live a life that is pure which should be our desire as well. God's will for our life is to Love God first, and then Love one another, be pure in our walk and seek His path through prayer for His guidance. He will direct our paths as we do. Be Blessed today as you walk in His will.

May 1st

The Forgiveness of Sins

We know we have all sinned and continue in the world with a sinful nature. That doesn't mean we have the desire to continue to sin as Christ's followers. Rather, we have a new life in Christ which is one that strives to live in a way that is pleasing to God and without sin. Colossians 1:13–14 says, *"Who hath delivered us from the power of darkness, and hath translated us into the kingdom of His dear Son; In whom we have redemption through His blood, even the forgiveness of sins."* As God's people, it is not our destiny to live under the cloud of darkness which comes from a life of sin. Rather, we walk in the light each day as our faith in Christ transforms our life and lights our path.

We know that sins have and will occur in our lives. The human nature is not perfect and, as such, will lead us into moments out of which we will do that which is not of God. Romans 3:23 tells us, *"All have sinned and come short of the glory of God."* We are not called to be perfect, but we are all called to be forgiven. First John 1:9 affirms: *"If we confess our sins, He is faithful and just to forgive us our sins and to cleanse us from all unrighteousness."* We are not to walk with a burden of sin in our hearts. We are to live in a relationship with God, knowing with confidence that He has forgiven us of sins as we confess those sins to Him. With that being said, we have a new spirit that seeks His righteousness as a follower of Christ. Second Corinthians 5:17 teaches us: *"Therefore, if a man be in Christ, he is a new creature; old things are passed away; behold, all things become new."* As we walk with Christ in our hearts and lives, we seek a new life without sin.

Know you are forgiven if you have asked for such forgiveness from God. Romans 4:7–8 calls those who are forgiven blessed: *"Blessed are they whose iniquities are forgiven; and whose sins are covered. Blessed is the man to whom the Lord will not impute sin."* May we each be so blessed today!

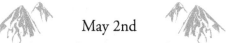

May 2nd

Using the Gift That God Gave You

The Bible describes many unique gifts of the Spirit that God gives to each of us. These gifts were given to each of us with a purpose and a plan from God our Father to be in service to those whom He gives to us in our lives. First Peter 4:10 teaches us: *"As every man hath received the gift, even so minister the same one to another, as good stewards of the manifold grace of God."* One may wonder, what is this gift that I have been given? I don't feel I have any special qualities which God bestowed upon me. Think of what you do especially well in your life. Maybe you simply care for others, for caring is a gift. My wife is constantly giving of herself to others by providing care and support, which is her gift from God.

In a spiritual sense, the body of believers, which is also known as the church, is given diverse gifts from the Holy Spirit. In 1 Corinthians 12:8–11, we are taught these:

> *For one is given by the Spirit the word of wisdom; to another the word of knowledge by the same Spirit; To another faith by the same Spirit; to another the gifts of healing by the same Spirit; To another the working of miracles; To another prophecy; To another discerning of Spirits; To another diverse kinds of tongues; To another the interpretation of tongues. But all these worketh that one and the selfsame Spirit, dividing to every man severally as He will.*

It is not intended for each of us to receive the same gifts. Rather, we are to receive a gift that is unique to each of us to be used in the service of God.

Ask for God's guidance in prayer for how He wants you to use His gift, which He has given to you. James 1:17 says, *"Every good and perfect gift comes from above, and cometh down from the Father of lights, with whom is no variableness, neither shadow of turning."* God is consistent, and He does not change. If you seek God to reveal His gift to you and how you are to use it, you will find the answer today. Be Blessed as you do so.

May 3rd

We Are Saved by the Grace of God

We may question the idea of how God could have chosen us to be called His children. We are not worthy in our hearts or minds to be called as such. Our works alone are not sufficient to make us worthy of such a calling. What the scripture tells us is that we achieve salvation by virtue of the "grace of God." Ephesians 2:8–9 says it this way: *"For by grace are you saved through faith; and that not of yourselves, it is the gift of God; Not of works, lest any man should boast."* It is the grace of God that opened to us the door of salvation through our faith in the Lord Jesus Christ. We can't earn our way into this gift by works.

Grace takes form in divine favor, Love, compassion, and clemency. It is manifest in a Spirit that is filled with Love that is unexpected and undeserved. Jesus was described as "full of grace" in John 1:14: *"And the word was made flesh, and dwelt among us, and we beheld His glory, the glory of the only begotten of the Father, full of grace and truth."* The grace of God was displayed in Christ's words and teachings as He walked with us in His life on earth. In the book of Acts 15:11, the apostle Paul writes: *"But we believe that through the grace of our Lord Jesus Christ, that we shall be saved, even as they."* Let us continue to embrace God's salvation and thank Him for His grace which sets us free from sin.

Paul went on to say in Acts 20:32: *"And now brethren, I commend you to God, and to the word of His grace, which is able to build you up, and to give you an inheritance among all them which are sanctified."* Today, let us thank our Heavenly Father for His grace which gives to each of us salvation and an inheritance among all those who are sanctified through our faith in Jesus Christ. Be Blessed today through the grace of God.

We Are Called to Care for the Elderly

In this world in which many people are working many hours to pay their bills and get caught up in the pursuit of money, we find those among us who are growing older with needs for special care. Often those are family members who lose their ability to care for themselves. In situations where specialized care is needed, with on-site nurses and twenty-four-hour care provided, we seek the help of professionals to deliver this care. The scriptures call for us to be there for these people and to honor them as they go through this time of their lives.

The scriptures are very specific when it comes to families taking care of widows. 1 Timothy 5:3–4 tells us, *"Honor widows that are widows indeed. But if any widows have children or nephews, let them learn first to show piety at home, and to requite their parents; for that is good and acceptable to God."* There is no question we have a responsibility to those who have raised us and have cared for us as little children growing up. In that same chapter in the Bible, we are told to care for all our family in 1 Timothy 5:8, which says, *"But is any provide not for his own, and especially for those of his own house, he hath denied the faith, and is worse than an infidel."* We are taught the importance of Loving one another, and the act of Love will direct us to care for those who are in need around us. The cost is time and money to do so is an investment in the Spirit of Love which will yield great returns in our lives on earth and our lives beyond.

The command to honor our father and mother is the first commandment with a promise. Ephesians 6:2–3 says it clearly: *"Honor thy father and mother; which is the first commandment with a promise; That it may be well with thee, and thou mayest live long on the earth."* As we Love these people, we do provide care for them for reasons beyond the promise of life going well and being extended. The promise of God shows us how important this is.

May 5th

The Glory of God is Manifest in the Elderly

When we are young and the world appears to remain all in front of you, it is easy to look upon the elderly among us as having less to offer us. However, the opposite is true. The excellence of wisdom that comes from years of experience is something to be sought and to learn from in our lives. Job 12:12 teaches us: *"With the ancient is wisdom; and in length of days understanding."* While we are young and have those who are such resources in our world, we can gain great insights into life that lies ahead by respectfully learning from them. To shy away from that opportunity is to miss much that God may want to teach us.

Visit those who are put on your path, who might be able to share God's Love and insights with you who are in their golden years. God has not forgotten them, nor has He forsaken them. Isaiah 46:4 tells us, *"I will be your God throughout your lifetime, until your hair is white with age. I made you, and I will care for you. I will carry you along and save you" (NLT).* It is a great comfort knowing God will carry us to safety as we approach the end of our time on this earth. First Peter 5:5 says, *"In the same way, you who are younger must accept the authority of the elders. And all of you, dress yourselves in humility as you relate to one another."* Let us find the humility and grace that God intends for each of us as we embrace each age God has planned for our lives and for the lives of those who we Love and who He puts on our path.

For those who live a long life, we have the encouragement that the Spirit will renew us day by day in 2 Corinthians 4:16–17, which reads: *"For which cause we faint not, but though our outward man perish, yet the inward man is renewed day by day. For our light affliction, which is but for a moment worketh for us a far more exceeding and eternal weight of glory."* Love those who God gives you who have lived a long and full life and learn the lessons they will teach you as you do. Their wisdom is a treasure in our lives.

May 6th
Have Faith Like a Child

Jesus Loved little children and told the disciples to allow them to come to Him when they sought to do so. He would teach the value of the faith of young children as being a key to those who want to enter the kingdom of heaven. In Mark 10:13–16, we are told of such a time when children tried to reach Jesus and were turned away:

> *And they brought young children to Him, that He should touch them; and His disciples rebuked those who brought them. But when Jesus saw it, He was much displeased, and He said unto them, Suffer the little children to come unto me, and forbid them not; for such is the kingdom of God. Verily I say unto you, whosoever shall not receive the kingdom of God as a little child, he shall not enter therein. And He took them up into His arms, put His hands on them, and blessed them.*

The Love and compassion that Jesus had for little children are evident in the way He handled this moment.

The Love and compassion that Jesus had for little children are evident in the way He handled this moment. The innocence of a child allows us to embrace new ideas without fear and doubt. When Jesus was in the temple, the chief priests got angry about the praises being sung to Jesus just prior to His arrest and crucifixion in Matthew 21:15–16, which says,

> *And when the chief priests and scribes saw the wonderful things that He did, and the children crying in the temple, and saying, Hosanna to the Son of David; they were sore displeased. And said unto Him, Hearest thou what these say? And Jesus said unto them, Yea; Have ye never read, Out of the mouths of babes and sucklings thou hast perfected praise?*

Jesus brought forth praise from the innocent lips of children while the church leaders of the time rejected Him despite the wonderful things they witnessed. May we embrace the message of the cross and the teachings of Jesus with innocence like a child.

May 7th
Teach Your Children the Way

One of the greatest joys in a person's life is the day of the birth of a child that God has given to them. Being a father or mother to a child in this world is an amazing blessing that comes with a significant obligation to nurture and teach that beautiful soul the truth of life as you know it to be. During your life, there is no other thing that is more important than being a parent and doing that which is right for the training and development of your child. Proverbs 22:6 tells us, *"Train up a child in the way he should go: and when he is old, he will not depart from it."* Instilling in the heart and mind of the child early in life the teachings of the Lord will build in the child the guardrails of the holy commandments as the guide for their life, which keep them on the path to find God.

Isaiah 54:13 says this: *"And all thy children shall be taught of the Lord; and great will be the peace of thy children."* We know this to be the way to lead your children to a happier life that follows the teaching of Christ our Savior. The best guide for the child is to see the parent as one who leads a life consistent with the teachings of God. If you tell a child to behave one way and live a life inconsistent with that, the child is going to immediately discount what is being said and model after the lifestyle lived by the parent. The importance of being taught the scriptures by a parent is reflected in 2 Timothy 3:14–15, which says, *"But continue thou in the things which thou hast learned and hast been assured of, knowing of whom thou hast learned them. And that from a child you have known the holy scriptures, which are able to make thee wise unto salvation through faith which is in Jesus Christ."*

The happiness and joy of having a child following on the path to righteousness through faith in Jesus is something that is a great reward for a parent. 3 John 1:4 says this: *"I have no greater joy than to hear that my children are walking in the truth."* This is your reward as you teach your children the way.

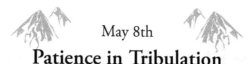

May 8th
Patience in Tribulation

Patience is a virtue that we all know to be true. It is a virtue that is elusive for those of us who want to be in control of all we do. High achievers are often the least patient of those among us and expect to get things done quickly and efficiently in dealing with issues in their life. Walking with God daily, we must understand that it is not our timing that is important, but, rather, God's timing we are waiting on for life's results we are after. We cannot see past the circumstances of the moment in which we live, but God sees what the consequences of each action will be. Hebrews 10:36 tells us, *"For ye have need of patience, that, after ye have done the will of God, ye might receive the promise."* We are always trying to get ahead of situations to the resolution of any potential conflict in which we find ourselves. God will deliver those resolutions in His time, and the promise of God will then be revealed.

Our faith is sometimes tested in this way. We are not always capable of waiting on the Lord as the scriptures require of us. Isaiah 40:31 reminds us: *"But they that wait upon the Lord shall renew their strength; they shall mount up with wings as eagles; they shall run and not be weary; they shall walk, and not faint."* The power and encouragement of that message are profound. While we are patient, we are to continue to work and serve others we are given by God on our journey. Romans 12:12–13 tells us, *"Rejoicing in hope; patient in tribulation; continuing instant in prayer; Distributing to the necessity of saints; given to hospitality."* During all our trials and tribulations of life, we are here to serve those who are part of our journey and who are in need.

Patience is often a virtue that can keep us from conflict with others. Proverbs 15:18 says, *"A wrathful man stirreth up strife; but he that is slow to anger appeaseth strife."* Patience gives us peace in relationships with others. May the virtue of patience be in your spirit on this day.

May 9th

Be Filled with Hope Each Day

We live in a world filled with much despair and forces of evil which are at work in lives of those who live around us. Many get caught up in despair and overcome by the news that streams into our hearts and lives each day. God has a plan which takes us beyond the reaches of the evil one who tries to ensnare us with thoughts that limit our vision of who we are and why we are here. Jeremiah 29:11 tells us, *"For I know the thoughts that I think toward you, saith the Lord, thoughts of peace and not of evil, to give you an expected end."* When you turn your life over to God, you have a future, and it is a bright one. We are passing through this land and on a journey that takes us beyond.

While we journey on this earth, we do not walk alone each day. Zephaniah 3:17 says, *"The Lord thy God in the midst of thee is mighty; He will save, He will rejoice over thee with joy; He will rest in His Love, He will joy over thee with singing."* God doesn't leave us alone to face trials and tribulations while we journey through this time. He is with us to support us and to lift us up during every step we take. Second Corinthians 4:17–18 tells us, *"For our light affliction, which is but for a moment, worketh for us a far more exceeding and eternal weight of glory. While we look not at the things which are seen, but at the things which are not seen. For the things which are seen are temporal; but the things which are not seen are eternal."* The promise of an eternal life with God in heaven awaits us as we hold fast to our faith through the hope God has given us.

The scriptures were provided to us to give us this hope. Romans 15:4 teaches this: *"For whatsoever things were written aforetime were written for our learning, that we through patience and comfort of the scriptures might have hope."* The more time you spend reading your scriptures each day, the more your hope and trust in God grow. May you embrace this hope and trust on this day fully.

May 10th
The Power of Positive Thinking

We encounter those each day who are clearly optimistic and those who allow negative thoughts to rule their thinking. We are certainly influenced by the events of our lives at times which cause us to drift in one direction or the other. Ultimately, we can control our destiny by guiding our minds to positive thoughts, which will then direct our energy accordingly. Proverbs 17:22 teaches us: *"A merry heart doth good like a medicine, but a broken spirit drieth the bones."* The power of your attitude can affect your mental and physical health. As such, we need to embrace positive thoughts to live the life God has planned for us.

Our thoughts will translate into what we say and how we appear to others. Turning your words into positive expressions serve as a healing potion inside your own heart and soul. Proverbs 16:24 says, *"Pleasant words are as a honeycomb, sweet to the soul and healing to the bones."* Once again, attitude and health tend to be related. When we turn our thoughts into our words and express positive thoughts, it lifts us up as well as others around us. Proverbs 12:25 speaks to how anxiety pulls us down negatively: *"Heaviness in the heart of a man maketh it stoop; but a good word maketh it glad."* We need to pass along good words to those who we meet along the way each day who are suffering from their own anxiety, but we need to address our own with positive words and thoughts.

The best way to change your energy and thoughts into the mindset of one who is positive each day is through the Holy Spirit being alive in your heart and life. Ask God daily for the positive influence of the Holy Spirit to fill your heart. Ephesians 4:23 tells us this: *"And be renewed in the Spirit of your mind."* We live in the physical world as spiritual people. We are here to change the world around us as we walk with God and become His ambassadors to those, He gives us on our journey. May you be a blessing to those who cross your path with your positive energy today. Be Blessed as you do!

May 11th
Surround Yourself with Positive People

One of life's greatest blessings is to be surrounded by those who lift your spirits each day. God gives us those people along the path of our journey to help us to elevate our thinking and to nurture our spirits. We also will have encounters with those who drain our energy and infuse negativity into our thoughts. Their influence on our lives is less than positive. We need to do our best to help them overcome their negative attitudes toward life and others, but we can't spend too much of our time in that type of environment if we intend to stay healthy and on course.

Romans 12:2 speaks of having a transformation of thought: *"And do not be conformed to this world, but be ye transformed by the renewing of your mind, so that ye may prove what is that good, and acceptable, and perfect, will of God."* When you surround yourself with those who share the desire to find a path that is pleasing to God, you will find that which is good and acceptable and perfect in God's will for your life. We are influenced by those who surround us each day. Proverbs 13:20 teaches us: *"He that walketh with wise men shall be wise; but a companion of fools will be destroyed."* As such, choose your friends carefully and be careful who you spend your time with each day.

The attitudes of others will be infectious in our lives as we spend time with them. Proverbs 22:24–25 says, *"Make no friendship with an angry man; and with a furious man thou shalt not go; Lest thou learn his ways, and get a snare to thy soul."* We are influenced by those we meet and can be a positive influence in the lives of others each day. Positive people have a spirit that is radiant in their countenance. Proverbs 15:13 says, *"A merry heart makes a cheerful countenance, but by sorrow of the Spirit is broken."* Be one of those who walk today with a cheerful countenance and become a positive influence on the lives you encounter this day. May those you meet lift you up as well.

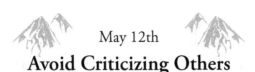

May 12th
Avoid Criticizing Others

It is human nature to find fault with those who are doing things or saying things that are different than the way we would conduct ourselves. In the world of politics, there are liberals and conservatives, and whichever side we are not on, we can deem their respective views to be wrong. When we take the action step of being critical of those people, we have set up our hearts in judgment of their beliefs. As the spirit of Love guides our hearts and souls, we find more tolerance for actions and words that are not consistent with our own.

The Bible teaches us in Ephesians 4:29: *"Let no corrupt communication proceed out of your mouth, but that which is good to the use of edifying, that it may minister grace to the hearers."* When we are critical and speak negatively about those who may see the world differently than we do, we attempt to put down their ways as being inferior to ours. When we speak in a manner to build them up, it gives more grace to those who hear us. We are not put here in this place to be the judge of others. James 5:9 says it this way: *"Grudge not one against another, brethren, lest ye be condemned, behold, the judge standeth before the door."* God's plan for our lives is to support one another with Love in our hearts. When we do so, we draw others into that spirit, and they grow with Love in their hearts as well.

When we walk with God and Love grows in our hearts, we have less need to concern ourselves with the shortcomings of those around us. Rather, we seek to build them up with our thoughts and words. First Peter 4:8 speaks to this as it says, *"And above all things, have fervent charity among yourselves, for charity shall cover a multitude of sins."* We all sin and fall short of the glory of God in our lives. The more tolerance we show towards others, the more it will be returned to us. May this spirit of Love guide us today and remove from our hearts the critical nature that tries to influence us. Be Blessed today in all that you do.

May 13th
Your Circle of Friends Is Important

We associate with friends who are like-minded. For successful people, there is an attraction to others who have produced success in their own lives. We tend to send our children to the same schools and go to the same social events. God puts people on our paths that we have an opportunity to learn from and grow with as we seek His will for our lives. Conversely, there are those which we will meet along that path that are not of the faith and will lead us away from the things of God. How you deal with those can determine the direction of the faith walk in your life.

We know the people we spend our time with will have influence on our lives. Psalm 1:1 speaks to this as it says, *"Blessed is the man that walketh not in the counsel of the ungodly; nor standeth in the way of sinners; nor sitteth in the seat of the scornful."* When our days are surrounded by those who have hearts that are wicked and spend their lives with sinful actions, we find ourselves drawn in that direction as well. Proverbs 12:26 tells it this way: *"The righteous is more excellent than his neighbor; but the way of the wicked seduceth them."* Look at the friends you have chosen. Which direction have they attempted to influence you on your journey as you spend your time with each of them? First Corinthians 15:33 says it plainly: *"Be not deceived; evil communications corrupt good manners."* Be selective with those who you choose to spend your time with each day.

If we seek to find those who God has put on our path to guide us to a closer walk with Him, He will bring them to us. Jeremiah 3:15 tells us, *"And I will give you pastors according to mine heart, which shall feed you with knowledge and understanding."* When our lives are surrounded by such pastors, we will find our paths taking us to a knowledge and understanding of God's will for our lives more clearly. Surround yourself with such people on this day.

May 14th
Finding Comfort in Times of Loss

We experience grief during times of loss in our lives. Jesus did when he saw Mary weeping when her brother, Lazarus, had died. John 11:35 tells us, *"Jesus wept."* Grief over lost Loved ones or other tragic moments we experience in our human lives is inevitable. Sadness occurs as we go through these times. Dealing with such sadness is very difficult regardless of your faith. The Bible speaks to this time of mourning and says in Matthew 5:4: *"Blessed are those who mourn, for they will be comforted."* God brings comfort to us through His Holy Spirit.

He uses us as vessels in our human relationships to comfort one another. Often a spoken word will soothe the troubled spirit of another as we direct thoughts to the eternal reward that awaits those who believe. Second Corinthians 1:3–4 speaks to this as it says, *"Blessed be God, even the Father of our Lord Jesus Christ, the Father of mercies, and the God of all comfort. Who comforteth us in all tribulation, that we may be able to comfort them which are in any trouble, by the comfort wherewith we ourselves are comforted of God."* The ministry God will give you in life is often designed for such a moment in the life of another. People are put on our path for a purpose for us to fulfill. God gives us the opportunity to invest Love into the life of one who needs to receive that gift of God through each of us. Many times God sends those to comfort us as well.

Know that in your darkest moments, God will be with you and shine His light upon you to heal your broken spirit. Psalm 34:18 says, *"The Lord is close to the brokenhearted and saves those who are crushed in spirit."* We know when we go through such difficult times, we do not walk alone. The spirit is with us to comfort us in our darkest hours. Be there for one another as comforters and share the Love God gives you in those difficult times to lift each other up. We pray for those who are suffering loss and pray for God to use you to bring comfort.

May 15th

Draw Your Strength from God

The daily struggles of life are continuous. We learn to work each day as young people in school, and it carries on through life as we build our careers and work at our jobs. The magnitude of trying to achieve at a high level in our workplace or school can add stress to our hearts and minds. Many people grow weary from the daily grind they face and need to renew their spirit and energy to build their strength to carry on. Those who exercise and eat the proper diet and get enough rest through sleep are in a better position to endure and grow in their lives. Even those who take great physical care may experience emotional stress and fatigue as they go through the years of work in striving for excellence in life.

The renewal of strength in our lives comes from God when we are spiritually connected to Him and when we daily walk with Him. Second Timothy 1:7 tells us, *"For God hath not given us the spirit of fear; but of power, and of Love, and of a sound mind."* This is a beautiful thought to hold onto and embrace in your life. Be bold and courageous in your life as you receive this power to Love—and exercise self-discipline. We cannot do this on our own, and it is not our strength, but the strength of God will sustain us each day. First Chronicles 16:11 says, *"Seek the Lord and His strength, seek His face continually."* When we turn our attention to that seeking God's will and seeking His face, our power to fight the battles we face in this world becomes easier each day. We never walk alone.

When you feel weak or need to be strengthened, reflect on what God tells us in Isaiah 40:29, which says, *"He giveth power to the faint; and to them who have no might, He increaseth strength."* We may feel weak, but He is strong. Take courage and faith in knowing He will deliver you in times when you are feeling weak if you turn to Him for your strength. Be courageous and strong today in your faith walk.

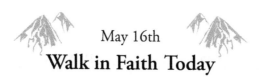

May 16th

Walk in Faith Today

We often refer to the idea of our journey as a "faith walk" as we go through this lifetime. When opening a conversation with another about their beliefs, we can do so by asking them, "How is your faith walk?" The way they answer is revealing and will lead us to the opportunity to plant seeds from which their faith can be discovered and grow. Faith in God is the basis of our relationship and our daily journey with God. Second Corinthians 5:7 tells us, *"For we walk by faith, not by sight."* We can't see God in a physical sense, but we see His evidence in all that is around us. To receive His blessings, we must open our hearts to the faith which comes through reading His Word. Romans 10:17 tells us this: *"So then faith cometh by hearing, and hearing by the word of God."* To deepen our faith and to live in it fully, we must engage in reading the Word of God and seek those who deliver the message of Christ through His Word.

If we are truly seeking a relationship with God each day, we are looking for ways to better understand His purpose for our lives. As we do, our faith is rewarded. Romans 1:17 speaks to finding God's righteousness in His gospel: *"For therein is the righteousness of God revealed from faith to faith; as it is written; The just shall live by faith."* The idea of living by faith is simply opening your heart to the Love and presence of God in your life each day. God wants to come into our lives. Revelation 3:20 says, *"Behold! I stand at the door and knock. If any man hear my voice and open the door, I will come in to him, and will sup with him and he with me."* If Jesus is knocking on your door, would you want Him to come in and dine with you?

The walk of faith is meaningful each day. It is how we take the steps required to come closer to God in our lives. Without faith, we cannot make this happen. By faith, we open the door for Christ to come in. Be Blessed as you do.

The Power of Prayer for God's Will to Be Done

The idea of talking with God through prayer is sometimes difficult for people to accept. We serve the creator of the universe and know that He seeks to have a personal relationship with us. When you take time to privately go to Him in prayer, you must accept the fact that He is faithful and just in listening to your prayers and will respond. When you pray, you must believe it will be answered by God, and He will do so. Mark 11:24 says, *"Therefore I say unto you, what so ever ye desire, when ye pray, believe that ye receive them, and ye shall have them."*

What if you are asking for something that is outside of the will of God for your life or for another? The answer you receive from God may not be that which you have asked Him for unless you pray that His will be done. Jesus made that prayer in the Garden of Gethsemane. Our prayer should always be to the Father that we wish for His will to be done on earth as it is in heaven. Jesus taught us to pray in this way. First John 5:14 confirms this as it says, *"And this is the confidence we have in Him; that, if we ask anything according to His will, He heareth us."* Aligning our prayers to seek His will for our life will carry great power and is what God wishes for each of us to do.

The prayers of God's people have healing power. Pray for those God gives to you who need a healing touch from our Father. James 5:16 says, *"Confess your faults, one to another, and pray for one another, that ye may be healed. The effectual fervent prayer of a righteous man availeth much."* Be confident that our God listens to your prayer and gives you the desires of your heart when you seek His will through your prayers. Be Blessed today as you do so.

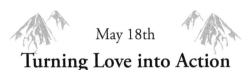

May 18th
Turning Love into Action

The scriptures teach us to Love one another as He Loved us. John 13:34–35 expresses it this way: *"A new commandment I give unto you; That ye Love one another; as I have Loved you, that ye also Love one another. By this all men shall know that ye are my disciples, if ye have Love one to another."* To be a "disciple of Christ," the evidence of His Love in us. As we Love, it is more than a feeling or an emotion. Love requires that we do things that will turn the Love into action in lives of those we meet. First John 3:18 speaks to this as it says, *"My little children, let us not Love in word, neither in tongue, but in deed and in truth."*

This is not a suggestion made by Christ, but it was a commandment. Jesus spoke with authority that this is how we are to live our lives. In the book of John, in chapter 21, Jesus appears to His disciples for a 3rd time following His resurrection. They had been fishing all night and had not caught anything. He told them to try again with their nets in verse 6: *"And He said unto them; Cast the net on the right side of the ship, and ye shall find. They cast therefore, and now they were not able to draw it for the multitude of the fish."* He went then with the disciples and had a meal with them. Following the meal, He asked Peter 3 times if he Loved Him in verses 15–17. When Peter responded "yes" each time, Jesus said these words: *"Feed my lambs…. Take care of my sheep….and…Feed my sheep."* The action of Love, as described by Jesus, was to care for those who are in need which we meet along the way. Feed those who are in need.

I believe God brings us into the lives of others who have such needs. Our role in life is not simply to Love those who Love us in return. Luke 6:35 tells us to Love those who come against us in life: *"But Love ye your enemies, and do good, and lend, hoping for nothing again, and your reward shall be great, and ye shall be the children of the Highest; for He is kind unto the unfaithful and to the evil."* God is Love, and His Love extends to all people, and we are to Love them as well.

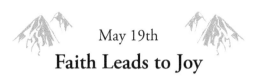

May 19th

Faith Leads to Joy

The source of pure joy in our life comes through having faith in our Lord and Savior, Jesus Christ. Without it, we are lost and searching for answers to the questions we face in life. There is an emptiness in the lives of those without faith, and their life has no sense of purpose until God unveils it for them. To find that sense of purpose, we must earnestly seek it in our quest to grow closer to God. The Bible discusses the power of faith in 1 Peter 1:8–9, which says, *"Whom having not seen, ye Love; in whom, though now ye see Him not, yet believing, ye rejoice with joy unspeakable and full of glory."* Knowing that by faith, we are given the gift of salvation and the treasure of eternal life by God is a pure source of joy for believers. It is a blessing beyond measure.

To say we have joy does not eliminate the grief, disappointment, and heartache we will experience during our time on earth. All humans have such moments during their lifetime journey. John 16:22 speaks of this as it says, *"And ye now, therefor, have sorrow; but I will see you again, and your heart shall rejoice, and your joy no man taketh away from you."* The experiences of life are temporal, but the joy of our spiritual journey is eternal, and therein lies the source of our joy. It is our calling to share our joy and happiness with others. Nehemiah 8:10 says, *"Then he said unto them, 'Go your way, eat the fat, and drink the sweet, and send portions unto them for whom nothing is prepared; for this day is Holy unto the Lord; neither be ye sorry, for the joy of the Lord is your strength."*

Be filled with the joy of the Lord on this day which is holy to our Lord. Be one who is a source of joy to those you meet along the path. Our faith leads us to a place where joy is abundant. Embrace it and share it with others on this day. Be Blessed as you do!

May 20th
Was That a Coincidence?

We have moments in our lives in which things appear to happen by an amazing coincidence. People may tell you about an amazing doctor they have had an experience with just at the time you may need one of that specialty. Perhaps it was a contractor that they used who was excellent when you were thinking of having work done on your home. There may have been a time you gave money to a homeless person, and soon thereafter, someone returned the favor of giving you support that was needed which appeared to be another of life's amazing coincidences. Albert Einstein, who was known as one of the world's smartest people, said, *"Coincidence is God's way of remaining anonymous."* Life is a series of events and all part of God's master plan for each of us. He directs those who cross our paths, and we are, in that way, given to one another for a purpose.

The scriptures tell of how God will orchestrate His plan. As followers of Christ, God is using us to do His work while we are in this world. As we journey in life, we have a plan which is unfolding around us and through us. The closer we get to finding the will of God for our lives, the more blessed we are as the plan unfolds. Ephesians 1:11 says, *"In whom we have obtained an inheritance, having been predestined according to the purpose of Him who works all things in accordance with the counsel of His own will."* As we open our hearts and minds to embracing His purpose and His will, we find things in our lives working together for good. Romans 8:28 says it best: *"And we know that all things work together for good to them that Love God, to them who are called according to His purpose."*

May we walk as one of those who Loves God today and be guided to seeking His purpose and will for our lives. There is no coincidence in our lives, but rather, God directing us in accordance with His will.

May 21st
We Live in God's Protection

There are dangers people face each day in this world around us. Those dangers are greater when you travel but exist on days when you stay at your home. Our God watches over us and provides us with His protection. Proverbs 2:8 teaches us, *"For He keepeth the paths of judgement, and preserveth the way of His saints."* This protection is something we should ask God for in prayer as we go through each day for ourselves and for those we Love. There is nothing to fear in this world, even death, as it will open the door for our journey beyond heaven.

As the people of God, we are to obey His commandments and live in accordance with His laws, and He will protect us from harm according to His Word. The scripture tells us in Genesis 28:15: *"And behold, I am with thee and will keep thee in all places whither thou goest and will bring thee back again into this land; for I will not leave thee, until I have done that which I have spoken to thee of."* With God as our protector as His plan for our life continues to unfold, we have nothing to fear from what lies ahead on our path. The journey we are on is not simply one of the flesh and blood but one of the spirit to our ultimate destination. Our battles along the way are spiritual more than they are physical. God's protection is there for us as we face these battles as described in 2 Timothy 4:18: *"And the Lord shall deliver me from every evil work and will preserve me unto His heavenly kingdom; to whom be the glory forever and ever."*

The journey we are on has an end in the earthly realm. The end of this time on earth will lead us to another kingdom that will be eternal for those who believe in Jesus Christ as our Lord and Savior. Nothing we face along the way can deter us from this destiny in our lives. As such, there is nothing to fear for those who walk with God each day. Be Blessed today as you do so.

May 22nd
How All Things Work Together

We go through so many different types of experiences in life. There are seasons of joy and great delight, such as when we are married or have our children born into our world. We share these moments with those around us who we have great Love for and experience much happiness as we do. There are also times of sadness and difficulty in dealing with the emotions of loss of Loved ones and sickness in our family or friends for whom we care deeply. In those moments, we find it hard to understand why we or others we Love must go through such times. It is truly impossible for us to understand all that life delivers to us along the journey. God is with us always to direct our paths and brings us comfort as we seek His presence in the most difficult of these moments.

In Ecclesiastes 3:1–4, we are told of these different times in our life we will go through:

> To every thing there is a season, and a time to every purpose under heaven: A time to be born, a time to die; a time to plant, and a time to pluck up that which is planted; A time to kill, and a time to heal; a time to break down, and a time to build up; A time to weep, and a time to laugh; a time to mourn and a time to laugh.

We clearly will and do experience it all during human existence. It is important to thank God for all that we face as we know He is with us each day of the journey in all phases of our life. We can't always understand why things are happening as a part of our human experience. There are going to be things that happen we will not fully understand in our time here.

God has a purpose for each of us as our life continues to unfold. We are here to seek His will and find His purpose for us each day. God is working for good for those of us who Love Him and are called to His purpose. Take comfort in that each day as you face the challenges of the various changes and seasons that life brings you. Romans 8:28 teaches us it is all working together for good.

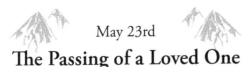

May 23rd
The Passing of a Loved One

We know it is our destiny to pass through this life into that life that lies beyond the veil of death. The most difficult experience we face along the way is the time when one of those we Love the most completes their journey on the earth and moves on. My neighbor called us to tell us about the sudden and unexpected loss of her father this week. I had my father pass without warning and can easily relate to such a feeling which happens when you don't have any expectations and don't get to say goodbye. The emptiness which comes at such a time is profound. I also lost my mother but in a totally different manner. She was bedridden at the end of her journey, and we knew for many days that her time to pass was at hand. I got to visit with her at her bedside and hold her hand and tell her how much I Loved her. It gave me a chance to feel closure when her moment arrived. All I know is it is God's plan for each of us to leave this earth when our time is done.

The scriptures talk about the passing from death into life in a positive way. Isaiah 57:1–2 says, *"The righteous perisheth, and no one layeth it to heart; and merciful men are taken away, none considering that the righteous is taken away from the evil to come. He shall enter into peace; they shall rest in their beds, each one walking in his uprightness."* The fear of death by one who is walking with God should not exist. Jesus speaks of death of the believer in John 11:25–26: *"Jesus said to her, 'I am the resurrection and the life. He that believeth in me, though he were dead, yet shall he live. And whosoever liveth and believeth in me shall never die. Believest thou this?'"* Jesus speaks with authority that we will never die if we believe in Him but live life everlasting with Him.

We will mourn the passing away of a Loved one who is a believer because we will no longer share time with them on earth but know they are with God. However the passing occurs, know God was with them till the end and beyond.

May 24th

God Is Merciful

We are offered the gift of salvation from a Loving God who has shown mercy to us as sinners. It is not earned by our good works but rather a gift from a merciful Father in heaven. We struggle daily with a sinful nature that strives to lead us away from the path to our Heavenly Father. We must willfully seek Him to draw closer each day. Though we have such a nature, God is gracious and forgiving of sins of the past when we seek Him. Isaiah 1:18 teaches us: *"Come now, let us reason together, saith the Lord. 'Though your sins are like scarlet, they shall be as white as snow; though they are red like crimson, they shall be as wool."* Don't let the evil one plant thoughts in your head of being separated from God because of sins of your past. Know God has forgiven them when you repent of those sins and ask for His forgiveness.

Our faith in Christ is the path to a new life. When we take that step, the world becomes a new one, and our life is born again with a fresh start. First Peter 1:3 speaks of God's mercy and our new life in Christ as it says, *"Blessed be the God and Father of our Lord Jesus Christ, which according to His abundant mercy has begotten us again unto a lively hope of the resurrection of Jesus Christ from the dead."* The magnificent truth of the faith we share is that Jesus Christ is alive today, and death could not hold Him. The gift of salvation is described in Titus 3:5: *"Not by works of righteousness which we have done, but according to His mercy He saved us, by the washing of regeneration, and renewing of the Holy Ghost."*

May we each be washed in the regeneration of God's Love and renewed by the Holy Spirit as we go through this day filled with the Blessings of God the Father. We are blessed to have this gift from God, who is merciful and Loving to all His people who Love Him. Be Blessed today as you walk with God!

May 25th

The Conversion of Paul

Saul of Tarsus was a zealot and a Pharisee who persecuted believers in Christ for the leaders of the Jewish church. He was active in participating in the stoning of Stephen as described in Acts 7:58–60, which describes the event: *"And cast him out of the city, and stoned him and witnesses laid down their clothes at a young man's feet whose name was Saul. And they stoned Stephen, calling upon God and saying, 'Lord Jesus, receive my spirit.' And he kneeled down and cried out with a loud voice, 'Lord lay not this sin to their charge.' And when he had said this, he fell asleep."* Paul's conviction to persecute the believers of Christ was intense, and he was committed to doing it full-time.

While on the road to Damascus to find and persecute other believers, we learn in Acts 9:3–7 the events which changed Saul's life forever: *"And as he journeyed, he came near Damascus, and suddenly there shined round about him a light from heaven; and he fell to the earth and heard a voice saying to him, 'Saul, Saul, why persecutest thou me?' And he said, 'Who are thou, Lord?' And the Lord said, 'I am Jesus whom thou persecutest: it is hard for thee to kick against the pricks.' And trembling and astonished he said, 'Lord what wilt thou have me to do?' And the Lord said, 'Arise and go into the city and it shall be told thee what thou must do."* The story of how he was guided to a life-changing belief in Jesus Christ is truly an amazing one. Paul transforms into the great evangelist who builds the early churches throughout the Middle East and into Europe. His letters to the churches account for thirteen of the books of the Bible, which we have today as our Holy Scriptures.

As passionate as Saul was in his life as one who persecuted the believers, he became totally committed to the faith in Jesus Christ as one of His most devoted followers and ministers as Paul the Apostle. That same power of the Holy Spirit is alive today and can transform each of us today into a powerful follower of God.

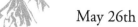

May 26th

Paul Wrestles with His Human Nature

The Apostle Paul was one of the most influential people in the history of the world. His 13 books of the Bible provide much of the foundation of the church of Jesus Christ for believers throughout history. His writings bring comfort to all believers today as we read his words and are taught by them. We all deal with a sinful nature, and Paul also faced that as a human. He writes of it in Romans 7:15, which says, *"I do not understand what I do. For what I want to do, I do not do, but what I hate, I do."* Further, in verses 17–18, he says, *"Now then it is no more that I do it, but sin that dwelleth in me. For I know that in me, that is in my flesh, dwelleth no good thing; for to will is present with me; but how to perform that which is good I find not."* Paul wrestles with him humanity.

This is a man who spent his life after his conversion teaching others throughout the world how to live a life of faith in seeking God's will for their lives. As righteous as he was, he dealt with the same 'sinful nature' which afflicts us all. His description of this in the seventh chapter of Romans is profound. He was troubled by his own sinful nature, which he faced. We face this same struggle each day. In verses 22–23, Paul continues: *"For I delight in the law of God after the inward man; But I see another law in my members, warring against the law of my mind, and bringing me into captivity to the law of sin which is in my members."* The struggle of the forces of sin against us is very real each day. We fight spiritual battles because of it all along the way in our lives.

We don't fight these battles alone. Paul speaks to the victory we have through Jesus Christ in verse 25: *"I thank God through Jesus Christ our Lord. So then with the mind I myself serve the law of God; but with the flesh the law of sin."* We overcome our sinful nature through Jesus Christ and following God's laws. We know this struggle is one that is ongoing in the human experience.

May 27th
You Can Do This!

We face challenges in life in all aspects of what we do. The challenge may be establishing and maintaining a healthy lifestyle with the disciplines required for proper exercise and nutrition. The challenge may be business related regarding an endeavor that stretches you beyond the comfort zone of knowing the outcome will be easily reached. The challenge of passing a specific class is required in which the instruction you are receiving is not clear to you. When we face challenges, we can become discouraged and want to pull back from embracing the opportunities which are there for us. How often do we take these concerns and possible anxieties to God in prayer to ask for His support as we face them? God is there for us to strengthen us in all we do and face.

Fear, anxiety, or doubt is not anything we need to embrace when facing difficult challenges in our lives. First Peter 5:7 tells us, *"Casting all your care upon Him for He careth for you."* Sometimes the elimination of fear and anxiety enables you to perform at your highest level and helps you take the steps needed to achieve great results. Isaiah 41:10 says it beautifully when we look to God for our strength and support: *"Fear thou not; for I am with thee, be not dismayed; for I am thy God; I will strengthen thee; Yea, I will help thee; Yea, I will uphold thee with the right hand of my righteousness."* This does not say that God is going to do it for us, but rather that He is going to give us the strength to do it.

Our confidence in our capabilities should grow each day as we seek God's will for our lives and endeavor to keep Him close in all we face. There is no test you cannot pass, nor is there any goal you cannot achieve, provided it is consistent with God's plan for your life and as you continue to seek His will. One of the greatest messages in the Bible is Philippians 4:13, which says, *"I can do all things through Christ which strengtheneth me."* On our own, we cannot achieve our goals, but while we walk with God each day, all things are possible!

May 28th

You Are a Child of God

As a believer in the Lord Jesus Christ, we have entered a new life as a child of God. The royal heritage that comes with the faith is significant in that our Heavenly Father watches over us as one of His children each day. His Love and mercy cover us in all we do as we walk with Him each step along the way of our lives. We are described as the "people of God" in 1 Peter 2:9–11, which says,

> *But you are a chosen generation, a royal priesthood, a holy nation, a peculiar people, that ye should show forth the praises of Him who hath called you out of darkness into His marvelous light. Which is time past you were not a people, but now you are the people of God; which had not obtained mercy, but now have obtained mercy. Dearly beloved I beseech you as strangers and pilgrims, abstain from fleshly lusts, which war against the soul.*

We are spoken of as a separate and holy nation separate from the world and are expected to act as such.

God's great Love for us is what brings us into a relationship as His children. This is made clear in 1 John 3:1–3, which describes our relationship to God this way: *"Behold, what manner of Love the Father hath bestowed upon us, that we should be called the Sons of God, and it doth not yet appear what we shall be; but we know that, when He shall appear, we shall be like Him; for we shall see Him as He is. And every man that hath this hope in Him purifieth himself even as He is pure."* The power of this message to each of us is that we are God's children, and as such, we are to purify our lives by following Christ's lead. The soul of the follower will seek that which will please God as His children.

On this day, declare the praises of Him who called you out of darkness and into His wonderful light. Abstain from the sinful desires which wage war against your soul and seek the purity which is like Christ, for you are a child of God!

May 29th
The Amazing Grace of God

There is a wonderful Christian hymn called *Amazing Grace*, which was written by an English poet and clergyman, John Newton. The words speak of the grace of God in a beautiful way. The first verse is: *Amazing grace, how sweet the sound, that saved a wretch like me. I once was lost, but now am found, was blind but now, I see.* " The message in this poem which became such a powerful Christian song, is how the grace of God saved us from a life of sin and despair and "did appear the hour I first believed."

When we stumble or fall on the path of our lives, the grace of God is sufficient to carry us through those times. Second Corinthians 12:9 tells us, *"And He said unto me, 'My grace is sufficient for thee; for my strength is made perfect in weakness. Most gladly therefore will I glorify in my infirmities, that the power of Christ may rest upon me."* When we are weak, He is strong enough to support us in all we face. God's grace shines brightest in the darkest places in our hearts and lives. When we need God's help, which is every day, we should feel confident in approaching Him for His help. Hebrews 4:16 tells us this: *"Let us therefore come boldly unto the throne of grace, that we may obtain mercy, and find grace to help in time of need."* God's Love for us as His children is absolute and is the reason; He will deliver us in these times.

We are made alive in Christ because of God's grace and His Love for us. Ephesians 2:4–5 says, *"But God, who is rich in mercy, for His great Love wherewith He Loved us, even when we were dead in sins, hath quickened us together in Christ, by grace you are saved."* His amazing grace saved a wretch like me, and He will be a power in my weakness today. May the grace of God be with you today in all that you do!

May 30th

May God Bless the Work You Have Been Chosen to Do

Our time on earth is spent doing work in support of our families and our lifestyle. May we seek to do the work God has called us to do in our lives. When we find that which God calls us to do, we find great blessings as a result. Psalm 90:17 says, *"And let the beauty of the Lord our God be upon us; and establish thou the work of our hands upon us; Yea, the work of our hands establish thou it."* When we seek that which the Lord calls us to do, He establishes the 'work of our hands.' The more we commit to doing God's work, the more God will direct us to the path of His calling. Proverbs 16:3 tells us, *"Commit thy works unto the Lord, and thy thoughts shall be established."*

God wants us to enjoy the work we are called to do each day. The scriptures tell us in Ecclesiastes 3:22, which says, *"Wherefore I perceive there is nothing better, than a man should rejoice in his own works; for that is his portion; for who shall bring him to see what is after him?"* We don't know what the future will bring, but we know where we find ourselves today. As such, we should embrace the moment in which we live with contentment. We keep in mind that the work we do has the goal of serving God and helping others. We are all ministers to one another regardless of the work we are chosen to do. Acts 20:35 says, *"I have showed you all things, how that so laboring ye ought to support the weak, and to remember the words of our Lord Jesus Christ, how He said it is more blessed to give than receive."* In all walks of life, we can lift up those who God gives to us each day and give of ourselves to help them.

May God richly bless you in the work you have today. May you find enjoyment in what you have been chosen to do. Actively seek God's plan for you and commit to the Lord each day. As we do, His rich blessings will be upon us.

How to Build on Your Faith

The scriptures teach us to believe in the Lord Jesus Christ as the Son of God, and we will be saved. One of the greatest scriptures in the Bible is John 3:16, which many believers can recite, which says, *"For God so Loved the world that He gave His only begotten Son, that whoever believeth in Him shall not perish but have everlasting life."* It is our faith that sets us free from eternal damnation and gives us life. If, then, we are believers in Jesus as the Son of God, how can we continue to build on this faith walk each day?

First, we must understand the meaning of faith as it pertains to our spiritual walk. Hebrews 11:1 tells us, *"Now faith is the substance of things hoped for, the evidence of things not seen."* This is what makes it most difficult for non-believers. We believe in Jesus at a time when He has ascended to heaven in the flesh but abides in our hearts in His spirit. His words and His truth last forever in the hearts and souls of the believer. To get closer to Christ and to build on our faith, we must seek greater knowledge of those words which He spoke. Romans 10:17 teaches us: *"So then faith cometh by hearing, and hearing by the word of God."* If you desire a closer walk, you will seek out those teachers of His Word, which God will make available to you on your path. It may be attending services in churches or listening online to scriptural messages delivered by ministers of God that bring messages of God's Love to your heart and soul.

God takes pleasure in us as we grow in our faith. Hebrews 10:38–39 says this: *"Now the just shall live by faith; but if any man draw back, my soul shall have no pleasure in him. But we are not of them who draw back unto perdition; but of them that believe to the saving of the soul."* Reading God's Word and hearing the word taught by ministers will help us grow our faith. Adding prayer and meditations daily strengthens our faith and brings us close to God. Be Blessed today as you do so!

June 1st
A Strong Faith Gives You Power

The significant battles of life are those in which the forces of good versus evil take place. The battlefield is often inside our heart, soul, and mind. We find ourselves engaged in these struggles often, and they may be very subtle as they occur. We face moments where the enemy of our souls may try to minimize a compromise from doing that which is right and good, to seek to draw us away from God's true path for us. Ephesians 6:12 talks about this battle in our lives as it says, *"For we wrestle not against flesh and blood, but against principalities, against powers, against the rulers of darkness of this world, against spiritual wickedness in high places."* The fight is on for our souls each day.

When you walk with strong faith, you will be strong in the heat of this battle. First Corinthians 16:13 says, *"Watch ye, stand fast in the faith, quit you like men, be strong."* When we walk with God, there is nothing we fear in dealing with the enemy. Ephesians 6:16 assures us of the power of faith as a shield against the power of the forces of evil as it says, *"Above all, taking the shield of faith, wherewith ye shall be able to quench all the fiery darts of the wicked."* Your faith is your source of strength and your protection against all the evil one can throw at you.

Take comfort in all that you do, knowing that because of your faith, God is in you and will help you to overcome all the obstacles you face. First John 4:4 makes it clear when it says, *"Ye are of God, little children, and have overcome them; because greater is He that is within you, than he that is in the world."* This scripture speaks of the power of our faith in God, delivering us from the forces of the evil one. May we each take comfort in the presence of God today as we walk in faith with Him. Be Blessed and filled with His power as you do!

June 2nd
Jesus Promises He Will Do This

During His ministry on earth, there were many times Jesus made the promise that He "will do" a certain thing to His disciples and those who followed Him. As He made these promises, we can have absolute confidence in knowing if Jesus said, "He will do it," it will be done. One of these moments talks about those who God directs to Jesus to follow Him in John 6:37, which says, *"All the Father giveth me shall come to me, and him that cometh to me, I will in no wise cast out."* If you are reading this and you have chosen to 'come to Jesus' in your heart, know that He will 'never drive you away' from Him. Rather, He will walk with you on your journey.

Another powerful message and promise from Jesus to His followers is given in Matthew 4:19, which says, *"Then He saith unto them, 'Follow Me and I will make you fishers of men.'"* These men to whom He was speaking were career fishermen. All they knew was their life's vocation was how to net fish and how to sell them in the market. Jesus offered them a higher calling. We all have other professions we choose along life's path. His promise to make us 'fishers of men' still applies to us today. If we truly are following Jesus today, we will want to share His glorious story with others God gives to each of us on our journey. The Good News of the gift of eternal life is something all need to hear. The Holy Spirit will direct you to those who need to hear it from you. Planting seeds of His message daily is what we are here to do.

The great message Jesus gave to those who believe in Him is written in John 14:1–3, in which He says, *"Let not your heart be troubled; ye believe in God, believe also in me. In my Father's house are many mansions; if it were not so, I would have told you. I go to prepare a place for you. And if I go and prepare a place for you, I will come again, and receive you unto myself; that where I am, there ye may be also."* Jesus will come again and take us to our heavenly home.

June 3rd
Sowing Seeds for Jesus

One of the parables that Jesus used to teach the multitudes who followed him was that of the sowing seeds for the harvest. In this parable, the seeds fall on rocky soil, along the path with no roots, amid thorns, and some fall in fertile soil. The message is about planting the seed, which is the word of God. Luke 8:11 tells us, *"Now the parable is this: The seed is the word of God."* We are all called to be laborers in the field to harvest souls for the kingdom of God. The seeds we are given to plant are the message we receive in God's Word. Jesus further describes the meaning of the parable in Matthew 13:38, which says, *"The field is the world, and the good seed are the children of the kingdom; but the tares are the children of the wicked one."*

The choice of sowing seeds is up to each of us each day. Galatians 6:9 teaches us: *"And let us not grow weary in well doing, for in due season we shall reap, if we faint not."* Doing good is simply the planting of seeds for the harvest as we spread the word of God to those we are given along the way. We may not be there to nurture these seeds we have planted along the way, but we need to trust that God will do so. First Corinthians 3:6–9 says, *"I have planted, Apollos watered, but God gave the increase. Now he that planteth and he that watereth are one; and every man shall receive his own reward according to his own labor. For we are laborers together with God; ye are God's husbandry; ye are God's building."*

We are called to be ministers to one another. We plant the seeds of life into the harvest field each day if we are committed to being followers of Jesus. May our harvest be bountiful. Second Corinthians 9:6 tells us, *"But this I say; He that soweth sparingly shall reap also sparingly; and he that soweth bountifully shall also reap bountifully."* May your harvest be bountiful for the seeds you sow today!

June 4th

Be Bold and Confident in Your Faith

Our faith in Jesus Christ carries us to a new dimension in our relationship with God the Father. As we seek to do God's will in our lives, we face times in which we must speak out boldly and confidently against that which we see as wrong or evil in the world around us. We know that God walks with us, and the Holy Spirit is in us. Philemon 1:8 speaks to this as it says, *"Wherefore, though I might be much bold in Christ to enjoin thee that which is convenient."* We cannot be timid in dealing with issues of good versus evil and right and wrong. The Holy Spirit is our guide in how we conduct ourselves. Second Timothy 1:7 tells us, *"For God hath not given us a Spirit of fear; but of power, and of Love, and of a sound mind."* Those qualities empower us to face anything on our path.

We are taught to approach God boldly through Christ in the Spirit as well. Our access to God through Jesus is described in Ephesians 3:11–12: *"According to the eternal purpose which He purposed in Christ Jesus our Lord; In whom we have boldness and access with confidence by faith of Him."* What amazing access we can bring our needs to God directly because of our faith in Jesus. There is no one who you are required to go through to talk with God. Hebrews 10:19 says this again: *"Having therefore, brethren, boldness to enter into the holiest by the blood of Jesus."* With such access to God, we can seek His will directly daily.

The message of Jesus and the meaning of His sacrifice for our sins is in our hearts. We are commissioned with the responsibility to plant seeds in the world around us. Be bold and confident in your faith as you do so. Proverbs 28:1 tells us, *"The wicked flee when no man pursueth; but the righteous are as bold as a lion."* As we seek God's will and plant seeds of the faith in the lives of others, may we be as bold as a lion as we walk with God today!

June 5th

God Wants Us to Be Happy

The human mind will experience all emotions in life as we go through all the experiences life has for us. Some days are filled with joy, and others bring us sadness due to the trials and tribulations we might face. During our journey in this world, we look to God in faith and gratitude for the life He has given us. When we do so, we find happiness and joy. Psalm 144:15 tells us, *"Happy is the people, that is such a case; Yea, happy is the people, whose God is the Lord."* With God walking with us each day, we have no reason to be unhappy. We don't fight our battles alone. Nehemiah 8:10 says, *"For the joy of the Lord is your strength."* Whatever we face, when we turn to the Lord, we gain strength and joy.

Jesus speaks of how we can keep His joy in our hearts in John 15:10–11: *"If you keep my commandments, you will abide in my Love; even as I have kept my Father's commandments and abide in His Love. These things have I spoken unto you, that my joy might remain in you, and that your joy might be full."* As we face the daily issues that life gives to us, keeping the commandments of Loving God and Loving others which Jesus directed us to do, will give us the joy which is complete in our lives. First Peter 1:8–9 teaches us: *"Whom having not seen, ye Love; in whom, though ye now see Him not, yet believing, ye rejoice with joy unspeakable and full of glory."* Knowing this, we celebrate the faith we have in Jesus with joy and happiness in our hearts and souls each day.

There is no reason to dwell in sadness while we walk with God this day. As Psalm 37:4 says, *"Delight thyself also in the Lord, and He shall give thee the desires of thine heart."* When we take such delight in the Lord, we will experience a sense of joy and happiness that will radiate into the lives of those we meet this day. Be Blessed as you do so!

June 6th

Clothe Yourself in Kindness

Our lives are filled with moments in which we may disagree with one another, and in such moments of conflict, it is easy to answer sharply to prove our points. When we do, we face similar responses and arguments take place which result in harsh words taking place which are not filled with a loving spirit. Those experiences pull us apart and put a shadow on our Loving of one another. God has chosen us to be different in our manner and our approach to each other. Ephesians 4:29 tells us, *"Let no corrupt communication proceed out of your mouth, but that which is good to the edifying, that it may minister grace unto the hearers."* It is more important to be Loving than it is to win in an argument.

If we are to be God's chosen people, we are to lead our lives in a way that is different from how we conduct ourselves in relationships with others. Colossians 3:12 speaks to this: *"Put on therefore, as the elect of God, holy and beloved, bowels of mercies, kindness, humbleness of mind, meekness, longsuffering."* Those characteristics enable us to live in harmony and peace with those God has brought into our lives. It is taught to us that we *"reap what we sow,"* and as such, when we sow the seeds of kindness into the hearts of others, we reap the rewards of kindness in return.

Later in the book of Ephesians 4:32, Paul writes these words: *"And be ye kind one to another, tenderhearted, forgiving one another, even as God for Christ's sake hath forgiven you."* When we commit to taking on the spirit of kindness toward others in our life, we are walking in the light of God's spirit. First Peter 3:9 teaches us: *"Not rendering evil for evil or railing for railing; but contrariwise blessing; knowing that ye are thereunto called, that ye should inherit a blessing."* Be kind to all you meet today and inherit the blessing of God.

June 7th

The Humble Will Be Exalted

We know from the scriptures that God resists the proud and gives grace, and lifts up the humble. The more we choose to take credit for the good in our lives, the less we give credit to God for the blessings He bestows on us. James 4:6 tells us, *"But He giveth more grace. Wherefore He saith, God resisteth the proud, but giveth grace to the humble."* As believers, we are blessed each day with His presence and His abundant mercy. The things we accomplish in our lives are directly the result of His plans and gifts to us. As His people, we are to be humble and seek His way for our life. Psalm 25:9 says, *"The meek He will guide in judgement; and the meek He will teach His way."* Our path is made clear as we humbly walk with God each day.

The more we seek to do that which is good for others, the more we are doing what God has called us to do in this world. Philippians 2:3–4 tells it this way: *"Let nothing be done through strife or vainglory; but in lowliness of mind let each esteem other better than themselves. Look not every man on his own things, but every man also on the things of others."* God values the service we give to the lives of those He gives to us. In humble service to others, we find victory in our lives. Psalm 149:4 says, *"For the Lord taketh pleasure in His own people; He will beautify the meek with salvation."* To live a life filled with victory, we must humbly walk with God and do His will.

Be humble in all you do and say, and God will exalt you. Luke 14:11 teaches us: *"For whosoever exalteth himself will be abased; and he that humbleth himself will be exalted."* Doing that which brings glory to God will yield His mercy in our hearts and lives. As we do, we grow closer to Him each day. Be humble and kind on your journey today, and find His blessing in your life as you do.

June 8th
The Holy Spirit Is with You

When Jesus sat at the last supper with His disciples, He told them about His death which was about to happen. He also told them He was going to ask the Father to send His Holy Spirit to be with those who believe in Him and keep His commandments. In John 14:15–17, Jesus says, *"If ye Love me, keep my commandments. And I will pray the Father, and He shall give you another comforter that He may abide with you forever; Even the Spirit of truth; whom the world cannot receive, because it seeth Him not, neither knoweth Him; but ye know Him; for He dwelleth in you, and shall be in you."* The Holy Spirit dwells inside of us as believers and gives us strength and understanding

The power of the Holy Spirit is from God and is with us as a comforter in times of trials. John 14:26 says this: *"But the Comforter, which is the Holy Ghost, whom the Father will send in my name, He shall teach you all things, and bring all things to your remembrance, whatsoever I have said unto you."* As we go through this and every day on our journey in this world, we know that the Holy Spirit of God is with us and in our hearts and souls. When we seek the answers to questions in life, He is here to teach us of God's ways and direct our paths. Embrace His spirit in your life. You can recognize the fruit of the spirit in your own life and in that of others. Galatians 5:22–23 says, *"But the fruit of the Spirit is Love, joy, peace, long-suffering, gentleness, goodness, faith, meekness, temperance; Against such there is no law."* When we see these fruit manifest in our lives and that of others, we know the Holy Spirit resides therein.

The Holy Spirit is a gift from God you will receive when you repent of your sins and accept Christ as your savior. Acts 2:38 says, *"Then Peter said unto them, Repent, and be baptized every one of you in the name of Jesus Christ for the remission of sins, and ye shall receive the gift of the Holy Ghost."* What a beautiful gift we have received from God our Father. His Spirit lives within us.

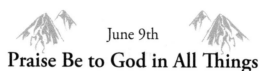

June 9th

Praise Be to God in All Things

It is easy to offer praise to God when things we face in this world are going our way. It is more difficult to fill our hearts with praise for God when we face difficulties. What we should understand is God is directing our paths if we have given our hearts to Jesus Christ and all things work together for good as His people. Romans 8:28 tells us this: *"And we know that all things work together for good to them that Love God, to them who are called according to His purpose."* That doesn't mean we will always understand why things happen as they do. We must learn to trust in Him as we face different things in life.

First Peter 4:16 says, *"Yet, if any man suffer as a Christian, let him not be ashamed; but let him glorify God on this behalf."* There is going to be suffering in this world. Our Lord and Savior Jesus Christ suffered for the sins of the world. The gift of eternal life is ours because of His sacrifice. Our sacrifice should be that we praise God in all things. Hebrews 13:15 tells us, *"By Him, therefore, let us offer the sacrifice of praise to God continually; that is, the fruit of our lips giving thanks to His name."* We know our God is pleased with us when we praise His Holy Name. We can embrace the opportunity to praise Him in all things as we read 1 Thessalonians 5:18, which says, *"In everything give thanks; for this is the will of God in Christ Jesus concerning you."*

The life we live is not our own but that which is given to us by our God. May our hearts sing praises to God on this day and every day. Psalm 9:1–2 says this: *"I will praise thee, O Lord, with my whole heart; I will shew forth thy marvelous works. I will be glad and rejoice in thee; I will sing praise to thy name, O thou Most High."* May this spirit of praise and rejoice in our hearts as we walk with God today! Be Blessed as you do!

June 10th

God Is with Us as We Go Through Changes in Our Lives

We will experience many changes in our lives significance. Those may be job-related changes, personal relationship changes, or physical locations we change as we grow and develop in our time on earth. Those moments can add anxiety or concern about whether the decision to do so is right for us. Turn these questions over to the God who walks beside us every day. The Holy Spirit is here to guide you as you seek His wisdom and direction. Our instincts on what to do may not be enough to choose the right path, but God will guide us always.

God has a plan for us that is unfolding each day. His plan is for us to prosper and grow as we seek His will for our lives. Jeremiah 29:11 affirmative states that: *"For I know the thoughts I think toward you, saith the Lord, thoughts of peace and not of evil, to give you an expected end."* The peace in your heart that comes from trusting God in all things is available when we turn our lives over to following the path God provides us. Proverbs 19:21 says, *"There are many devices in a man's heart; nevertheless, the counsel of the Lord, that shall stand."* When you seek God's direction for your life, He will guide you in what steps to take. Proverbs 16:9 teaches us: *"A man's heart deviseth his way; but the Lord directeth his steps."* When you seek God's direction and guidance, He will be there to open doors for you and, in doing so, establish your steps to take.

Throughout the scriptures, we are reassured by God that He is with us to guide us and to direct our paths when we walk with Him and are His people. Psalm 32:8 tells us, *"I will instruct thee and teach thee in the way you should go. I will guide thee with mine eye."* We don't travel alone through the various changes in our lives. Turn to God for comfort, peace, and guidance, and your path will become clear to you as you do. Be Blessed in all of life's changes.

June 11th

Walk Upon the Land as God Directs You

There are many illustrations in the Bible in which God directs the path of those who were devoted to Him. In those stories, God told them to act and to go places they had not been to receive the blessing and the inheritance He had chosen for them. In our lives, we face similar opportunities as we follow God's direction for our lives. We must walk upon the land in faith for the promise to be realized in our lives. In Hebrews 11:8, Abraham has such an experience: *"By faith Abraham, when he was called to go out into a place which he should after receive as an inheritance, obeyed; and he went out, not knowing whither he went."* What amazing faith he had to relocate his family and himself knowing God would direct his path.

When Moses led the children of Israel out of Egypt, he guided them to the land promised to them by God. To possess the land, they had to walk upon it in faith. Deuteronomy 11:22–24 tells us,

> *If ye shall diligently keep all these commandments which I command you, to do them, and to Love the Lord your God, to walk in all His ways, and to cleave unto Him; Then will the Lord drive out all these nations from before you, and ye shall possess greater nations and mightier than yourselves. Every place whereon the soles of your feet shall tread shall be yours; from the wilderness and Lebanon, from the river, the river Euphrates, even unto the uttermost sea shall your coast be.*

The scripture teaches us that every place they walked in faith, they took possession over. We are all called upon in our lives to take a walk of faith along the way to possess what God is giving to us.

We will find moments where we are to walk upon the land God has called for us to possess, and He will deliver it to us. Allow your faith to be strong when you are called to walk upon the land in those moments. May God's guidance be with you today on your journey and bless you in all that you do.

June 12th

May We Grow in Our Spiritual Walk Today

As Christian followers, God wants us to grow in our spiritual walk each day. The growth gives us confidence in our relationship with God as well as intimacy in the way we prayerfully talk with Him. We grow through the grace of God and through the knowledge we gain as we read the word of God. 2 Peter 3:18 teaches us: *"But grow in the grace and in the knowledge of our Lord and Savior Jesus Christ. To Him be the glory now and forever! Amen."* As we continue to walk on this path toward God, the time we spend in His Word helps us better understand His will for us and our purpose in what He has planned for our life. Spiritual growth is the direct result of this discipline.

Spiritual growth brings us to a deeper understanding of Jesus and matures us in how we are to deal with the issues we face in life. Hebrews 6:1 guides us to this growth and maturity as it says, *"Therefore, leaving the principles of the doctrine of Christ, let us go on unto perfection; not laying again the foundation of repentance from dead works, and of faith toward God."* The more we invest in gaining knowledge of God's will through His Word, the more we live a life that is worthy and one that pleases God. Colossians 1:9–10 says this: *"For this cause, since the day we heard it, do not cease to pray for you, and to desire that ye might be filled with the knowledge of His will in all wisdom and Spiritual understanding. That ye might walk worthy of the Lord unto all pleasing, being fruitful in every good work, and increasing in the knowledge of God."*

Our spiritual growth leads to wisdom and the understanding of what God's will is for us each day. As we grow in Christ, we become stronger in Loving and serving one another. May the Holy Spirit guide you on this day on the path to spiritual growth. Seek the knowledge that comes from reading His Word each day. Be Blessed as you do so!

June 13th
Using Your Gift for Christ

The great commission spoken by Jesus to His followers was to go into all the world and to teach the gospel of Christ. Jesus told His disciples this after His resurrection just prior to His ascension into heaven in Matthew 28: 19–20, which says, *"Go ye therefore and teach all nations, baptizing them in the name of the Father, and of the Son, and of the Holy Ghost. Teaching them to observe all things whatsoever I have commanded you; and, Lo, I am with you always, even unto the end of the world."* Jesus has called us to teach others in our world. He brings people to us for that purpose. We bear witness to His spirit in the way we lead our lives which should be by Loving those He has put on our path.

As you grow spiritually, this becomes easier to do. We are not all destined to be teachers but minister in the way God gives us the gifts to use in His service to others. First Peter 4:10 tells us, *"As every man hath received the gift, even to minister the same one to another, as good stewards of the manifold grace of God."* What we need to seek from God is a better understanding of what gift He has given us to use in His ministry and service to others. Romans 12:6–7 says, *"Having the gifts differing according to the grace that is given to us, whether prophecy, let us prophesy according to the proportion of faith; or ministry, let us wait on our ministering, or he that teacheth, on teaching."* What we know is that God uses each of us in a unique way to reach others. Embrace the opportunities to use your gift as such.

We are working together to share His truth with the world in which we live. Ephesians 4:16 says, *"From whom, the whole body fitly joined together and compacted by which every joint supplieth, according to the effectual working in the measure of every part, maketh increase of the body unto the edifying of itself in Love."* Be Blessed as you do your part in Love on this day!

June 14th

The Power of Hope

Each day that passes brings us different influences which have impact on our perspective. We have periods of fulfillment and periods of concern and grief. It is all a part of the human experience. The one thing we must hold on to through it all is our hope in the deliverance we have through our faith in Jesus Christ our Savior. May we remain steadfast in holding on to that hope each day. Hebrews 10:23–24 teaches us: *"Let us hold fast to the profession of our faith without wavering for He is faithful that promised; And let us consider one another to provoke unto Love and to good works."* The scripture is twofold; one point is we have our hope to hold on to always. The second point is for us to help one another to produce greater Love and good deeds as we walk with God each day.

Our good works and doing the will of the Father each day is the direct result of our faith, Love, and hope we have in our hearts and souls. We don't do these because of our human nature, but this is the result of the desire to follow Christ and His teachings in our lives. First Thessalonians 1:3 says, *"Remembering without ceasing your work of faith, and labor of Love, and patience of hope in our Lord Jesus Christ, in the sight of God our Father."* We continue the path each day inspired by the hope we hold in our Lord Jesus Christ. God watches over us as we retain our hope in Him. Psalm 33:18 says, *"Behold the eye of the Lord is upon them that fear Him, upon them that hope in His mercy."* May our hope be eternal as we seek God each day.

As hope fills our hearts, we experience great joy and peace while we live in this world. Romans 15:13 speaks to this: *"Now the God of hope fill you with all joy and peace in believing, that ye may abound in hope, through the power of the Holy Ghost."* May hope fill our hearts on this and every day and bring us peace and joy through the Holy Spirit. Be Blessed today in your hope!

June 15th
Do Everything with Love in Your Heart

Whatever you are called to do today, whether it is business-related, family time, schoolwork, or other personal matters you must attend to, take the approach that we will embrace and engage in the spirit of Love or charity, as Love is described in the King James version of the Bible, in all that we do on this day. As we do so, we find ourselves growing closer to God and find ourselves in harmony with all that is in our lives. Colossians 3:14 tells us this: *"And above all these, put on charity, which is the bond of perfectness."* The more we Love others and express our Love to those we meet each day, the more we receive the spirit of Love in return.

We look past the shortcomings of others when we Love, and they will find it easier to do so with us. First Peter 4:8 says, *"And above all things, have fervent charity among yourselves; for charity shall cover the multitude of sins."* When we Love each other, we don't focus on issues we see which are imperfections in other people's lives. The spirit of Love leads us to being humble and kind toward one another and seek unity rather than division in our relationships. Ephesians 4:2–3 says it well: *"With all lowliness and meekness, with longsuffering, forbearing one another in Love; endeavoring to keep the unity of the Spirit in the bond of peace."* When we strive to approach all with humility and gentleness with Love in our hearts, we find a spiritual flow of Love that is genuine always.

If we are looking to do that which is pleasing in God's sight, we will strive to be filled with Love in all we do. Jesus gave us this command as is written in 1 John 4:21: *"And this commandment we have from Him; That he who Loveth God Love his brother also."* This Spirit of Love is to be pervasive in all we do. First Corinthians 16:14 says it plainly: *"Do everything in Love."* May those be our marching orders as we go through this day, and Be Blessed as you walk in Love!

June 16th

Be the Source of Love, Peace, and Comfort in Times of Conflict

It is human nature to want to be right in all we do and to want to win battles in which we find ourselves. Arguments with others stem from this desire which is placed in our hearts by a spirit that is not the Holy Spirit of God. We become indignant in such times and will dig our heels in and try to prove we are right and justify our decision to engage in these battles accordingly. We need to ask ourselves, "What would best please God in such moments?" The scriptures are clear on this when we read Matthew 5:9, which tells us, *"Blessed are the peacemakers, for they shall be called the children of God."* It is interesting to note the scripture makes no reference to who wins the conflict as the "sons of God," but rather the one who makes peace being called in such a way.

As we live close to those we Love the most and spend most of our time with them, we can find moments of conflict with our Loved ones. It is not God's plan for us to prevail over one another but, rather, to help support and elevate one another in all we do in Love. When we maintain a spirit of humility, gentleness, and patience with one another, we find peace growing in the relationship. Ephesians 4:2–3 speaks to this: *"With all lowliness, and meekness, with longsuffering, forbearing one another in Love; Endeavoring to keep the unity of the spirit in the bond of peace."* As we seek to maintain this unity of the Spirit in the bond of peace, we forego the urge to prove we have gained a superior advantage or the need to win in the arguments or conflicts our minds may engage in with others in our lives.

Invest tenderness and a Loving Spirit in the moments of such conflicts. As you do, the Holy Spirit will minister through you to the other person who is fighting to be right on the other side of the issue. Bring peace and resolution to every conflict in all your relationships right away. God will bless you as you do!

June 17th
Avoid Jealousy and Selfish Ambition

The Spirit of man can be enticed to look at what others have and want more than what God has given to us. It is good to have ambition to strive to achieve goals in our life. It guides us to disciplines required to create growth and for the opportunity to provide for our families. However, when our hearts turn that ambition into greed and a lust for that which others have, it can cause us to envy and lose perspective on what God's plan for our life might be. We are cautioned to be wise in this respect in James 3:14–16, which teaches us: *"But if ye have bitter envying and strife in your hearts, glory not, and lie not against the truth. This wisdom descendeth not from above, but is earthly, sensual, devilish. For where envying and strife is, there is confusion and every evil work."* As we envy the possessions of another, we are filled with a desire and longing which is not going to draw us closer to the God we serve. Rather, it takes our attention away from the Love and appreciation for all that God has given us in our life.

God is with each of us as we strive to walk with Him daily. He wants us to prosper but not to be caught up in the love for money. Hebrew 13:5 tells us, *"Let your conversation be without covetousness; and be content with such things as ye have: for He hath said, 'I will never leave thee nor forsake thee.'"* When you walk with God and are appreciative of His blessings in your life, you find peace and contentment. God wants us to prosper in all we do and get rewarded for the labor we invest in our work. Trust in the Lord, and you will be enriched in your life. Proverbs 28:25 says, *"He that is of a proud heart stirreth up strife; but he that putteth his trust in the Lord shall be made fat."*

Our hard work is to be rewarded by God. Psalm 128:2 says this: *"For thou shalt eat the labor of thine hands; happy shalt thou be, and it shall be well with thee."* Be Blessed and find contentment as you walk with God this day!

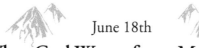

June 18th

What God Wants from Me Today

God designed each of us for His purpose, and we are called to do His will. We are not here by chance but rather by design. King David wrote these words to celebrate God's creation of his life in Psalm 139:13–14: *"For thou hast possessed my reigns; thou hast covered me in my mother's womb. I will praise thee, for I am fearfully and wonderfully made: marvelous are thy works; and that my soul knoweth right well."* We should praise God for all He does for us in our lives. We should especially have praise in our hearts for God choosing to create us in His image for a purposeful life on earth.

To fulfill that purpose, what is God's plan for me today? Certainly, it is to read His Word and have prayerful and meaningful communications with Him. Giving worship to our God is opening our hearts and lives to His blessings. Psalm 95:6 says, *"O Come, let us worship and bow down; let us kneel before the Lord our maker."* God is worthy of our praise and worship. What else is expected of us? It is our duty to obey His commandments on earth. Ecclesiastes 12:13 says this: *"Let us hear the conclusion of the whole matter; Fear God and keep His commandments; for this is the whole duty of man."* As we worship God and keep His commandments, we know He is pleased with us and walks with us on our path. Micah 6:8 tells it this way: *"He hath showed thee, O man, what is good; and what doth the Lord require of thee, but to do justly, and to Love mercy, and to walk humbly with thy God."* These are simple directives aimed at guiding us to a deeper relationship in following the will of God.

As we do these things, we are being transformed into His image as described in 2 Corinthians 3:18: *"But we all, with open face beholding as in a glass the glory of the Lord, are changed into the same image from glory to glory, even as by the Spirit of the Lord."* May God transform each of us as we walk with Him today!

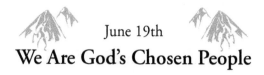

June 19th
We Are God's Chosen People

As a believer in Jesus Christ as the Son of God who died for our sins on the cross and was resurrected, and He lives forever, we are forgiven of our sins and have become children of God. We are chosen by God to be His people. First Peter 2:9 says, *"But ye are a chosen generation, a royal priesthood, an holy nation, a peculiar people; that ye should show forth the praises of Him who hath called you out of darkness into His marvelous light."* This is a beautiful spiritual calling that carries with it responsibilities on how we should live our lives.

A great guide on what God expects from His chosen people is found in Colossians 3:12–17, which says,

> *Put on therefore, as the elect of God, holy and beloved, bowels of mercies, kindness, humbleness of mind, meekness, longsuffering; Forbearing one another, and forgiving one another, if any man have a quarrel against any; even as Christ forgave you, so also do ye. And above all these things, put on charity, which is the bond of perfectness. And let the peace of God rule in your hearts, to the which also ye are called in one body; and be ye thankful. Let the word of Christ dwell in you richly in all wisdom; teaching and admonishing one another in psalms and hymns and spiritual songs, singing in grace in your hearts to the Lord. And whatsoever ye do in word or deed, do all in the name of the Lord Jesus, giving thanks to God and the Father by Him.*

The power of this passage can guide us each day to a lasting and blessed relationship with our Lord and Savior as God's chosen people.

As God's chosen people, may we live together in harmony and Love one another as God has Loved us. May gentleness and patience be our calling card as we lift one another up on this day. Be Blessed today as one chosen by God!

June 20th

Meditate on the Word

When we spend time in meditation on the word of God, we grow closer to Him in spirit and in understanding His will. It may come from reading a single scripture and asking God to help you understand the meaning for you in your life on this day. I believe when you concentrate on a chapter of His Holy Bible each day, you are blessed with insights into His Word and your growth is continual. Joshua 1:8 teaches us: *"This book of the law shall not depart out of my mouth, but thou shalt meditate therein day and night, that thou mayest observe to do according to all that is written therein; for then thou shalt make thy way prosperous, and then thou shalt have good success."* God's Word is a roadmap for our lives to take us to the place of prosperity God has prepared for us.

As we meditate on God's Word, we are protected from sin in our heart. Psalm 119:11 says, *"Thy word have I hid in mine heart, that I might not sin against thee."* As the seeds of truth are planted in our hearts and nourished in our souls, we are drawn closer to our God and Father as we learn more about how He wants us to live our lives each day. Our source of strength and the power of the Holy Spirit is revealed as we meditate on God's Word. Let us delight in the words of the Lord as expressed by David in Psalm 111:2: *"The works of the Lord are great, sought out of all them that have pleasure therein."* Be among those who delight in Him on this day and take time to study His Holy Word to build your spiritual walk further. The treasure you discover in your heart is worth the time.

The more time we spend in meditation on the word of God, the more we reflect it in all we do and say. The words of David in Psalm 19:14 are a beautiful expression of his desire to please God as he says, *"Let the words of my mouth and the meditation of my heart be acceptable in thy sight, O Lord, my strength and my Redeemer."* May this thought dwell in each of our hearts as we meditate on the Word of God on this day! Be Blessed as you do so!

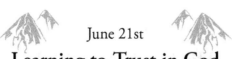

June 21st
Learning to Trust in God

The experiences of life daily bring us anxiety and stress along the way. As we face these moments, fear tries to enter our hearts to put doubts there to occupy space which pulls us away from the faith we have in God our Father. Where there is faith, there is no place for fear. The power of trusting in God is profound in our lives. If we believe in God, we must learn to trust Him in all things we do and all we face in life. Isaiah 12:2 says, *"Behold, God is my salvation; I will trust, and not be afraid; for the Lord Jehovah is my strength and my song, He also has become my salvation."* Trust and faith in God remove fears and anxieties from our lives. There is power in that trust.

Regardless of what you face in life, there is joy and peace that comes to you from trusting in God to carry you through it. Romans 15:13 tells us, *"Now the God of all hope fill you with all joy and peace in believing, that ye may abound in hope, through the power of the Holy Ghost."* If you are overflowing with hope, you have no room in your heart or your mind for fear and doubts to enter in. Peace and joy replace fears and doubt as you build on that trust. Psalm 56:3–4 says this: *"What time I am afraid, I will trust in thee. In God I will praise His word, in God I have put my trust; I will not fear what flesh can do unto me."* Our faith in God gives us a foundation on which to build our trust in Him. He will never leave you, nor will He forsake you in your times of trouble.

God provides us with His shelter and protection from the storms of life. Psalm 91:1–2 says, *"He that dwelleth in the secret place of the Most High shall abide under the shadow of the Almighty. I will say of the Lord, He is my refuge and my fortress; my God, in Him will I trust."* May we grow in our trust in God as our refuge from the storms of life we face each day. As we do so, our life is filled with joy and peace, and we will overflow with hope by the power of the Holy Spirit. Be Blessed today as you trust in the Lord our God!

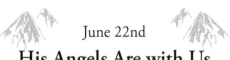

June 22nd
His Angels Are with Us

Throughout the scriptures, there are references to angels watching over the chosen people of God. Know that each of us is among that group as we go through each day. Psalm 91:11 tells us this: *"For He shall give His angels charge over thee, to keep thee in all thy ways."* The life of those who choose to follow God has benefits that extend beyond this world. We know God walks with us daily in all we face and do. It is an added blessing that He sends His angels to guard our way as well.

As we travel on the road of life, we may meet those who God places on our path as strangers who are sent as angels to us as well. How we treat them is a measure of our character and the spirit of Love in our hearts and souls. Hebrews 13:2 says, *"Be not forgetful to entertain strangers; for thereby some have entertained angels unawares."* We live in a spiritual world as well as a physical world. There is more that is unseen around us than that which we can see. In Hebrews 12:1, the scripture describes a "cloud of witnesses," which surrounds us each day: *"Wherefore, seeing we also are compassed about with so great a cloud of witnesses, let us lay aside every weight, and the sin which doth so easily beset us, and let us run with patience the race which is set before us."* This cloud of witnesses includes angels who are sent to watch over and protect us as well as the humans who are on our path as we travel.

Angels are often God's messengers to people on earth. He has spoken His Word to prophets and saints and shepherds through angels. They will carry messages to all the people on earth as it is written in Revelation 14:6: *"And I saw another angel fly in the midst of heaven, having the everlasting gospel to preach unto them that dwell on the earth, and to every nation, and kindred and tongue, and people."* God uses angels in many ways and could put one on our path today. They are here to protect the people of God and to bring His messages.

June 23rd
We Are Called to Care for Those Less Fortunate

Giving of ourselves in service to others is a calling for all who believe in Jesus Christ. For faith to be alive, we must work according to James 2:17, which tells us, *"Even so, faith, if it hath not works, is dead, being alone."* When we do things to support and lift one another up in Christ, we are living in accordance with Jesus's teachings. Act 20:35 tells us, *"It is more blessed to give than receive."* As we give of ourselves in service to others, we receive blessings from God. Living such a life of giving to the support of others draws us closer to the God we serve. Philippians 2:4 suggests that we are to look to caring for the needs of others as it says, *"Look not every man on his own things, but every man also on the things of others."* Watch after one another in Christ.

God gives us strength and prosperity so that we may be used in this service to others. Romans 15:1–2 teaches us this as it says, *"We then that are strong ought to bear with the infirmities of the weak, and not to please ourselves. Let everyone of us please his neighbor for his good to edification."* The more we approach our lives as one giving of himself to others, the more God blesses us with prosperity and growth in our spirit each day. You can't outgive God. He will reward you for your generosity to others. Proverbs 19:17 teaches this as it says, *"He that hath pity on the poor lendeth to the Lord; and that which he hath given He will pay Him again."* All we have is due to the blessing of the God we serve. As we give to others, He will give to us in abundance in return.

Once again, in Proverbs 22:9, we are told of the blessing of giving to the poor: *"He that hath a bountiful eye shall be blessed; for he giveth of his bread to the poor."* Be generous in all you do for those who are in need, and God will richly bless you. May God open doors for each of us to do so today!

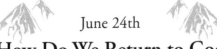

June 24th

How Do We Return to God
When We Have Strayed Away?

There is a beautiful song by Rascal Flatts entitled the *Broken Road*. The lyrics written describe a journey of one's life that lead him back to the one he Loves. The song starts out with this verse: *"I set out on a narrow way, many years ago. Hoping I would find true Love along the broken road. But I got lost a time or two, wiped my brow, kept pushing through, I couldn't see how every sign pointed straight to you."* The story of the song tells of how this sojourner had every experience of his life leading him back to this woman he Loves. In the reality of each of our lives, this song could easily be describing a similar journey back to God. His Love for us has always been and will continue always to be there for us. It is each of us who gets lost a time or two in our lives as we journey each day.

The broken road of each life carries us toward selfish and temporary motives which take us away from God and His purpose and will for our lives. He is always waiting for us to turn back to Him. Lamentations 3:40 says, *"Let us search and try our ways, and turn again to the Lord."* The soul of man longs for God when we are away from Him. We will never find peace and Love which satisfies our soul when we are apart from our Father in Heaven. God puts in your heart the desire to know Him as described in Jeremiah 24:7: *"And I will give them a heart to know me, that I am the Lord, and they will be my people, and I will be their God, for they shall return unto Me with their whole heart."* The choice is ours alone as to whether we seek to return to God with our whole heart. He is waiting for us to do so when we have lost our way.

The journey back to God may be due to distress in our life. Second Chronicles 15:4 says, *"But when they in their trouble did turn unto the Lord God of Israel, and sought Him, He was found of them."* The broken road of our lives will take us back to God if we seek Him. May God bless road that leads us back to Him.

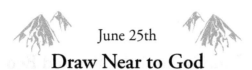

June 25th

Draw Near to God

As the road on which we travel brings us back to God, we are blessed and received by God in the fullness of His Love for us. God wants His people to be close to Him and to trust Him in all we do. When we pull away and stray from the Lord we serve, we find no happiness in the course we are on, and He is ready to restore us when our hearts turn back to Him. James 4:8 tells us, *"Draw nigh to God and He will draw nigh to you. Cleanse your hands, ye sinners, and purify your hearts, ye double–minded."* When we draw closer to God, we must ask His forgiveness for the sins we have committed and purify the hearts and minds which attempt to pull us away from Him.

To draw nearer to God, we must breathe the life-giving messages He delivers to us through His Holy word. The scriptures are given to us as a pathway in our journey back to Him each day. Second Timothy 3:16 teaches us: *"All scripture is given by inspiration of God, and is profitable for doctrine, for reproof, for correction, and for instruction in righteousness."* When we inhale the freshness of this breath of life, we want more to inhabit our hearts and souls, and as such, we seek it more and more. Our faith in God and His Son, our Lord and Savior Jesus Christ, is the cornerstone of the foundation of our relationship with Him. Without this faith, it is impossible to draw close to God. Hebrews 11:6 says, *"But without faith it is impossible to please Him, for he that cometh to God must believe that He is, and that He is a rewarder of them that diligently seek Him."*

Our walk in faith will take us to a place where God will inhabit our souls with His Holy Spirit and strengthen us each step along the way. May we call upon God to be with us on this day and to draw us closer to Him. Psalm 145:18 tells us, *"The Lord is nigh to all them who call upon Him, to all that call upon Him in truth."* May the blessings of God pour out on you today as you do so.

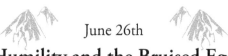

June 26th

Humility and the Bruised Ego

What we do when someone makes a comment which appears to make us feel less important or makes a statement that tends to disparage us in any way in a reflection of how prepared our spirit is at that moment. Our egos try to rise up in response quickly to point out the invasion emotionally and how it is not right. The ego tries to protect your self-esteem and, in doing so, can allow indignation and anger to invade your thoughts. This feeling causes separation and division among us with others who we are supposed to be Loving each day. It may be those who we truly Love the most who cause us occasional pain with such thoughts and words. How does God want us to react in such circumstances?

We are often taught about humility as the characteristic which God Loves in His people. James 4:10 teaches us: *"Humble yourselves in the sight of the Lord, and He shall lift you up."* You are not in need of proving you are right in such circumstances, rather, God will lift you up, and you are not gaining anything by taking an argumentative role in response. Philippians 2:3 says, *"Let nothing be done through strife or vainglory, but in lowliness of mind let each esteem other better than themselves."* Rather than taking a position with someone that denies the thing said about you, it may be better to defuse the moment by saying, *"You are probably right in your assessment of me, I value your opinion greatly."* What happens then is the other person must pause and reflect on such an answer in their own hearts.

We are tempted to engage in negative moments by the one who wants to pull us away from the path to God. When someone says something inappropriate to you, it is wrong. How we respond is up to us. First Thessalonians 5:15 teaches us: *"See that none render evil for evil unto any man; but ever follow that which is good, both among yourselves and to all men."* As we do, the Spirit of Love and Peace will fill our hearts with Joy as we avoid conflicts in our heart.

June 27th

Control That Which Leads You to Good Health

While we know there will come a time when our journey on earth will be over, as God's people, we have a Father in Heaven who wants us to do that which we can do to maintain our health and to seek His will in restoring our health when we face times of sickness. Our bodies are the temple of the Spirit. First Corinthians 6:19–20 tells us, *"What? Know ye not that your body is the temple of the Holy Ghost, which is in you, which ye have of God, and ye are not your own? For ye are bought with a price; therefore, glorify God in your body, and in your spirit which are God's."* How do we "honor God with our bodies"? The important thing for us to know is that we need to be moderate in all we eat and drink.

Third John 1:2 says, *"Beloved, I wish above all things that thou mayest prosper and be in good health, even as thy soul prospereth."* We should pray for one another in this way and ask God to bless our lives with good health as well. We control how much we eat and drink as well as how much time and energy we devote to exercise. The scriptures explicitly caution us about overindulgence in alcohol as it says in Ephesians 5:18: *"And be not drunk with wine, wherein is excess. But be filled with the Spirit."* Again, alcohol is mentioned in Proverbs 20:1, which tells us, *"Wine is a mocker, strong drink is raging; and whosoever is deceived thereby is not wise."* The excess of such consumption leads to an unhealthy life.

Proverbs 23:20–21 cautions us about eating too much as well as drinking too much: *"Be not among winebibbers; among riotous eaters of flesh; For the drunkards and glutton shall come to poverty; and the drowsiness shall clothe a man with rags."* God empowers us with the right to make those choices, but moderation in eating and drinking leads to a healthier lifestyle. Let us make the right choices today to lead us to good health.

June 28th
Providing Care Pleases God

There is joy one receives when we can give care to one who God gives to us. Whether it be a parent, or another Loved one, when God places someone on our path who needs help and support, we are blessed immeasurably when we are giving care and Love to that person. We may not have the capacity to be a full-time caregiver, and those who do are special in the way God has prepared their hearts to embrace such a ministry. To put a Loved one in a place where they can be receiving such full–time care can be a blessing from God. God puts angels on the earth to walk among us and to provide such Love and care for those in need.

As we age, we have physical, emotional, and spiritual needs which are greater than those we may face as a younger person. In such cases, the family is stressed in trying to provide 24-hour care, seven days a week, and must find additional support at times like this. We are directed by God to do all we can for those in our families who go through such times. Psalm 71:9 tells us, *"Cast me not off in the time of old age; forsake me not when my strength faileth."* With respect to caring for our family, 1 Timothy 5:4 instructs us: *"But if any widow hath children or nephews, let them learn to shew piety at home, and to requite their parents; for that is good and acceptable before God."* Our lives become busy will so many other things, but the value of caring for those who are part of our family is truly directed by God and pleasing to God.

One of the laws of God is for us to do unto others as we want done to us. Our day may well come when we need help and support as we age. Matthew 7:12 teaches us: *"Therefore, all things whatsoever ye would that men should do to you, do ye even so to them: for this is the law and the prophets."* We know we are doing that which pleases God to care for those in need. Be Blessed today as you do so.

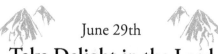

June 29th
Take Delight in the Lord

We will cross the path with people who profess to be a follower of Christ and who live their lives seemingly in an unhappy state of mind. It is hard for me to understand why they can't discover the joy of life that Christ gives us with His Holy Spirit. It is written that our salvation should bring us joy in Isaiah 12:3, which says, *"Therefore, with joy shall ye draw water out of the wells of salvation."* The life of a Christian should be one filled with the joy of the Lord in our hearts. Psalm 37:4 speaks boldly about this as it says, *"Delight thyself also in the Lord; and He shall give thee the desires of thy heart."* As we walk with God and take delight in Him, there should be happiness in our soul as we face any issue which comes our way.

Not all we go through in our lives will be "happy times," and we will experience sad moments as we travel through this time and space. Our hearts need to take comfort in that our ultimate destiny is to be one with Jesus Christ and our Heavenly Father. First Peter 4:13 tells us, *"But rejoice inasmuch as ye are partakers of Christ's sufferings, that when His glory shall be revealed, ye may be glad also with exceeding joy."* Any suffering we will experience will be temporary, but the joy we must look forward to is eternal. Knowing God is with us as we travel on life's path gives confidence in overcoming any obstacle along the way on our pathway to our heavenly home.

The more joy and happiness you bring into your day, the more you nourish your own spirit and others who you might encounter throughout each day. Proverbs 17:22 speaks to this as it says, *"A merry heart doeth good like a medicine, but a broken spirit drieth the bones."* Our mental attitude can have a direct impact on our physical well-being. Bring happiness into your heart and a smile to your lips, and you will be getting smiles and happiness returned to you from others you meet. Take delight in the Lord on this day!

June 30th

Serve One Another

God gives us the freedom of choice to live the life we wish to live. He offers us guidelines on what He wills us to do. Jesus taught us to Love God with all our hearts and souls and to Love one another as we Love ourselves. If we are to Love one another, we should devote our lives to supporting and providing service to others in our lives. Galatians 5:13 speaks to this: *"For, brethren, ye have been called unto liberty; only use not liberty for an occasion to the flesh, but by Love serve one another."* As God gives us the freedom to decide on the path we take, He also gives us the directive to be Loving in the way we give back to others.

God will smile upon you as you help those who are in need. Your life will be blessed by God as you do. Hebrews 6:10 says, *"For God is not unrighteous to forget your work and labor of Love, which ye have showed toward His name, in that ye have ministered to the saints, and do minister."* Jesus spoke of those who provide service to others as being the greatest among us. In Matthew 23:11, He spoke these words: *"But he that is greatest among you shall be your servant."* We are called to give to others the gifts we have received from God. As we do so, we are described as faithful stewards of God's grace in 1 Peter 4:10: *"As every man hath received the gift, even so minister the same one to another, as good stewards of the manifold grace of God."* We are each given unique gifts and are called to use them in service to others.

As we do these things, we are receiving an abundance of Love and support from others in return. Luke 6:38 tells us this: *"Give, and it shall be given to you; good measure, pressed down, and shaken together, and running over, shall men give into your bosom. For with the same measure ye mete, withal it shall be measured to you again."* As we bless and serve others, God is faithful and just to bless us richly. Be Blessed today as you give of yourself in service to others.

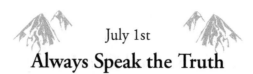

July 1st
Always Speak the Truth

The ego of mankind often will tempt us to embellish our story to make us sound more important and/or accomplished in what we might be telling another. There is no benefit to such a misstatement of fact, and God does not approve us when we vary from the truth. In fact, God detests lying lips as is said in Proverbs 12:22: *"Lying lips are an abomination to the Lord, but they that deal truly are His delight."* When people try to gain favor or stature by creating lies about themselves, they are going against the path of truth which God intends for us to follow in our lives. Be who you are and not a person you want others to think you should be.

God holds us close in His presence as we are truthful. Psalm 41:12 says it this way: *"And as for me, thou upholdest me in mine integrity, and settest me before thy face forever."* That is where we all want to spend our time, in the presence of God our Father. Second Timothy 2:15 guides us with this message: *"Study to show thyself approved unto God, a workman that needeth not to be ashamed, rightly dividing the word of truth."* There should be no compromise with our integrity, nor should there be any compelling reason to turn away from the truth of our lives in the face of others. The God we serve has blessed us with the life He has given us, and we should be thankful and praise Him for it.

We do battle with the enemy of our souls daily as the tempter tries to lure us away from the path of righteousness. The scriptures are there to lead us to that path and to empower us with the weapons with which we are to win that battle each day. Ephesians 6:14 tells us how we are to stand firm in the truth: *"Stand therefore, having your loins girt about with the truth, and having on the breastplate of righteousness."* There is no honor in deceitfulness. There is no glory in lies. Be truthful in all you do and say, and God will be with you and will draw you near to Him. Be Blessed as you speak the truth to all this day!

July 2nd

Seek the Lord Continually

As we begin each day, we have the opportunity to choose what to do in our lives that day. Our work becomes a mainstay of our lives, consuming much of the time we spend. Our family commitments are important and deserve much of our focus each day as well. God does not force His way into our lives as much as He waits quietly for us to seek Him. He gives us the ability to choose how much of our hearts and lives we want to give to Him and to seek His presence. There are so many other things that will clamor for our attention; it is easy to put off seeking God unless we create the mindset and discipline to do so.

When we begin each day with scripture reading and meditation, and prayer. It sets the tone for our lives that this is the most important thing we are to do each day. Matthew 6:33 tells us, *"But seek ye first the kingdom of God and His righteousness and all these things shall be added unto you."* Making the priority of your life each day, seeking God, puts in place all other things which must happen. First Chronicles 16:10–11 says, *"Glory ye in His holy name; let the heart of them rejoice that seek the Lord. Seek the Lord and His strength, seek His face continually."* People wait to ask for God's help only in times of trouble. He is waiting on each of us to find refuge in His strength in His name daily. Psalm 34:10 describes the importance of seeking God this way: *"The young lions do lack and suffer hunger; but they that seek the Lord shall not want any good thing."*

The scriptures are filled with passages about how good God is to those who seek him diligently. If you want God to be good to you always, seek Him always. Lamentations 3:25 says this: *"The Lord is good unto them that wait for Him, to the soul that seeketh Him."* May we learn to seek Him every day and in all we do. Psalm 14:2 says, *"The Lord looked down from heaven upon the children of men, to see if there were any that did understand, and seek God."* Be among those who seek after God our Father in heaven on this day and be blessed as we do.

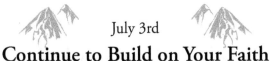

July 3rd

Continue to Build on Your Faith

The power of faith is life-changing. As Jesus walked on the earth, He touched the lives of many, and miracles followed Him. People were healed because they believed they would be. It was because of their faith that Jesus gave sight to those who were blind. In Mark 10:52, the scripture tells of one of those events: *"And Jesus said to him, 'Go thy way; thy faith hath made thee whole.' And immediately he received his sight and followed Jesus in the way.'"* The power of faith is manifest in many of the stories of the ministry of Jesus and His healing of those who were afflicted. He teaches us we can do all things when we believe. Mark 9:23 says, *"And Jesus said unto him, 'If thou canst believe, all things are possible to him that believeth."*

Continuing to build on your faith is the way you grow in your spiritual walk with God. We can't allow our faith to waiver. If we do, we are unable to stay the course as described in James 1:6, which says, *"But let him ask in faith, nothing wavering. For he that wavereth is like a wave of the sea that is driven by the wind and tossed."* When we are steadfast in our faith, there is nothing we cannot do in this world as God strengthens us and walks with us. Deuteronomy 31:6 tells us, *"Be strong and of good courage, fear not, nor be afraid of them, for the Lord thy God, He it is that doth go with thee; He will not fail thee, nor forsake thee."* We are blessed with a God who Loves us and will never leave us.

May we each build our faith like the woman who was ill who believed if she would only touch the hem of His garment as he walked by, she would be healed. Jesus knew when she did so and turned to her and said in Matthew 9:22: *"But, Jesus turned Him about, and when He saw her, He said, 'Daughter, be of good comfort, thy faith hath made thee whole. And the woman was made whole from that hour."* As we learn more to trust and believe in God, all things are possible. May our faith grow on this day as we open our hearts and believe!

July 4th
Celebrate Your Freedom

We live in a country that celebrates its freedom on this day each year. That freedom we enjoy as a people certainly comes with a price, and many men and women died as we fought and obtained this freedom at the beginning, and many men and women throughout the world fight to the death today in their struggle to gain freedom in their countries. May God bless richly on this day those families as they struggle for the prize of freedom. It is truly a treasure to be free. Spiritually we are blessed with freedom as a gift from God. This is a freedom to live beyond the bonds of doubt and fear, which comes from a life of sin which separates us from God. Second Corinthians 3:17 tells us, *"Now the Lord is that Spirit, and where the Spirit of the Lord is, there is liberty."* When God is with you, you are totally free and able to be who God intends for you to be.

We are given freedom from sin through our faith and belief in our Lord Jesus Christ. John 8:36 says it clearly: *"If the Son therefore shall make you free, ye shall be free indeed."* Jesus set us free from sin with His death on the cross and His resurrection as He conquered the grave. Galatians 5:13 tells us how to use this freedom from God: *"For, brethren, ye have been called unto liberty; only use not liberty for an occasion to the flesh, but by Love serve one another."* The joy of our freedom is found as we Lovingly serve one another as God has directed us to do.

Through Jesus Christ, we are given our freedom from sin. As we turn our lives over to God, we become His to do His will in our lives. Romans 6:22 says it this way: *"But now being made free from sin, and become servants to God, ye have your fruit unto holiness, and the end everlasting life."* For us to find our lives served as "slaves to God" will lead us to holiness and eternal life. Celebrate your freedom and choose the path which leads you to God this day.

July 5th

We Are Free to Walk in the Spirit

We live in a world of freedom due to the gift of God because of the sacrifice Jesus made on the cross. The law that was given by God to guide mankind through Moses as the children of Israel journeyed out of Egypt still is a guide for us today. The Ten Commandments teach us to Love God the Father and to follow His directions on how to live in peace with one another. Romans 13:8–10 teaches us this:

Owe no man anything, but to Love one another; for he that Loveth another hath fulfilled the law. For this, Thou shalt not commit adultery; Thou shalt not kill; Thou shalt not steal; Thou shalt not bear false witness; Thou shalt not covet; and if there be any other commandment, it is briefly comprehended in this saying, namely, Thou shalt Love thy neighbor as thyself. Love worketh no ill to his neighbor; therefore Love is fulfilling the law.

The sinful nature of man makes him a slave to sin. The law gave way to the Spirit when Christ came, and now is our guide in all things. Romans 7:6 speaks to this as it says, *"But now we are delivered from the law, that being dead wherein we were held; that we should serve in the newness of Spirit, and not in the oldness of the letter."* The Holy Spirit will guide you as you seek His way in your life. We are not able to earn our way into heaven's gate, but rather salvation is a gift from God for those who believe. Galatians 5:18 tells us, *"But if ye be led by the Spirit, ye are not under the law."* Such freedom of the Spirit is not a license to do that which is wrong or sinful. It is the opposite in that it lets us find God directly through the Holy Spirit, guiding us to the path which leads us to righteousness in our lives.

When we turn our lives over to following Jesus Christ, we put away our old nature and turn toward our Spiritual nature. Galatians 5:24–25 says, *"And they that are Christ's have crucified the flesh with the affections and lusts. If we live in the Spirit, let us also walk in the Spirit."* May we choose to walk by the Spirit in our lives on this day. God walks with us as we do.

July 6th

Bring Honor to Your Father and Mother

My father on earth was born on this day, and for me, it is a delight to think about him and the life he led as an example set for me to follow. I was blessed and fortunate to have a man who Loved God and his family as my father. He held high standards in demonstrating his faith by the way he lived. Honesty and integrity were without compromise in his life. He taught his children to maintain those values and took us to church regularly to enable us to learn of God and the teachings of our Lord Jesus Christ. I know how fortunate I am to have had such a father, and many didn't experience that kind of an example in their early life.

The scriptures are very clear on how we are to bring honor to our parents. Deuteronomy 5:16 gives us this commandment and a promise from God: *"Honor thy father and thy mother, as the Lord thy God hath commanded thee, that thy days may be prolonged, and that it may go well with thee in the land that the Lord God giveth thee."* To honor is to pay high respect or great esteem to another. We know we are to Love our neighbors as Christ taught us, and to Love our family is also a commandment. When we add 'honor' to the commandment of God, we are to praise those who are our parents for all they do for us. Proverbs 20:20 warns us: *"Whoso curseth his father or his mother, his lamp shall be put out in obscure darkness."* God directs us to be respectful and to treat our parents with great esteem.

Your responsibility as a parent is great as well. Proverbs 22:6 tells us, *"Train up a child in the way he should go, and when he is old, he will not depart from it."* That which we teach our children becomes their values for life. As a child, we are to listen to this instruction and take it to heart. Proverbs 1:8–9 teaches: *"My son, hear the instruction of thy father, and forsake not the law of thy mother: For they shall be an ornament of grace unto thy head and chains about thy neck."* May we bring honor to those who raised us always in our lives.

July 7th
Overcoming Fear

There are times when we face certain fears which can creep into our hearts and minds about uncertainty that we face. The source of the fear may be related to the health of a Loved one, or it may stem from financial pressures which arise. Regardless of the source, those fears can take hold of you and direct your thoughts into high anxiety that inhabits your mind and robs you of your perspective as you are pulled away from thoughts of your comfort, which comes from God. When we seek God, He will deliver us from these fears. Psalm 34:4 says, *"I sought the Lord, and He heard me; and delivered me from all my fears."* While we hold on to our faith, we have no reason to fear.

The enemy of our souls wants fear to reside in our hearts. God wants us to walk in His presence and never to fear. John 14:27 says this: *"Peace I leave with you; my peace I give unto you; not as the world giveth, give I unto you. Let not your heart be troubled, neither let it be afraid."* As we walk daily with God, we have no cause for fear to enter our hearts. His will is being done as we seek it in our lives. As Joshua 1:9 emphatically says, *"Have not I commanded thee? Be strong and of good courage; be not afraid; neither be thou dismayed; for the Lord thy God is with thee whithersoever thou goest."* Knowing that to be the case, there is no fear that should cause us any concerns in life.

When Jesus Christ is your Lord and Savior, you cannot be separated from the Love of God our Father. Romans 8:38–39 tells us this: *"For I am persuaded, that neither death, nor life, nor angels, nor principalities, nor powers, nor things present, nor things to come, nor height, nor depth, nor any other creature, shall be able to separate us from the Love of God, which is in Christ Jesus our Lord."* As we walk in the confidence of this truth, we have nothing to fear, whatever we face on this or any day. Be Blessed as you walk in this truth today! Have no fears, and let the Love of God reign in your hearts always!

July 8th

When Sickness Afflicts His People

As God's people, we will face times in this world in which sickness will afflict us. It is a part of the human experience for such to occur. In those times, as well as in all times, God is with us. Why do people who trust in God get sick? There are questions such as this one which is not easy to answer. It happens for reasons beyond our comprehension. In those situations, people can minister to others and bring them to a relationship with God. The Bible describes our lives as being surrounded by a cloud of witnesses. In all we do, others are watching us and studying how we deal with the challenges of life. Perhaps God has a lesson for one of those which is being taught through us.

There is healing power in the word of God, and through faith, you will be delivered. The Bible tells of many healing miracles performed through faith throughout the scriptures. James 5:14–15 teaches us: *"Is any sick among you? Let him call for the elders of the church; and let them pray over him, anointing him with oil in the name of the Lord; And the prayer of faith shall save the sick, and the Lord shall raise him up, and if he have committed sins, they will be forgiven him."* The healing power of God extends beyond the physical side of our life and will heal you from emotional and spiritual scars and transgressions. We must turn over these things to God in prayer, believing we will be healed, and it will be done. Too often, people only call upon the Lord when sickness or strife comes into their life. It is best to be in a daily walk with God so your faith grows and your relationship with Him in your prayer life is always healthy.

Even when you face sickness, keep your spirits positive, and your healing will be made quicker and more complete. Proverbs 17:22 says, *"A merry heart doth good like medicine."* There is nothing that comes our way in life that should poison our attitude as we seek God's will in our lives. If any are sick among us, we should lift them up in prayer, believing always.

July 9th

How and When to Pray

The idea of talking to God on a personal level is a difficult one for many to grasp. Yet it is a fundamental element of Christian living. We are provided with direct access to God through the life of Jesus. He taught us to pray during His time on earth by teaching us the Lord's prayer, which is found in Matthew 6:9–13. In this prayer, Jesus says, *"Our Father which art in heaven, hallowed be thy name; Thy kingdom come; Thy will be done, on earth as it is in heaven. Give us this day our daily bread. And forgive our debts, as we forgive our debtors. And lead us not into temptation but deliver us from evil; for thine is the kingdom, and the power and the glory forever. Amen."* This prayer should be a guide to how to speak to God and pray it as part of our prayers to God each day.

The more often we talk to God, the less likely we are to fall into the temptations of the flesh. Matthew 26:41 tells us this: *"Watch and pray that ye enter not into temptation; The spirit indeed is willing, but the flesh is weak."* The world is filled with temptations each day. Our hearts and minds will be focused on God's will the more we spend our time in communion with Him. We are called upon to pray for others in our lives who may have needs or simply to lift them up for God's blessing to be upon them. Ephesians 6:18 says, *"Praying always with all prayer and supplication in the Spirit and watching thereunto with all perseverance and supplication for all saints."* God will put people in your heart to pray for as He does mine. Lift them up daily.

Whatever comes your way in life, rejoice in it and pray to the God who made you, for it is His will being done in your life. First Thessalonians 5:16–18 says, *"Rejoice evermore. Pray without ceasing. In everything give thanks; for this is the will of God in Christ Jesus concerning you."* As we walk with God, let us embrace in joy every moment He has given us. His Spirit is with us and will guide us to the place He has planned for us. Be Blessed on your walk with God today!

July 10th

Dealing with Prejudice in Our Hearts

Feelings of prejudice will enter our hearts from many different sources. If we are conservatives, we may feel less toward those who are more liberal in their political views. Certainly, the feeling of racial prejudice is and has always been widespread in our world. The world is filled with people of a variety of ethnic groups from cultures that are diverse and completely different from the one in which we might have been raised. Those differences can cause our hearts and minds to position other people in a less favorable way to those who may look like us or think like us because of our cultural upbringing. How would you think God would feel about such prejudice in our hearts?

As we grow Spiritually, we should know that all people of the earth draw strength, wisdom, and understanding from the same Spirit. First Corinthians 12:13 tells us, *"For by one Spirit we are all baptized into one body, whether we be Jews or Gentiles, whether we be bond or free; and have been all made to drink into one Spirit."* We tend to paint with a broad brush those from the nations we may find to conflict with our own nation. Once again, such a prejudicial view is not wise. Acts 17:26 says, *"And hath made of one blood all nations of men for to dwell on all the face of the earth, and hath determine the times before appointed, and the bounds of their habitation."* God is in control of our world, know He has devoted followers who are our brothers and sisters in every land.

There is no room in your heart for hate. First John 2:11 teaches this: *"But he that hateth his brother is in darkness, and walketh in darkness, knoweth not whither he goest, because that darkness hath blinded his eyes."* We are called to be the light of the world. Leviticus 19:34 says, *"But the stranger that dwelleth with you shall be unto you as one born among you, and thou shalt Love him as thyself. For ye were strangers in the land of Egypt; I am the Lord your God."* Love all those God puts on your path on this and every day! Be Blessed as you do!

July 11th

Take a Stand for the Elimination of Prejudice Around You

It is easy to look the other way when our friends, neighbors or those with whom we are associated speak against others in disparaging ways. I believe God calls upon us to take a stand against such acts of discrimination and prejudice in the world. We are called by God to be the light of the world. Matthew 5:16 says, *"Let your light so shine before men, that they may see your good works, and glorify your Father which is in heaven."* When you make a stand for that which is right, you are also planting seeds that may come into fruition in the hearts and lives of others. Many walk in darkness around us and are in their own hearts seeking the light of understanding and spiritual awakening. You may have been chosen to provide that seed for growth in their hearts and souls.

We know God Loves us all, whatever our political persuasion, ethnic background, race, creed, or color. As His children, we must also embrace all people with Love in our hearts as well. Acts 10;34–36 teaches us: *"Then Peter opened his mouth and said, Of a truth I perceive that God is no respecter of persons; But in every nation that feareth Him, and worketh righteousness, is accepted with Him. The word which God sent unto the children of Israel, preaching peace by Jesus Christ, He is Lord of all."* We have no room for taking a prejudicial view of any others and should stand for those who face such discrimination and prejudice around us.

Share with confidence and boldness your wisdom and understanding with others you meet on this and every day. Be the light when you meet with darkness on your path. Ecclesiastes 2:13 spells it out this way: *"Then I saw that wisdom excelleth folly, as far as light excelleth darkness."* May your light shine in the darkness which surrounds you today as we speak with wisdom against the prejudice of those in the world around us!

July 12th

Planting Seeds for the Harvest

Many times, in the scriptures, we learn about the need to plant seeds for the harvest to come. It is important to note that Jesus called upon us to do the work required to plant these seeds into the hearts and minds of others. The benefit of that work is the transformation of those who learn from the words we share and are converted to a life of victory in Jesus Christ as their savior. The "seeds" we are to plant are the message of God concerning our Lord and Savior Jesus Christ. Luke 8:11 says it plainly: *"Now the parable is this. The seed is the word of God."* It is our lives that demonstrate to others the power of the word of God coming alive in the world. We are surrounded by the "cloud of witnesses," as the Bible describes it. The first measure of your witness is the way you live and treat others. Next, it is what you say to others in translating the message of the word of God into the daily life you lead and share with those God brings to you.

God encourages us through His Word to be patient in the process of nurturing these seeds for the harvest to come. James 5:7 speaks to this: *"Be patient, therefore brethren, until the coming of the Lord. Behold the husbandman waiteth for the precious fruit of the earth, and hath long patience for it, until he receives the early and later rain."* We know that God is working in all the lives of those around us. Not all will receive Him in Spirit and in truth. Things are working in their lives to open the door for His message. We are simply called upon to deliver it in a way God will use us.

The benefit to you as one who sows seed for God and His kingdom is that you reap Love and righteousness in your soul. Hosea 10:12 teaches us this: *"Sow to yourselves in righteousness, reap in mercy; break up your fallow ground, for it is time to seek the Lord, till He come and rain righteousness upon you."* May the glory of God shine through our hearts, souls, and lives today as we plant seeds for the Kingdom of God into the hearts and lives of others!

July 13th

How Can I Plant Seeds for the Kingdom of God Today?

As we journey each day, we are engaging with those we meet along the way according to a plan that God has for us. Our interaction with the lives of others is not by accident but rather a part of the grand design God has for each life. What to say and when to say something about God's Love and purpose may be awkward for us as we begin to work in the harvest field of our lives. You may want to simply ask a friend or neighbor about 'How is your faith walk' or 'Do you believe in God?' You will quickly know whether they are open and receptive to such a conversation with you at that time. It may not be the time to open into a longer conversation, but a planted seed is now in place because of the question being asked.

Often, it is easy to simply say, "be Blessed today," or when someone is having a difficult time, let them know you will reach out to God for them in your prayers. When we do so, it is often responded to with a great feeling of appreciation. Following up with Love and care plants more seeds into the lives of those who God puts on your path. God supplies you with the seed and provides you with more as you use it. Second Corinthians 9:10 shares this: *"Now He that ministereth seed to the sower both minister bread for your food, and multiply your seed sown, and increase the fruits of your righteousness."* The blessings of God are bountiful for those who do His work.

We may plant a seed, and others may water it, but it is God who gives the growth to those who seek it in their hearts. First Corinthians 3:6–9 says,

> *I have planted, Apollos watered, but God gave the increase. So, neither is he that planteth anything, neither he that watereth, but God that giveth the increase. Now he that planteth and he that watereth are one; and every man shall receive his own reward according to his own labor. For we are laborers together with God; ye are God's husbandry; ye are God's building.*

July 14th

Nurturing the Seed Once It Is Planted

Once the seed of life, which is the word of God, is planted in our hearts and/or the hearts of others God brings into our lives, what is the next step in nourishing this seed to grow into the fulfillment of God's plan for our lives? To enable this seed to grow, we must turn from the ways of the world and seek God's will for our lives. Psalm 143:10 says this: *"Teach me to do thy will, for thou art my God; thy Spirit is good; lead me into the land of uprightness."* When we seek God's will for our lives, we will find it as He desires for us to follow it.

To achieve this, we must turn away from our pursuit of that which draws us further away from God each day. James 1:21–25 tells us,

> *Wherefore, lay apart all filthiness and superfluity of naughtiness, and receive with meekness the engrafted word, which is able to save your souls. But be ye doers of the word, and not hearers only, deceiving your own selves. For if any be a hearer of the word, and not a doer, he is like a man beholding his natural face in a glass; for he beholdeth himself, and goeth his way, and straightway forgetteth the manner of man he was. But whoso looketh into the perfect law of liberty, and continueth therein, he is being not a forgetful hearer, but a doer of the work, this man shall be blessed in his deed.*

Daily seeking God's will and understanding His way for your life through the reading of His Word daily puts you on the pathway to nourishing the seeds of His Word, which are planted in you.

May our lives become a living sacrifice that is holy and pleasing to God. Romans 12:1–2 says,

> *I beseech you therefore, brethren, by the mercies of God, that ye present your bodies as a living sacrifice, holy and acceptable unto God, which is your reasonable service. And be not conformed to this world; but be ye transformed by the renewing of your mind, that ye may prove what is good, and acceptable, and perfect will of God.*

God is waiting for us to seek His will today!

July 15th

The Foundation of Life

The words that Jesus taught us establish the foundation of life for the world. If you want your life to be built on solid ground, read and understand His teachings and live by those principles in your life. In Matthew 7:24–25, Jesus says these words: *"Therefore whosoever heareth these sayings of mine and doeth them, I will liken him unto a wise man, who built his house upon a rock. And the rain descended, and the floods came, and the winds blew, and beat upon that house, and it fell not because it was founded upon a rock."* Living your life without the foundation of God's Word and failing to put His truth into practice is a recipe for disaster when the storms of life come your way. When you are built on the word of God, you will endure all that the storms of life bring to you.

As you receive the word of God into your life, you become a new person and have been born again in the Spirit. First Peter 1:23 says, *"Being born again, not of corruptible seed, but of incorruptible, by the word of God, which liveth and abideth forever."* This rebirth leads to a renewal of your mind and gives an understanding of the values Jesus taught us in His ministry. We should seek daily the renewal of our minds consistent with God's Word and the transformation of our attitudes to be more like Christ. Ephesians 4:21–24 says, *"If so be that ye have heard Him, and have been taught by Him, as the truth is in Jesus. That ye put off concerning the former conversation the old man, which is corrupt according to the deceitful lusts; And be renewed in the Spirit of your mind; And that ye put on the new man, which after God is created in righteousness and true holiness."* To be born again is to be changed in our thoughts, actions, and nature to be more like the man or woman God has intended us to be.

Be Blessed as you build your life on the foundation of the word of God! Let us embrace the new man or woman God has intended for each of us to be. Be renewed in the Spirit of your mind on this day!

July 16th
Teach Me Your Paths

Hiking with my family is one of my favorite activities when we go on vacation. We get to see the beauty the Lord has created in the world around us and experience the joy of discovery together. Whether it be in the mountains or by the seaside, the magnificence of God's creation is amazing to behold. As we seek God's presence in our lives, we are guided by the Holy Spirit to the path God would have us on each day of our journey through this world around us. This path is not on a trail map we can fold up and put in our pockets. Rather, it comes from the Spirit, which serves to guide us as our own personal GPS system inside our hearts and minds. It is up to each of us to seek the path through prayer and meditation on the word of God.

A prayer each day could be said in our hearts consistent with what David wrote in Psalm 25:4, which says, *"Show me thy ways, O Lord, teach me thy paths."* It is a simple request to God for His direction from where we stand today. The book of Proverbs, which is written by King Solomon, who is called the wisest man to have ever lived, speaks of the path directed by God. Proverbs 4:11 tells us, *"I have taught thee in the way of wisdom; I have led thee in right paths."* He speaks of God's guidance in his life and the wisdom it has given to him. Solomon's father, David, wrote these words in the book of Psalm 16:11 about the path of life: *"Thou wilt show me the path of life; in thy presence is fulness of joy; at thy right hand there are pleasures forevermore."* The joy of the Lord is evident in the writings of these great men of God as they seek the path that God has chosen for each of them. May we continue to endeavor to seek the path God has chosen for each of us.

God will direct us to the path that leads to righteousness. Proverbs 2:20 positions it this way: *"That thou mayest walk in the way of good men, and keep the paths of the righteous."* May God direct our path today as we seek His will.

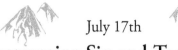

July 17th

Overcoming Sin and Temptation

As we seek to find the path to righteousness and to walk alongside God in our lives each day, we will still battle with the enemy of our souls along the way. The more we try to grow closer to God, the more the enemy will strive to pull us away from Him. Temptation and sin will surround us in the world as long as we live. It is a part of the ongoing battle between the forces of good and evil. Knowing this to be the case, how do we overcome sin and temptation in our life? First Corinthians 10:13 tells us, *"There hath no temptation taken you but such as is common to man; but God is faithful, who will not suffer you to be tempted above that ye are able; but will with the temptation also make a way to escape; that ye may be able to bear it."* Temptations don't control you. Rather, they attempt to allure you to a path that is not of God's will.

We need to always look at the company we are keeping. If you are surrounded by others who are seeking a righteous path in their lives, the amount of temptation you face is reduced considerably. First Corinthians 15:33 teaches this: *"Be not deceived. Evil communications corrupt good manners."* The choice you make of where you spend your time and with whom you are spending it will often determine the course of the path you are on spiritually. James 1:14–15 cautions us this: *"But every man is tempted, when he is drawn away of his own lust, and enticed. Then when lust hath conceived, it bringeth forth sin, when it is finished, bringeth forth death."* We face temptations daily in our lives as part of the human experience. We must be on guard in our hearts and minds to resist and overcome it. God always provides us with a way to escape it.

The choice of the path we are on each day belongs to each of us. We can either submit to sin, or we can submit to God. James 4:7 tells us, *"Submit yourselves therefore to God. Resist the devil, and he will flee from you."* God empowers you to be an overcomer. Be delivered from sin as you do so today.

July 18th

Are We Slaves to Sin or Righteousness?

The human nature is an addictive one. We grow in our habits in life to where we become addicted to certain behaviors. People find themselves addicted to things that hurt them, such as alcohol, porn, food, drugs, gossip, or simply television or movies that fill their minds with negative and evil thoughts. Others choose habits that become obsessive which lead to better health, such as exercise, proper dieting, meditations, and reading positive material, which build up their thoughts and energies and help their spiritual growth. As we turn from that which is pulling us from God, which we define as sin, to that which helps us grow closer to God, the scriptures suggest we are becoming "slaves to righteousness," as opposed to "slaves to sin."

Romans 6:12 tells us, *"Let not sin therefore reign in your mortal body, that ye should obey it in the lusts thereof."* When we subject ourselves to excesses in alcohol, drugs, porn, food, or other things which do us harm and take us further from God, we are slaves to it in our lives. It causes us shame and damages our spirit. By the death of Jesus on the cross and the grace of God, we are made free from sin if we choose to be so. Romans 6:14 says, *"For sin shall not have dominion over you; for ye are not under the law but under grace."* We remain addictive in nature but turning our behavior to that which is of God will eliminate the desire for the sin which pulls us away from God.

Paul concludes this chapter with this message in Romans 6:20–23: *"For when ye were servants of sin, ye were free from righteousness. What fruit had ye then in those things whereof ye are now ashamed? For the end of those things is death. But now, being made free from sin, and become servants to God, ye have your fruit unto holiness, and the end everlasting life. For the wages of sin is death, but the gift of God is eternal life through Jesus Christ our Lord."* May we turn away from sin and become the slaves of God on this day!

July 19th

May the Eyes of Your Heart Be Enlightened with Hope

With each day that passes, we grow closer to the day in which we will see God face to face. The spirit of Love and hope will guide us to the path which draws us closer to Him each day if we seek that path in our hearts. Ephesians 1:18 speaks to this enlightenment of our heart with hope as we seek His calling for our lives: *"The eyes of your understanding being enlightened, that ye may know what is in the hope of His calling, and what the riches of the glory of His inheritance in the saints."* We are all called as the people of God to a mission of service to Him. The inheritance that awaits us is called glorious, and that should be our hope in our life each day.

As we experience life on earth, we may have struggles from time to time, whether they be of a physical nature or perhaps emotional or spiritual struggles that we face. God is with us through it all, and He will strengthen us and lead us through such times. First Peter 5:10 teaches us: *"But the God of all grace, who hath called us unto His eternal glory by Christ Jesus, after ye have suffered a while, make you perfect, stablish, strengthen, settle you."* God gives us strength and builds our resolve as we need these qualities to overcome the issues we face in life. We are not reliant on our own ability to persevere in all we face.

As our heart is enlightened with the hope of what He has called us to attain, we are on a path to an eternal prize for which God has prepared for us. Philippians 3:13–14 tells us, *"Brethren, I count not myself to have apprehended; but this one thing I do, forgetting those things which are behind, and reaching forth unto those things with are before, I press forward to the mark for the prize of the high calling of God in Christ Jesus ."* We press on each day toward the ultimate goal of a life in heaven which is prepared for us. It is our hope, it is our goal, and it is our destiny as a believer in Jesus Christ. Be Blessed today as you press on to this goal in your life.

July 20th

All Things Work Together for the Good

One of my mother's favorite scriptures is found in Romans 8:28, which says, *"And we know that all things work together for good to them that Love God, to them who have been called according to His purpose."* When we read these words and meditate on their meaning, we see a God who is working in our lives always. The first three words ensure us by saying, *"And we know,"* that God is in it with us. We know we will face hardships and sicknesses along the way of our journey in life, but we can rest assured that God is with us while we pass through these times. He is working with us to create a good result in whatever we face.

This chapter of Romans has many scriptures which provide us with boldness and confidence in the spiritual walk we have with God as believers. Romans 8:1 opens the chapter by saying, *"there is no condemnation for them which are in Jesus Christ."* The chapter goes on to describe how we, through Jesus, have been set free from the bonds of sin. Romans 8:14 says, *"For as many as are led by the Spirit of God, they are the Sons of God."* As we walk in His spirit, we become His children. Verses 17–18 testify to this further: *"And if children, then heirs; heirs of God, and joint heirs with Christ, if so be that we suffer with Him, that we may also be glorified together. For I reckon that the sufferings of this present time are not worthy to be compared with the glory which shall be revealed in us."* We each have a "cross to bear" in our lives as we work to serve our God and Savior. He is with us as we do His will in our lives each day we live.

As we face the challenges of life, verse 31 tells us we have God on our side as it says, *"What shall we then say to these things? If God be for us, who can be against us?"* We have no reason to fear with God on our side. Romans 8:37 concludes: *"Nay, in all these things, we are more than conquerors through Him that Loved us."* Be a "conqueror" in all you face with God at your side! Be Blessed in all you do for Him today, knowing all things are working together for good!

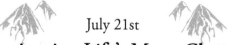

July 21st
Experiencing Life's Many Changes

There are many life-altering changes we experience on our journey. Some are the result of physical moves we make from place to place. Some are emotional changes resulting from births in our families or deaths which affect us with the passing of those who we have grown to Love. Some of life's changes are the result of sickness or health-related issues we may face or the health of those who we may care for. While we experience a whirlwind of emotions as these changes take place, we have the refuge of our God, who is with us through them all. Deuteronomy 31:6 assures us of this: *"Be strong and of good courage, fear not, nor be afraid of them; for the Lord thy God, He it is that doeth go with thee; He will not fail thee, nor forsake thee."* With this as our understanding, we can embrace any change we face with confidence that God will be there with us.

Some of life brings joy and other times bring us sorrow. The scripture tells of this in Ecclesiastes 3:1,4 as it says, *"To every thing there is a season, and a time to every purpose under heaven…A time to weep and a time to laugh, a time to mourn and a time to dance."* Our lives are filled with all phases of human experience. We share those moments with those God has given us as family and friends who share our lives and Love with us. We are blessed to be given to one another for support, comfort, and the sharing of joy or sorrow in all these moments. We face anxiety as some of our life's changes occur. We step outside of our comfort zone. Whatever changes you make, keep God at the center of your heart and mind and seek His will as you choose your path. Joshua 1:9 teaches us: *"Have I not commanded you? Be strong and of good courage; be not afraid, neither be thou dismayed; for the Lord thy God is with thee whithersoever thou goest."* God sends us this message throughout the scriptures.

Changes will happen throughout our lives. As they do, one thing remains the constant anchor for our souls. God walks with us, and He Loves us!

July 22nd

Live Each Day Within God's Purpose

God has a purpose for everyone He has created. It is our quest to seek His will and purpose for our lives for us to be fulfilled. We all will have plans and dreams of how we hope to live our lives, and it is good to explore those in our hearts and minds. To live in the center of God's will, we must seek it daily and yield to His Spirit as we do. Proverbs 19:21 tells us, *"There are many devices in a man's heart; nevertheless, the counsel of the Lord, that shall stand."* The vision we have for where we need to go is limited to what we see around us. God's vision of the world in which we live is unlimited, and He sees into our future in a way we cannot. As we learn to yield to His guidance, we find peace and joy.

The plan God has for you will not only impact your own life, but the lives of those He has given to you, such as your family, friends, and those He places on your path each day. Your life has a significance that extends beyond the years you spend on this earth as you live it consistent with His purpose. Psalm 33:11 teaches us this: *"The counsel of the Lord standeth forever, the thoughts of His heart to all generations."* As we seek to do His will, our lives become significant as part of His plan and bring value to us and to others around us. He plants the seeds of His purpose inside our heart. The more we actively seek His will and read His Word, the more that purpose is revealed. Proverbs 20:5 says, *"Counsel in the heart of man is like deep water; but a man of understanding will draw it out."*

We are created by God to do the works He has called us to do. It is our destiny, and we are to seek and find it each day. Ephesians 2:10 speaks to it as it says, *"For we are His workmanship, created in Christ Jesus unto good works, which God hath before ordained that we should walk in them."* As we seek His will, He reveals it to us. May we embrace the Holy Spirit and ask for His guidance as we seek to do His will on this and every day. Be Blessed today as you do so!

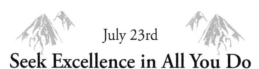

July 23rd
Seek Excellence in All You Do

As a child of God, it is our birthright to seek to be excellent in all He has called us to do in our lives. God did not call you to live a life of mediocrity but to find enthusiasm and to be fully invested in the work He has planned for you. Colossians 3:23–24 teaches us: *"And whatever ye do, do it heartily, as to the Lord, and not unto men. Knowing that of the Lord ye shall receive the reward of the inheritance; for ye serve the Lord Christ."* Whatever your job God has placed you in at this time in your life, bring passion and enthusiasm as you deliver excellence in all you do. The service you provide in the world in which you live should be beyond the expectations of those you serve. That will make an impact on the lives of those around you.

As you excel in all you do, may you continue to walk humbly, and may the glory be given to God as your testimony to others for the gifts He has given to you. Second Corinthians 8:7 says, *"Therefore as ye abound in every thing, in faith, and utterance, and knowledge, and in all diligence, and in your Love to us, see that you abound in this grace also."* In the witness your life has to others when your heart takes pride over your achievements, you lose the grace God intends for you to demonstrate to others. A humble spirit bears witness to God's presence in your heart and soul.

Seeking excellence in all we are called to do is what God intends for us in our daily walk. The most important aspect of your life to achieve excellence is to focus your mind on that which is of God each day. Avoid dwelling on negative thoughts. Philippians 4:8 tells us, *"Finally brethren, whatsoever things are true, whatsoever things are honest, whatsoever things are just, whatsoever things are pure, whatsoever things are lovely, whatsoever things are of good report; if there be any virtue, and if there be any praise, think on these things."* The more we think about things that are of God, the more we live a life that is excellent!

July 24th
Turn Away from Anger in Your Heart

Emotions of all kinds enter our hearts and souls from time to time. We experience joy and happiness, and hopefully, this is a spirit in our hearts that is prevalent often. There are times when sorrow occupies a place that casts a shadow over our lives for a period of time. The source of that sorrow can be coming from many places, such as sickness, or death of a Loved one, or from a conflict we have had with someone close to us. As a result of such a conflict, anger can invade our hearts, and as it does, any joy or happiness that resides there will be forced out by this dominating emotion. How do we best deal with replacing it with the spirit God would want us to carry us through the day?

The scripture talks about anger and encourages us to resolve it whenever it occurs. Ephesians 4:26 teaches us this: *"Be ye angry, and sin not; let not the sun go down on your wrath."* The message is clear that we will all experience anger in our lives. However, the message is to not let it linger in your heart, for it leads to sin, which comes as a result. We want to justify that we are right in those times of conflict. Winning the argument or the battle takes precedence over the feelings of humility and kindness toward the one with whom we have an issue. The scriptures lead us away from that in Ephesians 4:31, which says, *"Let all bitterness and wrath and anger and clamor and evil speaking be put away from you, with all malice."* None of these things bring us closer to God nor to one another in our lives. They only tend to separate us from the will of God.

We know this is not of God when we embrace this spirit. Psalm 37:8 says, *"Cease from anger and forsake wrath; fret not thyself, in any wise to do evil."* The more we engage in our angry moments, the more likely we are to do something we will regret. James 1:19–20 puts it this way: *"Wherefore my beloved brethren, let every man be swift to hear, slow to speak, slow to wrath. For the wrath of man worketh not the righteousness of God."* Let your anger subside.

July 25th

Put on a Heart of Compassion and Tenderness

As we continue to walk with God and we strive to further deepen our relationship with Him each day, we need to clothe ourselves in a spirit of tenderness and compassion for those we meet along the way. The light of our lives which shines through us should bring this spirit out in all that we do. Ephesians 4:32 says, *"And be ye kind, one to another, tenderhearted, forgiving one another, even as God for Christ's sake hath forgiven you."* When we carry forward, feelings of resentment or anger toward someone, those feelings reside inside our hearts and minds and are reflected in our actions toward the other. The poison of those feelings infects our own souls rather than the soul of the one for whom we harbor these thoughts. In any event, they will sustain the separation and further engage the animosity we experience for that person.

We seek harmony in our relationships with others rather than conflict. First Peter 3:8 says it this way: *"Finally, be ye all of one mind, having compassion one of another, Love as brethren, be pitiful, be courteous."* When we demonstrate these qualities, we are allowing the spirit of Love to flow through our hearts into our lives and lives around us. Colossians 3:12 says it as well about those who are chosen of God: *"Put on therefore, as the elect of God, holy and beloved, bowels of mercies, kindness, humbleness of mind, meekness, longsuffering."* These are all characteristics we should strive to achieve and will reflect someone who is walking on the path God would have for his life. When we demonstrate these qualities, we are doing what God would have us do.

The simplest guide we have in our lives is that we Love one another in all that we do. First Corinthians 16:14 teaches us: *"Let all your things be done with Love."* When we follow this verse and incorporate it into our lives, all the qualities and characteristics describing one chosen of God are going to be manifest in our lives. May you be Blessed today, and may everything you do, be done in Love!

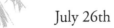

July 26th

Go Where God Leads You to Go

There are times in our lives when God is calling us to make a change and embrace a new phase of our lives. Those changes may include moving away from the place we have lived to embark upon a new path or taking a new job to put us where He wants us. God will direct us through His Holy Spirit to go and do that which He is calling us to do. When God needed a leader to bring His people out of slavery in Egypt, He called Moses to be that man. Moses felt inadequate and, at first, resisted God's calling. Exodus 4:10–12 tells us,

> *And Moses said unto the Lord, O my Lord, I am not eloquent, neither heretofore, nor since thou hast spoken unto thy servant; but I am slow of speech, and of a slow tongue. And the Lord said unto him, Who hath made man's mouth? Or who maketh the dumb, or the deaf, or the seeing, or the blind? Have not I, the Lord? Now therefore go and I will be with thy mouth and teach thee what thou shalt say.*

God gives us His gifts to do His work. When He calls us to do that work, it is not something He takes back. Romans 11:29 says this: *"For the gifts and the calling of God are without repentance."* When we embrace this life of service to God, we are His vessels to be used as He determines to be best. Our calling is to be serve others with Love and compassion for His glory. We may feel unworthy, and we, alone, do not have the power without God, but with Him, we have no limits. 2 Thessalonians 1:11 teaches us: *"Wherefore also we pray always for you, that our God would count you worthy of this calling, and fulfill all the good pleasure of His goodness, and the work of faith with power."*

Don't look at your limits in following God's calling for you. Look to the glory and excellence that comes from God. 2 Peter 1:3 says, *"According as His divine power hath given unto us all things that pertain unto life and godliness, through the knowledge of Him that hath called us to glory and virtue."* Seek His calling for your life today, and be confident that He will be with you always!

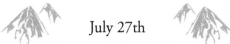

July 27th

God Has Chosen Us to Do His Work

We each are called to do the work that God has planned for our lives. God has a work for each of us to do to further the kingdom of God in the world around us. We are not on this earth to sit idly by as spectators but, rather, to be fully engaged in the work of the Lord as He directs us to do. First Corinthians 7:17 directs us: *"But as God hath distributed to every man, as the Lord hath called every one, so let him walk. And so ordain I all churches."* We must pray for His Spirit to enlighten us as to what His calling for our lives is as we develop further each day in our faith. Your role of responsibility may evolve as God further empowers you in your spiritual journey.

There are many roles and responsibilities that God has for His chosen people to fulfill in His work. God has determined a place for each of us in this ministry. First Peter 4:10–11 teaches us this: *"As every man hath received the gift, even so minister the same one to another, as good stewards of the manifold grace of God. If an man speak, let him speak as the oracles of God; If any man minister, let him do it as of the ability which God giveth; that God in all things might be glorified through Jesus Christ, to whom be praise and dominion for ever and ever."* Each of us has a role to play in the grand scheme of God's plan for His people. Prayerfully seek His plan for your life and know He has a calling for you.

We must seek God's enlightenment to understand fully His calling for each of us. May we seek, prayerfully, that calling and follow the path God has planned for us this day. The scripture tells us to seek, and we will find. God is waiting to help us develop the gift He has bestowed upon us. Be Blessed as you discover His gift and His purpose for your life today!

July 28th
The Simple Pathway to Salvation

Many people wrestle in their hearts and minds about the concept of salvation and what must happen for it to take place in our lives. We may not feel worthy due to the sinful nature of the human heart. Salvation is a gift from God for those who believe in Jesus Christ. Romans 10:9–10 puts it simply: *"That if thou shalt confess with thy mouth the Lord Jesus, and shalt believe in thine heart that God hath raised Him from the dead, thou shalt be saved. For with the heart, man believeth unto righteousness, and with the mouth confession is made unto salvation."* The pathway to salvation is a simple one that is based on our faith and our open declaration that Jesus is Lord.

The only path to salvation is through our faith in Jesus Christ. In Acts 4:12, the author, Luke, wrote these words: *"Neither is there salvation in any other: for there is none other name under heaven given among men, whereby we must be saved."* We know that Jesus is the truth and the light of the world. Our faith in Him is our key to finding the gift of salvation God offers to each of us. The journey with God and the experience of accepting His gift of salvation is a life experience and not just a momentary event. Our faith is to be sustained to the end of our lives. Some will come and "try out" a life of faith for a season, and they will drift away from it, lured by the sins of the world around them. First John 2:19 describes this happening: *"They went out from us, but they were not of us, for if they had been of us, they would no doubt have continued with us; but they went out, that they might be made manifest that they were not all of us."*

Salvation through our faith in Jesus Christ is a beautiful gift from God. Our choice of what path we take beyond the moment we accept Jesus into our hearts is what will determine if it is our lifetime commitment to faith. At the end of our lives, may our hearts hold this message from 2 Timothy 4:7: *"I have fought a good fight, I have finished my course, and I have kept the faith."*

July 29th

The Gift of Salvation Is Available to All People

God has made this beautiful gift of salvation available to all people who accept the truth that Jesus Christ died for their sins and was resurrected from the dead and lives forever as the Son of God. It takes faith as simple as that of a child to accept this truth in your heart and life. When you embrace the truth of the message of the gospel, you become one of God's chosen ones who are saved by His grace. Ephesians 1:13 says this: *"In whom ye also trusted, after that, ye heard the word of the truth, the gospel of your salvation; in whom also after that ye believed, ye were sealed with the Holy Spirit of promise."* His Holy Spirit is with you now as a believer to strengthen you in your faith.

When we accept Jesus as our Savior and ask God for the forgiveness of our sins, we become born again in the Spirit. We are in the infancy of our faith walk with God. To grow in the Spirit, we need to get our nourishment from the scriptures, which teach the life of Christ and His teachings to those who are to become His disciples. Through the reading of His Words, we become wise in what we then do. Second Timothy 3:5 teaches us: *"And that from a child thou hast known the holy scriptures, which are able to make thee wise unto salvation through faith which is in Christ Jesus."* To learn more about our Lord Jesus Christ enhances our ability to grow in our faith which leads to eternal life.

May our hearts sing joyfully to the God who has given us this gift of salvation and eternal life. David wrote in Psalm 95:1 these words: *"O come, let us sing unto the Lord; let us make a joyful noise to the rock of our salvation."* May your heart be filled with joy, and may your joy be shared with those around you as we celebrate the gift of salvation for our souls on this and every day. Be Blessed as you do so!

July 30th
God Is With Us in Times of Trouble

There will be times of trouble in every life. We deal with issues each day that will cause us stress which should give us the instinct to turn our hearts to God for strength and refuge. He is there with us in all these times. When we try to handle things on our own, we often find ourselves unable to create a resolution that is free from stress and one which brings us peace and prosperity. The scriptures teach us to seek God always, and He will bring us strength. First Chronicles 16:11 says, *"Seek the Lord and His strength; Seek His face continually."* When you seek God to take dominion over your life, you have His power to face adversity and will prevail.

There is no cause for fear when we face the challenges this world has to offer us. We don't go through tough times alone when we daily seek to walk with God in our lives. Though we face difficult times, we are never alone when we do so. Deuteronomy 31:6 assures us of this: *"Be strong and of good courage, fear not, nor be afraid of them; for the Lord thy God, He is that doth go with thee; He will not fail thee, nor forsake thee."* These words should be our source of comfort and give us the confidence to know we have His strength to empower us. There is nothing we cannot overcome with Him as our source of power.

David's relationship with God, as was revealed in the book of Psalms, was both intimate and deep. Psalm 50:11 expresses his faith this way: *"And call upon me in the day of trouble; I will deliver thee, and thou shalt glorify me."* In this verse, God is telling David to simply call upon His name, and He will be there to rescue him. God speaks to His people through Jeremiah 29:11, which says, *"For I know the thoughts I think toward you,' saith the Lord. 'Thoughts of peace and not of evil, to give you an expected end."* We walk under the protective covering of God. Be at peace and give thanks to Him each day as you do so.

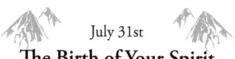

July 31st

The Birth of Your Spirit

Nicodemus was a prominent Pharisee and a member of the Jewish ruling council. He came to see Jesus at night and asked Him questions about who He was. Jesus told him that he must be "born again" to see the kingdom of heaven. Nicodemus questions that, and Jesus answers him in John 3:4–6, which says,

Nicodemus saith unto Him, 'How can a man be born when he is old? Can he enter a second time into his mother's womb, and be born?' Jesus answered, 'Verily, verily, I say unto thee, Except a man be born of water and the Spirit, he cannot enter the kingdom of God. That which is born of the flesh is flesh; and that which is born of the Spirit is Spirit.

Jesus spoke of the Spiritual awakening that gives your life awareness of the truth and light of His life. This is the beginning of your journey with God in the Spirit.

As the conversation with Nicodemus continues, Jesus points out to him that as people believe in Him as the Son of God, they are given the gift of eternal salvation. One of the most quoted scriptures in the Bible comes out of this conversation in John 3:16 which says, *"For God so Loved the world that He gave His only begotten Son, that whosoever believeth in Him shall not perish but have everlasting life."* This message resonates throughout the world today and will always be the foundation of the faith we have in Jesus Christ and the pathway to God and our eternal salvation. This belief leads to being born again in the Spirit.

John the Baptist speaks of Jesus later in the book of John 3:34–36 when he testifies to Jesus being the Son of God as he says,

For He whom God hath sent speaketh the words of God; for God giveth not the Spirit by measure unto Him. The Father Loveth the Son, and hath given all things into His hand. He that believeth on the Son hath everlasting life, and he that believeth not on the Son shall not see life; but the wrath of God abideth on him.

May our Spiritual birth lead us on the path to eternal life through our faith in Jesus Christ our Lord today!

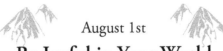

August 1st

Be Joyful in Your World

We bring an attitude in our lives to the world around us. As we do, people are influenced by it and bear witness to our Spirit through it. When we are dissatisfied with the condition of our life, it is reflected in what we do and say. People are less likely to want to be a part of that world alongside us and tend to shy away. When we bring happiness and joy to that world, people become attracted to it and want to have in their hearts what we possess from a Spiritual perspective. Ecclesiastes 9:7 tells us, *"Go thy way, eat thy bread with joy, and drink thy wine with a merry heart; for God now accepteth thy works."* When we see our lives as one of those who walk with God in our hearts each day, we are on the path He has chosen for us. Be happy as such and embrace the life you have been given.

Does this mean you won't face trials and tribulations along the way? We all know the answer is they will be a part of our journey. James 1:2–3 teaches us this: *"My brethren, count it all joy when ye fall into diverse temptations; knowing this, that the trying of your faith worketh patience."* We grow stronger when we are tested in life, and we overcome the enemy of our souls. God will give us the strength to be overcomers and to win these battles when we turn to Him. We must not shrink from these trials when they happen, but we welcome them with joy in our hearts.

Sharing your joy and prosperity with others is God's plan for all who believe in Him. Nehemiah 8:10 speaks to this: *"Then he said unto them, Go your way, eat the fat, and drink the sweet, and send portions to them for whom nothing is prepared; for this day is holy unto the Lord; neither be ye sorry, for the joy of the Lord is your strength."* May we each grow in the joy of the Lord, which gives us strength, and may our hearts be open to giving to others and sharing that joy each day. Your attitude is your choice to make today and always. Be joyful today!

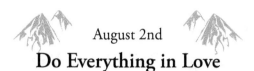

August 2nd
Do Everything in Love

Jesus taught us the greatest of all commandments is to Love the Lord your God with all your heart, and with all your soul, and with all your mind. The second commandment is to Love one another as yourself. All the law is fulfilled by these two Jesus described in Matthew 22:36–40. With that as our marching orders through the lives we lead, there should be a Spirit of Love present in all we do each day. The energy of Love is infectious, and those you embrace with this Spirit will draw strength and joy from it. As you invest this energy into the hearts and lives of others, you receive it back into your own heart, mind, and soul in return. First Corinthians 16:14 says it simply: *"Let all your things be done with Love."* When this becomes our mindset, we become one with God our Father.

If we intend to walk with God and be a disciple of Christ each day, we will witness to others what we are when we walk in the Spirit of Love. John 13:35 says, *"By this shall all men know that ye are my disciples, if you Love one to another."* Sharing Love with others is best described in what we call the "Love chapter" of the Bible, which is found in 1 Corinthians 13:4–7 (NIV), which shows us:

> *Love is patient, Love is kind. It does not envy, it does not boast, it is not proud. It does not dishonor others, it is not self-seeking, it is not easily angered, it keeps no record of wrongs. Love does not delight in evil but rejoices with the truth. It always protects, always trusts, always hopes, always perseveres.*

When you embrace this pattern of behavior in all your relationships, you bring an incredible Spirit of Love into the world.

This is the ultimate mission of our lives to be a source of Love in the world to all we meet. First John 4:7–8 tells us how important this is when it says, *"Dear friends, let us Love one another, for Love comes from God. Everyone who Loves has been born of God and knows God. Whoever does not Love does not know God, because God is Love."* Embrace this fully and do everything in Love always!

August 3rd

Continuing to Build Upon Your Faith

As we walk with God each day, it is our faith that continues to sustain us in our growth within our Spiritual life. The more we embrace the Holy Spirit in our lives in prayer, the closer we are drawn to the power of our faith in God. Jude 20–21 says this: *"But ye, beloved, by building yourselves on your most holy faith, and praying in the Holy Ghost, keep yourselves in the Love of God looking for the mercy of our Lord Jesus Christ unto eternal life."* Faith is what carries us forward to our destiny of eternal life, and everything we do to strengthen it will be to the glory of God.

We know the more time we spend reading and hearing the word of God, the more our faith is built and grows. Romans 10:17 says this clearly: *"So then faith cometh by hearing, and hearing by the word of God."* When we shy away from gathering with those who are believers, we are denying ourselves the opportunity to grow in our faith walk. Hebrews 10:38–39 tells us not to pull away from our faith: *"Now the just shall live by faith, but if any man draw back, my soul shall have no pleasure in him. But we are not of them who draw back unto perdition; but to them that believe to the saving of the soul."* The destiny of the believer is to persevere until the end and to build our faith throughout our journey.

We are guided in our faith walk in Hebrews 10:23–25, which teaches us: *"Let us hold fast to the profession of our faith without wavering; for He is faithful that promised. And let us consider one another to provoke unto Love and to good works; Not forsaking the assembling of ourselves together, as the manner of some is; but exhorting one another; and so much the more as you see the day approaching."* Our faith is being built as we journey together with the believers God has given to us in our lives. We are here to help one another by encouraging them in their faith walk as they do us. Be faithful in seeking other believers.

August 4th
Let Us Be Joyful This Day

As we embrace this day the Lord has given to us, let us be joyful and bring happiness into the lives of those we meet along the way. There is enough sadness around us with those who face adversity and have their minds filled with sorrow as a result. When you bring joy into their world, you may change their perspective to one of hope, if only for a moment, but that seed may grow into a Spiritual awakening as a result. Psalm 118:24 exalts: *"This is the day the Lord hath made; we will rejoice and be glad in it."* Simply knowing God has given us another day to walk upon this earth lets us know we have work to do in His name as we journey here. We always have the choice of how we think and feel, and it is God's plan to have us joyful in our hearts.

David writes in Psalm 30:11 a message we should all embrace: *"Thou hast turned my mourning into dancing; thou hast put off my sackcloth and girded me with gladness."* When we start each day prayerful and talking to God, we are reminded of His Holy Spirit in our lives, which is there to comfort and guide us. As such, we have no reason not to be joyful in all we do that day. John 15:11 says to us: *"These things I have spoken unto you, that my joy might remain in you, and that your joy might be full."* We are not despondent when we are filled with the joy of our Lord. Rather, we become a source of joy for all we meet along the way.

When you walk with joy in your heart and laughter on your lips, you bear witness to the blessings God has given you in your heart and soul. When you walk mournfully and are unhappy generally in your life, that, too, bears witness about your Spirit to others. Psalm 126:2 speaks to this witness of your soul as it says, *"Then was our mouth was filled with laughter, and our tongue with singing. Then said they among the heathen, 'The Lord hath done great things for them."* Let it be said by those in your world, "The Lord has done great things for them." Our lives bear witness to what is in our hearts and souls. May your joy be full!

August 5th

He Is Our Shelter from the Storms of Life

Living in Florida in the summer months, we are often reminded of the power of nature as hurricane season seems to grow in intensity each year. The power of the forces of nature is immense as our world moves forward with the influence of a changing climate. In our lives, we face storms of many kinds each year, some are literal and some figurative, as turbulence of some form invades the world around us. Preparation is said to be a key to mitigating the impact of such storms. Hurricane preparation may mean you have sandbags or generators ready to use and plenty of batteries for lamps and other electronic equipment. For those living in tornado areas, other preparations are required to escape from the fury of such storms. The only true shelter and protection from such storms come from God our Father.

When the storm approaches you, call upon the God who is the master of the universe to guide and protect you. Psalm 107:28–31 says,

> *Then they cry unto the Lord in their trouble, and He bringeth them out of their distresses. He maketh the storm a calm, so that the waves thereof are still. Then are they glad because they be quiet; so that he bringeth them unto their desired haven. Oh that men would praise the Lord for His goodness, and for His wonderful works for the children of men.*

There is nothing to fear in the midst of the storm when you walk with God in your heart. The peace and calm you receive are when fears flee, and His Love flows through you. The eye in the middle of a hurricane is symbolic of how we should remain calm as the fury of the storm swirls around us.

Going back to preparation, when we immerse our lives in the word of God and build our faith daily, we are prepared for all the storms life brings our way. We are then confident that God is with us in everything we face. As we grow ever closer to God, we lose the fear of the uncertainty of outcomes that lie ahead and know that we will be protected and guided by God to our destiny with Him.

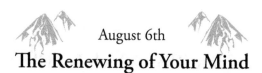

The Renewing of Your Mind

As believers in our Lord Jesus Christ and as we become His followers, we are taught in the scriptures to transform our thoughts and renew our minds. We are not simply viewing our lives as the world does. We think more about that which is eternal and not as much about that which is temporary. Colossians 3:2 says, *"Set your affection on things above, not on things on the earth."* We certainly have earthly things to deal with in our lives, and the things above are inherently more important, so we have to remain focused on the eternal aspects of our lives while living in the present.

There is a spiritual battle we face each day for control of our minds which tend to wander. Second Corinthians 10:3–5 talks about this:

> *For though we walk in the flesh, we do not war after the flesh. For the weapons of our warfare are not carnal, but mighty to God for the pulling down strongholds. Casting down imaginations, and every high thing that exalteth itself against the knowledge of God, and bringing into captivity every thought to the obedience of Christ.*

As we gain control of our minds and turn our thoughts to those which are consistent with God's Word, we become empowered to overcome the evil that tries to turn us away from the path God has for us.

Even as we live in this world, we are not conforming to the thoughts and patterns of the world around us. As our spiritual life grows stronger, we have the renewal of our minds to conform to the teachings of Christ and the power of the Holy Spirit, which guides us. Romans 12:2 tells us this: *"And be not conformed to this world; but be ye transformed by the renewing of your mind, that ye may prove what is good and acceptable, and perfect, will of God."* As we control our thoughts more effectively, we can more clearly discover in our hearts and souls God's perfect will for our lives. May God bless you today with a clear understanding of what His will is for you!

August 7th

Hate That Which Is Evil

The enemy of our souls tries to work his way into the hearts and minds of people by alluring them with temptations of the flesh each day. Whether these temptations are of a lustful nature or of coveting that which we don't have, it is trying to take our eyes from the path to righteousness. The devil will work in our minds to suggest it is okay to allow thoughts and actions to take place by convincing us they are not harmful and only a part of being human. The more we allow these to be present in our minds, the more of a stronghold the enemy creates in our lives. We must recognize this spirit as it comes to you and rebuke it for what it is.

The spirit of Love is what God calls for us to have in our hearts. He even tells us to Love our enemies. In Matthew 5:43–44, Jesus teaches us: *"Ye have heard that it hath been said, Thou shalt Love thy neighbor and hate thine enemy. But I say unto you, Love your enemies, bless them that curse you, do good to them that hate you, and pray for them that despitefully use you, and persecute you."* In this scripture, Christ is teaching us to Love the people who oppose us. He is not speaking to the enemy of our soul, which is evil. There exists good and evil in our world each day. Make no room for evil in your life. Romans 12:9 tells us, *"Let Love be without dissimulation. Abhor that which is evil; cleave to that which is good."* The spirit of evil is alive and trying to lure us from God each day. We can discern it when we seek God's will and allow His light to illuminate the path we are to travel.

Our lives are to be devoted to finding the path to righteousness that God has intended for us as His people. As we do so, we are anointed with the oil of joy. Hate that which is evil and Love that which is good. As you do so, may God fill you with the Spirit of joy on this day!

August 8th

His Blood Was Shed for the Sins of the World

The sacrifice of Jesus Christ on the cross was made for redemption of the sins of the world. God paid the ultimate price by sending His only Son, who was without sin, to die for the sins of mankind on the cross. As a result, we can now be reconciled with our Father in heaven if we believe in Him. It is a simple story for those who willingly accept it with childlike faith. This faith is the cornerstone of salvation to those who believe. First John 1:7 tells us, *"But if we walk in the light, as He is in the light, we have fellowship with one another, and the blood of Jesus His Son cleanses us from all sin."* The price for our sin has been paid at Calvary. The blood of Jesus was given for the remission of our sins.

The sacrifice of a living creature was practiced throughout the history of man to God for the atonement of sins prior to Christ coming. In Leviticus 17:11 we are told: *"For the life of the flesh is in the blood, and I have given it to you upon the altar to make atonement for your souls, for it is the blood which makes atonement for the soul."* The old covenant with God was the sacrifice of animals for sins. Jesus spoke to His disciples at the last supper and shared with them His sacrifice as the new covenant for the remission of sins in Luke 22:20 which says, *"Likewise also the cup after supper, saying, This cup is the new testament in my blood, which is shed for you."* Christ knew His life was designed to be the ultimate sacrifice and He gave it willingly for our sins.

As a result of His sacrifice, we are now cleansed to serve the living God. Hebrews 9:14 teaches this: *"How much more shall the blood of Christ, who through the eternal Spirit offered Himself without spot to God, purge your conscience from dead works to serve the living God?"* We are free from the life of sin and death because of the blood of Jesus having been shed for our lives. May your heart embrace the joy of this victory over death and seek how to best serve God in your life this and every day.

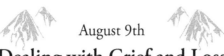

August 9th
Dealing with Grief and Loss

There are things that happen in this world that can only be described as evil and wrong. We cannot understand how they even happen other than knowing that evil exists, and we face it in the world around us. There was another sad story recently about a school shooting that happened in an elementary school in Texas. Many children and a couple of adults died during this tragic event. Our hearts mourn for the lives of those who were lost and for the families and friends of those who will never be the same because of their grief from this loss of Loved ones. It is incomprehensible to find an explanation for why these horrible acts continue to happen. We can only pray for the souls of those who are doing battle with the evil which turns them into such killers in our world.

We know this, we are only passing through this world, and our destiny goes beyond it. The Holy Spirit will bring comfort to those who seek Him in such times. Psalm 34:18 says, *"The Lord is nigh to them that are of a broken heart and saveth such as be of a contrite spirit."* The loss of life of a Loved one for any reason can crush your spirit and break your heart; when it happens because of pure evil stealing such a soul from our world, it is even more devastating. We comfort one another in such times with all the Love we have but need God's Love to wash our hearts and souls to bring peace in knowing these souls have gone to a place that has no more death or pain. When these events continue to happen, you must believe the end of this world as we know it is coming soon. The book of Revelation 21:4 tells us this: *"And God will wipe away all the tears from their eyes., and there shall be no more death, neither sorrow, nor crying, neither shall there be any more pain; for the former things are passed away."* A glorious day is coming when we see no more of the evil forces in our world and only that which is good through God our Father.

Pray for God's protection daily for you and your family always!

August 10th

Be Victorious Wearing the Armor of God

As we live our lives, we face many battles. The Spiritual battles are there daily with the enemy of our souls trying to steal our victory over sin and temptation. We have power through the Holy Spirit with which we can overcome the powers of darkness. First John 5:4 speaks to this: *"For whatsoever is born of God overcometh the world; and this is the victory that overcometh the world, even our faith."* As we walk with God, we do not face these battles alone. Rather, He is with us to fight for us against our enemies. Deuteronomy 20:4 tells us, *"For the Lord your God is He that goeth with you to fight for you against your enemies, to save you."*

We prepare our hearts and minds for the spiritual battles we face when we meet with God daily through the reading of His Word and our prayers in which we talk to God directly. God hears and answers our prayers. The scripture teaches us to go into our battles with the full armor of God as protection. Ephesians 6:11–16 describes this armor:

> Put on the whole armor of God, that ye may be able to stand against the wiles of the devil. For we wrestle not against flesh and blood, but against principalities, against powers, against the rulers of the darkness of this world, against spiritual wickedness in high places. Wherefore take unto you the whole armor of God, that ye may be able to withstand in the evil day, and having done all, to stand. Stand therefore having your loins girt with the truth and having on the breastplate of righteousness; And your feet shod with the preparation of the gospel of peace; Above all, taking the shield of faith, wherewith ye shall be able to quench all the fiery darts of the wicked.

As we go into battle empowered and protected by the full armor of God, victory is ours every time. Be victorious in your walk this day and every day, protected by the full armor of God!

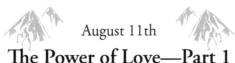

August 11th
The Power of Love—Part 1

Living a life filled with Love is the ultimate goal for our lives on this earth. There is power that comes to us from the Holy Spirit as we are engulfed in Love for our God and for others we meet on the path of our lives. The scriptures are clear that there is nothing more important than Love, nor is there anything more powerful than Love in our life's mission. First Corinthians 13 is the chapter in the Bible known as the Love chapter. We uncover a beautiful message from this book of the Bible on the Spirit of Love, or charity, as it is called in this book.

The message in verse 1 talks about various spiritual gifts people might possess when it says, *"Though I speak in the tongues of men and of angels, and have not charity, I am become as sounding brass or a tinkling cymbal."* The scriptures teach us that whatever message you are trying to deliver without Love in your heart is just noise. It carries no value. Verse 2 speaks of other gifts: *"And though I have the gift of prophesy, and understand all mysteries, and all knowledge, and though I have a faith so that can remove all mountains, and have not charity, I am nothing."* It is not a matter of how much you know or how insightful your mind becomes, nor is your faith alone sufficient to be of a great value to you or others without Love in your heart. The scripture teaches us that without Love, we are nothing in God's eyes. There are those who openly give of their time and their money to bestow gifts to the poor. Such benevolence is highly regarded. Verse 3 addresses this: *"And though I bestow all my goods to feed the poor, and though I give my body to be burned, and have not charity, it profiteth me nothing."* If all your charitable efforts are to simply gain you credit for your ego, it is of no value to God, who looks upon your heart.

We are measured by God in our lives by what we hold in our hearts and minds. Proverbs 21:2 tells us, *"Every way of man is right in his own eyes, but the Lord pondereth the hearts."* May Love guide your heart today in all that you do!

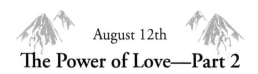

August 12th
The Power of Love—Part 2

The amazing power that Love brings to our lives is again described in 1 Corinthians as we read further. The virtues of Love are described in verses 4–5 in this book which allow us to distinguish Love from other emotions we may experience: *"Charity suffereth long, and is kind; charity envieth not; charity vaunteth not itself; is not puffed up; doth not behave unseemly, seeketh not her own, is not easily provoked, thinketh no evil."* As we see these virtues of Love, we see the way God intends for us to be. When we find ourselves in conflict with others, and those times will come to all of us, are we immersed in the spirit of Love, or is another spirit drawing us away from the Love God has intended for us to share with others in our lives? Patience, kindness, humility, and forgiveness are all characteristics of a life being lived which is filled with Love.

As we read further in the chapter, we see more of what is written to help us understand the power Love brings to the hearts of those who embrace it fully. Verses 6–7 speak to more of the characteristics of a person who allows Love to flow through their life when it says, *"Rejoiceth not in iniquity, but rejoiceth in truth; Beareth all things, hopeth all things, endureth all things."* When you Love someone, you will always be truthful to them and look out for them in all they face. You will trust in what they say and do and protect them from any harm or danger. You will lift them up when they need your support and want the best for them in all ways. To reject evil should always be in our hearts for all people.

When you experience the Spirit of Love in your heart for others, you gain a character that draws others to you. People will know they are able to trust you, and they can depend on you. As you Love God and you Love one another, your heart becomes pure in the sight of God. Matthew 5:8 says, *"Blessed are the pure in heart, for they shall see God."* May the Spirit of Love flow freely through your heart and soul on this and every day. May God bless you in all you do as it does!

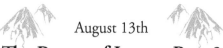

August 13th

The Power of Love—Part 3

The power of Love transforms our lives as we allow this Spirit to engulf us and fill our hearts and minds. As we read further in 1 Corinthians 13:8–10, the scriptures teach us that Love never fails, and it brings completeness to our life: *"Charity never faileth; but whether there be prophecies, they shall fail; whether there be tongues, they shall cease; whether there be knowledge, it shall vanish away; For we know in part, and we prophesy in part. But when that which is perfect is come, then that which is in part shall be done away."* With Love in our life, we find fulness of God's Spirit within us. It allows us to become one with the Father in our Spirit.

As you grow and mature in your body and your mind, you also grow and develop in your understanding of God's will and purpose for your life. As Love fills our hearts and minds, our wisdom and understanding of how God wants us to see the world changes.! Corinthians 13:11–12 speaks to this maturing perspective: *"When I was a child, I spake as a child, I understood as a child, I thought as a child. But when I became a man, I put away childish things. For now, we see through a glass darkly, but then face to face; now I know in part; but then shall I know even as also I am known."* God continues to open our eyes to His magnificent plan as we walk with Him in Love each day. We are learning more about His will, His purpose, and the kingdom of God as we deepen our Love.

There is no Spirit or power on earth greater than Love. It changes lives into that which we are all called to be. As 1 Corinthians 13 concludes with verse 13, we are taught this: *"And now abideth faith, hope, charity, these three; but the greatest of these is charity."* Of all the gifts God has bestowed upon mankind, the greatest of all is Love. We can each embrace and nurture this in our hearts, minds, and souls each day and grow closer to the God we serve as we do so. Be Blessed as your Love grows on this and every day!

August 14th
Loving Your Enemies

The is an ongoing battle for your mind and soul by the evil one who is our enemy. The devil is trying to get us off the path of righteousness by tempting us with thoughts that take us from Love into those of hate and prejudice toward others. This battle is an attempt to steal your soul and one which we must win each day. The path to righteousness is found when we Love all of those who God puts on our path. We are taught to Love our enemies in life by Jesus.

In Matthew 5:43–45, Jesus spoke these words:

> You have heard that it hath been said, "Love thy neighbor and hate thine enemy." But I say unto you, Love your enemies, bless them that curse you, do good to them that hate you, and pray for them who despitefully use you, and persecute you, that ye may be the children of your Father which is in heaven. For He maketh His sun to rise on the evil and the good, and sendeth rain on the just and the unjust.

Our minds and hearts resist the idea of Loving those who are enemies and lifting them up in prayer as Jesus directs us to do so. This is where the world is different from the children of God. Jesus is teaching us how to transcend the world in our hearts and souls. Using human logic, we will find this to be difficult to understand. When we do this, we eliminate thoughts of prejudice and replace those with Love.

We read on in Matthew 5:46–48 as Jesus challenges us to rise above the practice of others to embrace the Spirit God intends:

> For if you Love them which Love you, what reward have ye? Do not even the publicans the same? And if ye salute your brethren only, what do ye more than others? Do not even the publicans so? Be ye therefore perfect, even as your Father which is in heaven is perfect.

This call to Spiritual perfection through Love is one that will transform our lives into the lives in which we walk with God. Love is the light of the world. When we Love others, we become the light of the world. May your light shine brightly today and always as you Love all of those who are on your path.

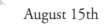

August 15th

Be Free from Racism and Discrimination

The enemy of our souls will plant thoughts in our minds to justify feelings of prejudice and discrimination to entice us away from the spirit of Love for one another. The negative thoughts that stereotype groups of people with certain characteristics which are perpetuated by our society lead us to feelings that are not of God. We are taught in the scriptures to embrace those who are different with Love and to lift those up with prayer. James 2:4 cautions us with this: *"Are ye not then partial in yourselves, and become judges of evil thoughts?"* When we start passing judgment on others because of the color of their skin or their ethnic heritage, we are allowing evil thoughts to enter our hearts and minds. John 7:24 says it this way: *"Judge not according to the appearance but judge righteous judgement."* We may be forming our opinions on how one dresses or how his or her physical stature may be.

We look at people and form opinions quickly as we measure them with our eyes. Peter gave a message about treating all people from all nations without favoritism in Acts 10:34–36 which says, *"Then Peter opened his mouth and said, Of a truth, I perceive that God is no respecter of persons: But in every nation he that feareth Him, and worketh righteousness, is accepted with Him. The word which God sent unto the children of Israel, preaching peace by Jesus Christ; He is Lord of all."* With our lives, we should minister His message unto all people.

The Holy Spirit is sent from God to guide us in bringing Love to the world in which we live. When we are directed to others who come from a different culture, we are the light of the world when Love flows through us. James 2:8–9 says this: *"If ye fulfill the royal law according to the scripture, 'Thou shalt Love thy neighbor as thyself,' ye do well: But if ye have respect to persons, ye commit sin, and are convinced of the law as transgressors."* May God free our hearts and minds from racism and discrimination always and let us Love one another freely.

August 16th

Be Fully Committed to the Lord

God will give each of us work to do, which may change from time to time as we complete our journey in this world. In all that we do, our goal is to be fully committed to giving to others in service to the God we serve. As we seek to understand the will of our Father for our lives, we must ask for His guidance each day to direct us to deliver that service to those who He puts on our path. If we are to live a life of fulfillment, we are to give all we have to His calling for us. First Kings 8:61 tells us, *"Let your heart therefore be perfect with the Lord our God, to walk in His statutes, and to keep His commandments."* His commandments are centered on Loving Him and turning our Love to others we meet each day. When we do, we become the light of the world and send His message to others.

We are to Love the Lord our God with all our strength. Deuteronomy 6:5 says this plainly: *"And thou shalt Love the Lord thy God with all thine heart, and with all thy soul, and with all thy might."* It is the foundation of your relationship with God, which allows you then to Love others as you Love yourself. Our work in this world is to be fishers of men. In Matthew 4:19, Jesus tells us, *"And He saith unto them, 'Follow me and I will make you fishers of men.'"* As we are being directed, we have a mission to bring others to Jesus who come into our world. This calling is the significant ministry of all believers. To share our faith with others is God's will for our lives.

The work we have remaining lies ahead, and God will direct our paths. Proverbs 16:3 says, *"Commit thy works unto the Lord, and thy thoughts will be established."* In all walks of life, God is using us to do that which is good. He is opening doors for us to become the light of the world. Be fully committed to the Lord, and He will use you to reach others for Him. Be Blessed today as you do the work He has called you to do!

August 17th

Be Free from the Shackles That Bind You

One of the great stories in the Bible was told in the book of Acts, chapter 16, which tells us about a time Paul and Silas were in prison for casting out a spirit from a girl who was a fortune teller. The owners of this girl made much money from her fortune-telling and were not happy with Paul and Silas and had them put in prison. They were put in shackles in this prison, surrounded by other men who were also bound. Instead of commiserating about their misfortune, Paul and Silas were praying and singing hymns to God. Verses 25–26 tell us what happened next:

> *At midnight, Paul and Silas prayed, and sang praises unto God: and the prisoners heard them. And suddenly there was a great earthquake, so that the foundations of the prison were shaken: and immediately the doors were opened, and everyone's bands were loosed.*

We can only imagine the energy and spirit of those prisoners in the room at that time. The jailer was the one who was fearful and was responsible for these men. Verses 27–31 tell us what happens next:

> *And the keeper of the prison awaking out of his sleep, and seeing the prison doors open, he drew out his sword, and would have killed himself, supposing the prisoners had fled. But Paul cried out with a loud voice saying, Do thyself no harm, for we are all here. Then he called for a light and sprang in, and came trembling, and fell down before Paul and Silas; And brought them out, and said, Sirs, what must I do to be saved? And they said, believe in the Lord Jesus Christ and thou shalt be saved, and thy house.*

As the story unfolds, this jailer then took them to his home, and he and all his family were saved as they believed in Jesus Christ that night.

Instead of complaining about their imprisonment, they were praising and worshiping God with prayers and singing. God delivered them with a powerful earthquake to enable them to serve as ministers to this family, and His will was done as they were all saved. As you praise God, your shackles are removed!

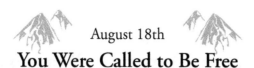

August 18th
You Were Called to Be Free

We live in a country where great freedoms are given to us. The price of freedom has been paid by the lives of many men and women who paid the ultimate price in fighting for those rights. In a spiritual sense, the ultimate price for our freedom was paid by Jesus Christ on the cross as He gave His life as a remission for the sins of the world. God's plan for us is to be free from the bondage of sin. Galatians 5:13–14 speaks to this freedom and the responsibility that goes with it. It teaches us not to use our freedom to pursue fleshly desires, but to humbly serve one another in the Spirit of Love." The freedom we have in the spirit gives us the power to choose how we live our lives. To serve one another humbly in Love is to live our lives consistent with the purpose God has for us.

As followers of Christ, we have freedom over sin and darkness. We have the right to do anything the spirit leads us to do. First Corinthians 6:12 cautions that not everything we might choose to do is beneficial: *"All things are lawful unto me, but all things are not expedient: all things are lawful for me, but I will not be brought under the power of any."* We live in a world in which our minds and spirits can be enticed to be mastered by things that pull us away from the God we are here to serve. Be wise in the use of your time and energy that it is devoted to Love and service to others each day. As you do so, you are following the plan and purpose God has for you.

As God's children, we are brought into a state of freedom. Romans 8:21 tells us, *"Because the creature itself also shall be delivered from the bondage of corruption into the glorious liberty of the children of God."* Be free from sin and filled with the glory of God who gives us liberty to choose that which good. Sin brings darkness to our hearts and lives, and God gives us the light to illuminate our path. Go follow His path, and you will be the light of the world around you.

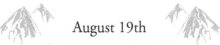

August 19th
Fear, Worry, and Anxiety Are Weapons of Satan

There are times in our lives when we are concerned about the future, and our hearts become filled with anxiety and uncertainty. The fears which are produced are not coming from our God, who walks with us and has His hand on our lives. God wants us to trust in Him always and know He will deliver us to the place He has for us. Philippians 4:6 tells us, *"Be careful for nothing, but in everything by prayer and supplication, with thanksgiving let your requests be made known to God."* As we walk in faith, we must learn to fully trust God in all things. He will be with us as we do.

When fear invades our hearts, it tends to be overwhelming, and it drives out the spirit of Love and peace, which resides there when our minds and hearts are tuned to God. When our minds and hearts embrace the Love of God fully, fear is pushed out of our lives. First John 4:18 makes it clear when it says, *"There is no fear in Love. But perfect Love casteth out fear because fear hath torment. He that feareth is not made perfect in Love."* When we experience fear, we are thinking we must face whatever is before us alone. When we know that God is with us, we have no reason to fear. Isaiah 35:4 assures us of God's protection: *"Say to them that are of a fearful heart, Be strong, fear not: behold, your God will come with vengeance, even God with a recompence; He will come and save you."* When God is with us, who can be against us? There is nothing to fear.

The Lord will deliver you from all your fears when you seek Him. Psalm 34:4 tells us this: *"I sought the Lord and He heard me, and delivered me from all my fears."* God is with us, and He will protect us. When we abide in His Love and seek His protection with our prayers, He will comfort us and take away the fears, worries, and anxieties which try to rule our hearts. May your heart be free from those negative feelings on this and every day. Be Blessed as God walks with you!

Blessed Is the One Who Trusts in God

The more we learn to trust in God, the more our lives become blessed by Him. God is patiently waiting for us to turn to Him with our prayers in seeking His will for our lives. As we do so, He will open our eyes to His will and give us His direction for us to take in our lives. Jeremiah 17:7–8 teaches us: *"Blessed is the man that trusteth in the Lord, and whose hope the Lord is. For he shall be a tree planted by the waters, and that spreadeth out her roots by the river, and shall not see when heat cometh, but her leaf shall be green, and shall not be careful in the year of the drought, neither shall cease from yielding fruit."* When you trust in the Lord, His springs of living water fill your life with joy and prosperity.

The human mind and heart are always trying to figure out what our next step must be. It leaves us with an uncertainty of what the best path is for our future. Proverbs 3:5–6 tells us to seek God's direction rather than our own: *"Trust in the Lord with all thine heart and lean not unto thine own understanding. In all thy ways acknowledge Him, and He shall direct thy paths."* What this simply means is to seek His will and His wisdom in all we do through prayer, and God will answer us and direct us to his path for our lives. David continually sought God in his life and put his trust in God to lead him. He expresses this faith again in Psalm 143:8 when he says, *"Cause me to hear thy lovingkindness in the morning; for in thee do I trust: cause me to know the way wherein I should walk; for I lift up my soul unto thee."* As we entrust our lives to God, He will direct our paths to righteousness.

God is our refuge in all times of trouble. He is the one who will shelter us from any evil. Psalm 62:7–8 tells us, *"In God is my salvation and my glory: the rock of my strength, and my refuge is in God. Trust in Him at all times; ye people, pour out your heart before Him; God is a refuge for us."* May our trust in God continue to grow in our hearts, and we will be blessed as it does.

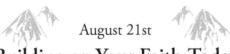

August 21st
Building on Your Faith Today

As we walk with God, we will be tested in our faith by those who do not believe in Him. Others may ridicule you for expressing your faith in Jesus Christ, who died for our sins. It is the way of the world to justify their unbelief by trying to destroy the faith of those who are on the path to salvation. We are called upon to Love those who come against us in the spiritual world and to show compassion and mercy to those who lack the faith which God gave to us through His grace.

The scriptures speak to this in Jude 18–22, which teaches us:

Hold that they told you there shall be mockers in the last time, who should walk after their own ungodly lusts. These be they that separate themselves, sensual, having not the Spirit. But ye, beloved, building up yourselves on your most holy faith, praying in the Holy Ghost; Keep yourselves in the Love of God looking for the mercy of our Lord Jesus Christ unto eternal life. And of some have compassion, making a difference.

As your faith continues to grow, you are given the strength to overcome these doubters who try to pull you away from that which God gives you through His Holy Spirit. God is always faithful to us. Hebrews 10:23 tells us not to waiver in our faith: *"Let us hold fast to the profession of our faith without wavering, for He who promised is faithful."*

Even His disciples lacked faith at times when the storms of life surrounded them. Jesus would speak the word, and the storms were made calm. Luke 8:25 tells us of a time when Jesus challenged them for their lack of faith when it says, *"And He said unto them, 'Where is your faith?' And they being afraid, wondered, saying to one another, What manner of man is this! For He commandeth even the winds and the water, and they obey Him."* Our faith is sufficient to overcome the storms and trials of life we face each day, knowing that God walks with us. Be bold in your faith and trust in our God, who is faithful to us as His children. May our faith grow today as we trust in Him fully! Be Blessed as you do!

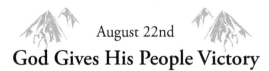

August 22nd

God Gives His People Victory

We will face many battles in life which take shape in many different forms. The struggles we face are emotional, physical, financial, and take place in all phases of our lives. The great confidence we have as we face these battles is that we do not fight alone as we go through them. We give credit to our God, who walks with us and who fights our battles for us. We simply cannot do it alone, and thanks be to God, who never fails in delivering us to victory over all our foes. Be humble as you give him thanks for His support in your life's toughest moments. Psalm 149:4 tells us, *"For the Lord taketh pleasure in His people, He will beautify the meek with salvation."*

If you are born again in the Spirit, God empowers you to overcome the forces you will face in this world. There is simply nothing that can defeat you as you put your trust in God our Father. First Corinthians 15:57 says, *"But thanks be to God! Which giveth us victory through our Lord Jesus Christ!"* The ultimate battles we face are the ones that lead to victory through Jesus Christ, who died for our sins and gave us eternal life. First John 5:4 says it this way: *"For whatsoever is born of God overcometh the world: and this is the victory that overcometh the world, even our faith."* If your faith in God and our Lord Jesus Christ remains strong, you will win all the battles you face in life as God walks with you.

The final battle which causes fear in those who are without faith is that of facing death as an unbeliever. For those of us who have held on to our faith, we have victory over death. First Corinthians 15:54–55 proclaims:

> So when this corruptible shall have put on incorruption, and this mortal shall have put on immortality, then shall it be brought to pass the saying that is written, 'Death is swallowed up in victory. O Death, where is thy sting? O grave, where is thy victory?

When you walk without fear of death, you live a life of victory each day! Live such a life today and every day, knowing God goes with you beyond the grave.

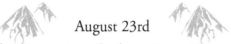

August 23rd
Walk Victoriously but Stay Humble

As God gives us the victory in life as we walk with Him, stay humble, knowing it is His victory we seek and not that of our own. We live to serve our Father in heaven, and He is the one who will deliver us as we overcome the forces we face in this world. As we remain humble, our spirit embraces gentleness, meekness, and kindness toward others. James 4:6 says, *"But He giveth more grace. Wherefore He saith, 'God resisteth the proud but giveth grace unto the humble."* God will favor us and elevate us when we are humble in our approach to others. When we try to take credit for all we accomplish, we are not pleasing to God, and He will oppose us as we do. Seek to be in His favor with a humble approach to all that goes well in your life.

Solomon was heralded as the wisest man on earth during his reign as King of Israel, and when he wrote the book of Proverbs, he put forth many teachings on how to best serve God with wisdom and humility in our hearts. Proverbs 11:2 shares this insight: *"When pride cometh, then cometh shame, but with the lowly is wisdom."* The only thing pride accomplishes is separation from the God who gives us our ability and strength to overcome that which we face each day. Proverbs 22:4 speaks to the fear of the Lord coming from our humble approach to Him: *"By humility and the fear of the Lord, are riches and honor and life."* God blesses those who honor and approach Him with a humble heart. Again, Solomon speaks of honor coming from humility in Proverbs 18:12, which says, *"Before destruction the heart of a man is haughty, and before honor is humility."*

God is with us. He walks with us each day and gives us victory in life. James 4:15–16 teaches us this: *"For that ye ought to say, 'If the Lord will, we shall live, and do this or that. But now ye rejoice in your own boastings; all such rejoicing is evil."* Let us not boast but walk in victory humbly with the God we serve and give him the glory for all the good things which come to us in our lives.

August 24th
Anger Is an Enemy of Righteousness

It is easy to unleash a spirit of anger in our hearts and minds when we feel we have been wronged by another. Our nature is to respond harshly and quickly to answer that person in a way that conflicts with the spirit of Love. That human emotion is one that resides inside of each of us and has a way to come forward quickly as our egos tell us we are right and they are the ones who are wrong. The scriptures often warn us to bring this beast under control. James 1:20 tells us, *"For the wrath of man worketh not the righteousness of God."* Knowing this to be true, how can we keep this side of our nature in check?

Is all anger wrong? When someone sins against another or causes harm to an innocent, I believe God intends us to be angry about the sin which takes place. To hate evil is consistent with God's Word. Our anger is against the evil and the sin, but our Love is to be alive in our hearts for the sinner who has sinned. Without God in our hearts, this is impossible for us to deliver on our own. We are guided by the scriptures to turn away from anger. Psalm 37:8–9 teaches us: *"Cease from anger, and forsake wrath; fret not thyself, in any wise to do evil. For evildoers shall be cut off; but those who wait on the Lord, they shall inherit the earth."* God doesn't want us to walk around with anger or evil in our hearts. We are taught to Love all people, even our enemies. Ecclesiastes 7:9 says, *"Be not hasty in thy spirit to be angry; for anger resteth in the bosom of fools."*

There are people in our lives who embrace anger as justification about being right in their own minds. We are taught to avoid being around these people in Proverbs 22:24, which says, *"Make no friendship with an angry man; and with a furious man thou shalt not go."* Those people will only seek your support for their position in their conflicts. Be slow to anger and find peace today. Being angry takes you away from righteousness and the presence of God. We are striving to move closer to God each day, and anger stops that from happening.

August 25th
Turn Your Eyes from Darkness to Light

It has been said that the eyes are the windows of the soul. When you look into someone's eyes, you can see the light that shines from within or the darkness which clouds their heart and soul. Joy and happiness are evident when you see the eyes of a Christ follower. The evidence seen coming from one's eyes reflects what thoughts they allow to dwell in their heart and soul. We need to be on guard as to what we turn our attention to in our lives and what we allow to enter our minds through our eyes. Matthew 6:22–23 tells us, *"The light of the body is the eye; if therefore, the eye be single, thy whole body shall be full of light. But is thine eye be evil; thy whole body shall be full of darkness. If therefore the light that is in thee be darkness, how great is that darkness!"* If our eyes are healthy, we are looking at that which brings us truth and steers us closer to God.

The things of this world entice us through our eyes to sin and separation from God. First John 2:16 cautions us: *"For all that is in the world, the lust of the flesh, and the lust of the eyes, and the pride of life, is not of the Father, but is of the world."* The more we gaze upon those things, the less we are dwelling in the Spirit of Love which is sent to comfort and guide us. It is within our power to turn our eyes from this darkness and into the light if we so choose. Acts 26:17–18 tells us,

> *Delivering thee from the people, and from the Gentiles, unto whom now I send thee. To open their eyes, and turn them from darkness to light, and from the power of Satan unto God, that they may receive forgiveness of sins, and inheritance among them which are sanctified by faith that is in me.*

Our eyes guide us to the path that we choose to be on in our lives. May we seek each day for our lives to be enlightened by the vision we see through the eyes which God has opened for us. Ephesians 1:18 says, *"The eyes of your understanding being enlightened; that ye may know what is the hope of His calling, and what the riches of the glory of His inheritance in the saints."*

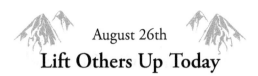

August 26th
Lift Others Up Today

As we journey through the time God has given us on this earth, we are here to serve a purpose and do the work God has given us to do. The life we lead is to be one in which we serve one another with the gifts God has given us. One of the greatest gifts we can offer to another is that of encouraging them in the Lord. Hebrews 3:13 gives us this: *"But exhort one another daily, while it is call today; lest any of you be hardened through the deceitfulness of sin."* As a body of believers, God ministers to each of us though the hearts and lives of those who He puts on our paths. We need their encouragement as much as they need it from us.

We bring honor to those who we share our lives with as we lift them up. God intends for that to be our approach as we provide support to others daily. Philippians 2:3–5 tells us, *"Let nothing be done through strife or vainglory; but in lowliness of mind let each esteem other better than themselves. Look not every man on his own things, but every man also on the things of others. Let this mind be in you, which was also in Christ Jesus."* Jesus Christ washed the feet of His disciples and spoke of the servant being the greatest of all. As we serve others, we are doing the work of the Lord in our lives. Romans 12:10 guides us with this message: *"Be kindly affectioned one to another with brotherly Love in honor preferring one another."* God is Love, and the more devoted we become in Loving one another, the closer to God we grow in our lives.

Our responsibility Is to help one another in dealing with the power of sin. Galatians 6:1–2 teaches us this: *"Brethren, if a man be overtaken in a fault, ye which are spiritual, restore such an one in the spirit of meekness, considering thyself, lest thou also be tempted. Bear ye one another's burdens, and so fulfill the law of Christ."* Lift each other in Love up today and always.

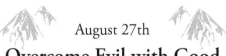

August 27th
Overcome Evil with Good

In all our lives, there are moments when darkness enters our hearts and minds. It can enter through a word spoken in anger as our ego responds to a thought or word from another which is not kind or appropriate. In some of those moments, we become retaliatory with harsh words of our own, resulting in division and hurt feelings of those we Love. Disparaging comments fuel the fires of division and cause increasing darkness to gain control of our hearts as we escalate such moments with evil and negative thoughts. First Peter 3:9 tells us to avoid these conflicts by repaying evil with blessings: *"Not rendering evil for evil, or railing for railing: but contrariwise blessing; knowing that ye are thereunto called, that ye should inherit a blessing."* How quickly we can turn a hostile and negative moment into a positive one if we approach our lives this way.

When these dark moments come into our hearts, it is the spirit of evil trying to take hold of us. We justify our feelings by our mind insisting we are in the right and the other with whom we are in conflict is in the wrong. This darkness can absorb you and blind you to the light of that which is good. Romans 12:21 tells us, *"Do not be overcome of evil but overcome evil with good."* Turning your heart to Love and expressing your Love for one another leads to goodness returning to the spirit at that moment. Words that we say bring hurt and pain to others. James 3:6 teach us: *"And the tongue is a fire, a world of iniquity; so is the tongue among our members, that it defileth the whole body, and setteth on fire the course of nature, and it is set on fire of hell."* We sometimes blurt out things that should never be said. Seek forgiveness quickly when you have done so.

The energy that comes from conflict with another is often coming from an evil source. We must turn away from the evil, turning our thoughts and words to good. Psalm 34:14 says, *"Depart from evil and do good; seek peace and pursue it."* As you do so, these conflicts are resolved, and peace is restored in your heart.

August 28th
Forgiveness Frees Your Spirit

As we harbor thoughts in our minds and hearts about another who has done something wrong to us, we become slaves to those negative energies that it creates inside us. The spirit of Love brings light into our hearts and souls, but darkness can enter when we feel these negative feelings for another person. God has forgiven us for the sins we have done in our lives when we ask Him for this forgiveness. Accordingly, we should be faithful to forgive others who have sinned against us. Colossians 3:13 tells us, *"Forbearing one another, and forgiving one another, if any man have a quarrel against any; even as Christ forgave you, so do ye."* When you allow yourself to forgive another person, you are freeing up your mind and heart to fill it with Love as God has intended for you.

Our hearts and minds want to pass judgment on others for their transgressions against us or their failures in the way they speak or act around us. While these thoughts are manifest inside us, we are un-willing to embrace that which is excellent, which comes from Loving them despite faults that we may see. We are not here to be their judges. Luke 6:37 says, *"Judge not and ye shall not be judged: condemn not, and ye shall not be condemned; forgive, and ye shall be forgiven."* When we allow ourselves to forgive, we can pass from darkness back into light inside our hearts and souls. Matthew 6:14–15 says it this way: *"For if ye forgive men their trespasses, your heavenly Father will also forgive you. But if ye forgive not men their trespasses, neither will your heavenly Father forgive your trespasses."* This is not an option but a directive to us.

When we foster Love, we look past some of the shortcomings of others. Mark 11:25 tells us, *"And when ye stand praying, forgive, if ye have ought against any: that your Father also which is in heaven may forgive you your trespasses."* The scriptures consistently tell us to forgive others so our sins may be forgiven. Forgiveness cleanses us and enables us to be free of our own sins.

August 29th
The Healing Power of God

As we journey through the days of our lives, we face many times when we are suffering physically, emotionally, or spiritually from damage that is done to us. That time of recovery is a time of healing when and if we turn to God for His healing power. Whatever aspect of our being is in distress, God has the healing power to help us through it and to heal the distressed part of our lives. In Jeremiah 17:14, the prophet prayed to God: *"Heal me, O Lord, and I shall be healed; save me and I shall be saved; for you are the one I praise."* Through God, all things are possible, and without Him, we are alone and incapable of delivering the healing we need.

When we are suffering emotionally from relationships that are not healthy or from disappointments or struggles we face in our life, God will restore us to peace and happiness when we turn to Him. Read His Words and meditate on them in times of trouble. They will bring you comfort and peace. Proverbs 4:20–22 tells us this: *"My son, attend to my words, incline thy ear to my sayings. Let them not depart from thine eyes; keep them in the midst of thine heart. For they are life unto those that find them, and health to all their flesh."* The word of God breathes life into our whole body. Keep it in your heart to draw from in times where you face troubles in your life. It will bring you healing. Isaiah 33:2 says, *"O Lord, be gracious unto us, we have waited for thee; be thou, their arm every morning, our salvation also in the time of trouble."* This is a great prayer.

God is there for us in times of trouble. Psalm 147:3 says, *"He healeth the brokenhearted and bindeth up their wounds."* In all we face, He is there to deliver us. Praise the Lord for His healing power and for being with us through all times of troubles we may face in our lives. Be Blessed as you walk with God on this day.

August 30th

Pray for Our Country and Our Leaders

The world is filled with darkness, and the battle between the forces of good and evil is going on every day. Our country has problems that result from choosing to follow a direction that takes us as a people further from God. The path we are on is a dangerous one. The scriptures speak of the people of God uniting in prayer and humility, and if we call upon His name, He will heal our land. 2 Chronicles 7:14 says it this way: *"If my people, which are called by my name, shall humble themselves and pray and seek my face and turn from their wicked ways, then I will hear from heaven, and I will forgive their sin and will heal their land."* This country was founded on faith, and we were a people who revered God, but we are now growing farther from Him as we seek our own means.

The key to a people united in a purpose is often the result of inspirational leadership to unite the people to rally to a common cause. May God raise such leaders in our land to bring us toward His purpose in this time. May we collectively pray for those who are now in authority in our land. We must get past the political party of those who lead us and pray for the spirits of our leaders to align with that which is of God. As God's people, we are more than just Democrats or Republicans or even Americans; we are God's people of the earth. Romans 13:1 says, *"Let every soul be subject to the higher powers. For there is no power but of God; the powers that be are ordained of God."* Knowing this, pray for those who are in such roles to listen to the God we serve and to seek His way for our people.

Our nation has been a light to the world and a beacon of that which is right. It can be again if we turn back to following God. Nations will fall when they fail to do so. Job 12:23 says this: *"He increaseth the nations, and destroyeth them: He enlargeth the nations, and straighteneth them again."* May the people of God unite in prayer for our nation and our leaders this day for God's will to be done.

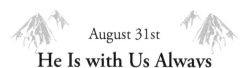

August 31st

He Is with Us Always

There are times in our lives when we feel alone in our struggles. It is at these times when we need those around us to lift us up with words of encouragement and prayerful support. The tendency of many of us is to withdraw and not let others know when we are hurting or feeling inadequate. Our human nature and our ego tell us to work through these times alone, even when we are surrounded by those who truly Love us. This time of isolation can lead to depression and feelings of anxiety which can only worsen such a situation. These are the times when it is especially important to turn to God for refuge.

God is walking with us even when we are feeling alone. In Matthew 28:20, Jesus assures of this: *"I am with you always, even unto the end of the world."* Jesus walks within us by virtue of His Holy Spirit, which was sent to us as a comforter and a counselor. He is our guide and our source of well-being when we open our hearts to Him. Psalm 46:1 speaks to this presence of God when we face difficult times: *"God is our refuge and strength, a very present help in trouble."* We are not only to turn our attention to God in times of trouble but to walk in the light of His Love every day. He is the rock of our salvation and the source of our strength each day. Psalm 18:2 tells us, *"The Lord is my rock, my fortress, and my deliverer; my God, my strength, in whom I will trust; my buckler, the horn of my salvation, and my high tower."* We have no reason to feel like we are alone. We only need to open our hearts to the God of our salvation.

When we feel the separation from God which leads to solitude and sadness, we can replace that with a spirit that comes from God, which will fill our hearts with joy. Romans 15:13 speaks of this: *"Now the God of hope fill you with all joy and peace in believing, that ye may abound in hope, through the power of the Holy Ghost."* The key to this transformation into hope, peace, and joy is to trust in God fully, and His Spirit will fill us with joy as promised.

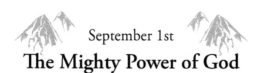

September 1st
The Mighty Power of God

We walk every day in a magnificent world and universe created by the mighty and powerful God who we serve. The majesty of His creation is evidenced in every flower and sunset we behold. We look upon the world and see His creation as it unfolds before our eyes, and we marvel as its witness. The miracles which flowed through Jesus Christ as He ministered on earth were further evidence of God's amazing power. From water turning into wine, the healing of the many sick people who Christ touched to the raising of the dead, and Jesus's resurrection and subsequent ascension into heaven are all recorded in the scriptures with multiple witnesses who became devout followers to their deaths on this earth. A small group of disciples changed the world forever as they bear witness to the wonderful story of Jesus Christ to others who became His church.

While the mighty power of God is without limits, He still cares for each of us on a personal level. It is through His amazing power; we can do all things as He strengthens us. 2 Peter 1:3 tells us, *"His divine power hath given us all things that pertain unto life and godliness, through the knowledge of Him that hath called us to glory and virtue."* God has given us the power to live the life He has chosen for us. Second Timothy 1:7 teaches us this: *"For God hath not given us the Spirit of fear; but of power, and of Love, and of a sound mind."* The power of God flowing through us in His Holy Spirit gives us the Love and self–discipline to lead the life which is pleasing to God. Opening our hearts to the guidance of the Holy Spirit takes us to where God intends us to go in our lives.

Ephesians 3:17–19 speaks of this power in us: *"That Christ may dwell in your hearts by faith; that ye being rooted and grounded in Love, may be able to comprehend with all the saints, what is the breadth and length and depth and height; and to know the Love of Christ, which passeth knowledge, that ye may be filled with all the fulness of God."* May the power of God fill your heart today!

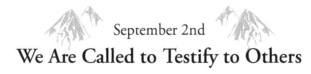

September 2nd

We Are Called to Testify to Others

God has called each of us as believers to share our testimony of how Jesus Christ and His Holy Spirit are at work in each of our lives. The purpose of such a testimony is to enable others to embrace this spirit as the path to their own eternal salvation. Our life and the way we lead it is evidence of the change which occurs when you believe in Jesus and walk on the path of righteousness. If the words you speak are not consistent with the life you lead, your testimony will mean nothing in the hearts of those you try to reach. God is Love, and that Spirit of Love must flow through you for His message to be genuine as seen by others. Luke 21:13 directs us to do this: *"And it shall turn to you for a testimony."* We are the messengers of God's Love to the world around us each day.

The testimony of Jesus Christ is the message we are to carry to the world. It is a simple message as directed in 1 John 5:11, which says, *"And this is the record, that God hath given to us eternal life, and this life is in His Son."* Our faith is built on a simple truth, and this truth sets us free and apart from the world. This truth, when shared, becomes a seed planted in the hearts of others. The seed will grow as they seek to embrace the gift of eternal life and witness the change in their own lives. As you discover the truth of God's Love and it resides in your heart, you will want to share it with those who God directs to your path. John 19:35 tells it this way: *"And he that saw it bare record, and his record is true; and knoweth that he saith true, that ye might believe."* If we truly Love others and have God's gift of eternal life, we want all we meet to enjoy this gift as well.

We walk boldly in the truth and without any shame that we believe in the Lord Jesus Christ. Second Timothy 1:8 says, *"Be not therefore ashamed of the testimony of our Lord, nor of me His prisoner; but be thou a partaker of the afflictions of the gospel according to the power of God."* Tell others about Him!

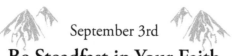

September 3rd

Be Steadfast in Your Faith

The enemy of our soul is always trying to question our faith and plant seeds of doubt in our minds. It is his purpose to separate us from God in every way he can. He is the master of deceit and the enemy of truth. John 8:42–45 says this about Satan as the master of lies as Jesus was talking to the Pharisees who challenged Him:

> *If God were your Father, ye would Love me, for I proceeded forth and came from God, neither came I of myself, but He sent me. Why do ye not understand my speech? Even because you cannot hear my word. Ye are of your father, the devil, and the lusts of your father ye will do. He was a murderer from the beginning, and abode not in the truth, for there is no truth in him. When he speaketh a lie, he speaketh of his own, for he is a liar and the father of it. And because I tell the truth ye do not believe me.*

We are promised to have peace in our hearts and minds as we remain steadfast in our faith in Isaiah 26:3: *"Thou will keep him in perfect peace, whose mind is stayed on thee; because he trusteth in thee."* We will be measured, and there will be trials we face along the way, but the scripture says we will be blessed when we remain faithful in those times in James 1:12, which says, *"Blessed is the man who endureth temptation; for when he is tried, he shall receive the crown of life, which the Lord hath promised to them that Love him."* God empowers us to overcome the world, and we are strengthened as we do so.

Our faith is not without work that we are called to do. As we remain steadfast in our faith, we engage effectively in the work He has called us to do. First Corinthians 15:58 says, *"Therefore, my beloved brethren, be ye steadfast, unmovable, always abounding in the work of the Lord, forasmuch as ye know that your labor is not in vain in the Lord."* As we do the work of the Lord, He blesses that work and blesses us for doing it. Be steadfast in your faith today and give yourself fully to the work of the Lord, and be blessed as you do so!

September 4th
Conquering Your Enemies

There are people who oppose us in life, and they come up against us in things we attempt to do and accomplish. They may simply be talking about us in a negative way to others in an attempt to diminish us and our reputations. How are we to deal with these people, and are they truly our "enemies?" Jesus teaches us to Love our enemies as we Love ourselves. In Matthew 5:44, Jesus says, *"But I say unto you, Love your enemies, bless them that curse you, do good to them that hate you, and pray for them that spitefully use you, and persecute you."* During human existence, those who oppose us are humans who face the same battles we face. Ultimately, our war is a spiritual one in which good does battle with evil for power over our souls.

If we Love our enemies, how do we conquer them or turn them away from trying to hurt us? God walks with us and will fight our battles for us to bring peace in those relationships if we do that which is pleasing to Him. In Exodus 23:22, it says, *"But if thou shalt indeed obey His voice and do all that I speak; then I will be an enemy unto thine enemies; and an adversary unto thine adversaries."* The trouble that others bring to us will turn into peace as we let God rule and direct our paths with Love in our hearts. Proverbs 16:7 speaks to this as it says, *"When a man's way pleases the Lord, He maketh even his enemies to be at peace with him."* If we want someone to stop coming against us in our lives, we turn our hearts to Love toward them and pray for them, and God will deal with their hearts, and peace will return to our relationships.

The true enemy of our life is not another person. The true enemy of our life is the evil one who seeks to destroy our hearts and souls and turn us away from God. It is the same evil one who is working in the hearts of other people we meet in our lives. As we share Love with each of those, we plant seeds for God, and He will nourish them. Perhaps in doing so, we help them find God in their life.

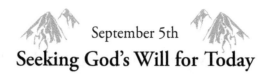

September 5th
Seeking God's Will for Today

As we journey each day, it is our purpose to seek God's will for our life for that day which He has given to us. We know He is in our hearts and lives through His Holy Spirit, which He sent to be our comforter and our spiritual guide. We are His messengers of light to those who He brings to us each day when we are doing the work of the Lord. When we pray the Lord's prayer, we ask that "His will be done," and that should be the hope and prayer for each of our hearts every day. The scriptures teach us of His will throughout the Bible. In Hebrews 13:20–21, we are told: *"May the God of peace...make you perfect in every good work to do His will, working in you that which is well pleasing in His sight, through Jesus Christ; to whom be the glory for ever and ever."* God will equip us with everything we need to do His will today and always if this is what we seek.

It is God's will that we rejoice and be thankful for all the blessings He has given to us and for where He has placed us in this world to do His work. First Thessalonians 5:16–18 speaks to this: *"Rejoice evermore. Pray without ceasing. In everything give thanks; for this is the will of God in Christ Jesus concerning you."* To walk with God and to be in His will, we are not walking in sorrow or commiserating about the life we have been given. Rather, we are rejoicing and giving thanks for His grace and realizing He is with us each step along the way. It is God's will that we seek purity in our life and do that which is right in His eyes. First Thessalonians 4:3 says, *"For this is the will of God, even your sanctification, that ye should abstain from fornication."* The temptation of the flesh is one of the ways the evil one uses to attempt to separate us from our God who Loves us.

It is God's will for us each day that we simply do that which is good and right in His sight. As we do so, we are ministering to those we meet each day to share the good news of Jesus Chris and the path to salvation.

September 6th

May God Prosper You as You Do His Work

As we walk with our God and do His work in our lives, He has promised us that He is with us and will reward us and provide for us. One of my favorite scriptures is found in Matthew 6:33, which tells us, *"But seek first the kingdom of God and His righteousness, and all these things shall be added unto you as well."* The condition of being able to receive these blessings and benefits is to seek His kingdom and righteousness first. To prosper and have success in life, you must be fully invested with hard work and commitment on your part. The reward of success and prosperity is the by-product of diligence and perseverance. Proverbs 10:4 teaches us: *"He becometh poor that dealeth with a slack hand; but the hand of the diligent maketh rich."* If prosperity is what you seek in all you do, you must be fully invested in that outcome.

We must remain focused on God's kingdom and His righteousness as we strive for success in our lives. To provide for our families in a way that allows us to give them nice things and a great house is not a sin, nor is it unpleasing to God. Make sure to give the glory to God for your success and prosperity and to give to the poor and needy when you are so blessed. 1 Timothy 6:17–19 says,

> *Charge them that are rich in this world, that they not be high–minded, nor trust in uncertain riches, but in the living God, who giveth us richly all things to enjoy. That they do good, that they be rich in good works, ready to distribute, willing to communicate. Laying up in store for themselves a good foundation against the time to come, that they may lay hold on eternal life.*

As God blesses you, be generous to others and humble, knowing all we have is a gift from God.

Let us not fall prey to the mindset of having Love for money to the extent we lose sight of the purpose of serving God and seeking His righteousness in our hearts. Be Blessed and content with God's blessings in your life and thank Him and give Him the glory for all you have. May He prosper you as you do His work.

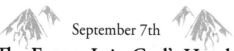

September 7th

The Future Is in God's Hands

There are times when we face an uncertain future in our lives. Whether it is the result of life changes, such as retirement, a job change, family changes coming from having a baby, or going through a divorce. Life has moments of emotional and physical changes which cause us to stress and feel anxious about what the future might hold. As a believer, God is with us through all these moments and will bring peace to your heart as you put your trust in Him. Zephaniah 3:17 tells us, *"The Lord thy God in the midst of thee is mighty; He will save, He will rejoice over thee with joy, He will rest in His Love, He will joy over thee with singing."* There is nothing to fear in our lives when we walk with God and trust in Him. He will take joy in our well-being always.

Whatever you are facing as your life goes through changes, God is there to supply you with the Love and support you need to go through it. Philippians 4:19 tells us, *"But my God supply all your need according to His riches in glory by Christ Jesus."* We do not serve a God who is limited with what He can deliver to us in our time of need. We walk each day in total confidence, knowing God will be with us throughout our lives and beyond. Philippians 1:6 says this: *"Being confident of this very thing, that He which hath begun a good work in you will perform it until the day of Jesus Christ."* Our journey is not one we take alone, and the God we serve is working in us each day as we seek His will. There is no room for fear about our future when we have faith in the God we serve.

The more we trust in God and do that which is good in the work we do for Him, the greater the peace we have in what is now and what is to come. Psalm 37:3–4 tells us, *"Trust in the Lord and do good, so thou shalt dwell in the land, and verily thou shalt be fed. Delight thyself also in the Lord, and He shall give thee the desires of thy heart."* May His peace fill your heart with joy as you trust in Him for all that is to come in your life. He is with us and will protect us always!

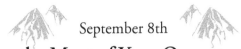

September 8th

Make the Most of Your Opportunities

As we walk with God each day, He provides us with opportunities in our life. Some of these opportunities are designed to allow us to best serve Him and be of service to others He gives to us on our path. Other opportunities may be for the betterment of our own lives and the lives of those in our family circle. God blesses us with opening such doors of opportunity, and it is up to us to make the most of them as they appear. Ephesians 5:15–17 tells us this: *"See then that ye walk circumspectly, not as fools, but as wise. Redeeming the time because the days are evil. Wherefore, be ye not unwise, but understanding what the will of the Lord is."* The message cautions us to measure each opportunity we face with what the will of our Father would be regarding it.

The most significant opportunity we will have in our lives is to accept the gift of salvation by repenting of our sins and believing in Jesus Christ as the Son of God. That faith is our path to eternal life. Ephesians 2:8–9 tells us, *"For by grace are ye saved through faith; and that not of yourselves, it is the gift of God; Not of works, lest any man boast."* Our time of opportunity to accept this gift of God is the moment of truth in our life. At that moment and for all eternity, we can walk with God, and our lives are in His hands. As God's people, we are here to do good things on earth and to serve those to who God gives to us. Galatians 6:10 teaches us: *"As we have therefore opportunity, let us do good unto all men, especially unto them who are of the household of faith."* Our opportunity to do good to others will be there for us as God opens those doors.

Our goal and calling as we walk with God each day is to be faithful to our Lord and Savior, Jesus Christ. Revelation 14:12 calls for us to do this: *"Here is the patience of the saints; here are they that keep the commandments of God, and the faith of Jesus Christ."* That is the opportunity we have. Let us make the most of it on this day and every day. Be Blessed as you keep the faith!

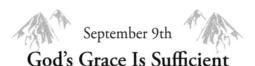

September 9th

God's Grace Is Sufficient

We continue to be blessed each day by the grace of God, which has offered salvation to all people. Salvation is not something that we deserve or earn by our good works but rather a gift that comes from our Holy Father out of His Love for each of us. While we lived a life deep in sin, He Loved us and brought us this amazing gift through His Son, Jesus Christ. Titus 2:11–12 tells us this: *"For the grace of God that bringeth salvation hath appeared to all men, Teaching us, that denying ungodliness and worldly lusts, we should live soberly, righteously, and godly, in this present world."* Through this amazing gift of God, when we accept this gift of salvation, we turn our hearts toward God and away from that which separates us from Him.

God's grace is sufficient to give us the power to overcome those areas in our lives which are weak. Everyone struggles in their spiritual life and needs God's power and strength to overcome the temptations we face along the way. Second Corinthians 12:9 tells us, *"As He said to me, "My grace is sufficient for thee, for my strength is made perfect in weakness.' Most gladly therefore will I rather glorify in my infirmities, that the power of Christ may rest upon me."* We do not battle in this spiritual world alone. God and His Holy Spirit are there to fight with us and for us. God has freed us from having to earn our way to heaven by His grace. Romans 6:14 says this: *"For sin shall not have dominion over you; for ye are not under the law, but under grace."*

We should thank God daily for His grace which has given us access to His mighty throne when we are in times of trouble. Hebrews 4:16 teaches us: *"Let us therefore come boldly unto the throne of grace, that we may obtain mercy, and find grace to help us in our time of need."* Thank you, my God, for your wonderful mercy and grace always.

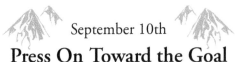

September 10th
Press On Toward the Goal

As we rise every morning to face the challenges and the opportunities which will come our way each day, we choose the path on which we travel. We can spend our time working out our own plans and schemes to try to bring about those things we desire and feel we need to accomplish. In doing so, are we pausing to reflect on whether that which we pursue is consistent with God's will for our lives? If we begin each day with the reading of His Word and spending time in prayer, the probability of us seeking His will for that day is increased exponentially.

Often, we may find ourselves reflecting on something which happened yesterday or sometime in the recent past, which is influencing the direction we are considering taking to deal with certain issues. It is understandable that we are influenced by all that happens in our lives which makes us who we are. However, it is sometimes in our best interest to leave things in the past behind us and to move on to what remains ahead with God's guidance and blessing. Paul wrote to the Philippians in 3:13–14 these words: *"Brethren, I count not myself to have apprehended: but this one thing I do, forgetting those things which are behind, and reaching forth unto those things which are before, I press toward the mark for the prize of the high calling of God in Christ Jesus."* Ultimately, that is where we need to be focused each day. We are all called to a destiny that goes beyond the temporary issues we face each day, and God has called us to keep our minds focused on this prize that lies ahead.

It is God's purpose for our lives that we are here to discover and serve. Proverbs 19:20–21 teaches us: *"Hear counsel and receive instruction, that thou mayest be wise in thy latter end. There are many devices in a man's heart, nevertheless, the counsel of the Lord, that shall stand."* May we press on to find His purpose on this day and listen intently for the counsel of the Lord.

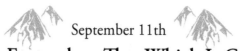

September 11th

Stay Focused on That Which Is Good

On this day in the year 2001, nineteen terrorists hijacked four planes and attacked our country, killing thousands of innocent people. We should always pause to reflect on those who were lost in this horrible and senseless series of events. Our thoughts and prayers should be with those families who lost Loved ones in this terrible attack. It is difficult for us to forgive those who have such evil in their hearts to want to unleash such evil in the world. We are taught to hate evil in Proverbs 8:13, which says, *"The fear of the Lord is to hate evil; pride and arrogancy, and the evil way and the froward mouth do I hate."* There is evil in our world today, and there always has been. We are told again in Romans 12:9 to hate that which is evil: *"Let Love be without dissimulation. Abhor that which is evil, cleave to that which is good."*

We must keep this in perspective in that we hate that which is evil, but we do not hate people who have evil in their hearts. Luke 6:27–28 teaches us this: *"But I say unto you which will hear, Love your enemies, do good to them which hate you, Bless them that curse you, and pray for them which despitefully use you."* We must overcome the darkness which comes from presence of evil in this world. When we think of the evil that is done to innocents, we are filled with anger and rage. Ephesians 4:31 guides us: *"Let all bitterness, and wrath, and anger, and clamor, and evil speaking, be put away from you with all malice."* This is not the purpose God has for us in our lives.

Philippians 4:8–9 tells us,

> *Finally, brethren, whatsoever things are true, whatsoever things are honest, whatsoever things are just, whatsoever things are pure, whatsoever things are lovely, whatsoever things are of good report; if there be any virtue, and if there be any praise, think on these things. Those things, which ye have both learned and received, and heard, and seen in me, do. And the God of peace shall be with you.*

This is the mindset to seek and to find God's will.

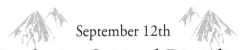 September 12th
Developing Spiritual Disciplines

There are disciplines many learn as a child to live a life that is orderly and wholesome. Whether it is brushing your teeth each morning and night or making your bed and cleaning up after yourself, these disciplines create a system from which you become more structured in your life, which leads you to better health and hygiene. As you age, you might add the discipline of eating more nutritious foods and exercising regularly to further enhance your health and well–being. From the perspective of being a good student, simply going to all classes, paying attention to the lessons, and studying the material will lead you to being your best in each of the subjects you take. When you engage in your career, performing your duties beyond the expectations of those with whom you work will allow you the opportunity to excel in all you do.

When it comes to the development of your spiritual growth, there are disciplines required for you to be your best and to accelerate your growth as well. First Timothy 4:7–8 speaks to the need for spiritual training: *"But refuse profane and old wives' fables and excuse yourself rather unto godliness. For bodily exercise profiteth little, but godliness is profitable unto all things, having the promise of the life that now is, and of that which is to come."* The importance of being trained for spiritual development is, without question, that the disciplines needed are simple. We need to read His Word daily. We need to spend time daily in prayer. We need to turn our minds from that with is temporal to that which is eternal.

Learn that which is going to lead you to a deeper spiritual walk. By reading God's Word, we will grow in our understanding and abide by His will. Joshua 1:8 teaches us:

> *This book of law shall not depart out of my mouth; but thou shalt meditate therein day and night, that thou mayest observe to do according to all that is written therein; for then thou shalt make thy way prosperous, and then thou shalt have good success.*

Read, learn, meditate, prosper and grow!

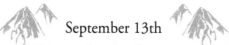

September 13th

The Spiritual Discipline of Prayer and Worship

We know we have been taught to pray continually for our own lives and for the lives of others. We should often pray for all of those in our own families and for those who are fellow believers who God puts on our path. It is a conversation we have with God, who will listen and respond to the earnest prayer of His children. In Colossians 4:2–4, Paul writes to the members of the church there to be devoted to prayer: *"Continue in prayer and watch in the same in thanksgiving; Withal praying also for us, that God would open unto us a door of utterance, to speak the mystery of Christ, for which I am also in bonds; that I may make manifest, as I ought to speak."* As we pray for that which God is doing in our lives, we should pray for those He has given to us as teachers and ministers who are leading us in spiritual understanding and growth.

As we live our lives for Christ, we are taught by Paul to offer our bodies as a living sacrifice in worship to our God in Romans 12:1–2, which says, *"I beseech you, therefore, brethren, by the mercies of God, which is your reasonable service, that ye present your bodies a living sacrifice, holy, acceptable unto God, which is your reasonable service. And be ye not conformed to this world but be ye transformed by the renewing of your mind, that ye may prove what is that good, and acceptable, and perfect will of God."* Our God is the master of the universe and worthy to be praised and worshipped by us daily. When we spend time in prayer and devote time to worshiping God for all He is and for all He has done, our Spirit grows closer to the God we serve.

Psalm 86:9–10 tell us this: *"All nations thou hast made shall come and worship before thee, O Lord: and shall glorify your name. For thou art great and doest wondrous things, thou art God alone."* Be focused on your praise and worship of God as part of your discipline for spiritual growth each day.

September 14th
Trust in God's Timing

As we go through changes in our lives, we want to see the big picture of where we are going and how soon we will be able to get there. We have to need to be in control and want to see each step as it unfolds. The anxiety of not knowing how all things will develop causes us stress and worry. If we truly trust in God for His plan to work in our lives, we must learn to be patient and know that it is in His hands each moment as it develops. Peace only comes to our hearts and minds when we surrender to trusting in God in all things. Isaiah 26:3 tells us, *"Thou wilt keep him in perfect peace, whose mind is stayed on thee; because he trusteth in thee."* Our hearts and minds are only troubled when we fail to trust in God.

The more confident you become in the relationship you have with God, the easier it is to be willing to let Him direct our paths and lead us to where He is guiding us to be. There is no room for fear and anxiety when we have faith and trust in our hearts, minds, and souls. Psalm 37:5 says this: *"Commit thy way unto the Lord, trust also in Him and He shall bring it to pass."* This unwavering declaration of faith is what is required for us to be committed to as we fulfill the faith and trust required of us. Let there be no uncertainty in your heart when it comes to your trust in God. Isaiah 12:2 tells us, *"Behold, God is my salvation; I will trust, and not be afraid; for the Lord, Jehovah, is my strength and my song, He also is become my salvation."*

Let us pray to God that He shows us the way we should go and trust in Him for this guidance. Psalm 143:8 speaks to this: *"Cause me to hear thy lovingkindness in the morning; for in thee do I trust; cause me to know the way wherein I should walk; for I lift up my soul unto thee."* When we put our trust in God, He is faithful to deliver us and strengthen us in all we do each day. Be Blessed today and trust in Him, and in His timing, He will deliver us.

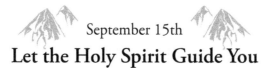

September 15th
Let the Holy Spirit Guide You

There are many choices we must make in life to get on the path to where God intends us to go. We have choices pertaining to our career path, which begin as early as college classes we select or job training programs we undertake. Those choices include the mate we choose to spend our lives with who will be with us through all phases of our lives. The place selected for where we build our homes is a major decision we reach along the way. There are daily choices that are impactful as well as we journey through this world. Our destiny is the by-product of all these moments rolled into the story of our lives.

When we walk with God and seek His wisdom and guidance in these decisions, He will empower us with His Holy Spirit to guide us as much as we allow Him to do so. John 16:13 teaches us: *"Howbeit, when He, the Spirit of truth is come, He will guide you into all truth; for He shall not speak of Himself, but whatsoever He shall hear, that will He speak; and he will show you things to come."* The power of listening to the whispers of the Holy Spirit as you go through each day is life-changing. We must understand that we are spiritual beings living in the flesh of our bodies. Romans 8:9, 11, 16 says this:

> *But ye are not in the flesh, but in the Spirit, if so be that the Spirit of God dwell in you. Now if any man hath not the Spirit of Christ, he is none of His. But if the Spirit of Him that raised Jesus from the dead dwell in you, He that raised Christ from the dead shall also quicken your mortal bodies by His spirit that dwelleth in you. The Spirit itself beareth witness with our Spirit, that we are the children of God.*

When you commit your life to Christ and believe in Him, you become a child of God and have been given the gift of eternal salvation. The Holy Spirit dwells in you and will guide you in all you do. As a child of God, listen to His leading in your spirit. Romans 8:14 tells us, *"For as many as are led by the Spirit of God, they are the Sons of God."* May God's Holy Spirit lead you in all you do!

September 16th
Seek to Please God Today

Each day of our lives is a gift from God. We have a purpose that God has given to each of us for that day as well. We will meet those God puts on our path to deliver His message of salvation and to minister to the needs of those who He chooses for us to serve each day. God will give us joy and peace as we seek to do His will and live according to His purpose. All that we do or say should be done with an attitude of seeking to please God with our lives. Pleasing God begins with having faith in God and living consistent with His commandments. Hebrews 11:6 tells us, *"But without faith, it is impossible to please Him, for he that cometh to God must believe He is, and that He is a rewarder of them that diligently seek Him."* God rewards those who seek Him each day.

We have been given the gospel of Jesus Christ and have the mission to share it with others. As we do, we please God and will receive His rewards. First Thessalonians 2:4 says, *"But just as we were allowed of God to be put in trust with the gospel even so we speak, not as pleasing men, but God who trieth our hearts."* The more we speak boldly of the glory of Jesus Christ and His story of victory over death, the more God is pleased with our ministry and will continue to bless it and our lives. There are many blessings God will bestow upon us as He is pleased with us, and peace is one of those. Proverbs 16:7 teaches us this: *"When a man's ways please the Lord, He makes even his enemies to be at peace with him."* What a great blessing that is in our lives.

As we seek righteousness and increase our knowledge of how God wants us to live, we are able to do that which is pleasing to God. Colossians 1:10 speaks to this as it says, *"That ye might walk worthy of the Lord unto all pleasing, being fruitful in every good work, and increasing in the knowledge of God."* When we walk in a manner which is worthy and seek to gain knowledge of God, He is pleased with us each day. Be Blessed today as you do so today!

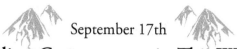

September 17th

Finding Contentment in This World

While we live in a world where success is often measured by the cars we drive and the homes in which we live, it is natural to want the best that life can give you. We strive in our careers to achieve the maximum results with the hopes of providing the best of all these material things to our families and to ourselves. The scriptures tell of God's desire to enrich His people as they trust in Him but cautions against greed in Proverbs 28:25. *"He that is of a proud heart stirreth up strife, but he that putteth his trust in the Lord shall be made fat."* Our God plans for us to prosper in our lives but to be content with that which He has given to us.

When you walk with the knowledge that God is with you, you need to know He will provide for your needs as you go through each phase of your life. Hebrews 13:5 tells us, *"Let your conversation be without covetousness; and be content with such things as ye have; for He saith, I will never leave thee nor forsake thee."* There is great comfort in knowing we have a God who will never forsake us on our journey. The scorecard of life is not based on who gains the most worldly possessions. Luke 12:15 says this: *"And He said unto them, 'Take heed, and beware of covetousness; for a man's life consisteth not in the abundance of the things which he possesseth."* God wants us to prosper, but He doesn't want us to be caught up in attaining that which we don't already have.

As we desire more material things, we can easily be pulled away from God and His righteousness. First Timothy 6:10–11 says, *"For the love of money is the root of all evil; which while some coveted after, they have erred from the faith, and pierced themselves through with many sorrows. But thou, O man of God, flee these things, and follow after righteousness, godliness, faith, Love, patience, and meekness."* As we seek these things, all other things will be added by God. Find contentment in all God has given you, and He will continue to bless you and provide you with prosperity in your life as you trust in Him.

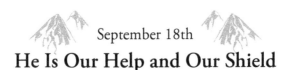

September 18th
He Is Our Help and Our Shield

As we face trials and times of uncertainty in our lives, we must have full confidence that God is with us always. The storms of life will come, and as they do, we feel the anxiety of not knowing when they will pass and what will be the result of the aftermath of the storm. It is at times like these when we need to have an anchor of our souls to give us protection and shelter. Hebrews 6:18–19 says these words to encourage us in such times:

> *That by two immutable things, in which it is impossible for God to lie, we might have a strong consolation, who have fled for refuge to lay hold on the hope before us; Which hope we have as an anchor for our soul, both sure and steadfast, and which entereth to that which is within the veil.*

Our hope is God will always be with us and protect us. When we face trials and go through moments of darkness in our lives, we hold steadfast to the knowledge and hope of God's deliverance in His time. In 1 Peter 5:6,7,10, we are encouraged by these words:

> *Humble yourselves, therefore, under the mighty hand of God, that He may exalt you up in due time. Casting all your care upon Him for He careth for you…But the God of all grace, who hath called us unto His eternal glory by Jesus Christ, after ye have suffered a while, make you perfect, establish, strengthen, settle you.*

The mighty hand of God will empower us with His strength to restore our energy to carry on through all the storms we face in life. God's eyes are on us as Psalm 33:18–22 assures of this:

> *The eye of the Lord is upon them that fear Him; upon them that hope in His mercy; to deliver their soul from death, and to keep them alive in famine. Our soul waiteth for the Lord, He is our hope and our shield. For our heart shall rejoice in Him because we have trusted in His holy name. Let thy mercy, O Lord, be upon us, according as we hope in thee.*

May God be with each of us today as we put our hope in Him.

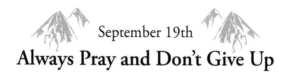

September 19th

Always Pray and Don't Give Up

We live in a time when we expect instant gratification, and we want our messages to be responded to quickly. In a world in which text messages are used daily to tell another about something which happens in our life, and we expect the other person to respond to us immediately, it is easy to translate that urgency into our relationship with God. When we pray, we often think God's response will be coming soon thereafter. Patience is not a virtue many of us possess in the modern world and one which we must have with our Heavenly Father, who sees and knows all things. Psalm 27:14 says this: *"Wait on the Lord; be of good courage, and He will strengthen thy heart; wait, I say, on the Lord."* There is no question He hears your prayer. Now, wait for Him to do His work in your life.

Know that God is listening to your prayers and will answer them according to His will for our lives. First John 5:14 tells us this: *"And this is the confidence we have in Him, that, if we ask anything according to His will, He heareth us."* It is our desire to find ourselves in the perfect will of God in all we do. As we seek His will in that which we pray for each day, know with confidence God hears us and will respond. Psalm 5:3 speaks to this: *"My voice shalt thou hear in the morning, O Lord, in the morning will I direct my prayer unto thee, and will look up."* There is no better way to start each day than to be in communication with our Heavenly Father. God is near to those who earnestly seek Him. Psalm 145:18 makes this clear: *"The Lord is nigh unto them that call upon Him, to all who call upon Him in truth."* Daily prayer is the path to a deepening relationship with God.

The more we pray in every situation, the more we find that God guards our hearts against the evil one. Philippians 4:6–7 says,

> *Be careful for nothing, but in everything by prayer and supplication with thanksgiving let your request be made know unto God. And the peace of God which passeth all understanding, shall keep your hearts and minds through Christ Jesus.*

September 20th

Be Thankful Always to God

We pray to God for the moments when we find ourselves facing issues of concern. When we find that those moments are resolved, we should pour our hearts in thanksgiving to the God who works with us as we go through these times. Quietly and masterfully, God is always working in our lives. We are provided daily with what we need, and our health and well-being are the direct result of blessings from God. We should create in ourselves in a perpetual state of thanksgiving to God for every moment we spend our time on this earth. First Thessalonians 5:16–18 tells it this way: *"Rejoice evermore, pray without ceasing; In everything give thanks; for this is the will of God, in Christ Jesus concerning you."* That doesn't mean there won't be moments in which you face difficulties or stressful times. That means you are in God's will as you go through these times. He is with you if that is what you are seeking for your life.

The scriptures teach us to always give thanks to God for all we have and for all we are able to do. Ephesians 5:20 says this: *"Giving thanks always for all things unto God and the Father in the name of our Lord Jesus Christ."* As we do this, we are drawing closer to God each day. The scriptures speak of how we move closer to God through our thanksgiving and praise in Psalm 100:4, which says, *"Enter into His gates with thanksgiving and into His courts with praise; be thankful unto Him and bless His name."* God is worthy of our praise, and His will be done in our lives is something we all can and should be thankful for each day. Those who fail to thank God and give Him the glory for their lives are drawn away from the light into darkness. Romans 1:21 tells us, *"Because that, when they knew God, they glorified Him not as God; neither were thankful; but became vain in their imaginations, and their foolish heart was darkened."* As children of the light, this cannot be the path we choose to take.

Give thanks to the Lord on this and every day, and be blessed as you do!

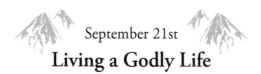

September 21st
Living a Godly Life

We are all sinners who have been saved by the grace of God. No one will lead a perfect life as we witnessed in the life of Jesus Christ. That being said, it should be our goal to be more "Christ-like" in all we do on this earth. The great evangelist Billy Graham once said, *"Make it your goal to be more like Christ by refusing to let sin have its way and pursuing instead that which is pure and good in the sight of God."* As we strive to achieve this life in which we turn our hearts and minds away from sin, we must embrace that which is good and pure in our thoughts and our actions each day, knowing we will not be perfect in this life.

We walk with God in the spirit each day. As we walk in the spirit, we are to turn our hearts away from the desires of the flesh. Galatians 5:16–17 tells us this: *"This I say then; Walk in the Spirit, and ye shall not fulfill the lust of the flesh. For the flesh lusteth against the Spirit, and the Spirit against the flesh. And these are contrary the one to the other; so that ye cannot do the things that ye would."* As we walk with our God in the Spirit each day and have received our salvation, we are directed to seek the path to righteousness and live a Godly life. Titus 2:11–13 teaches us this: *"For the grace of God that bringeth salvation hath appeared to all men; Teaching us that, denying ungodliness and worldly lusts, we should live soberly, righteously, and godly, in the present world. Looking for the blessed hope and glorious appearing of the great God and our Savior Jesus Christ."* As we wait upon the Lord, our desire is to become more like Him during our walk on this earth.

As we walk each day in this world, which is filled with sin and evil, we seek the presence of a God who is pure and good in our hearts and in our lives. The evil one wages war within us. First Peter 2:11 teaches us: *"Dearly beloved, I beseech you as strangers and pilgrims, abstain from fleshly lusts, which war against the soul."* May God direct your path to be more like Christ this day!

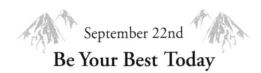

September 22nd

Be Your Best Today

We are all called to do work that is uniquely ours to do. It may change as we go through the evolution of our own life, and God may place us in different roles along the way. He has a plan and a purpose for us each day, and all we are asked to do is to be our best in that role that He has given us to accomplish. The fundamental work we are here to do is based on our Loving one another and being of service to God and mankind in spreading the gospel message. That role can be fulfilled whether you are a gardener, a laborer, or a priest. It is God's will that you be in the role you now have to fulfill His plan for you on this day.

Colossians 3:23–24 tells us, *"And whatsoever ye do, do it heartily, as to the Lord, and not unto men. Knowing that of the Lord ye shall receive the reward of the inheritance; for ye serve the Lord Christ."* We may find ourselves in a job that seems relatively unimportant in the grand scheme of things with respect to God's kingdom, but we are reminded that we are surrounded by a "cloud of witnesses" who observe how we live our lives each day. It is a ministry to do that which is right and to testify of God's grace and His salvation message to those who are placed on our path. Second Timothy 2:15 says, *"Study to show thyself approved unto God, a workman that needeth not to be ashamed, rightly dividing the word of truth."* We know the truth of God's message, which we carry in our hearts. Let our lives reflect that truth daily, and let us continue to study it.

We are all called to be diligent and hard-working and directed to not be lazy in the work we do here. Romans 12:11 directs us: *"Not slothful in business; fervent in Spirit; serving the Lord."* Laziness is not a quality that brings positive results. Be diligent and excellent in all you do this day, and dedicate the day to service to our Lord and Savior Jesus Christ. You will be rewarded as you always commit to being the best you can be.

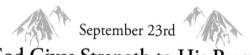

September 23rd

God Gives Strength to His People

We fight battles in life and often need help in overcoming that which we face. At times we feel unable to win these alone, but the great news is that we are never alone as children of God. Whether the battle you face be one which is physical in nature due to health-related problems, spiritual in nature as the enemy of your soul tries to steer you away from God, or emotional in the fact it is a conflict that arises in human relationships or the loss of a Loved one, God is with you and will strengthen you to go through the difficult times. Alone, we are weak, but with God, we overcome the world and all its hardships. Psalm 46:1 says, *"God is our refuge and our strength, a very present help in times of trouble."*

When we trust in our God, we have no room for fear in what we face in life. He is our source of strength and our salvation, regardless of what comes our way. Isaiah 12:2 tells us, *"God is my salvation; I will trust and not be afraid."* If God is with us, who can possibly be against us in our lives? With God as our source of strength, we can go places we could never go on our own and do things we would never be able to do without Him. Habakkuk 3:19 speaks to this: *"The Lord God is my strength, and He will make my feet like hinds feet, He will make me to walk upon my high places."* We live without limits as we walk with God and gain His strength each day. He gives us the power to speak for Him and to be of service to those who He gives us to serve each day. First Peter 4:11 teaches us:

> *If any man speak, let him speak as the oracles of God; if any man minister, let him do it as of the ability which God giveth; that God in all things might be glorified through Jesus Christ, to who be praise and dominion for ever and ever.*

May we trust God for His strength and power as we walk with Him today and always. He is faithful to deliver His strength to those who call upon His name. His power will flow through us as we walk with Him and do His will. Be Blessed as you do so!

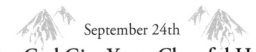

September 24th

May God Give You a Cheerful Heart

We live in a world with many stresses which come our way. It is part of the human experience and can steal your joy if you allow that to happen. God wants His people to have joy and happiness in their hearts as they serve him and are called according to His purpose. People who turn their hearts to positive energy and happiness are forever fed by God in their soul. Proverbs 15:15 says this: *"All the days of the afflicted are evil, but he that is of a merry heart hath a continual feast."* Our attitudes determine so much in our lives each day as to what the outcome will be in our hearts and souls. When we embrace joy in all we face, we find our lives pouring joy and happiness into the lives of others we meet each day. In return, we face smiles and positive energy coming from those as well.

One of the great moments of my life is when I can hear a member of my family laugh out loud as they experience joy from someone or something in their lives. God intends for us to have laughter in our hearts and on our lips. In Job 8:21, the scripture talks about this: *"Till He fill my mouth with laughing, and my lips with rejoicing."* When others around you see your laughter and the joy you have in your hearts, they recognize that you are blessed by God and that your life is different from those who are overwrought with the burdens of this world. Psalm 126:2 tells us, *"Then our mouths were filled with laughter, and our tongue with singing; then said they among the heathen; The Lord hath done great things for them."* Our demeanor bears witness to our Spirit, and we should be filled with happiness as we walk with God in our lives.

Not every day will be filled with happiness, and we will endure times of sadness in our lives. We know God will be with us through it all and will direct our paths to a place where joy and happiness are restored. Ecclesiastes 3:4 says, *"A time to weep, and a time to laugh; a time to mourn, and a time to dance."* May today be filled with times of laughter and dancing as God Blesses You!

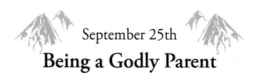

September 25th
Being a Godly Parent

There has been no greater joy in my life than that of being a father to two great sons who were truly gifts from our Heavenly Father God. The joy of such a role carries with it great responsibility and puts one in a position to be an example of how to live your life. It is less what you say and more how you live that translates into the hearts of those children God has given to you. If you speak of Love and don't demonstrate it throughout your life, you are less likely to carry the message to those children in a meaningful way. Proverbs 20:7 teaches us: *"The just man walketh in his integrity; His children are blessed after him."* When you speak of things like honesty and integrity to your children, you must follow through and live a life that is filled with integrity to bear witness to what is in your heart. As you do, your children are truly blessed by your example.

Our children become our greatest joy and a true treasure as they follow the path set before them to seek God's will for their lives. As a parent, it is our greatest responsibility to plant the seeds in their hearts to seek this path. Proverbs 22:6 says, *"Train up a child in the way he should go, and when he is old, he will not depart from it."* We do this by our words and our actions which teach them of the way God intends for a righteous man to live. As the child seeks a righteous life, the parent is filled with joy. Proverbs 23:24 speaks to this: *"The father of the righteous shall greatly rejoice; and he who begetteth a wise child shall have joy in him."* We all want the best for our children, and the best life is one that is dedicated to following the plan God has for us and seeking His will.

As a parent, we must talk often about the value of following God's commandments in our lives. Deuteronomy 6:6–7 says, *"And these words which I command thee this day, shall be in thine heart. And thou shalt teach them diligently unto thy children."* Keep God's Word in front of your children daily, and they will grow up and follow on the path to seek God's will for their lives.

September 26th

God Wants Us to Succeed and Prosper

It is God's plan for each of our lives that we do His work and follow a plan He has laid out for each of us. It is in God's plan that we prosper and find success as we diligently do that which He has given us to do. It is imperative that we conduct our lives consistent with His laws. His laws were established in the days of Moses when we were given his Ten Commandments. 1 Kings 2:3 guides us when it says, *"And keep the charge of the Lord thy God to walk in His ways, to keep His statutes, and His commandments, and His judgements, and His testimonies, as it is written in the law of Moses, that thou may prosper in all that thou doest."* Establishing a foundation in being obedient to God is how we can then build upon it a life filled with prosperity in His plan for our lives.

God gives us the ability to produce wealth but cautions us not to seek it by dishonest means. Deuteronomy 8:18 teaches us: *"But thou shalt remember the Lord thy God, for it is He who giveth thee power to get wealth, that He may establish His covenant which He sware unto thy fathers, as it is this day."* We thank God for the ability which He gives us to achieve success. His covenant with us requires that we do all things consistent with His laws and commandments. Luke 16:10–11 talks about how we are tested with the handling of worldly prosperity when it says, *"He that is faithful in that which is least is faithful also in much; and he that is unjust in the least is unjust also in much. If therefore ye have not been faithful…who will commit to your trust the true riches?"* The more we are given by God, the greater the opportunity we have to be able to give back to those in need that God places on our path.

We are here for a season, and our true reward will be that which we receive in heaven. Matthew 16:26 says, *"For what is a man profited, if he shall gain the whole world and lose his own soul? Or what shall a man give in exchange for his soul?"* Focus on the true riches God has planned for us in our eternal lives.

September 27th
Run a Good Race Today

There are many scriptures in the Bible which speak of the race we run as humans in our lives. We all face obstacles and stumbling blocks along the way, but our goal is to reach the end successfully with our eyes on the ultimate prize of eternal life with God our Father. When God is with us, we can advance each day against all levels of resistance in our battles. Psalm 18:29 tells us, *"For by thee I have run through a troop; and by my God I have leaped over a wall."* The author, David, was a fearless warrior, and he led his men into many battles where they were outnumbered, but his God went with him and gave him the strength to conquer those who he fought against. He will do the same for each of us.

Don't let anyone steer you away from the path you are on with respect to your faith journey. The evil one will put others in your path to do that as you strive to live a life that is pleasing to God. Galatians 5:7 cautions us: *"You did run well. Who did hinder you that you should not obey the truth?"* It is our quest to remain faithful to our God to the end of our journey and to run the race before us. First Corinthians 9:24–25 says this:

> *Know ye not that they which run in a race, run all but one receiveth the prize? So run, that ye may obtain. And every man that striveth for the mastery is temperate in all things. Now they do it to obtain a corruptible crown, but we an uncorruptible.*

The finish line of the race we run will be leading us to the prize of eternal life with God the Father and His Son Jesus Christ. What could be a more blessed prize to win?

Set aside everything that keeps you from running the race God has given to you, and victory will be yours in the end. Hebrews 12:1 says this:

> *Wherefore, seeing we are compassed about with so great a cloud of witnesses, let us lay aside every weight, and the sin which doth so easily beset us, and let us run with patience the race that is set before us.*

Be victorious in your race today!

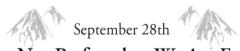

September 28th

We Are Not Perfect, but We Are Forgiven

It is easy to fall prey to the thought that, as believers, we will now lead a perfect life in Christ. It is our goal and daily quest to turn our lives from sin and to find the path to righteousness in Jesus Christ. With that desire in our hearts and minds, we will still find moments along the way where we stray from that which is pure and righteous, and we will need to ask forgiveness for those things which separate us from the God we serve. There was only one perfect man, and He died for the sins of the world. First John 2:2 says this: *"And he is the propitiation for our sins, and not for ours only but also for the sins of the whole world."* As Christ died on the cross for the sins of the world, we are free from the bondage of sin.

The path to righteousness will take us away from the sinful nature that is of this world. When we believe in Jesus Christ as our savior, we become a new creation as described in 2 Corinthians 5:17: *"Therefore, if any man be in Christ, he is a new creature, old things are passed away, behold, all things are become new."* When we turn toward the light, we leave that path that led us into darkness in our soul. When we live in the light of Christ, we turn away from the life of sin. First John 3:6 says this: *"Whosoever abideth in Him sinneth not; whosoever sinneth hath not seen Him, neither known Him."* We are His chosen people when we believe in Jesus Christ. Our goal is to never sin, but if we should, Jesus Christ is our advocate to God the Father. First John 2:1 tells us this: *"My little children, these things write I unto you, that ye sin not. And if any man sin, we have an advocate with the Father, Jesus Christ the righteous."*

We strive daily to live a life that is pleasing to God. We are not perfect in this world, but we press on to be made perfect in our Love through Jesus Christ. Philippians 3:12 teaches us: *"Not as though I had already attained, either were already perfect; but I follow after, if that I may apprehend that for which also I am apprehended of Christ Jesus."* May God keep us close in His perfect Love.

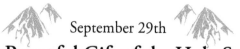

September 29th

The Powerful Gift of the Holy Spirit

Jesus spoke to His disciples about the Holy Spirit, which would come to be with us when he went to heaven to be with His Father God. The Holy Spirit is now with us to give us comfort and to teach us of the ways which please God. In John 14:26, Jesus says this: *"But the Comforter, which is the Holy Ghost, whom the Father will send in my name, He shall teach you all things, and bring all things to your remembrance, whatsoever I have said to you."* This living Spirit of God lives inside of each of us who believes in Jesus Christ and follows His path. The scriptures tell us that our bodies are His temple in 1 Corinthians 6:19, which teaches us: *"Know ye not that your body is the temple of the Holy Ghost which is in you, which ye have of God, and ye are not your own?"* This is a powerful message about God's Holy Spirit living in each of us.

Jesus spoke of this Spirit in His Words to His disciples as He prepared them for His upcoming death. In John 14:15–17, He describes it this way:

> *If you Love me, keep my commandments. And I will pray the Father, and He shall give you another Comforter, that He may abide with you forever. Even the Spirit of truth, whom the world cannot receive, because it seeth Him not, neither knoweth Him; but ye know Him; for He dwelleth in you and shall be in you.*

Jesus says clearly that the Holy Spirit will live inside of each of us as believers. The Spirit inside us guides us to a life of peace as described in Romans 8:5–6, which says,

> *For they that are after the flesh do mind the things of the flesh; but they that are after the Spirit the things of the Spirit. For to be carnally minded is death; but to be Spiritually minded is life and peace.*

Let our minds always be led by His Holy Spirit.

May the Holy Spirit be our guide on this day, and may the fruit of the Spirit be evidence in our lives of His presence. His presence and guidance will take us to the path that leads us closer to God every day. Be Blessed in His Spirit today!

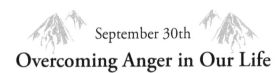

September 30th

Overcoming Anger in Our Life

We face many struggles as we go through the days of our life. We have moments of anger, disappointment, and frustration, which can lead to conflict, which lead us far from the path which God has chosen for us to be on. James 1:19–21 teaches us: *"Wherefore, my beloved brethren, let every man be swift to hear, slow to speak, slow to wrath; For the wrath of man worketh not the righteousness of God."* These are the moments in our lives in which we simply must trust in God our Father for our deliverance to help us resolve such conflicts with Love in our hearts. As we do so, we become the light of the world we are called to be.

One of the easiest traps the devil will use to take us away from the path of righteousness is to engage us in arguments with others which lead to an angry spirit that is not filled with Love. Ecclesiastes 7:9 says, *"Be not hasty in thy Spirit to be angry; for anger resteth in the bosom of fools."* Always be slow to anger and quick to forgive those who say things that unsettle our egos. The Spirit of Love will forgive and forget such momentary intrusions in our lives. Second Timothy 2:23–24 (NIV) teaches us this: *"Don't have anything to do with foolish and stupid arguments, because you know they produce quarrels. And the Lord's servant must not be quarrelsome but must be kind to everyone, able to teach, not resentful."* If we are to be the Lord's servant and the light of the world, we cannot be one who engages in meaningless arguments with others to prove a point or win a battle.

First Corinthians 13:4–5 (NIV) says, *"Love is patient, Love is kind, it does not boast, it is not proud. It does not dishonor others, it is not self-seeking, it is not easily angered, it keeps no record of wrongs."* Love is the answer; anger is not and is a weapon used by the evil one to pull us away from the path has for us. Don't let anger stand between you and God and the path to righteousness.

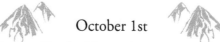

October 1st

Let Peace Rule Your Heart and Mind

One of the tricks of the enemy of our soul is to bring anxiety and fear into the hearts of believers. He seeks to plant seeds of doubt in our minds about our relationship with God and His hand of protection which is on our lives. The enemy will draw our attention to issues that may be financially related, our health, or the health of a Loved one. Satan wants us to have thoughts that trouble us and cause us stress in our hearts and lives. Philippians 4:6–7 teaches us not to worry about things but to turn them over to God through prayer, and He will bring us through them and fill our hearts with peace driving out all fear and anxieties.

Jesus spoke the words of peace to those who became His disciples. In John 14:27, He tells us, *"Peace I leave with you; my peace I give unto you; not as the world giveth, give I unto you. Let not your heart be troubled, neither let it be afraid."* We are His people, and He will deliver us from any evil which tries to come into our lives as we turn toward Him in every situation we face. We are assured of this peace that comes from Jesus Christ is Colossians 3:15, which says, *"And let the peace of God rule in your hearts, to the which also ye are called in one body; and be ye thankful."* We have been called to peace, and we should be giving thanks to God for this spiritual gift of peace in our hearts and souls.

The gift of peace is a blessing from our Lord. 2 Thessalonians 3:16 expresses it this way: *"Now may the Lord of peace Himself give you peace always by all means. The Lord be with all of you."* May God's blessing of peace reside in your hearts and minds as you journey today and every day! It is God's plan for our lives that we dwell in this spirit of peace as we live our lives with Him. The enemy of our souls will try to steal the peace God gives to us. When the darkness of the enemy comes, may the light of Christ fill your heart and soul with the Spirit of peace and Love.

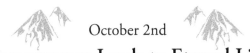 October 2nd

Perseverance Leads to Eternal Life

We have a journey that will take us to that place where our Spirit is able to cross over to be with God eternally in heaven. Our daily quest to reach that destination is filled with momentary struggles and challenges we must face, which bring us adversity that will lead to spiritual strength as we overcome that which is on our path. Each day we are here to do that which is righteous and good in dealing with others God places in our lives on our journey. We must not grow weary in doing good for those we meet. Romans 2:7 tells us this: *"To them who by patient continuance in well doing seek for glory and honor and immortality, eternal life."* There is a reward which is a gift from God of eternal life for doing His work and believing in our Savior Jesus Christ.

We will face trials along the way and must persevere in the faith through each one that comes into our life. Our faith will be tested by the evil one who only wants to see us fall short of delivering that which is good in times of stress. James 1:12 teaches us this: *"Blessed is the man who endureth temptation; for when he is tried, he shall receive the crown of life, which the Lord hath promised to them that Love Him."* Be joyful when you are tested and know you will be given the strength you need to overcome any such test by our God who Loves us. Second Timothy 4:18 says this: *"And the Lord will deliver me from every evil work, and He will preserve me unto His heavenly kingdom, to whom be glory forever and ever."* We know God wants us to be with Him eternally, and He will deliver us from the evil one when we are under attack. Praise God for His mercy and for His strength which He gives to His people.

We know the work is not yet finished in our lives as we get up each day to face the challenges and opportunities which lie ahead. God is not done with us and will be with us till the end of our time on this earth. Be happy in knowing God continues to work each day in your life.

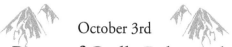

October 3rd

The Power of Godly Relationships

We have many relationships with people in our lives that carry significant influence on who we are. It begins as children with the relationships we establish with our parents. It is a great blessing from God when we are raised in a family in which prayer and faith are practiced, and we begin to see life through the eyes of Godly parents. Not everyone gets this early benefit in life, but in all cases, children are directed by God to give honor to their parents. Exodus 20:12 says, *"Honor thy father and thy mother, that thy days may be long upon the land which the Lord thy God giveth thee."* This is the first commandment of God with a promise. That promise is for you to live a long life because of the honor you give your parents.

When Love blossoms in your life and you enter a marriage relationship, Proverbs 31:10–11 talks about the great value and treasure of a wife of good character as it says, *"Who can find a virtuous woman? For her price is far above rubies. The heart of her husband doth safely trust in her."* Husbands are directed to Love wives and to be gentle with them in Colossians 3:19: *"Husbands Love your wives and do not be bitter against them."* It is easy at times to be harsh and unkind to those who we Love the most. God directs us from this spirit to one who is humble and kind if we are to live a Godly life. Ephesians 4:2–3 says it this way: *"With all lowliness and meekness, with longsuffering, forbearing one another in Love; Endeavoring to keep the unity of the Spirit in the bond of peace."* The more we approach one another with humbleness and gentleness, the less we allow egocentric conflicts to arise.

Godly relationships in all human interactions should be our objective. We sometimes focus on the shortcomings of one another in human relationships. As we live Godly lives, we must look past those shortcomings and allow Love to flow through us. First Peter 4:8 teaches us: *"And above all things, have fervent charity among yourselves, for charity shall cover a multitude of sins."* Let Love Flow!

October 4th

We Live in the Moment with Our Eyes on Our Eternal Home

As we walk in each moment of our lives, we have the rich blessing of our God walking with us. As we face the challenges that life brings our way, He is there to fight for us and to comfort us in times of sorrow and distress. We are told to take courage and be strong in all we do as He is with us. As we live in each moment of time, we must embrace it with God's will in our hearts and in our prayers as we seek to do that which He would have us to do. Deuteronomy 31:6 instructs us: *"Be strong and of good courage, fear not and be not afraid of them; for the Lord thy God, He it is that doth go with thee, He will not fail thee nor forsake thee."* As God walks with us, there is nothing we should fear.

We find ourselves making our plans for the future as we try to create the desired path for ourselves and our families. It is appropriate for us to do so with the understanding that our plans are to be at the center of God's will for our lives. James 4:13–15 tells us,

> *Go to now, ye that say, Today or tomorrow, we will go into such a city, and continue there a year, and buy and sell, and get gain. Whereas ye know not what shall be on the morrow. For what is your life? It is even a vapor, that appeareth for a little time, and then vanisheth away. For ye ought to say, If the Lord will, we shall live and do this or that.*

When we plan to do that which is consistent with the Lord's will, we are centering our life on Him. The plans we make should be with the stipulation that if it is the Lord's will, we will do these things in our lives.

We have a destiny that is eternal. While on this earth, Deuteronomy 30:16 instructs us:

> *I command thee this day to Love the Lord thy God, to walk in His ways, to keep His commandments, and His statutes and His judgements, that thou mayest live and multiply; and the Lord thy God shall bless thee in the land whither thou goest to possess it.*

Wherever we go, God goes with us and will bless us as we walk with Him with Love in our hearts.

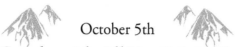 October 5th

Be Gentle with All You Meet Today

It is easy to be strong and affirmative in our dealings with others in life. We know when we are right and to assert ourselves as such is part of our human nature. Being strong does not mean that we must overcome others with our human spirit in an effort to prove we are right and they are wrong about an issue. The best way to unlock a human's heart to welcome in the spirit of Love is to try a little tenderness and gentleness with them. The scriptures speak often about the power of gentleness in our dealings with one another. Titus 3:2 teaches us this: *"To speak evil of no man, to be no brawlers, but gentle, showing meekness unto all men."* For us to live our lives in peace, we must be peaceable, considerate, and gentle to others we meet and try a little tenderness with all.

God finds great value in a gentle spirit as it is told to us in 1 Peter 3:4, which says, *"But let it be the hidden man of the heart, in that which is not corruptible, even the ornament of a meek and quiet spirit, which is in the sight of God of great price."* Our egos will often try to direct us to be bold in our conversations with others in attempts to rule over them in arguments and conflicts. A gentle spirit will win most of those battles without such conflicts occurring when you demonstrate Love rather than a spirit of dominance. Words with Love carry great power with others who are trying to convince you they are right. Speaking gently and humbly, you can defuse their wrath and turn their thoughts to positive resolutions.

Jesus taught us to be gentle and humble in our lives in Matthew 11:29–30 when He says, *"Take my yoke upon you and learn from me, for I am meek and lowly in heart: and ye shall find rest for your souls. For my yoke is easy and my burden in light."* When we follow the path to which Jesus is guiding us, we will be at peace and will embrace others with gentleness and humility, which will lead them to a place where they will want more of the Love we are taught to give.

October 6th
Our Heavenly Home

As Jesus ministered to His disciples, He spoke of going ahead of us to the place we would follow and that He would prepare a place for us in Heaven. When one of our Loved ones who is a believer passes away from this world, we have confidence in knowing they have left their earthly bodies and have been transported in the Spirit to be with Jesus and our Heavenly Father in His kingdom. Jesus said in John 14:2–4:

> *My Father's house are many mansions; if it were not so, would I have told. I am go to prepare a place for you. And if I go and prepare a place for you, I will come again and receive you unto myself; that where I am, there ye may be also. And whither I go ye know, and the way ye know.*

We are on our journey to that place each day of our lives.

There is often sadness for those of us who have been left behind when a believer graduates to the Spiritual world that lies ahead. Once they reach heaven, the tears are wiped away, and there will be no more death in heaven. Revelation 21:4 tells us, *"And God shall wipe away all tears from their eyes; and there shall be no more death, neither sorrow, nor crying, neither shall there be any more pain; for the former things are passed away."* For those of our Loved ones on earth who had been suffering from physical pain or discomfort, they now have taken on celestial bodies which have no more pain or sadness. We have cause to celebrate this time of their new lives as the children of God. Revelation 21:7 says this: *"He that overcometh shall inherit all things; and I will be his God, and he shall be my son."* What a glorious promise and victory we will have with our Father God when that day arrives for each of us.

We, too, will one day take our place at the feast in the kingdom of God as described in Luke 13:29, which says, *"And they shall come from the east and from the west and from the north and from the south and shall sit down in the kingdom of God."* We will be joyous on our arrival at that celebration with God.

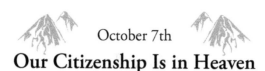

October 7th

Our Citizenship Is in Heaven

While on earth, we are citizens of a specific country and take pride in that allegiance. Our soldiers will defend the country against those who would attempt to do it harm. We fight for our collective freedoms and establish governments to try bringing justice and freedoms to all who live here. As believers in our Lord Jesus Christ, our true citizenship is beyond the borders of our earthly homes. Our destiny is to transform our earthly bodies into celestial ones as we become citizens of heaven. Philippians 3:20–21 teach us this: *"But our conversation is in heaven, from whence also we look for the Savior, the Lord Jesus Christ. Who shall change our vile body, that it may be fashioned like unto His glorious body, according to the working whereby He is able to subdue all things unto Himself."* Our bodies are the temples of our Spirit, but at the end of the time we spend on this earth, we are transformed into a heavenly body that is like that of Christ.

Our earthly home is not our eternal one. We are simply passing through this world as described in 2 Corinthians 5:1: *"For we know that if the earthly house of this tabernacle were dissolved, we have a building of God, a house not made with hands, eternal in the heavens."* We are going to a place where there we will live forever in a place where God has created for us all who believe in Jesus Christ. We have no fear of death as believers in Jesus Christ. John 11:25–26 tells us these words spoken by Jesus: *"Jesus said unto her, 'I am the resurrection and the life; He that believeth in me, though he were dead, yet shall he live, and whosoever liveth and believeth in me shall never die. Believest thou this?"* Jesus taught us the way to salvation and eternal life, which is through faith in Him. All who believe in Him will be given the gift of eternal life without death.

Our faith in Jesus Christ gives us citizenship that goes beyond the borders of this world with an eternal home in heaven. May God bless us as we journey toward that home on this and every day!

October 8th
Life After Death

The enemy of our souls tries to bring fear and doubt into our hearts and minds to separate us from the Love and faith we have for Jesus Christ and our Heavenly Father. When we are filled with faith and Love, we have no fears, and our doubts disappear as the light of our lives causes the darkness to flee. Jesus made it clear that those who believe in Him will live beyond the death we face on this earth. In John 11:25, Jesus says this: *"Jesus said to her, 'I am resurrection and the life. The one who believes in me will live, even though they die.'"* His Words are clear that the death of the body does not translate into the death of the Spirit. Again, in John 5:24, we are told this by Jesus:

> *Verily, verily, I say unto you, he that heareth my word and believeth on Him that sent me, hath everlasting life, and shall not come into condemnation, but is passed from death unto life.*

There is a judgment day coming when our life is over here on earth. The scripture is clear that we will all appear before the judgment seat to be measured on how we lived while in our earthly bodies. Second Corinthians 5:8–10 speaks of this as it says,

> *We are confident, I say, and willing to be absent from the body and to be present with the Lord. For we must all appear before the judgement seat of Christ, that everyone may receive the things done in his body, according to that he hath done, whether it be good or bad.*

If you believe in Jesus Christ and our Father God who sent Him to die for the sins of the world, you need not fear judgment, for your sins are forgiven. Hebrews 9:27–28 tells us this: *"And as it is appointed unto men once to die, but after this the judgment; So Christ was once offered to bear the sins of many; and unto them that look for Him shall He appear the second time without sin unto salvation."* Let your heart be waiting for Christ's return today, and may our lives be dedicated to spreading His gospel to those God gives to us along the way of our lives.

October 9th

May Our Hearts Be Pure on This Day

Our hearts and minds steer our souls and influence all we do in this world. We tend to think about those things which we read about or see on television, and our eyes are indeed the windows to our souls as they allow in those thoughts and desires. The more frequently we add the word of God into our daily diet of information, the closer we come to living a life with a heart that is pure. Meditation on the word and praying to the God we serve will purge our hearts and minds from the thoughts and influence of the evil one who wishes to destroy. Matthew 5:8 tells of what Jesus said about a pure heart: *"Blessed are the pure in heart, for they shall see God."* If we want to be among those who see God, we must strive to purify that which is in our hearts.

As we purify our hearts, we seek more earnestly to Love one another. First Peter 1:22 tells us this: *"Seeing ye have purified your souls in obeying the truth through the Spirit unto unfeigned Love of the brethren, see that ye Love one another with a pure heart fervently."* The more we willingly purify our hearts and souls, the closer we grow in our relationship with God the Father, who is pure. First John 3:3 speaks to this: *"And every man who has hope in Him purifies himself as He is pure."* The more we store the word of God in our hearts, the more we are able to create purity in all we do and say. Psalm 119:9 instructs us this: *"Wherewithal shall a young man cleanse his way? By taking heed thereto according to thy word."* Read God's Word each day!

As we do that which is good and right and live a life that is honest, we purify that which we do, and it becomes pleasing to God. Psalm 24:4–5 says this: *"He that hath clean hands and a pure heart; who hath not lifted up his soul into vanity, nor sworn deceitfully. He shall receive the blessing from the Lord, and righteousness from the God of his salvation."* May our hearts be pure on this day, and may the God of our salvation bless us richly as we do that which is righteous.

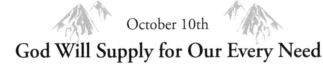

October 10th

God Will Supply for Our Every Need

As we enter a prayerful relationship with God our Father, we ask Him for things that we want to happen in our lives and in the lives of those we Love. Our hopes and prayers are for those to prosper and to be happy in all they face and do in their lives. We want the same for our own lives and know we serve a God who wants all the best for us as well. The scriptures teach us that God will provide for our every need. It does not say He will provide for our every "want." Philippians 4:19 specifically says, *"But my God will supply all your need according to His riches in glory by Christ Jesus."* There is a great difference between what we need and what we want as we journey in this world. There is also a great difference between our perspective on life and that of our Heavenly Father. He sees all and knows what is best for us when we do not.

We are directed to bring our requests to God and know that He will answer them. Philippians 4:6 directs us: *"Be careful for nothing, but in everything by prayer and supplication with thanksgiving let your requests be made known to God."* In some of these situations, the answer from God is to turn our hearts away from the desire for those things we might ask Him for. The future is not something we can see, but it is clear to God what will unfold in our lives as time passes. Second Peter 1:3 guides us with this understanding: *"According as His divine power hath given unto us all things that pertain unto life and godliness, through the knowledge of Him that hath called us to glory and virtue."* When we are seeking His will and following the path He has chosen, we will be given all we need to live the life which leads us to godliness.

When we get wrapped up in what we want rather than what we need, we lose sight of what God intends for us. Psalm 34:10 says, *"The young lions do lack and suffer hunger; but those who seek the Lord shall not want any good thing."* Seek the Lord, and He will meet all your needs as we are promised in His Word.

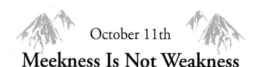

October 11th
Meekness Is Not Weakness

The scriptures are full of references to those who are meek and lowly and how God favors this spiritual nature. We are taught to receive God's Word with meekness in our hearts which will save our souls. James 1:21 teaches us this: *"Wherefore lay apart all filthiness and superfluity of naughtiness, and receive with meekness the engrafted word, which is able to save your souls."* As we do our work in this world with a quiet and gentle spirit in our dealings with others, we are demonstrating the qualities which are pleasing to God as said in 1 Peter 3:4, which says, *"But let it be the hidden man of the heart, in that which is not corruptible, even the ornament of a meek and quiet Spirit, which is in the sight of God of great price."* God highly values us when we take on a meek spirit.

The meek are described as blessed by God in Matthew 5:5, which tells us, *"Blessed are the meek, for they shall inherit the earth."* In this scripture, God speaks to the victorious life of those who are humble and meek in how they behave. Psalm 37:11 also speaks of this inheritance and the peace and prosperity which come with it: *"But the meek shall inherit the earth; and shall delight themselves in the abundance of peace."* As we approach God and others with meekness and humility, He can teach us His way to follow. Psalm 25:9 speaks to this as it says, *"The meek will He guide in judgement, and the meek will He teach His way."* Being meek is viewed by God as a strength in our character, and His blessings flow into us as we live His way.

As we embrace a spirit of meekness and demonstrate kindness and gentleness in our lives, we are demonstrating wisdom in the eyes of God. James 3:13 says it this way: *"Who is a wise man and endued with knowledge among you? Let him show out of a good conversation his works with meekness and wisdom."* May we demonstrate a life that is humble and kind today, and we will inherit the world as we become meek in our spiritual walk each day.

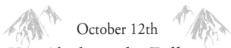

October 12th

May You Abide in the Fullness of Joy

Everyone wants to be happy each day as we travel through this life we have been given. Happiness is somewhat fleeting and can turn to sadness with the circumstances of the world happening around us each day. The soul, which is rooted in God, has a source of joy that takes us beyond fleeting happy moments and into a state of joy that can endure forever. We can choose to be joyful when our hearts are in tune with God. Psalm 16:11 tells us this: *"Thou wilt show me the path of life; in thy presence is fulness of joy, at thy right hand there are pleasures for evermore."* When God is at the center of your life, you will have joy in His presence always.

The more we build our trust in God, the more we are filled with joy, peace, and hope in our lives each day. Romans 15:13 makes this clear as it says, *"Now the God of hope fill you with all joy and peace in believing, that ye may abound in hope, through the power of the Holy Ghost."* The Holy Spirit dwells inside of each of us as believers in Jesus Christ. He was sent to be our comforter and brings us strength to overcome spiritual obstacles we face in our journey. Matthew 6:33 says, *"But seek first the kingdom of God and His righteousness, and all these things shall be added unto you."* It is not material things the scripture is talking about, but rather spiritual things of true value which will be added, such as joy in our hearts. Romans 14:17 teaches us: *"For the kingdom of God is not meat and drink, but righteousness and peace, and joy in the Holy Ghost."* These are true treasures that come from God our Father.

Jesus taught us to have a joyful heart, and His Words, when planted in our heart, gives us true joy, hope, and peace. In John 15:11, Jesus told His disciples: *"These things have I spoken unto you, that my joy might remain in you, and that your joy might be full."* May the joy Jesus spoke of be complete in our lives today and always, and may we share it with those He gives to us on our path today.

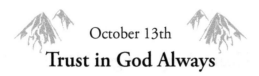

October 13th
Trust in God Always

We walk in faith and believe in our Heavenly Father, and seek to discover His will for our lives as believers. When we face the adversity and trials that this life has to offer us on our journey, we must turn to Him for strength, comfort, and understanding as to what direction we need to go to stay on the path He has chosen for us. Proverbs 3:5–6 tells us this: *"Trust in the Lord with all thine heart and lean not unto thine own understanding; In all thy ways acknowledge Him, and He shall direct thy paths."* We all face moments in our lives where we are not sure what we should do next. These are the times to put our trust in our God, who Loves us and will guide us when we seek His will for our lives at that time.

When we need His strength, He is faithful to deliver us and to give us His strength to fight every battle we face. Psalm 28:7 speaks to this: *"The Lord is my strength and my shield; my heart trusted in Him, and I am helped; therefore my heart greatly rejoiceth, and with my song will I praise Him."* We should always give thanks to the Lord for His goodness and mercy and for all He does to provide for our lives. The more we can trust God, the more He is willing to do that which is necessary for us to be triumphant in our lives. Psalm 37:5 teaches us this: *"Commit thy way unto the Lord; trust also in Him and He shall bring it to pass."* God is our refuge, and our hope, and our trust in Him is rewarded in times of trouble. There are many times when no one else can give you the comfort and hope you need. God is there in such times.

The solid foundation of your faith and trust in God will carry you through all the difficult moments you will face. His steady presence is the solid rock upon which our lives are built. Isaiah 26:3–4 says this: *"Thou wilt keep him in perfect peace, whose mind is stayed on thee; because he trusteth in thee. Trust ye in the Lord forever; for the Lord Jehovah is everlasting strength."* Trust in Him always.

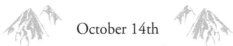

October 14th

May Our Hearts Sing Songs of Praise to Our God

The scriptures teach us to enter the gates with thanksgiving and into His courts with praise. Psalm 100:4–5 says this: *"Enter into His gates with thanksgiving and into His courts with praise; be thankful unto Him and bless His name. For the Lord is good; His mercy is everlasting; and His truth endureth to all generations."* The simple way to understand this message is we grow close to God when we give Him thanks and grow closer still when we offer Him praise for His goodness and His mercy to us each day. When we praise God, we are enveloping our mind and our heart in His greatness and the wonder of His Holy Spirit, which lives within us. He is truly worthy of being praised, and our hearts should rejoice in His Holy presence in our lives.

How can we best express this praise to our Heavenly Father? Certainly, we can freely express our praise and worship for our God in the moments in which we are alone with Him in our prayers. We should be praying throughout each day, and when we do, pause in our words to simply tell God, "I worship you and praise your Holy Name." These heartfelt expressions of our Love draw us closer to God. The scriptures often suggest that we open our hearts and lips to singing praises to Him. Jeremiah 20:13 tells us, *"Sing unto the Lord! Praise ye the Lord; For He hath delivered the soul of the poor from the hand of the evildoers."* David, who was a man after God's own heart, sang and danced before God in praising Him. He wrote this is Psalm 104:33, expressing His Love for our God: *"I will sing unto the Lord as long as I live; I will sing praise to my God while I have my being."* We should all embrace this attitude and philosophy toward our God.

Growing closer to God is a daily objective as a disciple of Christ. While we praise His Holy Name, we are doing exactly that. Isaiah 12:5 says, *"Sing to the Lord, for He has done excellent things; this is known in all the earth."* Freely open your hearts to God and sing His praises today and always.

October 15th

His Angels Watch over Us

The scriptures tell us how God will direct His angels to watch over and protect His people. He will send them as messengers, as is reported throughout the scriptures. He uses them to minister to His people as well. There are times when you might encounter an angel of the Lord and not know the person you have met is one. God works in mysterious ways, and His choice of how He uses angels is a mystery to us.

We know His angels are here to protect us as the scripture tells us this in Psalm 91:11: *"For He shall give His angels charge over thee, to keep thee in all thy ways."* Our protection by His mighty angels is a great comfort to us as believers. This protection of God through His angels is also referenced in Psalm 34:7, which describes it this way: *"The angel of the Lord enencampeth around them that fear Him, and delivereth them."* When God is with you, there is nothing on earth that can come against you to overpower you. His army of angels are there to keep you safe as you do the work of God. The scripture also speaks of the angels providing ministry for us on earth. Hebrews 1:14 teaches us this: *"Are they not all ministering spirits sent to minister for them who shall be heirs to salvation?"* The roles of the angels of God are to protect us and to minister to us.

David praises God for His angels in Psalm 103:20, saying: *"Bless the Lord, ye His angels, that excel in strength, that do His commandments, harkening unto the voice of His word."* As a believer, it is a blessing and gift from God our Father that we enjoy having His angels watching over us in our lives. Be comforted by the knowledge of their presence and mindful that you may be entertaining an angel when you have dealings with strangers you meet along the way. God is great in the way He watches over us and ministers to His people through His army of angels.

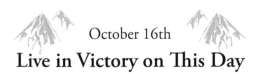

October 16th

Live in Victory on This Day

As we awaken to begin each day of our journey, we have a series of events that are about to unfold in our lives which become our challenges and our opportunities. We sometimes allow ourselves to get lost during the challenges and become entangled in the difficulties they present. When we stay focused on doing God's work and seeking His will, we find the solutions for the challenges to be easier to find. God will give us strength through His mighty power to win our battles while we go through each day. Ephesians 6:10 speaks to this as it says, *"Finally, my brethren, be strong in the Lord, and the power of His might."* As we stand strong in the Lord, we know He will deliver us. Our confidence in knowing God our Father will deliver us from all the snares of life should be absolute. When we understand that, we have victory in our heart and soul daily.

If you are born again in the Spirit of God and have the faith walk with Jesus Christ as your savior, you will live a life of victory and will overcome the forces of this world. First John 5:4 assures us of this when it says, *"For whatsoever is born of God overcometh the world; and this is the victory that overcometh the world, even our faith."* Living a life filled with faith, hope, and peace is victory in this world. The promise of life eternal with God our Father is the great reward of the faith we hold onto tightly in our lives. We are to give God thanks for the victories He gives to us each day, for our source of power to overcome is from Him. First Corinthians 15:57 tells us, *"But thanks be to God! which giveth us the victory through our Lord Jesus Christ."*

When Jesus Christ died on the cross and was resurrected from the grave, we were given victory over sin and death. There is nothing we face which can defeat us. First Corinthians 15:55 proclaims: *"Where, O death, where is thy sting? Where, O grave, where is thy victory?"* Live a life filled with victory on this day!

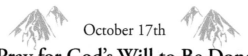

October 17th

Pray for God's Will to Be Done

When Jesus faced the final moments of His life, and He knew the persecution, pain, suffering, and death He was about to face, He went into the Garden of Gethsemane with His disciples to pray. As He prayed, He asked God to let the cup pass from Him if it were possible. He then added in His prayer to God that He wanted God's will to be done. Matthew 26:37–39 describes these moments:

> *And He took with Him Peter and the two sons of Zebedee, and began to be sorrowful and very heavy. Then saith He unto them, 'My soul is exceedingly sorrowful, even unto death; tarry ye here and watch with me. And He went a little further, and He fell on His face and prayed, saying, O Father, if it be possible, let this cup pass from me, nevertheless, not as I will, but as thou wilt.*

The power in this moment and in this prayer is Jesus continues to seek God's will while knowing all that was about to happen in His life.

When we face our moments of sorrow, we cannot fully understand that which will await us on the other side of those events as they unfold. Our true surrender to God will allow us to ask simply for His will to be done in our lives as we face these times. In the Lord's prayer, Jesus taught us to always ask God for His will to be done. Matthew 6:9–10 says, *"After this manner therefore pray ye: Our Father, which art in heaven, Hallowed be thy name. Thy kingdom come, thy will be done in earth as it is in heaven."* This prayer Jesus taught us is a simple one that calls for us to praise and worship our God and to seek His will. We will never have to face a moment such as the one Christ faced in the Garden of Gethsemane. However, each day of our lives, we live in a world that is filled with evil. Ephesians 5:15–17 teaches us: *"See then that ye walk circumspectly, not as fools, but as wise; Redeeming the time, because the days are evil. Wherefore be ye not unwise, but understanding what the will of the Lord is."*

Be Blessed as you prayerfully seek God's will for your life each day!

October 18th

The Eternal Moment of Today

We cannot change the experiences we had leading us to the time we are now in. The history of our lives is simply that. All the circumstances and events of our lives influenced our growth and development and provided us with the wisdom we now possess. We have become the people we are now because of having traveled on the road, which led us to this day. If we spend time dwelling on what we did wrong in our past, we are missing the renewal of the spirit God has for us this day. Second Corinthians 5:17 speaks to this: *"Therefore, if any man be in Christ, he is a new creature; old things are passed away; behold, all things are become new."* Embrace the new creature you have become in Christ on this day.

The future is not something we can control, but it is something we can prepare ourselves for in many ways. We prepare financially for the future by setting aside money today. We help build our health which can result in a higher quality of life by eating well and engaging in a meaningful exercise program today. We live in this moment we have been given today as a blessing of God. It is up to each of us to make the most of it. Matthew 6:34 teaches us this: *"Therefore, take no thought for the morrow: for the morrow will take thought for the things of itself. Sufficient unto the day is the evil thereof."* Jesus said these words and is telling us to focus our attention and energy on the things we need to do on this day. There will be more challenges and opportunities each day we face.

May we each renew our minds and seek God's will for our lives on this day as described in Romans 12:1–2:

> *I beseech you brethren, by the mercies of God, that ye present your bodies as a living sacrifice, holy, acceptable to God, which is your reasonable service. And that you be not conformed to this world, but transformed by the renewing of your mind, that you may prove what is that good, and acceptable, and perfect, will of God.*

Live today seeking God's will for your life, and His blessings will be great in your life as you do.

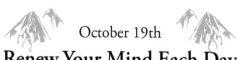

October 19th
Renew Your Mind Each Day

The journey of life is filled with many influences each day which come from all the things we face and do. Some are based on interactions with our family and Loved ones. Others come our way because of the career path we are engaged in or the school activities we face that day. All of these bring our focus to the whirlwind which surrounds us, which we call our life. During this collaboration of energy, we need to take some time each day for a renewal of our spirit and our mind. To pause and reflect and turn our attention to what God would have us dwell on will bring about a rejuvenation of the spirit and a refocus on that which is important. Ephesians 4:23 calls upon us to do this as it says, *"And be renewed in the spirit of your mind."* As we dwell on the things God would have us be tuned in to, we gain power and strength from our God each day.

The stresses of the outside world cannot control the spirit which lives inside of us. The Holy Spirit, which lives within us, is there to guide us and comfort us in all times of trouble or distress. Second Corinthians 4:16 tells us that nothing happening in the world around us should be able to overcome the inner man as it says, *"For which cause we faint not; but though our outward man perish, yet the inward man is renewed day by day."* How do we renew the inward man? It is by prayer and the reading of God's Word daily. The time spent with our Lord is the time we get to experience His renewal which brings us strength, wisdom, and understanding. Isaiah 40:31 says it best: *"But they that wait upon the Lord shall renew their strength; they shall mount up with wings as eagles; they shall run and not be weary; they shall walk, and not faint."* This renewal of our spirit and mind is needed for us to face the struggles that life can bring. We wait upon the Lord when we pray to Him and read and store His Word in our hearts each day.

Find the time today to be alone with God, and as you d,o He will renew your mind and spirit to face any and all challenges that life has to offer to you today!

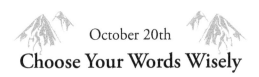

October 20th
Choose Your Words Wisely

There are many times we find ourselves in situations where some-one will say or do something, which causes us to respond in a way that is spoken in a moment of passion. Those words which we choose to unleash are often combative in nature or intended to correct the person to whom they are directed. We must question the source of the response to measure whether it is pride speaking through us or is it the manifestation of Love that dwells in our hearts? The significance of the words you speak is addressed by Jesus in Matthew 12:37 when He says this: *"For by thy words thou shalt be justified, and by thy words thou shalt be condemned."*

The words which come out of our mouths are either filled with Love or will cause divisions among us to those God gives us each day. If we are to be witnesses of our faith, we must be guarded in what we say. Often it is best to look past momentary transgressions of oth-ers and keep in perspective that we don't gain anything in truth by proving we are right. Solomon, in his wisdom, says this in Proverbs 17:9: *"He that covers a transgression seeks Love; but he that repeated a matter separates good friends."* Is making a correction with someone you Love and care for being done in the spirit of Love, or is it the ego that needs to rule over that person causing you to speak out in that moment? Solomon also added this guidance in Proverbs 26:20: *"Where no wood is, there the fire goes out: so where there is no talebearer, the strife ceases."* We can end strive and arguments and allow for Love to flow by simply not engaging in disagreements with others and refusing to prolong such discussions.

It only takes a few words to ignite a destructive fire in a relation-ship. James 3:5 teaches us this: *"Even so the tongue is a little member and boasts great things. Behold how great a matter a little fire kindleth!"* Refrain from igniting a hostile fire with words. Let Love flow through your words to all you meet today!

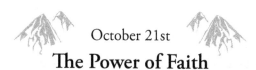

October 21st
The Power of Faith

Our faith in God the Father and in our Lord Jesus Christ is the key that unlocks the door to the kingdom of God for our lives. We have to develop our ability to grow our faith as we surrender to the power of God in our lives. Hebrews 11:1 tells us this about faith: *"Faith is the substance of things hoped for, the evidence of things not seen."* Embracing our faith is not relying on that which is seen, but to trust the unseen world in which God dwells in our lives. To place our trust in God and to know He is with us as we face the trials and tribulations of our lives is the door we must pass through to allow faith to grow.

Knowing faith is a critical piece to the relationship we have with God, we must find the path to establishing and growing our faith experience. Romans 10:17 teaches us: "So faith comes from hearing, and hearing through the word of Christ." The more often we read God's Word or listen to the teaching of those who are ministering to us about God's Word and sharing Christ's teaching, the more we will build our faith. Jesus said these words in Mark 11:22–23: *"And Jesus answered and saith unto them, 'Have faith in God. For verily I say unto you, That whosoever shall say unto this mountain, Be thou removed, and be thou cast into the sea and shall not doubt in his heart, but shall believe that those things which he saith shall come to pass; he shall have whatsoever he saith. Therefore, I say unto you, What things soever ye desire, when ye pray, believe that ye receive them, and ye shall have them."*

Faith comes by transforming thoughts and prayers into beliefs. When you trust in God and ask Him what you desire, He will receive that which is consistent with His will. Our faith grows as we learn from His word what His will for our lives will be. May our faith grow on this day and every day as we seek to find God's perfect will for our lives. Be Blessed as you do so.

October 22nd

Humility Comes Before Honor

The scriptures are filled with references to how God will exalt the humble and tell us the meek will inherit the earth (Matthew 5:5). The ego is always looking for an opportunity to build itself up with pride and arrogance, but it works against us in spiritual growth and well-being. Proverbs 18:12 cautions us with this: *"Before destruction the heart of man is haughty; and before honor is humility."* When things are going well for us, and we are accomplishing much due to the gifts and blessings of God, we should always give Him the glory and honor for all He has done in our lives. Micah 6:8 tells us, *"He hath showed thee of man what is good; and what doth the Lord require of thee? But to do justly, and to Love mercy, and to walk humbly with thy God."* God guides us to do that which is right, and He blesses us as we do so.

As we follow our path as humble servants of the Lord God, he will direct our paths and exalt us in His time. First Peter 5:6 tells us in these words: *"Humble yourselves therefore under the mighty hand of God, that He may exalt you in due time."* Our mighty God will choose His time in which we are exalted in our lives. Solomon speaks of this also in Proverbs 22:4, which says, *"By humility and fear of the Lord are riches, and honor, and life."* That which we seek to find as blessings from God our Father comes to us when we walk humbly with fear for the Lord. The things we can achieve are the result of following His path and doing that which we are called to do in His will.

Let us continue to give glory to God for all He has done for us in our lives. When we are being recognized for our earthly achievements, may we pause to give thanks and honor to God in those moments for all to hear. Philippians 4:20 tells us, *"Now unto God and our Father be glory for ever and ever."* On this and every day, we thank God from whom all blessings come, and to Him be the glory forever!

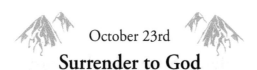

October 23rd
Surrender to God

The idea of living a life that is in total surrender to God sounds great and is something we should all aspire to achieve. The difficulty we face in this spirit of surrender to the Almighty who created us is the mind, and the ego tells us regularly that we've got this and don't need any help. As we embrace that mindset, we tend to be less humble and more ego–driven and turn more to our own initiative and less to submitting our hearts and lives to the will of God. There is no question that God wants us to humbly approach Him will all things and to seek His will in all that we do. Jeremiah 10:23 teaches us this: *"O Lord, I know that the way of man is not in himself; it is not in man who walketh to direct his steps."* If we can embrace this mindset, we find that living in our submission to our Lord allows us to find His path each day rather than our own.

We all must learn the value of trusting in our God to direct us in our lives. That sounds simple enough, and in theory, we have no problem accepting this in our hearts. The human mind and heart long for control which makes it difficult to accept that we are yielding that control to our God in all we do. He has promised us to direct our steps when we have such trust in Proverbs 3:5–6, which tells us this: *"Trust in the Lord with all thine heart and lean not unto thine own understanding. In all thy ways acknowledge Him, and He will direct thy paths."* We often ask God to give us His strength and guidance when we are in troubled times. It is important to understand we are to seek His way and ask for His guidance when times are filled with success and prosperity as well.

Being submissive to God does not make you weak. Rather, it is a source of strength and boldness in our lives when we yield to His holy presence and direction. The more you yield to the Holy Spirit of God and allow it to be in control of your destiny, the more you grow in power, Love, and self-discipline (2 Timothy 1:7). May we surrender to the Spirit of God and seek His guidance in all we do!

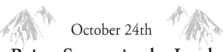

October 24th
Being Strong in the Lord

We are not designed by our God to be weak as we walk with Him each day. Rather, it is God's plan for each of us to be strong and to draw our strength from Him every day to help us fight the battles we face. When we are directed to be humble and meek, it is not a sign of weakness or inability but evidence that we give the glory and honor to our God, who delivers the strength and ability for us in all we do. Psalm 29:11 tells us this: *"The Lord will give strength unto His people; the Lord will bless His people with peace."* Knowing God is our source of strength should give us each great comfort. He is mighty with His power, and there is nothing that can come against Him and win. This mighty power He gives to those who believe in Him and His son Jesus Christ.

We are reassured of God's willingness to give us strength throughout the scriptures. Isaiah 40:29 says it this way: *"He giveth power to the faint; and to them who have no might, He increases strength."* We are never at a loss to overcome that which we face with God at our side. He is there as a source of strength, and His mighty power will rule in any situation. One of the greatest scriptures in teaching us this is found in Philippians 4:13, which speaks boldly as it says, *"I can do all things through Christ which strengtheneth me."* We should walk fearlessly and boldly with this attitude as we face the challenges which come our way each day.

We are taught to seek the Lord and His strength continually. As we do, He is quick to deliver His mighty strength to us. As He does so, we should sing His praises to all to let it be known that our strength comes from the God we serve. Ephesians 6:10 tells us to be strong in the Lord always: *"Finally, my brethren, be strong in the Lord, and in the power of His might."* We have this amazing power God intends for us to draw from each day. Be bold in approaching Him for strength when you need it. He is faithful to deliver it to you.

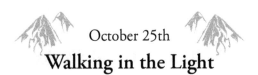

October 25th
Walking in the Light

The Bible makes many references to the importance of the Christian believer being the "Light of the World." Jesus told His followers that He is the light of the world, and those who follow Him would be so as well. In John 8:12, He said this: *"Then spake Jesus again to them, saying, 'I am the light of the world; he that followeth me shall not walk in darkness, but shall have the light of life.'"* Jesus tells us that we who are following His path and who are embracing His teachings possess the light of life. This means we possess the truth of His Word and have the capacity to light up the world around us with this truth which brings life to the world which is lost.

If we walk in His light and are saved by our faith, does this mean we will no longer have moments in which we sin? That is not what the word of God tells us. We have all sinned and come short of God's glory. If we repent of our sins, God is faithful and just to forgive us of our sins. First John 1:7–9 speaks to this:

> *But if we walk in the light, as He is in the light, we have fellowship with one another, and the blood of Jesus Christ His Son cleanest us from all sin. If we say we have no sin, we deceive ourselves, and the truth is not in us. If we confess our sins, He is faithful and just to forgive us our sins, and to cleanse us from all unrighteousness.*

What a beautiful promise of God that He will forgive us when we repent and confess our sins before Him. We are not sinless but forgiven. As we confess our sins, He will cleanse us from all unrighteousness through His Love!

We are here to let our light shine to bring illumination to the world in which we live each day. Jesus spoke to us as His followers and directed us to do so in Matthew 5:16, which tells us, *"Let your light shine before men, that they may see your good works, and glorify your Father which is in heaven."* When we walk in the light, we do the works of God, which is good, and bring His message of truth to those He gives us on our path each day. Let your light shine before all on this day!

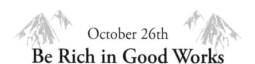

October 26th
Be Rich in Good Works

We all strive for a measure of excellence in life, and we often measure the success of a man by the things he has achieved. We consider those who live in fine homes and who drive the finest cars as being successful people in this world. It is easy to want to emulate them in our own lives as we work to provide what is best for our families and for ourselves. The scriptures caution us not to take pride in the uncertain riches of this world but rather to be invested in being 'rich' in good works. First Timothy 6:17–19 speaks to this:

> *Charge them that are rich in this world, that they not be high minded, nor trust in uncertain riches, but in the living God, who giveth us richly all things to enjoy; That they do good, that they be rich in good works, ready to distribute, willing to communicate; Laying up in store for themselves a good foundation against the time to come, that they may lay hold on eternal life.*

The riches of this world are only temporary, but the good works we do each day will establish the foundation for eternal life.

We are taught in the scriptures that having faith without doing that which is good is dead and not true faith. James 2:14–17 spells it out this way:

> *What doth it profit, my brethren, though a man say he hath faith, and have not works? Can faith save him? If a brother or sister be naked, and destitute of daily food, And one of you say unto them, Depart in peace, be ye warmed and filled; notwithstanding, ye give them not those things which are needful to the body; what doth it profit? Even so, faith, if it hath not works, is dead, being alone.*

It is easy to say that 'I believe in something,' but the scriptures tell us to take the faith and do that which is good to support the faith to give it life inside you.

The scriptures tell us we were created by God to do good works in Ephesians 2:10, as it says, *"For we are His workmanship, created in Christ Jesus unto good works, which God hath before ordained that we should walk in them."* Be rich in the good works that God has called you to do on this day!

October 27th
Overcome Evil with Good

If you turn on the evening news, you quickly see stories of the evil that is in the world today. It has always been with us and will be in this world until the return of Jesus Christ. While it exists in the world, we can overcome the evil that surrounds us and have victory over it in our lives. The scriptures assure us of this victory and know our victory is in Christ, who won the battle on the cross and through His resurrection. John 16:33 tells us to have peace in knowing of this victory as it says, *"These things I have spoken to you, that in me ye might have peace. In the world, ye shall have tribulation: but be of good cheer; I have overcome the world."* This verse tells us we will have tribulation in the world. It also gives us encouragement and tells us to be of good cheer, for in Christ, we can have peace, for He has overcome the world.

We fight our battles with Jesus Christ and the Holy Spirit inside us. The war is between the forces of good versus the forces of evil, which are at work in this world. When we are at work doing that which is good that God places on our path each day, we give light and Love to the world, which defeats evil. Romans 12:21 encourages us in the fight by saying: *"Be not overcome of evil but overcome evil with good."* The evil one wants you to question your faith, but God gives us victory over the evil one through our faith. First John 5:4–5 tells us how faith in Jesus gives us this victory: *"For whatsoever is born of God overcomes the world: and this is the victory that overcomes the world, even our faith. Who is he that overcomes the world, but he that believes that Jesus is the Son of God?"* That is our faith, and therein lies our victory over the world.

This victory over evil has a promise from Jesus to sit on the throne with Him. Revelation 3:21 says, *"To him that overcomes will I grant to sit with me on my throne, even as I also overcame, and am set down with the Father on His throne."* May you overcome the evil one with your faith and claim your victory!

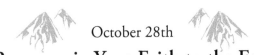

October 28th
Persevere in Your Faith to the End

None of us knows how long the journey of our lives will be. For some, the path is shorter than that of others. It is in God's plan and His hands how long we are placed upon this earth. Our purpose is fulfilled when He has decided to end our time here. It is not our final resting place but rather a time and place we are simply passing through on our spiritual journey to a destiny with God our Father in our heavenly home, which is coming soon. While we journey here, there will be temptations and trials we will face continually. James 1:12 teaches us this: *"Blessed is the man that endureth temptation: for when he is tried, he shall receive the crown of life, which the Lord has promised to them that Love Him."* These temptations and trials are temporary, and we will overcome them if we keep our eyes on God and stay on the path that He has chosen for us.

In Matthew 14:22–33, the scriptures tell of the time Jesus walked on the water, and Peter asked for Jesus to let him walk on the water to Him. When he stepped out of the boat and began to walk to Jesus, he lost sight of the Lord and began to see the wind and the turbulence around him. As he did so, he began to sink. Jesus reached out and touched him, and together, they walked back to the boat. Our lives are like this. When we lose sight of Jesus and our Heavenly Father and see only the turbulence that surrounds us, we begin to sink spiritually, and our faith wavers. First Chronicles 16:11 tells us, *"Seek the Lord and His strength, seek His face continually."* When our hearts and minds are actively seeking God and His will for our lives, we can do anything through our faith. When we lose sight of God and His plan for our lives, we sink into the sea which surrounds us.

It is our faith that will allow us to endure all that this world has to challenge us with, and through God, we can overcome it all. In doing so, Matthew 24:3 gives us this promise: *"But he that shall endure to the end, the same shall be saved."* May we persevere in our faith to the end of our journey!

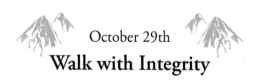

October 29th
Walk with Integrity

When we engage with others in our lifetime, we leave an imprint on the lives of those we meet and interact with in life and in our business dealings. As a man of God, our dealings with others must be done with the highest levels of integrity maintained. We are a witness of our faith as we demonstrate to the world around us what a life in Christ is supposed to be. Absolute integrity means being truthful always and giving all that is fair and just in everything we do and say. Proverbs 20:7 says this: *"The just man walketh in his integrity; his children are blessed after him."* The scriptures tell us we are surrounded by a cloud of witnesses, and our children and others observe us as we deal with others in our lives. If we conduct ourselves with high integrity, our children will learn to do the same in their lives.

Your integrity is a treasure in your life that goes beyond the material gains and things we can acquire in this world. The character and reputation of a man are far greater than the riches one can gather. Proverbs 28:6 teaches us this: *"Better is the poor that walketh in his uprightness, than he that is perverse in his ways, though he be rich."* We are taught many lessons in the scriptures on being open and honest with our words and actions in our lives. We cannot compromise on the truth. Proverbs 12:22 tells us, *"Lying lips are an abomination to the Lord; but they that deal truly are a delight."* May we always strive to be a delight to the Lord God we serve each day.

We strive to live a life of honesty and integrity for all around us to see. In doing so, we are in the will of God our Father. Pray each day for one another to live in such a way. Hebrews 13:8 speaks to this: *"Pray for us; for we trust we have a good conscience, in all things willing to live honestly."* May the lives we live and the desires of our heart be filled with honesty and integrity in all we do today and always. God will continue to Bless our lives as we do!

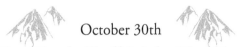

October 30th

The Truth Shall Make You Free

The scriptures often refer to the "truth" and tell us how God's Word is the truth. We know from lips of Jesus Himself; He described His life as the way, the truth, and the life in John 14:6, which clearly says, *"Jesus saith unto him, 'I am the way, the truth, and the life; no man cometh to the Father, but by me."* The only access we have to God our Heavenly Father is through faith in Jesus. Therefore, the foundation of all we believe in this spiritual walk is built on our faith in Jesus as the Son of God. He is the truth, and through Him, we are set free from sin. John 8:32 teaches us: *"And ye shall know the truth, and the truth shall make you free."* This is the freedom that sets your soul free from all the cares of this world.

The deeper we dig into God's holy scriptures as the Word of God, the more we can see the truth of His message to us. The deeper we walk in His Word, the closer to God we can become as one with Him in our spiritual walk. Second Timothy 2:15 tells us, *"Study to show thyself approved unto God, a workman that needeth not to be ashamed, rightly dividing the word of truth."* Knowing the Bible intimately plants the seeds in your heart from which the truth will enlighten your heart and soul. The more we become immersed in His Word, the more we are made perfect in His will for our lives. Second Timothy 3:16–17 speaks to this: *"All scripture is given by inspiration of God, and is profitable for doctrine, for reproof, for correction, for instruction in righteousness. That the man of God may be perfect, thoroughly furnished unto all good works."* The deeper we travel into the depths of His Word, the greater our understanding of living the life of righteousness which is pleasing to God, can be.

Let us walk freely in the light of His message and truth. John 4:24 says this: *"God is a spirit; and they that worship Him must worship Him in spirit and in truth."* May His truth fill our hearts and souls each day as we worship our Father. Be Blessed as you do so on this day!

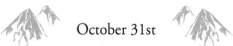

October 31st
Discern Between the Good and Bad

Each day our hearts and minds are presented with opportunities to act upon situations that will alter the path on which we travel. There will be those situations where we are enticed to go in a direction that appears to lead us to greater prosperity and a life filled with the pleasures of this world. God truly wants us to prosper but not at the cost of our righteousness. We need to continually seek His will in these moments when such decisions arise. We have the Holy Spirit alive in our souls to help us with the power of discernment to sort through these times. It is up to each of us to earnestly seek God's will and to open our hearts to the Spirit to guide us.

When we seek God and ask Him to give us the wisdom to understand what is best for our lives, we are taught that He will give this to us. James 1:5 says it plainly: *"If any of you lack wisdom, let him ask of God, that giveth to all men liberally, and upbraideth not; and it shall be given to him."* God is not going to withhold that which you need or that which you seek. He is there to strengthen you in all these ways. We seek God's knowledge on how to proceed in our life. Proverbs 2:1–5 tells us this:

> *My son, if thou wilt receive my words, and hide my commandments with thee; So that thou incline thine ear to wisdom, and apply thine heart to understanding; Yea, if thou cry after knowledge, and lift up thy voice for understanding; If thou seek her as silver, and search for her as hidden treasures; Then shalt thou understand the fear of the Lord, and find the knowledge of God.*

When we earnestly seek the knowledge of God with all our hearts, we will find it and be able to follow the path to what is His will.

When we let Love be our guide in all we decide to do, we follow the direction Christ gave us. Philippians 1:9–10 says,

> *And this I pray, that your Love may abound yet more and more in knowledge and in all judgement; That you may approve all things that are excellent.*

Love will guide us to God's will.

November 1st

The Holy Spirit Brings You Life and Power

The energy we seek each day to bring us to the place God would have us to be coming from His Holy Spirit and will deliver us the power we need to carry on living according to His will for us. There are times when we feel exhausted and unable to generate the power needed to accomplish what we have in front of us for that day. Spend time in meditation and prayer and seek God's Holy Spirit to engulf you, and all the needed energy will appear in your heart and soul. Psalm 27:14 says, *"Wait on the Lord; be of good courage, and He shall strengthen your heart: wait, I say, on the Lord."* Sometimes we lack the patience needed to restore our souls for the fight we may face. God has it all under control, and He is able to deliver us in His timing as we go through each day.

Our own ability to muster the energy needed at times may fall short. When the Spirit of God comes upon you, there is no limit to what you can achieve. John 6:33 teaches us this: *"It is the Spirit that quickeneth; the flesh profiteth nothing; the words that I speak unto you, they are spirit, and they are life."* We want that Spirit of God to energize our lives to bring us to full capacity and strength. Then our human weakness is overcome with the great power of God, which allows us to accomplish all we need as He directs our paths. God guides our thoughts as well as He enlivens us with His Spirit as described in Proverbs 16:3: *"Commit thy works unto the Lord, and thy thoughts shall be established."* We have to want this and be committed to the Lord, and he will be with us and direct our thoughts and actions to do that which He has for us to do.

Let us serve our God in the business we have before us each day. God has put us each in a place to be of service and minister to those He has given us on our path. Romans 12:11 tells us this: *"Not slothful in business; fervent in Spirit, serving the Lord."* Be fully invested in what you are called to do in service to God. God will empower you with His Holy Spirit to do all He has for you to do this day!

November 2nd
Why Are People Drawn to Evil?

The spiritual battle between Good and Evil is taking place in the hearts and minds of all people. It is ongoing and will take place again today and each day on this earth. We find so many people drawn into the snares created by the evil one to steal their souls, just like a moth is drawn into the flame, which will ultimately destroy it. We wonder why it is so common to witness this all around us. The evil one entices humans with lust for flesh, money, and power. He appeals to egos and fills hearts with desires for things which turn hearts away from that which is of God. He instills hatred where the heart should be filled with Love and blinds the eyes of many people with prejudice and fear. The scriptures teach us in 1 John 5:19 that evil rules this world: *"And we know that we are of God, and the whole world lieth in wickedness."*

As we are surrounded by wickedness and evil, we face the forces of evil spiritually each day in the world in which we walk. We see things and people around us which ignite passions and thoughts which are impure, but the source of those thoughts comes from the evil one working inside us. Mark 7:21–22 teaches us: *"For from within, out of the heart of men, proceed evil thoughts, adulteries, fornications, murders, thefts, covetousness, wickedness, deceit, lasciviousness, an evil eye, blasphemy, pride, foolishness."* All these evil thoughts come from within a man's heart placed there by the evil one. This happens when we allow darkness to reside within our soul. Romans 6:12 cautions us: *"Let not sin therefore reign in your mortal body, that ye should obey it in the lusts thereof."* When you turn your heart over to God, you want to do that which is good in your life. As we do so, we replace all evil thoughts with Love, and the light of Love chases away the darkness of evil.

As children of God, we bring our Love and light into the world, and evil will flee from us. The battle lines are drawn. May God rule in our hearts always!

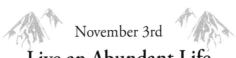

November 3rd
Live an Abundant Life

As a believer in God and His Son Jesus Christ, we are given His mighty power to live a life filled with His grace and Love. As He walks with us, there is nothing in the world that can conquer or defeat us. There is a confidence that we possess when we walk with God and His Holy Spirit in our lives. Mark 9:23 tells us these words from Jesus: *"Jesus saith unto him, 'If thou canst believe, all things are possible to him that believeth."* When we walk in faith with God, we have no limits on what we can and will do in our lives. The enemy of our soul wants to limit us in all ways and is called a thief in John 10:10, which says, *"The thief cometh not but to steal, and to kill, and to destroy: I am come that they may have life, and that they may have it more abundantly."* Jesus spoke these words to let us know that as we walk with Him, our lives will be lived to the fullest measure of what they should be.

The evil one will whisper in our ears and try to limit us on what we can accomplish in our lives. Let us not be dismayed by such thoughts but rather turn to the positive energy God gives us in Philippians 4:13, which clearly states: *"I can do all things through Christ which strengtheneth me."* Don't let thoughts of your limits crowd your mind with negativity. Rather, turn your thoughts to seeking the will of the Father who can guide you to the path He has chosen for you and know you can do all things He has chosen for you to do. As we take our delight from the Lord, He promises to give us the desires of our heart. Psalm 37:4 tells us this: *"Delight thyself also in the Lord; and He shall give thee the desires of thy heart."*

God wants us to experience life to the fullest. His plans for us are that we find power and Love in His Word and His presence in our lives. Second Timothy 1:7 tells us, *"For God hath not given us a spirit of fear; but of power, and of Love, and of a sound mind."* We live a life of victory in all we do with this spirit inside us.

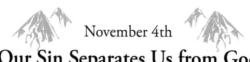

November 4th

Our Sin Separates Us from God

If we truly believe in God and His Son Jesus Christ, our hearts and minds are drawn to Him, and we will have the desire in our hearts to please Him and to grow ever closer to Him each day. The separation one feels from God is the direct result of the sin in our lives that causes it. Isaiah 59:1–2 teaches us this: *"Behold, the Lord's hand is not shortened, that it cannot save; neither His ear heavy, that it cannot hear: But your iniquities have separated between you and your God, and your sins have hid His face from you, that He will not hear."* When we walk through this world living a life filled with sin, we cannot grow close to the God we seek to serve. His light does not dwell in the presence of darkness.

God waits for us to call upon His name and to seek forgiveness for the sins we have committed. First John 1:9 tells us how easy it is to receive redemption from God for our sins: *"If we confess our sins, He is faithful and just to forgive us our sins, and to cleanse us from all unrighteousness."* The willful act of asking for forgiveness is our responsibility if we are seeking a life filled with God's presence. He will forgive those who are lost. Jesus describes this act of redemption as being "born again." John 3:3 tells us this: *"Jesus said unto him, 'Verily, verily, I say unto thee, except a man be born again, he cannot see the kingdom of God.'"* When we are born again, we seek to live our lives without sin and be closer to God.

Christ died for our sins to give us the opportunity to be closer to God. First Peter 3:8 speaks to this: *"For Christ hath once suffered for our sins, the just for the unjust, that He might brings us to God, being put to death in the flesh, but quickened in the Spirit."* The price for our sins has been paid. God waits for us to seek His forgiveness which He will freely give to all who seek Him. Living each day close to God opens the door to joy unspeakable in His presence. Turn away from the sins of this world and toward the eternal blessing of God the Father on this and every day! Be Blessed as you do so!

November 5th

Don't Harbor Unforgiveness

We want to have God's forgiveness of all our own transgressions. The scripture is very clear that we must also forgive others who have done things we feel were wrong toward us. This spirit of forgiveness is one that is taught to us throughout the scriptures and is required by God for us to receive forgiveness from Him. When we fail to forgive another person, it is a spirit of darkness that can live inside of our hearts and minds where Love should reside. Matthew 18:35 clearly makes this point: *"My heavenly Father will also do the same to you, if each of you does not forgive your brother from the heart."* Don't allow this negative thought or energy to separate you from a brother or sister. As it does so, it causes you to be separated from God as well.

If someone continues to do things that you feel are sins against you, our Lord teaches us to continue to forgive them. Luke 17:4 says this: *"And if he sins against you seven times a day, and he returns to you seven times and says, I repent. Forgive him."* To hold inside of us resentment toward another only poisons our own soul. Turn loose of it and be free from it. Replace resentment with Love, and your soul will prosper as a result. Daniel 9:9 says this: *"To the Lord our God belong compassion and forgiveness, for we have rebelled against Him."* May we turn from any rebellion we might have in our hearts and turn toward compassion and forgiveness for all people in our lives. The power that comes from such a choice is immeasurable.

The conflicts which come along between those we meet in this world are only temporary battles brought to us by the evil one who seeks to destroy us. Ephesians 4:32 guides us on how to best act: *"Be kind to one another, tender-hearted, forgiving each other, just as God in Christ has forgiven you."* As we embrace this spirit, such conflicts disappear, and the light of Love illuminates our path and flows through into the lives of those we meet on our journey.

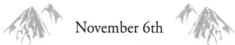

November 6th

He Forgives Our Sins and Frees Us from Guilt

God is merciful and will forgive us of our sins as we confess them before Him and ask Him for forgiveness. Our sins are washed away in the blood of Jesus Christ, who died on the cross for the sins of the world. Our human nature will allow guilt to creep into our hearts and minds to make us feel unclean for sins of the past. This is the work of the evil one who is always trying to separate us from God our Father. Once you have been forgiven, the sins of the past have been taken away by the Father. Psalm 32:5 teaches us this: *"I acknowledged my sin unto thee, and I have not hid my iniquity. I said, I will confess (against myself) my rebellions unto the Lord, and thou shalt forgive the iniquities of my sin."* Once we have confessed our sins, He is faithful and just to forgive them as the scriptures tell us often.

The work of the evil one is to try and make us feel unworthy of the relationship we have with our God. The gift of God of eternal life is not one which we have earned by our works but rather one which is given to us because of our faith in Jesus Christ as the Son of God. Romans 8:1 tells us, *"There is therefore no condemnation to them which are in Christ Jesus, who walk not after the flesh, but after the Spirit."* Once you turn your heart and life over to Jesus Christ and become one of His followers, you are no longer condemned by the sins of this world. Don't let your heart condemn you as a child of God who has been forgiven. First John 3:19–20 says this: *"And hereby we know we are of the truth and shall assure our hearts before Him. For if our heart condemns us, God is greater than our heart, and knoweth all things."*

God knows what goes on in our hearts. He knows when the evil one tries to separate us from the Love of God. Let your Spirit and heart be free from guilt if you have confessed your sins before God. Psalm 103:12 promises this: *"As far as the east is from the west, so far hath He removed our transgressions from us."*

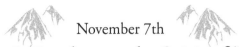

November 7th

There Is Freedom in the Spirit of Truth

One of the greatest things about living in our country is the freedoms we get to enjoy. We have the freedom of speech and the freedom to choose who we are and what we believe. Our blessings of such freedom came with the price of men who gave their lives for our right to enjoy such freedom. In the spiritual world, we have been given freedom that goes beyond the freedoms granted by any country in the world. This freedom comes from the God we serve through the Spirit. Jesus gave us this freedom when He gave His life for our sins, and the bondage of sin was taken away from us on the cross. Galatians 5:1 speaks to this as it says, *"Stand fast therefore in the liberty wherewith Christ hath made us free and be not entangled with the yoke of bondage."* This bondage describes a life of sin that ensnares your heart and soul in the devil's grip.

This freedom allows us to live a life of serving others for Christ. We get to choose how to provide such support and service in the Spirit. God will direct our paths as we seek His will for our lives. First Peter 2:16 speaks to this freedom as it says, *"As free, and not using your liberty as a cloke of maliciousness, but as the servants of God."* The more of our lives we give in service to our God, the more we gain from the sense of purpose that life offers us. Our God rewards us in all ways as we live such a life. Romans 6:22 describes this freedom this way: *"But now being made free from sin, and become servants to God, ye have your fruit unto holiness, and the end everlasting life."* To receive holiness, which leads us to everlasting life, is truly a wonderful gift that results from our freedom from sin.

The freedom of the Spirit is freedom from sin. The world around us is filled with sin and evil. We find this freedom when we find Jesus Christ to be the master of our lives. When you discover this truth of Jesus, you are free indeed. John 8:32 says it plainly: *"And ye shall know the truth, and the truth shall make you free."* Live freely and share the truth of Jesus with all you meet on the path today.

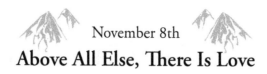

November 8th

Above All Else, There Is Love

When we strive to find the perfect will of God for our lives, our search always brings us back to the basic commandments which were given to us by our Lord and Savior Jesus Christ in Mark 12:30–31, which says,

> *And thou shall Love the Lord your God with all your heart, and with all thy soul, and with all thy mind, and with all thy strength: this is the first commandment. And the second is like, namely this; Thy shall Love thy neighbor as thyself. There is none other commandment greater than these.*

Jesus built the foundation of our faith and then directed us to build our lives on these two commandments. As we do so, the will of our Father is attained in our lives.

Love takes many forms in our lives. The Love of our God is the first one we should pursue, which restores our soul to a place where all else can be developed in human relationships fully. The Love for our chosen one with whom God blesses our hearts and lives to spend our time on this earth's journey would be the most significant Love in our lives after our Love for our God. In Genesis 2:24, the scriptures describe the relationship with one's spouse as that they become one flesh: *"Therefore a man shall leave his father and mother and hold fast to his wife, and they shall become one flesh."* We are called to Love and protect one another in such relationships always. It is an amazing blessing to find a spouse who shares your Love and your faith as you journey in this world.

When you experience Love for your fellow man and woman who journey in this world alongside you, the Holy Spirit of God lives in you. First John 4:16 speaks to this clearly: *"So we have come to know and to believe the Love God has for us. God is Love, and whoever abides in Love abides in God, and God abides in him."* There is nothing we can do in our lives that is more significant in doing the will of our Father than to Love all of those he brings to our path. May God enrich your heart and life with an outpouring of Love for all you meet on this day!

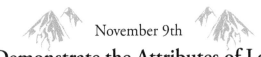

November 9th

Demonstrate the Attributes of Love

When we talk about Loving one another, it should be in our hearts to take this Love and turn it into actions as we have interactions with those God has given to us each day. What are some of the attributes of Love in these experiences we have with each other? The scriptures often refer to Love and how we conduct ourselves as we express it freely. One of the key factors about Love is how we can look past another's imperfections and shortcomings when we have Love in our hearts. First Peter 4:8 (ESV) describes this when it says, *"Above all, keep Loving one another earnestly, since Love covers a multitude of sins."* When we talk about the shortcomings or weaknesses demonstrated by another, we are focusing on their sins rather than looking past them. We know we are all sinners saved by grace. We need to Love others who may have sinned against us or someone else in their lives but need our Loving kindness to help them learn from those sins.

When we are abiding in the Spirit of Love, we are tender-hearted and kind to one another, and we demonstrate humility in the way we approach each other. Our prideful moments are not the times when Love flows through our hearts as it should. Ephesians 4:2 (ESV) reminds us of this: *"With all humility and gentleness, with patience, bearing with one another in Love."* The evil one tries to push our ego into the middle of moments of disagreement with others in our lives to steal away these attributes and replace them with a vigorous desire to be the one who is right in an argument that only carries us away from the Spirit of Love. Prevailing over another is not Loving that person; rather, it is a snare of the enemy. Colossians 3:14 (ESV) says this about Love: *"And above all these put on Love, which binds everything together in perfect harmony."*

As we Love one another on our journey, may the attributes of Love keep us humble, gentle, patient, and kind with all the people God puts on our path today.

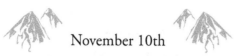

We Determine the Direction We Take Each Day

When I was young, and we went as a family on a trip, we would take with us a paper map, and often, we had been to AAA to have them route one for us to our destination. It would be highlighted in yellow as to what roads we would take along the way. That mapping system gave way to programs such as MapQuest, which would do that on the computer, allowing us to plot our own route with a similar paper map and write out directions on which way we were to travel. Today each car has such a mapping system in it and will audibly tell you when a turn is upcoming, and all personal cell phones do the same with GPS systems that adjust to traffic congestion that may lie ahead on our route. These systems even now tell us of police activity ahead to caution those who might be speeding along the way.

The journey of the Spirit each day is taking each of us in a direction as well. We choose the path on which we are traveling in our hearts and souls with the freedom God allows each person to enjoy as they live out their lives. At the end of each day, and with each moment that passes, we are either moving closer to God or further from him with the road we choose to take. Proverbs 4:18 says this about the path on which we travel: *"But the path of the righteous is like the light of dawn, that shines brighter and brighter until the full day."* Is the path on which you are traveling today shining brighter as you go along? If not, we can see what we are doing to take us away from the light of Christ, which shines brightly in our hearts when we turn toward Him.

Every day of our lives, we have a choice to make. We either turn our Spiritual journey to taking us closer to God, or we allow our Spirit to drift further away. We control the steering mechanism that directs our path. In Matthew 7:14, Jesus teaches: *"For the gate is small and narrow is the way that leads to life, and there are few who find it."* Let us steer our course in this narrow way always.

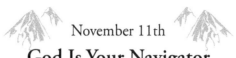

November 11th

God Is Your Navigator

When we travel, and we depend on our GPS to steer us to our course and to direct us on our journey, a voice will prepare us for the turns as they are upcoming. As you immerse yourself in the word of God and spend your time in prayer daily, you are growing closer to Him and will find He is there to guide you through life's journey. The road ahead is often filled with uncertainty, and we need to know which direction to choose as we approach the intersections of life. If you are seeking God's will and His guidance and then listen for His small voice to help you understand what is best, He will speak to your soul and direct your path. Isaiah 30:21 speaks to this: *"And thy ears shall hear a word behind thee, saying, This is the way, walk ye in it, when ye turn to the right hand, and when ye turn to the left."* The voice is there for us. Are we listening to it?

God is the light that illuminates our path and is the guide who will instruct us on the way to go when we are attuned to His Holy Spirit. We seek God's way through reading His Holy Word and praying for Him to guide us each day. That will open our hearts to receive His guidance and to hear His Words when He speaks to us. Luke 1:78–79 talks to us of God's guidance and His light which illuminates our way as it says,

> *Through the tender mercy of our God, the dayspring from on high hath visited us. To give light to them that sit in darkness and in the shadow of death, to guide our feet into the way of peace.*

The path of the righteous will lead us to peace and eternal life. That is the direction God intends for us to travel, and He will guide us to this path if we allow Him to do so.

We should all want to be on the path that God has chosen for each of our lives. If we seek His will and ask for His guidance, we will be shown the path we should follow each day. Psalm 25:4–5 says, *"Show me thy ways, O Lord, teach me thy paths."* This is the prayer we should have on our lips as we seek the will of God for each day of our lives. When we earnestly seek His way, we will find it.

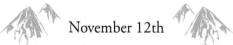

November 12th

We Have Seen the Dawning of the Light

Light symbolizes the radiance of God in the scriptures. It is also a symbol of our faith and righteousness as we walk toward God on our journey in this world. The closer to God's path we travel, the more the light of His holiness will shine through our lives each day. Prior to our discovery of Jesus Christ and His message, we lived in a land of darkness in our souls. Matthew 4:16 describes it this way: *"The people which sat in darkness, saw a great light; and to them which sat in the region and shadow of death, light is sprung up."* The dawning of a new age came when Christ appeared on the earth. The light of life moves in where there was only darkness as the dawning of a new world.

While Jesus walked on this earth and ministered to the people He met along the way, He often spoke of Himself as being the light of the world. His illustration of this light was to demonstrate the darkness of the evil one, which was keeping the world separated from God our Father. In John 8:12, Jesus told the people: *"Then Jesus spoke unto them saying, 'I am the light of the world; he that followeth me shall not walk in darkness but shall have the light of life."* When you walk in darkness, you cannot find the way to the truth. Jesus gave us His light to enable us to walk with His light inside our hearts to be able to bring light into this world through our own ministry as we share His truth with others. Matthew 5:16 says this: *"Let your light so shine before men, that they may see your good works, and glorify your Father which is in heaven."*

As we walk in a world filled with darkness, we bring a message of Jesus Christ in our hearts that illuminates our souls with the power of His light. The more we fill our hearts with His Word, the more we see where He leads us to go to walk in His light. Psalm 119:105 tells us, *"Thy word is a lamp unto my feet and a light unto my path."* May your light shine brightly on the path God has planned for you on this day. May your light shine before others and glorify God as you do.

November 13th

Patiently Waiting on the Lord

We live in a world of instant communications, gratification, and even our foods are designed around being delivered fast to our plates. When we reach out to others through our text messages and other forms of communication, we expect to be answered quickly and wonder what is wrong when the response comes slowly. Our attention span is quickly diminishing in the world around us as we live in a world of sound bites on the news of the world and don't want to wait for answers. We use Google or other search systems to immediately find out the answers we seek to questions that enter our minds. The days of looking up things in a word document or book such as a dictionary or encyclopedia have long since passed.

In such a world, we are exasperated when we have to wait for an answer or a response. We have become conditioned to expect that our timing is the only timing that truly matters. In the world in which we live spiritually, we are often asked to wait upon the Lord and submit to His timing on those things we ask for. This is not an easy thing for us to do. Second Thessalonians 3:5 tells us, *"And the Lord direct your hearts into the Love of God, and into the patient waiting for Christ."* The idea of being in a hurry for God or Christ to answer our prayer requests is not one that comes from God or Christ. It is our human nature to want it all now. God's timing is not our timing, but when we patiently wait upon Him, we find we will receive what He has promised to deliver. Hebrews 6:15 teaches us this: *"And so, after he had patiently endured, he obtained the promise."* Our efforts should not be to hurry things along but rather to seek God's will in all we do.

God hears our prayers and knows what is in our hearts. He understands what is best for us each day. Psalm 40:1 says, *"I waited patiently for the Lord; and He inclined unto me and heard my cry."* God is with us and wants to give us all we need. When we learn to wait upon the Lord, He will deliver what we need.

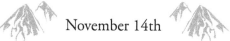

November 14th

Seek Wisdom and Understanding from the Lord

We have been taught that which we seek from the Lord is that which we will find. When Solomon was made king of Israel, he prayed to God for wisdom to be a just ruler of his people. This pleased God as he could have asked for riches, wealth, or personal honor but sought that which was of great value to God. Second Chronicles 1:11–12 tells of God's response to this prayer of Solomon:

And God said to Solomon, Because this was in thine heart, and thou hast not asked for riches, wealth, or honor, nor the life of thine enemies, neither yet hast asked long life; but hast asked for wisdom and knowledge for thyself, that thou mayest judge my people, over whom I have made thee king: Wisdom and knowledge is granted unto these; and I will give thee riches, and wealth, and honor, such as none of the kings have had that have been before thee, neither shall there any after thee have the like.

God clearly chose to reward Solomon for his unselfish desire to be a wise and faithful leader of his people.

As Solomon later wrote the book of Proverbs, he wrote many verses describing the value he learned through his pursuit of wisdom and how he gained wisdom through listening to the teachings of the Lord. In Proverbs 4:7–8, he wrote these words: *"Wisdom is the principal thing; therefore, get wisdom: and with all thy getting, get understanding. Exalt her, and she shall promote thee to honor, when thou dost embrace her."* The more we seek wisdom and embrace understanding, the more we are honored in our lives. As we gain wisdom and understanding from the Lord, we also will gain the benefit of happiness in our spirit. Proverbs 3:13 tells us this: *"Happy is the man that findeth wisdom, and the man that getteth understanding."*

Wisdom and understanding come from the reading of God's Word and meditating on His scriptures in prayer while seeking God's message to us. Ask God for His wisdom in your heart and soul today.

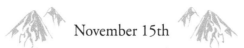

November 15th

Be Swift to Hear and Slow to Speak

It is easy for us to be quick to form opinions and judgments on people and situations in which we may not know all the facts of the matter involved. As people share their perspective on things or on other people, we are inclined to jump into the conversation to offer our own perspective or insights on how we feel those situations need to be addressed. In other instances, we may form quick opinions of people based on how they look or what they are wearing. When we say things that are less than complimentary about those people, we are falling into a trap for our spirit of not looking into their hearts and souls but rather at the outward appearance, which is not how God views us all.

The scriptures caution us as spiritual people about this type of behavior. James 1:19 says, *"Wherefore, my beloved brethren, let every man be swift to hear, slow to speak, and slow to wrath."* Avoid the instinct to allow anger to well up in your heart and soul quickly when something happens to bruise your ego. That spirit is not of God. Proverbs 18:6–7 teaches us this: *"A fool's lips enter into contention, and his mouth calleth for strokes. A fool's mouth is his destruction, and his lips are a snare of his soul."* Engaging in arguments or divisive conversations will only lead to separation from God as we let our anger cause damage to those with whom we battle. Love allows us to pass over these moments with grace in our heart rather than angry words.

The less we talk at times, the wiser and smarter we appear to others. When our tongues are unleashed, the opposite may happen. Proverbs 17:28 speaks to this as it says, *"Even a fool, when he holdeth his peace, is counted wise; and he that shutteth his lips is esteemed a man of understanding."* It is clear we should let some things go unsaid, and others will think we are wise in doing so. As we listen more and speak less, we gain wisdom and understanding and enter into fewer moments of conflict in our lives.

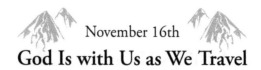

November 16th
God Is with Us as We Travel

As we travel to various places in our lives to visit with family and friends or to conduct business in various destinations, God is there with us each step along the way. He never leaves us, nor does He forsake us as we journey through this world. Keep Him close in your thoughts and prayers, and your Spirit is comforted through the trials and challenges that travel brings upon you. Keeping Christ at the forefront of our thoughts and allowing Love to flow freely in all human experiences and interactions brings added blessing to our journeys. Psalm 121:7–8 lets us know that God watches over us and protects us always while we are on these journeys as it says, *"The Lord shall preserve thee from all evil; He shall preserve thy soul. The Lord shall preserve thy going out, and thy coming in from this time forth, and even for evermore."* As we leave and as we return to our earthly homes, He is with us forevermore.

There are multiple scriptures that confirm God's presence with us as we take to the road, air, or sea for journeys in our lives. There is no place where God is not going to be there to guide and protect us. Psalm 139:9–10 says this: *"If I take wings of the morning and dwell in the uttermost parts of the sea; Even there shall thy have lead me, and thy right hand shall hold me."* We serve a God who Loves us and will be always with us, and He sends His angels to watch over us in all we do. Psalm 139:7 assures us of His eternal presence when it says, *"Whither shall I go from thy Spirit? Or whither shall I flee from thy presence?"* He has promised to be with us always, even to the end of the earth. Feel the blessing of His Holy Spirit as it leads you through each day of your journey.

As we trust in God, He will direct our paths to wherever we should go. As He does so, we should not lean on our own understanding but submit our hearts to the God who sees it all. Proverbs 20:24 says, *"Man's goings are of the Lord; how can a man understand his own way?"* Travel with God's guidance always.

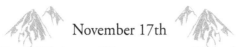

November 17th

When Bad Things Happen to Good People

We face trials and tribulations in this world. It is hard to understand why bad things happen to the good people around us or why we suffer pain or experience accidents and injuries in our lives. We are the children of God and expect only the best in our lives as we follow the path He has ordained for us. When we look to Jesus, we see that He faced the ultimate suffering as He lived His life in this world filled with evil ones. With each trial we face, we are presented with an opportunity to minister to others and bear witness to the Love God has given to us, and bring light into this world of darkness.

We are told in the scriptures we will face difficult times. It is part of the human experience. John 16:33 says it plainly: *"These things I have spoken to you, that in me ye might have peace. In the world, ye shall have tribulation; but be of good cheer; I have overcome the world."* There is no suffering you will face that you will go through alone. Jesus Christ and His Holy Spirit go with us through all aspects of our journey through this world. We are told that God will deliver us from all the afflictions we face in Psalm 34:19, which says, *"Many are the afflictions of the righteous; but the Lord delivereth him out of them all."* When Jesus prayed in the garden of Gethsemane, He prayed that God takes away the cup from which He was to drink. After those words, Jesus' prayer said, *"But not my will but thine be done."* If it is God's will that we drink from the cup we have been given, our prayer must be the same. May His will be done as we do so.

As we go through such trials and tribulations moments, we are given opportunities to minister to others. Second Corinthians 1:4 tells us, *"Who comforteth us in all our tribulation, that we may be able to comfort them which are in any trouble, by the comfort wherewith we ourselves are comforted of God."* As we experience such moments in our lives, God is preparing us to minister to others. He brings us to Love through such times in their lives. Be Blessed as you do so.

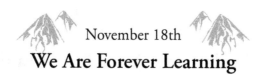

November 18th
We Are Forever Learning

The mysteries of life continue to be revealed as we travel life's highway. We will never know all that is in God's plan for us until He reveals it in His own time for us. The fact we are remaining in this world is evidence that God has work for us to do in His plan for us. When our work is finished, He will call us home. As we open our hearts for His guidance through His Holy Spirit, we discover new truths and reaffirm the truth which has set our souls free from the bondage of sin in this world. In Psalm 32:8, we are told this message: *"I will instruct thee and teach thee in the way which thou shalt go; I will guide thee with mine eye."* When we seek God's guidance through His Holy Spirit, we will receive it, and our paths will be illuminated with His light.

We have been given the Holy Spirit to guide us and to teach us the way God will direct us in our lives. He abides within us as we follow the will of God for our lives. John 14:16 tells us this: *"But the Comforter, which is the Holy Ghost, whom the Father will send in my name, He shall teach you all things, and bring all things to your remembrance, whatsoever I have said to you."* As we read God's Word and reflect on the teachings of Jesus Christ, we hear the truth, which will open our hearts to the understanding of God's plan for our lives. The Holy Spirit will teach us the meaning of God's will as we do so. David, who sought God's will in all that he did, wrote this in Psalm 86:11: *"Teach me thy way, O Lord; I will walk in thy truth; unite my heart to fear thy name."* We are to respect and fear the Lord our God and to walk in His truth, and He will bring us understanding.

As we seek knowledge from God to do the will of our Father, He will lead us to the path He has chosen for us. Psalm 143:10 tells us, *"Teach me to do thy will; for thou art my God; thy Spirit is good; lead me into the land of uprightness."* May this be our prayer today, for God to teach us His will and to lead us to the place He would have us go. Be Blessed as you do so.

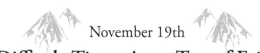 November 19th

Difficult Times Are a Test of Faith

When our lives are filled with happy moments and good health and prosperity, it is easy to believe in our God, who blesses us in such times. When we face times in which troubles arise, and we discover health-related issues or face financial stress, we want our God to rush in a cure that is wrong and restore us to health and prosperity. Life is not about God being a magic genie who caters to every wish we make in our lives. Rather, life is a series of events leading to eternity with God if we keep His will in focus and learn to trust in Him always. We face times of testing along the way in our faith walk. Those times will strengthen us as we walk through difficult times and maintain our trust in God.

There is an old expression that things that don't kill you will only make you stronger. There is a measure of truth in this saying, but that truth is better expressed in James 1:3, which teaches us: *"Knowing this, that the trying of your faith worketh patience."* We need to have and develop our patience as we go through trials and tribulations in our lives. We know they will come and that they are a part of the human experience in life. We all prefer the times we spend on the mountaintop rather than the times spent walking through the valley. In life, there will be times for each. As David said so beautifully in Psalm 23:4: *"Yea, though I walk through the valley of the shadow of death, I will fear no evil: for thou are with me; thy rod and thy staff they comfort me."* In whatever state we find ourselves, know that God is with us and will protect us on our journey.

There are times in our lives we must look past the moment and hold on to our faith in our eternal destiny with God. Second Corinthians 4:17–18 tells us,

> *For our light affliction which is but for a moment, worketh for us a far more exceeding and eternal weight of glory. While we look not at the things which are seen, but at the things which are not seen; for the things which are seen are temporal, but the things which are not seen are eternal.*

Keep your faith strong in God daily.

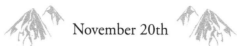

November 20th

God Will Heal Your Heart and Your Body

There will be times in our lives in which we need to experience healing for wounds of the heart and for our bodies that may be afflicted. Often, when the body is suffering, so will the spirit of the man or woman. God is with us in all these times and can and will deliver us as we wait upon the Lord and seek His healing power to come upon us. The scriptures direct the elders of the church to pray over those who are suffering sickness and to join together in lifting up one another in intercessory prayer for deliverance. James 5:14 teaches us this: *"Is any sick among you? Let him call for the elders of the church; and let them pray over him, anointing him with oil in the name of the Lord."* This is one of many benefits of belonging to a body of believers in a church family. When one is in need, we can all come together to support and pray for those who need a touch from God.

Faith is a key to the healing power of the Holy Spirit. This is true for emotional healing as well as that of the physical body. We are promised His healing in Jeremiah 33:6, which says to us: *"Behold, I bring it health and cure, I will cure them, and I will reveal unto them an abundance of peace and truth."* God will restore our health in all ways as we believe in Him for this. Jesus spoke about the power of faith in the healing of the woman who touched the hem of his garment, which is recorded in Mark 5:34, which says, *"And He said unto her, 'Daughter, thy faith hath made thee whole; go in peace and be whole of thy plague.'"* The importance of faith in healing was also revealed when Jesus went back to his hometown, and people lacked faith in Him as the Son of God. Matthew 13:58 speaks to their unbelief: *"And He did not many mighty works there because of their unbelief."* For God to do mighty works in our lives, we must have faith and trust in the power of His Holy Spirit to work in us.

God is here to heal our bodies when we ask Him for deliverance. We are His children, and He will deliver us from all afflictions we face on our journey.

November 21st
God Will Direct Your Paths

There are many intersections we will come to on our road of life that will give us options to go one way or another. Those choices may be whether to engage in personal relationships or the pursuit of a job or career choice which presents itself to us. The choice we face may be related to options on physical locations to move our families or to stay in the place where we find ourselves. These choices will be very impactful on our lives in this world, and we need to seek God's will for our lives as these choices are made. When you ask for God's direction, He will direct your paths and give you His assurance on where you should travel on the road of life. The key to making the right choice is to be seeking God's will as you choose. Psalm 143:10 says, *"Teach me to do thy will; for thou art my God: thy spirit is good; lead me into the land of uprightness."*

As we approach God with a humble spirit, He is faithful to guide us to the place which He has chosen for us to be. Proverbs 3:5–6 teaches us this: *"Trust in the Lord with all thine heart: lean not to thine own understanding. In all thy ways acknowledge Him, and He shall direct thy paths."* It is human nature to want to figure out what is best for our own lives. The more we proudly try to do so, the more often we find ourselves in the snares that life's journey can produce. The more we seek God's will and His path, the more we are delivered from the traps that pull us away from our Father in heaven. Our prayer should be simple and direct to God as was written in Psalm 25:4: *"Show me thy ways, O Lord; teach me thy paths."* As we pray this, He will do so for us.

The more we are immersed in the word of God daily, the easier it is to find the path that God has for us. His Word is designed to illuminate the path to God and to help us find His will for our lives. The words written in Psalm 119:105 says this: *"Thy word is a lamp unto my feet, and a light unto my path."* Choose the path on which God illuminates for you, and you will be blessed each day.

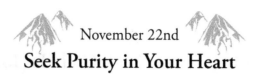

November 22nd
Seek Purity in Your Heart

When Jesus taught the multitude while giving His sermon on the mount, He spoke of those who were called "blessed by God." In His sermon, as recorded in Matthew 5:8, He said: *"Blessed are the pure in heart, for they shall see God."* As we seek to be one with the Father, this goal of seeing God is always in our heart and soul. The purification of our heart is a process and not an event. It happens over time as we strive to eliminate those thoughts and temptations which cause corruption in our minds. The more we turn our hearts to pleasing God and seeking to fill our hearts and minds with His Word, the closer we come to the purity of thought which turns our hearts to His will for our lives.

The path to purity is by following the teachings in the word of God. It is a journey we are all on each day. The purification of our heart is something we must desire and seek as we grow in our walk with God. Psalm 119:9 tells us this: *"Wherewithal shall a young man cleanse his way? By taking heed thereto according to thy word."* When we seek the path to righteousness and purity, it is by learning from the word of God and abiding by the teachings we find there. The applications and disciplines taught in the scriptures take us to the path God has chosen for us. It is on that path that we will see Him.

As we seek God's will for our lives each day, and we pray to Him for strength and guidance, we should pray for Him to give us purity in our hearts and minds and anchor our thoughts on His Word to build us up. Psalm 51:10 is such a prayer that David prayed to God: *"Create in me a clean heart, O God, and renew a right spirit within me."* If we choose to seek this daily in our hearts and minds, God will truly bless us, and we shall see God as we move closer to Him. Be Blessed as you do so today!

Preparing for the Work God Has for Us

Anything of value in our lives takes time to develop. Education and training for a job or career is typically something we study for over an extended period of time. Doctors and lawyers, and many high-level professionals are required to invest many years in their education prior to entering the workforce. Beyond the time spent in school, once we are engaged in our professional lives, we spend many years as we prepare to attain excellence in whatever field we have chosen. In fact, there is never an end to the learning phase of our life as we seek to be better in our chosen field of endeavor.

As we travel on whatever path we have chosen to do God's will, we are learning each day what God has for us to accomplish on that journey. Our spiritual training comes from His Holy Word as we seek to fill our hearts and souls with the message God has for us each day. Whatever it is you are called to do for God in your life, be fully invested in the success each day. Colossians 3:23–24 tells us this: *"And whatsoever ye do, do it heartily, as to the Lord, and not unto men; Knowing that of the Lord ye shall receive the reward of the inheritance, for ye serve the Lord Christ."* We learn from the scriptures the things God gives us to prepare us for His work. Romans 15:4 teaches us this: *"For whatsoever things were written aforetime were written for our learning, that we through patience and comfort of the scriptures might have hope."* The scriptures will prepare us for the work God has for us today.

We are to lift up one another in prayer that God will use each of us in a mighty way. Colossians 1:9–10 says,

> For this cause we also, since the day we heard it, do not cease to pray for you, and to desire that you might be filled with the knowledge of His will in all wisdom and spiritual understanding. That you may walk worthy of the Lord unto all pleasing, being fruitful in every good work, and increasing in the knowledge of God.

Be great with God in your heart today!

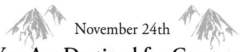

November 24th

You Are Destined for Greatness

God did not create you in His image and put you on this earth to live a life destined for mediocrity. He has a life filled with greatness which is available for each of us if we do that which is in His will for us each day. What we choose to do and how we choose to develop spiritually will determine whether that ultimate destiny is fulfilled. There are no limits to where you can go and or what you can do. One of the most powerful and uplifting scriptures in the Bible is Philippians 4:13, which professes: *"I can do all things through Christ which strengtheneth me."* Don't let the negative thoughts of the evil one try to limit you in what you can do. God can and will empower you as your faith embraces your potential.

The measurement of being great in the eyes of God is described in simple terms in Matthew 5:19, which tells us,

> *Whosoever therefore shall break one of these commandments, and shall teach men so, shall be called the least in the kingdom of heaven: but whosoever shall do and teach them, the same shall be called great in the kingdom of heaven.*

As we keep God's commandments and teach others to do so, we are called great in His eyes. Jesus taught us to Love God with all our hearts and to Love our neighbor as ourselves. He said these two commandments would lead us to fulfill all others in our lives (Matthew 22:37–40). Psalm 71:21 says, *"Thou shalt increase my greatness, and comfort me on every side."* It is God's will and plan for us to make us stronger in that which we are called to do. We are called to be a witness to others and a light shining in the darkness of this world. When we seek His will and follow His path, he enables us with His strength to carry His message forward to the world around us.

If we seek greatness in our lives, we learn to serve others in Christ. Jesus spoke of this in Matthew 23:11 as He said: *"The greatest among you shall be your servant."* May we embrace the role of service which God has for each of us as we Love our God and others He places on our path. Be Great Today as you do so.

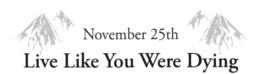

November 25th
Live Like You Were Dying

Tim McGraw sings a great country song entitled *"Live Like You Were Dying,"* written by songwriters Craig Wiseman, James Nichols, and Tim Nichols, which contains a very powerful message about a man who has been told he is dying by his doctors while in his early forties. The lyrics ask him, "What did you do?" In this song, the man does all those things he wanted to do, such as skydiving, riding a fierce bull, climbing mountains, and living a full life. The songwriter writes of loving deeper and speaking to others more sweetly as we express our Love to others more meaningfully each day. The song speaks of tomorrow being a gift, and we would have eternity to think about what we do with it. This is a song that ministers to my soul each time I hear it played. I hope it does to each of us as we think about this day which we were given as a gift.

Hebrews 11:13 talks about how we are simply passing through this earth as pilgrims, and our eternal destiny lies beyond. If our time on earth is limited in the number of days we have here, let us make each one count as it should for the God we serve. Psalm 90:12 says this: *"So teach us to number our days, that we may apply our hearts unto wisdom."* With our number of days having a limit, let us embrace the fullness of what we can do to yield the highest result in each one we have. If we Love deeper, speak sweeter, and give forgiveness, we have been denying. We might find the message in the song will lead us to a closer walk with God and serve our fellow man more completely in the days we have.

The messages we find in music and literature direct our thoughts to that which God would have us embrace. To learn to Love our God and one another more completely as we journey is our ultimate goal in life. If this is our last day on earth, may we do exactly that with all our heart and soul. May God richly bless you today as you do so!

November 26th
God Is Our Comfort and Joy

All families experience times of loss and grief as they journey in this world. In my family, my wife's mother recently went home to be with the Lord. We gathered together as a family to celebrate her life and mourn her passing from this world. There is always a mixed emotion when one who is a believer passes away, knowing she has gone on to be with the Lord, but we know that person will be missed by those of us who remain here in this world. Matthew 5:4 speaks of the comfort we are given from the Lord in such times: *"Blessed are they that mourn, for they shall be comforted."* There is great comfort in the Lord, knowing that God has taken the soul of the believer home to be with Him. For a non-believer, it is hard to feel such comfort at a time of loss.

There are many times in life when sadness engulfs your spirit. Those times certainly include the moments when we have lost a Loved one. Other times might be when one is sick and dying or fighting through a period of treatment for cancer or some other affliction. When we are in such periods of duress in our lives, we may mourn and feel great sadness in our human experience. As a believer in our faith journey, we know that God draws close to us in such times if we seek Him to do so. Psalm 34:18 tells us, *"The Lord is nigh unto them that are of a broken heart; and saveth such as be of a contrite spirit."* God is there for us and with us when we need Him the most. We are never alone when we open our hearts to receive Him. When we stumble and fall, God is there to restore our hearts and souls. Psalm 73:26 says, *"My flesh and my heart faileth; but God is the strength of my heart, and my portion forever."*

When God is needed most in our lives to bring us comfort and restore our hearts to peace and joy, He is there to bring us the strength to carry on. It has been said, "Joy is not the absence of suffering, but, rather, the presence of God." May we seek God's presence in our hearts and lives always and receive His joy.

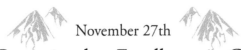

November 27th

Be Committed to Excellence in Christ

There is a work we have each been called to do in service to one another through Jesus Christ our Lord. As we seek God's will for our life, He will reveal to us that which He has chosen for us to do. Jesus spoke of the harvest of souls as He took compassion on the multitude of people which surrounded Him as He ministered in this world. In Matthew 9:36–38, we are told:

> *But when He saw the multitudes, He was moved with compassion on them, because they fainted, and were scattered abroad, as sheep having no shepherd. Then saith He unto His disciples, "The harvest is truly plenteous, but the laborers are few; Pray ye therefore the Lord of the harvest, that He will send forth laborers into His harvest."*

How God plans to use each of us in this harvest will differ from person to person. He will clearly have a plan for each believer to serve in His harvest.

It is our calling to commit to excellence in our work for Christ while we are on our journey here. If we commit to doing that which God calls us to do, He will give us the understanding of what He has for us in His plan. Proverbs 16:3 teaches us this: *"Commit thy works unto the Lord, and thy thoughts shall be established."* When we truly seek God's will for our lives and ask Him to direct our paths, He will do so and guide us to understand His purpose in our hearts. As we discover more fully the work we are each called to do, be fully invested in it with all your heart. Colossians3:23–24 speaks to this: *"And whatsoever ye do, do it heartily, as to the Lord and not unto men; Knowing that of the Lord ye shall receive the reward of the inheritance, for ye serve the Lord Christ."* When our hearts embrace the thought we work for God, not for men, each day, our energy and enthusiasm for our work should be intensified accordingly. Be all in on what it is He has called you to do.

As Jesus told us, the harvest field is filled with opportunities for souls needing to find salvation. Be an excellent laborer for God in all you do today!

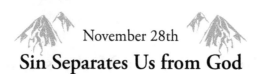

November 28th

Sin Separates Us from God

Our God Loves us and wants what is best for us. Nonetheless, when we live a life of sin, He will turn His face from us, and we walk alone during those times. The evil one wants to separate us from the power and strength that comes to us from walking with the Lord. The devil will lure us away from God by appealing to our lust for desires of the flesh or other worldly pleasures and appeals to our ego by turning our attention to the riches and things of the world that we don't already have. Isaiah 59:1–2 says it this way:

> *Behold, the Lord's hand is not shortened, neither is His ear heavy, that it cannot hear. But your iniquities have separated between you and your God, and your sins have hid His face from you, that He will not hear.*

Our God is a jealous God who wants us to be fully devoted to Him in all we do. Sin takes us down the path further away from Him, and His commandments are forsaken in exchange for things used by the devil to lure us into his trap for our souls.

We are taught to turn our hearts away from the things of this world and to seek the will of our Father, which is in heaven. In doing so, we are embracing that which is eternal as we turn away from that which will pass away. First John 2:15–17 teaches us this:

> *Love not the world, neither the things that are in the world. If any man Love the world, the Love of the Father is not in him. For all that is in the world, the lust of the eyes, and the pride of life, is not of the Father, but is of the world. And the world passeth away, and the lust thereof; but he that doeth the will of the Father abideth forever.*

The choice is a simple one in our lives, we pursue that which will take us further from God, or we pursue the path of righteousness which draws us ever closer to Him each day.

The path to the Father is through our faith in Jesus Christ as His Son. John 14:6 says, *"Jesus saith unto him, 'I am the way, the truth, and the life; no man cometh to the Father but by me."* We know the way we must travel each day!

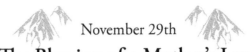

The Blessing of a Mother's Love

There is no greater gift from God our Father than the gift of parents who Love us and teach us the way to salvation early in our lives. Not everyone is fortunate enough to be born into such a family. Love is the essence of God's presence in a home, and having a mother who gives you the blessing of Love each day builds your heart with joy and happiness and lifts you up with confidence and self-esteem. Unfortunately, not all mothers are filled with the Love and virtue which gives them the Love of God in their hearts to pass along to the children in their homes. Proverbs 31:10–12 talks about the value of a virtuous woman:

> *Who can find a virtuous woman? For her price is far above rubies. The heart of her husband doth safely trust in her, so that he shall have no need of spoil. She will do him good and not evil, all the days of her life.*

Such a woman in a family is a treasure and one of God's greatest gifts. When such a woman is the mother of a family, Proverbs 31:25–28 says this about her:

> *Strength and honor are her clothing; and she shall rejoice in time to come. She openeth her mouth with wisdom; and her tongue is the law of kindness. She looketh well in the ways of her household, and eateth not the bread of idleness. Her children arise up, and call her blessed; her husband also, and he praiseth her.*

Women of this virtue and character change the lives of those around them for the better. For those of us who were raised in such a family by a mother who poured out Love into our lives each day along the way, we need to reflect on the impact they have had on our lives today and often. We need to speak to them and thank them for their Love and leadership if they are still with us in this world. We also need to thank our God for this glorious gift, whether they are still with us or have gone home to their reward in heaven.

Be blessed today as you think about your mother and the mother of your children. Express your Love today to those who are still on the journey with us.

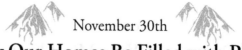

November 30th

May Our Homes Be Filled with Peace

Our God blesses us in so many ways. One of the greatest blessings He gives to those who follow Him is a home that is filled with His peace as a refuge for our lives in the midst of a turbulent world that surrounds us. When Jesus sent out His disciples, He instructed them to go to various cities and preach the Good News of His life to the world. When they were to enter cities, they found people to take them into their homes while they visited that city. Jesus instructed the disciples to bless the homes as they entered, as reported in Luke 10:5: *"And into whatsoever house you enter, first say, Peace be to this house."* The idea of a home that is blessed with peace is one that we need to appreciate and value. Peace comes from working together in the Spirit of Love to forgive one another and look past issues that can cause conflict. The more we do so, the more our lives become filled with peace and joy.

It is God's intention that His people dwell in homes filled with peace. Isaiah 32:18 tells us this: *"And my people shall dwell in peaceful habitation, and in sure dwellings, and in quiet resting places."* The importance of such a place of rest and peace is not lost on the God we serve. When you find the spirit of divisiveness at work in our homes, it is up to each of us to find the willingness to make peace and to rebuke such a spirit that is not of God. The scriptures tell us, "Blessed are the peacemakers, for they shall be called the children of God." When you sow peace, that is what you also reap. When you have peace in your home, your heart and soul can be restored and rejuvenated for the challenges life brings your way each day. When there is no peace in the home, the energy is spent, and we become weaker in all we face in the world around us.

As we walk with God and seek His will, His blessings over our house will be given to us and our families. Seek His peace in your heart each day and make peace with those who live in your homes through forgiveness and Love.

December 1st
Find Renewal in Your Mind Each Day

The mind of man is often tempted and pulled away from thoughts of God as the evil one tries to create separation in our heart and soul from God's plan and purpose for each of us. The path to righteousness is one that is described as "straight and narrow," and we know God will direct our paths if we seek Him and ask Him to do so. To renew our minds daily is to meditate on the word of God and spend time in prayer as we wait upon the Lord for energy and direction. Second Corinthians 4:16 speaks to this renewal daily as it says, *"For which cause we faint not; but though our outward man perish, yet the inward man is renewed day by day."* This renewal comes from the strength given to us by the Holy Spirit of God working in our hearts and souls.

As we seek to follow Christ in our lives, we are taught to put on the mind of Christ in how we approach the lives we live. Learning from the scriptures what He taught and praying for God to open our hearts and minds with understanding, renews our minds, and we become new and refreshed in the Spirit. Colossians 3:10 teaches us this: *"And have put on the new man, which is renewed in knowledge after the image of Him that created him."* The more we learn about the Lord and the more we seek His ways, the more our Spirit is renewed and rejuvenated to become more like Him. David wrote in Psalm 51:10: *"Create in me a clean heart; and renew a right Spirit within me."* May this be our prayer as we approach this day, and may we seek purity in our heart to draw ever closer to the God we serve.

As we renew our minds and set our hearts to follow Him, we have the power of the Holy Spirit working within us. Titus 3:5 tells us this; *"Not by works of righteousness that we have done, but according to His mercy He saved us, by the washing of regeneration, and renewing of the Holy Ghost."* May your Spirit be renewed, and your heart be cleaned as you go through this day.

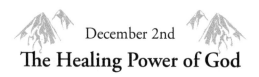

December 2nd

The Healing Power of God

We often take our health for granted until and unless we face a time when we must deal with sickness or injury. It is a time when we look to God for one of His miracles in delivering us from the affliction with His cure and His comfort while we recover. God has promised to be with us and to restore our health as His people. Jeremiah 30:17 says this: *"For I will restore health unto thee, and I will heal thee of thy wounds, saith the Lord."* God is called the Great Physician and has the power to heal and deliver us from all we face. As God's plan for our lives unfolds, there are many mysteries as to why things happen beyond our control which affect our physical, mental, and emotional health. We know we face many trials. One thing is a certainty; we don't go through these times alone.

God has a purpose in all moments of our lives. We go into situations that bring us to a time where we need His healing touch without fully understanding the opportunities we are afforded to minister to others during such times. God places us in the care of others to allow us to receive ministry and blessings from those around us and for us to provide such ministry and blessings to those who are providing us with care. Our Spirits are engaged always in work He has for us. We must accept the challenges we face as health-related issues arise, knowing God is in control of the plan for our lives as it develops. We know if we call upon the Lord for healing, He will hear our cries and answer in His time. Psalm 30:2 tells us this: *"O Lord my God, I cried unto thee, and thou hast healed me."*

When Jesus walked on the earth and healed the multitudes of their sicknesses and afflictions, the key to their ability to be healed was their faith. In Mark 10:52,, we read about a blind man who was given his sight because of his faith: *"And Jesus said unto him, 'Go thy way; thy faith hath made thee whole.' And immediately he received his sight and followed Jesus in the way."* When we turn to our God with true faith in our hearts, we will be healed as we believe.

December 3rd
God Gives Us Victory over Death

There are many battles we fight along the way as we go through this journey called life. We face forces and powers which try to lure us away from the path of righteousness and doing that which we know is pleasing to the God we serve. He blesses His people with many gifts to be used in His work on this earth in service to those who He puts on our path. Our commission is to Love our God with all our hearts, minds, and souls and to Love one another fully as well. The end of the journey for Christians is not the same as it is for those who are non-believers. God has given us the ultimate gift, which is victory over the grave.

There is no reason to fear death for one who believes in Jesus Christ as the Son of God and who has asked our Heavenly Father for the forgiveness of our sins. We have been promised a life eternal as the gift of salvation by the grace of God. First Corinthians 15:54 tells us, *"So when this corruptible shall have put on incorruption, and this mortal shall have put on immortality, then shall be brought to pass the saying that is written, Death is swallowed up in victory."* The journey just begins again as we pass through the veil of death into the life that goes beyond for eternity as a believer. Death has no power over us through Christ, who lives today. First Corinthians 15:55 exclaims: *"O Death, where is thy sting, O grave, where is thy victory?"* Through Christ, we have this victory won.

The promise of this victory was written in Isaiah 25:8, which says, *"He will swallow up death in victory; and the Lord will wipe away tears from off all faces; and the rebuke of His people shall He take away from off all the earth; for the Lord hath spoken it."* We trust in Him that created us and know that His Word is true. Death is nothing to be feared but, rather, a portal into the land which God has promised to us as His people. Live a life filled with victory, knowing we are in His hands as we do so. Be Blessed today on your journey!

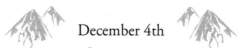 December 4th

He Is Our Refuge and Our Strength

When you face times that are difficult, and you feel alone or that you are trying to survive against forces that are overwhelming, God is there with you always when you turn toward Him. We often want to win all our battles by our own initiative and move forward without pausing to reflect on the power of the God we serve. It is His desire for us to humble ourselves and be willing to ask Him to guide us and strengthen us in such times. There is nothing in this world that He can't help us to overcome. He has given us victory over death and the grave, and as we are conquerors over the final enemy, we will likewise be conquerors in all other battles we face.

God provides us with a refuge from the storms of life, and He gives us strength and capabilities beyond those we can produce on our own. Psalm 46:1–2 promise us this: *"God is our refuge and strength, a very present help in trouble. Therefore, we will not fear, though the earth be removed, and though the mountains be carried into the midst of the sea."* David is telling us that we have nothing to fear with God at our side as we face such moments of distress along the path of our lives. In Lamentations 3:22–23, we are told of God's mercies and compassions for us: *"It is of the Lord's mercies that we are not consumed, because His compassions fail not. They are new every morning; great is thy faithfulness."* God is faithful and Loves His people fully. Every day He will renew His Love and compassion for us, and all we must do in life is trust in Him.

We must wait on the Lord for His timing in our lives which is a difficult thing for many to do. His plan for our lives is unfolding in His time and as His will is being done. Psalm 27:14 teaches us: *"Wait on the Lord: be of good courage, and He shall strengthen thy heart: wait, I say, on the Lord."* As we trust in God and wait for Him to deliver us, He will strengthen our heart and comfort our soul. He is with us today and always. Be Blessed as you walk with Him today!

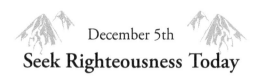

December 5th
Seek Righteousness Today

Seeking the path to righteousness must be our daily quest as a follower of Jesus Christ. Jesus taught us in the sermon on the mount to hunger and thirst after righteousness in our lives. In Matthew 5:6, Jesus called those who do blessed: *"Blessed are they which do hunger and thirst after righteousness; for they shall be filled."* Being righteous in the eyes of God is to do that which is good and filled with Love to those He brings to us each day. When we are righteous, we sow the seeds of peace in all that we do. James 3:18 teaches us this: *"And the fruit of righteousness is sown in peace of them that make peace."* When we avoid conflict and bring resolution to conflicts that we encounter along the way, we are sowing seeds of peace in the troubled world around us.

We are taught in many scriptures and books of the Bible to follow the path to righteousness. Solomon writes to us in Proverbs 21:21 this message: *"He that followeth after righteousness and mercy find life, righteousness, and honor."* When you seek to do that which is right in the eyes of God to others and show mercy in your dealings with people, God will fill your life with honor and righteousness. The commandments of God were directing our paths to a life which is righteous in His eyes. The commandment Jesus gave us to Love our God with all our hearts and to Love others as we Love ourselves fulfills all the commandments and puts us on the path to righteousness each day.1 Timothy 6:11 reinforces this again as it says, *"But thou, man of God, flee these things; and follow after righteousness, Godliness, faith, Love, patience, meekness."* When others describe us as having these characteristics, we are living a life that is righteous and is pleasing to the God we serve.

God hears the prayers and the cries of a righteous man. Psalm 34:15 tells us, *"The eyes of the Lord are upon the righteous; and His ears are open unto their cry."* The path to righteousness brings us closer to God each day!

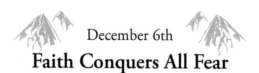

December 6th
Faith Conquers All Fear

One of the key measurements of the strength of our faith is how well we have overcome fear in our life. Whether the fear is based on issues we face in life that are related to the stresses which come from business or financial needs or those fears which are about the security and well-being we might face related to our future. When we fear, we are overshadowing our faith with the darkness of doubt in our hearts. We are to dwell in the Spirit of Love, which is the Spirit of God in our hearts and lives each day. When we are in that Spirit, we have no cause for fear. Second Timothy 1:7 says it clearly: *"For God hath not given us the Spirit of fear; but of power, and of Love, and of a sound mind."* Since God did not give us the Spirit of fear, those fears that try to occupy space in our minds come from another source which is the evil one. Rebuke it and let the power of the Spirit of God, which is Love, flow through you to take the place of fear.

There will be times when anxiety and fear try to take hold of each of us. It is the work of the one who tries to weaken your faith as it troubles your heart and mind. David wrote these words in Psalm 56:3–4, which says, *"What time I am afraid, I will trust in thee. In God I will praise His word, in God I have put my trust; I will not fear what flesh can do to me."* When great men of God, such as David, face their fears, learn to trust in God, and fear goes away. The more we fill our hearts and minds with Love, the less we feel the energy of fear. Love makes us strong as described in 1 John 4:18: *"There is no fear in Love; but perfect Love casteth out fear; because fear hath torment. He that feareth is not made in perfect Love."* May we strive each day to find perfect Love in our hearts and minds and ask God to bring this Spirit fully into our lives each day. As we do so, there is no room for fear of having a place.

There is nothing to fear in this world. Cast all your cares upon God, for He cares for you as is told to us in 1 Peter 5:7. There is no room for fear when you do.

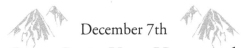

December 7th

May Peace Be in Your Heart and Soul

We live in a world filled with war, strife, and evil which surrounds us. The tribulations and conflict swirl around us and attempt to draw us in. Our egos stand up proudly when we hear others say things that cause damage to our pride, and we can easily engage in conflict to prove we are right and another is wrong in what is being said. In such moments we are given a choice to win the battle with our will or to choose the path to peace through humility and patience. The one who makes peace is called by Jesus blessed as a child of God in Matthew 5:9: *"Blessed are the peacemakers, for they shall be called the children of God."* We all know those who are in this category in our lives. The ones who continually strive to end conflicts with those around them even when they are not one of the combatants. They are truly a blessing to be around in the way they bring peace to our world.

The great advantage of being one who creates peace is that peace now resides inside your heart and soul. The blessing of peace is not feeling the anxiety and stress of carrying on a spirit of conflict and divisiveness inside you. It is God's will that we have peace in our hearts and souls. First Thessalonians 3:16 tells us, *"Now the Lord of peace Himself give you peace always by all means. The Lord be with you all."* As God Himself gives us peace, we must embrace it and pursue it with all we do. As we focus our minds on God, we find peace in the process as we trust Him more fully. Isaiah 26:3 teaches us this: *"Thou will keep him in perfect peace, whose mind is stayed on thee; because he trusteth in thee."*

The Love of God and our Love for others is what we lean upon as the foundation for peace in our lives. When we Love others, we look past their shortcomings and look upon them as we should. Hebrews 12:14 says, *"Follow peace with all men, and holiness, without which no man shall see the Lord."* May the peace of God engulf your heart, mind, and soul on this day and every day. Be Blessed as you find His peace in your life today!

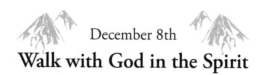

December 8th
Walk with God in the Spirit

The idea of walking with God in the Spirit each day is one that comes from the scriptures as it guides us to the path to take us closer to God in our hearts. As we dwell more in the Spirit, we turn away from the flesh and the desires which entrap us in this journey we are on. We learn of those who were able to grow close to God in the history books of the Bible, such as Noah. In Genesis 6:9, Noah is described: *"Noah was a just man, and perfect in his generations; and Noah walked with God."* How many people today would describe any of us as someone who "walked with God?" Wouldn't that be an amazing legacy to leave as we make our mark on this world!

There are various scriptures written to describe what such a "walk with God" should be and how it should appear to the cloud of witnesses that surround us, which we read about in Hebrews 12:1: *"Wherefore seeing we also are compassed about with so great a cloud of witnesses, let us lay aside every weight, and the sin which doth so easily beset us, and let us run with patience the race which is before us."* In this passage, we are taught to turn away from sin and move forward with patience in our lives. The walk with God is described in Micah 6:8: *"He hath showed thee, O Man, what is good; and what doth the Lord require of thee, but to do justly, and to Love mercy, and to walk humbly with thy God?"* Do that which is right by others, be merciful with Love in your heart, and walk humbly with God, and you draw closer to Him each day.

We are to follow the teachings of Jesus in our hearts fully on our journey. Colossians 2:6 teaches us this: *"As ye therefore received Jesus Christ the Lord, so walk ye in Him."* Imagine Jesus Christ walking alongside you in the flesh each day. How would you conduct yourself? In fact, His Holy Spirit is inside of us as we walk each day. His Spirit is there to guide us and to minister to us. We do walk with God each day and, as such, we must follow His commands and Love one another.

December 9th
Earnestly Seek the Path to Righteousness

There are days we wake up with high energy and enthusiasm for what lies ahead. It is easy to imagine such a day when you have planned to do something which is fun and exciting for you and/or your family. Whether it be a travel experience or a sporting event, you have a renewed vigor for that which lies ahead for your day. Do we take the same energy and passion to the day in search of our Spiritual awakening for each day? Passion, energy, and enthusiasm should flow through our hearts and lives as we seek the path to righteousness that draws us ever closer to the God we serve. As we humbly walk with Him, our world is made complete, and His care for us develops into an eternal reward. How can other things take a higher level of importance than this?

We are on a path that is leading us in the direction of light or darkness. As we draw closer to God's way, the brightness of the path becomes more intense each day. Proverbs 4:18–19 tells us this: *"But the path of the just is as the shining light; that shineth more and more upon the perfect day. The way of the wicked is darkness, they know not at what they stumble."* The more we earnestly seek God's will and His plan for our lives, the brighter the light becomes, which illuminates the path on which we journey. With energy, enthusiasm, and passion, we should daily be engaged in the pursuit of what God's will is for us for each day. The pleasures and joy which come from following God's path are unlike any others we could ever find on our journey. Psalm 16:11 says this: *"Thou wilt show me the path of life; in thy presence is fulness of joy; at thy right hand there are pleasures forevermore."* As David writes these words, you can feel the passion he had for the Love he felt for God.

May we pray for God to teach us His will for us today. Psalm 143:10 says this: *"Teach me to do thy will; for thou art my God; thy Spirit is good; lead me into the land of uprightness."* May this be the prayer in our hearts for this day.

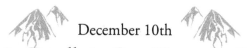

Christ Dwells in Our Hearts by Faith

We seek to find ways to build on our faith as we journey each day. God is with us, and His Holy Spirit is there to guide us and minister to us while we live in this physical world. Hebrews 11:1 teaches us: *"Faith is the substance of things hoped for, the evidence of things not seen."* If we have faith, we believe in things we cannot see with our eyes but rather know is real in our hearts and souls. It is difficult for the mind of man or woman to embrace this thing called faith as such. Those who lack faith, they scoff at the idea we believe in a God they cannot see. Those same people believe in the wind, which blows the leaves in the trees all around them but remains invisible to the eye. They see evidence of it with the rustling of the leaves. The evidence of our faith in God is in life all around us as well.

There is power in faith for those who believe. When you earnestly pray for God's blessing and direction, He will give you that which is in your heart when your faith in Him is strong and present. Mark 11:24 tells us this: *"Therefore I say unto you, What things soever you desire, when ye pray, believe that ye receive them, and ye shall have them."* Jesus spoke these words in response to a comment by Peter about the fig tree which He had cursed, which quickly withered. He went on to talk about the unlimited power of prayer for those who believe and have a strong faith. Ephesians 3:16–17 speaks of the power of faith and being rooted and grounded in Love:

> *That He would grant you, according to the riches of His glory, to be strengthened with might by His Spirit in the inner man; That Christ may dwell in your hearts by faith; that ye, being rooted and grounded in Love.*

Be rooted and grounded in Love with strong faith as you walk with God.

The life of a man or woman of God is one that is filled with faith. Second Corinthians 5:7 says, *"For we walk by faith, not by sight."* May your faith guide your walk today and always.

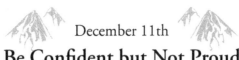

December 11th

Be Confident but Not Proud

The scriptures teach us to be confident through our faith in the Lord God, who can deliver us through any situation and will empower us to be able to do all things through Christ, who strengthens us. Conversely, the scriptures caution us to give glory to God and not to try to take credit for what God does for us in our lives. God favors those who are humble and meek and will not bless those who are prideful. First Timothy 6:17 speaks to this: *"Charge them that are rich in this world, that they be not high-minded; nor trust in uncertain riches, but in the living God, who giveth us richly all things to enjoy."* When we are blessed by God with prosperity in our lives, we know that He is the one who has blessed us with His gifts. We always should approach our lives with a thankful heart giving Him the glory for all His blessings which He bestows upon us.

Know that your ability to achieve in life is the direct result of God giving you the gifts to produce positive results and any prosperity you enjoy. Second Corinthians 3:5 teaches us this: *"Not that we are sufficient of ourselves to think anything as of ourselves; but our sufficiency is of God."* The idea of taking pride in what you accomplish is not consistent with what pleases God. However, God intends for us to be confident in Him and His promises to empower us to do His will. Hebrews 10:35–36 speaks to this as it says, *"So do not throw away your confidence; it will be richly rewarded. You need to persevere so that when you have done the will of God, you will receive what He has promised."* We are here to do His will and to walk with Him on the path as we do so. There is confidence in our hearts as we know He will be with us always and help us overcome any obstacles on our path.

We can approach God in confidence through our faith in our Lord Jesus Christ. He will listen to our prayers and will answer them according to His will. Ephesians 3:12 tells us, *"In Him, and through faith in Him we may approach God with freedom and confidence."* Let us do so today freely and confidently!

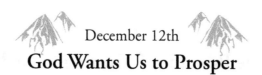

December 12th

God Wants Us to Prosper

It is God's desire for His children to prosper and to be in good health. That is not to say that we won't go through times that are difficult, either financially or physically. Rather, it is to say we are His children and, in His time, and as we strive to abide in the center of God's will for our lives, we are destined to prosper and be in good health according to His scriptures which promise us this. A Godly man does not seek worldly gains and wealth as his primary objective in life. Matthew 6:33 teaches us this: *"But seek ye first the kingdom of God, and His righteousness, and all these things shall be added unto you."* As we walk with God, our purpose and plan are to do His will and seek His righteousness. As we do, He will give us the desires of our hearts.

We are taught to give, and it shall be given unto us. We are taught also in the word that you reap what you sow. Luke 6:38 says it clearly:

Give and it shall be given unto you; good measure, pressed down, and shaken together, and running over, shall men give into your bosom. For the same measure that ye mete withal it shall be measured to you again.

You can't outgive God. This pertains to the gifts you make to the church and the people in need who God puts on your path each day. Be generous in Love and in service to others, and you will prosper in your life. Second Corinthians 9:8 tells us, *"And God is able to make all grace abound toward you; that ye, always having all sufficiency in all things, may abound to every good work."* God provides for us all we need to prosper and do well all the good work we have been chosen to do for Him in our lives.

We are all blessed to serve a God who only wants what is best for us in our lives. He expresses this to us in 3 John 1:2, which says, *"Beloved, I wish above all things that thou mayest prosper and be in good health, even as thy soul prospereth."* Our God does not want His people to suffer and be sad. Rather, He is our source of joy, peace, and prosperity in all we do. May you prosper today!

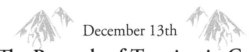

December 13th

The Rewards of Trusting in God

The greatest reward that comes from trusting in God is the gift of eternal life. There is nothing on earth that can compare with this gift of life which comes to us through God's Love and grace toward His people. The gift is the result of our faith in His Son Jesus Christ, who died for our sins, and the belief and Love we have for our Heavenly Father. As we walk with God in this world, we do so with a desire to do His will each day and to serve His purpose in our lives. As we live in such a way, God bestows His blessings upon us as His people. Philippians 4:19 promises us this: *"But my God shall supply all your need according to His riches in glory by Christ Jesus."* As we follow the path He has chosen for us, we will not want for anything nor be without what we need according to His promise.

We each have work God has called us to do in our lifetime. He has called us to be of service to one another in Love. We are taught in the scriptures to give to the poor. Proverbs 19:17 says, *"He that hath pity on the poor lendeth unto the Lord; and that which he hath given will He pay him again."* Our service to others in God's name is the work we are to do continually while we walk on this earth. Jesus spoke of greatness among men as being the one who is the servant to others. Matthew 23:11 tells us this: *"But he that is greatest among you will be your servant."* As we serve, we give of ourselves to others which is what Christ did for all of us. God will reward the work we do for others. Second Chronicles 15:7 says, *"Be ye strong therefore and let not your hands be weak; for there is reward for your labor."* God will prosper us in the work we do for Him in service to others. Do with vigor that which you are called to do in His service.

As we commit our lives to the path God has chosen for us to follow, we are rewarded with the desires of our heart. Psalm 37:4–5 promises this:

> *Delight thyself also in the Lord; and He shall give thee the desires of thy heart. Commit thy way unto the Lord; trust also in Him; and He shall bring it to pass.*

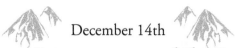

December 14th

Patience, Perseverance, and the Promise

The scriptures are often reminding us to be patient in dealing with people and issues we face in our lives. This is one of the most difficult things to achieve for people who are high achievers and want to get things done quickly to move on to other challenges and opportunities. I count myself among those who wrestle with my ability to demonstrate patience as one of my virtues. God calls us to persevere on our path in doing good, seeking His will, and being diligent in our praying to Him for all things. The promise of eternal life to come is there for those who follow this path to the end. Hebrews 10:36 teaches us: *"For ye have need of patience, that, after ye have done the will of God, ye might receive the promise."*

When we suffer through trials and tribulations in our lives, we learn to experience and develop the ability to be patient in going through these times. Romans 5:3 tells us this: *"And not only so, but we glory in tribulations also; knowing that tribulation worketh patience."* Instead of fearing such moments which are difficult in our lives, we need to embrace them, knowing the value of gaining patience is a result of such times. When going through such times, always let Love fill your heart as you engage with others in doing good despite the challenges you face. Second Thessalonians 3:5 says, *"And the Lord direct your hearts into the Love of God, and the patient waiting for Christ."* Christ will be with us and will deliver us from all that we face as we trust in Him to do so.

The journey of life will be one in which trials and tribulations will come to each of us. The will of God continues to be alive through such times in our lives as well. When we stay focused on praying for His will to be done and continue to Love one another as we are commanded to do, His promise will be fulfilled, and our lives will be ever drawn closer to the God we serve. May we pray for God's will to be done as we wait patiently for His strength to carry on today, as always.

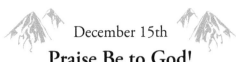

December 15th
Praise Be to God!

We need to be filling our hearts with praise for the God we serve always. When good things happen to God's people, praise should be raised for God's blessings upon us. The glory belongs to God for the strength He gives to us each day to carry on in this world. It is heartwarming to me when young athletes are first giving the glory to God for their abilities to play the games they Love to play. As we prosper in business and in life, we need to be humble and give the praise to God for such blessings as well. We should praise God for our good health each day and not only seek Him when we face afflictions and need His healing power. It is easy to take things for granted when we are doing well, rather than praising Him for the goodness he bestows upon us.

David sings the songs of praise continually in the book of Psalms. Psalm 150:6 says, *"Let everything that hath breath, praise the Lord. Praise ye the Lord."* We are taught that God inhabits the praises of His people in Psalm 22:3, which tells us, *"But thou art holy, O thou that inhabitest the praises of Israel."* We have a God that has given us all we own and lives within us through His Holy Spirit each day. Isaiah 12:4 declares to us: *"And in that day shall ye say, Praise the Lord, call upon His name, declare His doings among the people, make mention that His name is exalted."* We should make it known to others around us that God is to be praised for what He does for us in our lives.

The greatest thing we must praise God for is the gift of Jesus Christ, His beloved Son, who died for our sins and gave us access to our Father in heaven. Ephesians 1:3 speaks to this: *"Blessed be the God and Father of our Lord Jesus Christ, who has blessed us with all spiritual blessings in heavenly places in Christ."* May we praise God for all He has done in each of our lives on this day. As Psalm 34:1 says, *"I will bless the Lord at all times; His praise shall continually be on my mouth."* Praise be to God! For He is worthy to be praised always!

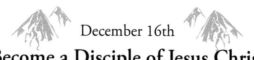

December 16th

Become a Disciple of Jesus Christ

When Jesus called His disciples from the work they were doing, He told them He would make them "fishers of men." That same calling is for those of us who choose the path of discipleship in our lives today. We are called to do work and to follow His teachings and to Love one another each day as He Loves us. The path of discipleship begins with faith in Jesus Christ as the Son of God. We believe He died for our sins on the cross and was raised from the dead three days later, and lives today. This simple faith is the door through which we must travel in our Spiritual walk to be on the journey to eternal salvation.

Jesus spoke of the absolute commitment of becoming one of His disciples in Matthew 16:24–25, which says, *"Then said Jesus to His disciples, 'If any man will come after me, let him deny himself, and take up his cross, and follow me. For whosoever shall save his life shall lose it, and whosoever shall lose his life for my sake, shall find it."* The idea of losing the life you led before Christ and dedicating your life to the work of the gospel is the total commitment it takes to being a disciple of Christ. When you "find your life," you have found your purpose and have entered into God's will for your life. The work we are called to do as the disciples of Christ is described in 2 Timothy 2:2, which teaches us this: *"And the things that thou hast heard of me among many witnesses, the same commit thou to faithful men, who shall be able to teach others also."* The message calls for us to spread the word of God and tell others of the truth of Jesus Christ as our Lord, and those you teach will teach others also.

As you learn of God's Word through the teachings of Christ and you continue to study it each day, you are becoming one of His disciples. Jesus spoke about this in John 8:31–32, which says, *"Then said Jesus to those Jews who believed upon Him, 'If you continue in my word, then ye are my disciples indeed; And ye shall know the truth, and the truth shall make you free.'"*

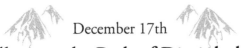

December 17th

Following the Path of Discipleship

The path of discipleship is a journey that lasts for a lifetime. We are forever moving toward the light of Christ, which guides our lives as we make such a journey, and we become the light of the world as we walk on this path. Each soul that you touch along the way has an opportunity to choose to join you on this path and find eternal life at the end of their journey on this earth. There is no greater calling than to be one of God's children who spread His Word to others. Matthew 5:14–16 tells us this:

> *Ye are the light of the world. A city that is set on a hill cannot be hid. Neither do men light a candle, and put it under a bushel, but on a candlestick; and it giveth light unto all that are in the house. Let your light shine before men, that they may see your good works, and glorify your Father which is in heaven.*

We are here to bring illumination into the world which is around us each day.

A disciple of Christ is one who Loves those God puts on his path. The commandment to Love one another came from Jesus, and His disciples must demonstrate Love in all they do to draw others to the path as a follower of Christ. John 13:34–35 teaches us this: *"A new commandment I give unto you, that ye Love one another; as I have Loved you, that ye also Love one another. By this shall all men know that ye are my disciples, if ye have Love one to another."* The significance of Love cannot be understated in the life of a true believer. Love is the foundation of a walk as a disciple of Christ. We are to Love those who are our enemies as well as those who Love us in return. Jesus had compassion and Love for all walks of life and healed the sick daily, and lifted up those who were lost.

As we do the work God calls us to do, we bear fruit in the lives of others who are placed on our path. We glorify God with this work as described in John 15:8: *"Herein in my Father glorified; that ye bear much fruit; so shall ye be my disciples."* May God open doors for each of us today as His disciples.

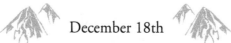

December 18th

We Look to God and His Holy Spirit for Guidance

As we rise to face another day on our journey, we face many moments which will give us the opportunity to travel in more than one direction in our lives. These opportunities may be related to our physical location but more often pertain to the spiritual path on which we find ourselves traveling. In our life's work, we may face business opportunities or obstacles that give us options to consider, out of which a Spiritual impact can occur. The choices we make on our journey will either take us closer to God in our hearts and souls or move us further from the path He has chosen for us to follow. Our hearts and minds need to be attuned to seeking His will for us in all we do daily.

As we walk with God each day, we must earnestly seek His will and guidance through prayer and the reading of His Word. Psalm 37:3–4 says, *"The steps of a good man are ordered by the Lord; and He delighteth in his way. Though he fall, he shall not be utterly cast down; for the Lord upholdeth him with His hand."* We know that God has His hand of protection and guidance on us as we follow His direction for our lives. He will never forsake us or abandon us on our journey. This journey we are on with God walking beside us is described beautifully in Isaiah 58:11, which says this: *"And the Lord shall guide thee continually, and satisfy thy soul in drought, and make fat thy bones; and thou shalt be like a watered garden, and like a spring of water, whose waters fail not."* It is God's plan to protect, guide, and prosper us on our journey with Him. We simply must trust in Him and seek His will and guidance in all we do.

When we have questions about which direction we need to take in a matter of importance in our lives, we simply need to ask God for His guidance and listen closely as He steers our minds to the thoughts He has for us. Isaiah 30:21 speaks to this: *"And thine ears shall hear a word behind thee saying, 'This is the way, walk ye in it, when ye turn to the right hand, and when ye turn to the left.'"*

December 19th

God Never Changes, But We Can

For those times in our lives when we feel like we are not close to God, and our journey seems lost, or without direction spiritually, we must choose whether we want to change our hearts to seek God earnestly. God is always there waiting for us to come to Him. If we stay on a path that is without God in our hearts, we are on the road to destruction. Luke 13:3 says this clearly: *"I tell you, Nay, except you repent, ye shall all likewise perish."* It is God's desire for all of us that we all be saved. The path to salvation begins with repentance of our sins and finding faith in God and our Lord Jesus Christ, which opens our hearts to the gift of salvation. First John 1:9 speaks to this simple path: *"If we confess our sins, He is faithful and just to forgive us our sins, and to cleanse us from all unrighteousness."* That door of life is always open for us to walk through.

God has endured many years of man walking the earth without Him in our hearts. He offers us the gift of His Holy presence in our lives if we choose the path to grow closer to Him. 2 Peter 3:9 says it this way: *"The Lord is not slack, concerning His promise, as some men count slackness; but is longsuffering to us, not willing that any should perish, but that all should come to repentance."* We know this to be God's desire for all mankind. It is up to each of us to accept His promise and turn to Him in Love and faith. Once we make such a decision, we truly do become a new man in Christ. Second Corinthians 5:17 tells us this: *"Therefore, if any man be in Christ, he is a new creature; old things are passed away; behold, all things are new."* Do you know anyone who might be ready to become new and fresh in their approach to the way they are living their life today?

Let us all put on the new man described in Ephesians 4:23–24: *"And be renewed in the spirit of your mind; And that ye put on the new man, which after God is created in righteousness and true holiness."* As we do so, let us also share this opportunity for renewal with those God gives to us on our journey always.

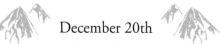 December 20th

Stories of Faith: Touching the Hem of His Garment

There are many stories of faith in the Bible which reveal the power of faith in healing of the body and the spirit. There may be none more compelling about the power of faith than the ones we find in fifth chapter of the book of Mark. Jesus was approached by Jairus, who is described as one of the rulers of the synagogue, who fell at Jesus' feet and begged Him to come to lay hands on his twelve-year-old daughter, who was sick and near death. Jesus felt compassion for him and went to go with him to his home to heal this sick young girl.

As they journeyed to the home, they were encompassed by a throng of people who pressed in to Jesus, and many sought healings and were drawn in by His reputation for doing good works and possessing great power. One of those in the crowd had been ill for over twelve years and had spent all her money on physicians to try to cure this issue of blood as was described in the Bible. Her faith led her to believe if she could only touch the hem of His garment, she would be healed. Mark 5:27–30 describes what happens:

> *When she heard of Jesus, came in the press behind, and touched the garment. For she said, If I should touch but His clothes, I shall be made whole. And straightway the fountain of her blood was dried up; and she felt in her body that she was healed of the plague. And Jesus, immediately knowing virtue had gone out of Him, turned Him about in the press, and said, "Who touched my clothes?"*

Imagine the moment for this woman. She was being singled out by Jesus as having touched His garment for her healing, and she feared how He would respond. The disciples tried to downplay the moment and said many have touched Him. When she admitted to her reason for the touch, Jesus says in verse 34: *"And He told her, 'Daughter, thy faith hath made thee whole; go in peace and be whole of thy plague.'"*

When we seek His will for our lives or healing for our body and or spirit, it is our faith which brings us healing and the ability to be made whole.

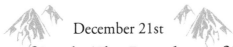

December 21st

Stories of Faith: The Daughter of Jairus

Jesus proceeded to go with Jairus to his home to visit the young daughter of this man when a messenger came to meet them to tell them the young girl had died. Mark 5:35–36 tells us this happens while Jesus was speaking to the woman who had been healed from her plague:

While He yet spoke, there came from the ruler of the synagogue's house certain which said, "Thy daughter is dead: Why troublest thou the Master any further?" As soon as Jesus heard the word that was spoken, He saith unto the ruler of the synagogue, "Be not afraid, only believe."

We can only imagine how this man felt when he heard his daughter had died. The most devastating moment of his life had happened, and Jesus spoke to him and told him not to fear but only to believe. What a test of faith this would be for anyone!

Jesus told all those who were with Him not to follow them. He took with Him only Peter, James, and John to go to this home with the father, Jairus. When they got to the home, there was much "tumult," as the Bible describes it, with people weeping and wailing. Mark 5:39–40 describes what happens as Jesus enters the home:

And when He was come in, He saith unto them, "Why make ye this ado, and weep? The damsel is not dead, but sleepeth. And they laughed Him to scorn, but when He put them all out, He taketh the father and the mother of the damsel and them that were with Him and entereth in where the damsel was lying."

To imagine this moment and to put ourselves in the position of these parents is difficult to do. Jesus had told the ruler not to be afraid, "only believe."

As the story concludes, Jesus told the young girl to "arise," and she did, and she walked and was made whole. This young girl was healed by the faith demonstrated by her father and mother. We need to learn to not fear but believe. When we do, anything is possible for God to do for us and through us.

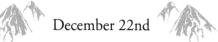

December 22nd

The Christmas Story Begins with Mary and the Angel

The beautiful story of Christmas begins with the angel Gabriel being sent by God to be the messenger to Mary, who He had chosen to be the mother of our Lord Jesus Christ. Gabriel had been sent to her cousin Elisabeth and her husband *Zacharias to tell them that God was sending them a son to be named John six* months prior to this. That would become John the Baptist, who would preach of the coming of the Lord in the wilderness prior to Christ beginning His ministry. When Gabriel appears to Mary, he says this in Luke 1:28: *"Hail, thou are highly favored, the Lord is with thee, blessed are thou among women."* Mary is said to be troubled by this greeting, and the angel continues: *"Fear not, Mary, thou hast found favor with God. And, behold, thou shalt conceive in thy womb, and bring forth a son, and shalt call His name Jesus."* The angel goes on to tell Mary how Jesus will take the throne of David and reign over the "house of Jacob forever."

Mary is taken aback by all of this, and we can only imagine what is running through her mind at this time. She questions the angel on how she can conceive as a virgin, and the angel responds in verse 35: *"The Holy Ghost shall come upon thee, and the power of the Highest shall overshadow thee; therefore, also that holy thing that shall be born of thee, shall be called the Son of God."* The angel then spoke of her cousin Elisabeth who was barren but now bearing a son in her old age, and then said this in verse 37: *"For with God, nothing shall be impossible."* Mary, who is clearly a woman of devout faith, then responds to the angel this way in verse 38: *"Behold, the handmaid of the Lord: Be it unto me according to thy word. And the angel departed from her."* The most powerful moment in the history of mankind has begun with this exchange. Mary received the blessing from God to be the mother of our Lord and Savior Jesus Christ.

The Christmas story had begun, and Jesus was on His way to save the world. Be Blessed in your heart as you contemplate this season of Christ's birth.

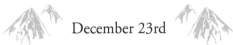

December 23rd

Joseph and Mary Responding to the Calling

Mary was said in Luke 1:27 to be *"espoused to a man whose name was Joseph of the house of David."* These young people were planning to marry and were engaged to one another. Joseph was a good man who wanted to do what was right for Mary when he discovered she was with child, as it is described in Matthew 1: 18–25, which tells us how he was informed of the conception of the child in a dream. Beginning in verse 20, we are told this:

> But while he thought on these things, an angel appeared to him in a dream saying, Joseph, thou son of David, fear not to take unto thee Mary thy wife; for that which is conceived in her is of the Holy Ghost. And she shall bring forth a son and thou shalt call His name Jesus; for He shall save His people from their sins.

This had to be a lot for a young carpenter to comprehend and accept. However, Joseph was a man of faith and trusted his wife and the message brought to him by the angel in his dream.

Joseph took Mary to be his wife and cared for her as such. The scriptures tell us that she remained a virgin until the birth of Christ, as told to us in Matthew 1:25. God chose this couple and brought them compelling visits from angels to prepare their hearts for this miracle of life. Mary went to visit her cousin, Elizabeth, to share with her the experience of the life God had called her to embrace. We are told of this visit in Luke 1, starting with verse 40: *"And entered the house of Zacharias, and saluted Elizabeth. And it came to pass when Elizabeth heard the salutation of Mary, the babe leaped in her womb; and Elizabeth was filled with the Holy Ghost."* The two women were bonded in the spirit with the blessings of God upon them and their children. John the Baptist and Jesus would forever change the world through their ministry.

The first gift of Christmas was the gift of the child to Mary from God. He is the reason we celebrate this moment each year as we should. God has given us a path to eternal life with this child, which was born on this day and lives forevermore.

 December 24th

Wise Men Seek Him

Christmas Eve is a day of great energy and excitement. It begins in our lives as young children as we anticipate the celebration of Christmas the following day, and we look forward to the joy of opening presents and sharing the Love and laughter that is associated with that special day. For Christians, we celebrate much more than a mystical "Santa Clause" who is told to ride a magical sleigh around the world delivering presents. We celebrate the glorious story of the birth of our Lord and Savior Jesus Christ. As we read about the events leading up to this wonderful day on which Jesus was born, we discover the story of the wise men who came from far away to worship our Savior at the time of His birth.

The story of the wise men is found in Matthew chapter 2, which tells of these men coming from the east following a star that guided them. They came seeking the one who was to be the "King of Jews," as it was told in verse 2, which says, *"Where is He that is born, the King of the Jews? For we have seen His star in the East and we are come to worship Him."* The story tells us of King Herod hearing of this and being troubled by the idea of a new king being born. He told the wise men to go and find Jesus and to return and tell him where He was so he could go and worship him as well. The men followed the star to the exact location where the child was born, and they worshiped Jesus and gave Him gifts of gold, frankincense, and myrrh, which were great treasures of their time. They were warned by God not to return to King Herod, and they went home another way.

These men were seeking the one who could set the heavens ablaze with the glory of His birth. They were inspired by God to come and see the magnificence of this child who would change the world forever. Their journey to seek God in the flesh is recorded so we can understand the power of this moment in time. Wise men still seek Jesus in the world today. Be guided by the light of His Word, which draws us to Him. Follow the light in your heart today to be near Him.

December 25th

A Child Is Born

The holiest days of the year for those of us who live as Christian followers are the day when Christ was born and Easter when we celebrate the resurrection of our Lord and Savior. The story of this birth is told in Luke chapter 2, which details Mary and Joseph traveling to Bethlehem, the city of David when everyone had to go to the city of their ancestors to be taxed. Jesus was born in a modest setting with a humble beginning in a manger because there was no room at the inn. That night, the world around them exploded with activity because of this young child coming into the world.

God chose witnesses to come and see the evidence of the birth of Jesus. The wise men came from the east to be there, and they brought great gifts to our Lord. Also chosen as witnesses were lowly shepherds who were abiding in the field with their flocks. Luke 2:8–14 tells us what happens:

> *And there were in the same country, shepherds abiding in the field, keeping watch over their flock by night. And, lo, the angel of the Lord came upon them, and the glory of the Lord shone round about them; and they were sore afraid. And the angel said unto them, Fear not; for behold, I bring you good tidings of great joy, which shall be to all people. For unto you is born, this day, a Savior, which is Christ the Lord. And this shall be a sign unto you; Ye shall find the babe wrapped in swaddling clothes, lying in a manger. And suddenly there was with the angel a multitude of the heavenly host praising God, and saying, Glory to God in the highest and on earth peace, good will toward men.*

What an incredible moment in the history of the world as God reveals His Son to these humble men. They became the first witnesses of Christ to tell the story of Christ on earth.

The story of the birth of Christ should live in our hearts on this Christmas day and always. This message, as it is told in Luke, is one of the most beautiful of all the scriptures as it relates to how Christ was born. May it Bless you today!

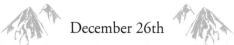

December 26th

Seek Righteousness through Christ

Jesus Christ was born and came into this world to teach us the path to righteousness and to eternal life with God. His message was one of Love and how we should Love our God with all our heart, soul, and strength. He taught us to Love one another as we Love ourselves. As we study His life and His teachings, we grow closer to being the people God wants us to become. His message is one we are to share with others as we journey through this time and space in our lives. We are called to plant the seeds of His gospel which is the holy word of God. We are destined to be the light of the world as we do so. The world around us is filled with darkness and evil, and the light of God's Word will chase away the darkness and illuminate the hearts and minds of those who receive it.

We are to seek righteousness which is doing that which is good in God's eyes. As we seek it, we will find it as we are told in the word of God. Proverbs 21:21 teaches us this: *"He that followeth after righteousness and mercy findeth life, righteousness, and honor."* As we journey on this path, God rewards us and brings honor to us. The path to righteousness is through Christ Jesus and His teachings. We need to learn from His life, and as we read His Word, we are put on this path by God. Second Corinthians 5:21 speaks to this as it says, *"For He hath made Him be sin for us, who knew no sin; that we might be made the righteousness of God in Him."* God's plan to overcome the sins of this world was to give His own Son as a sacrifice to die for our sins. As we follow Jesus and direct the path of our life to do so, we will turn from sin and seek that which is righteous.

The path to righteousness is through Christ Jesus, and He made clear the commandments to Love God and to Love one another, which fulfill the law. Romans 10:4 tells us this: *"For Christ is the end of the law for righteousness to everyone that believeth."* May your path lead to righteousness through Christ on this and every day. God will bless you richly as you follow this path!

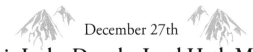

December 27th

This Is the Day the Lord Hath Made

With the dawning of a new day, we are awakening to a new sense of purpose with opportunities that are yet to unfold. We should approach this, and every day, with renewed excitement concerning the plan God has for us in our lives. The reason we have not yet been called home to be with Him is we have work yet to be done. When our work here is completed, we will be called to go to our heavenly home to be with the God we serve. Believing that, we can turn our thoughts to Psalm 118:24, which extolls: *"This is the day the Lord hath made; we will rejoice and be glad in it."* Let us embrace the spirit of rejoicing in this day that God has prepared for us. Let us enthusiastically live in the moment we have been given. As we carry that enthusiasm with us, the energy will translate into all we do, and others will respond with favorable energy in return.

Let us learn to Love the life God has given to us and avoid speaking evil about others we meet along the way. Turn to the positive in all things you face, and avoid the tendency to participate in negative words or thoughts as you go through this day. First Peter 3:10–11 teaches us this: *"For he that will Love life, and see good days, let him refrain his tongue from evil, and his lips that they speak no guile; Let him eschew evil, and do good; let him seek peace and ensue it."* The scripture teaches us to avoid those conflicts which take us away from the path of Love and to avoid speaking in a manner that is seen as evil in any respect. As we rejoice and find gladness in the day God has given us, we find no room for thoughts that take us away from this spirit of rejoicing.

May we approach this day with joy in our hearts as we embrace with Love all that is before us. Reflect on the message in Nehemiah 8:10, which proclaims: *"For this day is holy unto our Lord; neither be ye sorry; for the joy of the Lord is your strength."* Be joyous and be strong in the Lord on this day, and be filled with Love for all that God puts on our path on this and every day we live!

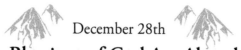

December 28th

The Blessings of God Are Abundant

As we move closer to the end of another year in our time on the earth, it is good to reflect on the many blessings which God has bestowed upon each of us. We often take for granted many of God's blessings until they are no longer there. Simple things like good health are often overlooked until we face a time of sickness. The same could be said for the peace we enjoy in the world around us. We don't appreciate such peace until a conflict arises that engulfs us in it. It is important to pause and reflect on the goodness of God our Father and to thank Him for His many blessings, which we enjoy each day and particularly as we begin to look back on a year we are close to completing.

In the book of Numbers, we find a passage that speaks of the blessings of God in verses 24–26, which says this: *"The Lord bless thee and keep thee; The Lord make His face to shine on thee, and be gracious unto thee; The Lord lift up His countenance upon thee, and give thee peace."* This is a blessing we may offer to another in parting or one which we claim for our own lives. Let us take stock of the many things God does for us on a daily basis. He gives us our "daily bread" and forgives us of our sins. He brings us peace and good health and will bring us prosperity as we do His work and are diligent in doing so. These are a few of the many blessings which flow from God into our lives daily. James 1:17 says, *"Every good gift and every perfect gift is from above, and cometh down from the Father of lights."* God is the giver of all gifts that flow into the lives of His people. When you seek to do His will, He will bless you beyond measure.

May God continue to bless you on this and every day. May our hearts be open to praising and thanking God for the gifts we receive. John 1:16 teaches us this: *"And of His fulness have we all received, and grace for grace."* May we learn to be filled with Love and appreciation for the blessings we receive from our God, who Loves us and who bestows His rich blessings of Love upon us.

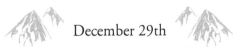

December 29th

Finish the Work God Has Called You to Do

As we near the end of the journey for this year, we realize there is work remaining that God has called for us to do. Let us do that which remains ahead of us and complete the work with excellence that is yet to be done. Jesus told His followers in John 4:34 that He has to finish the work He was given: *"Jesus said to them, 'My food is to do the will of Him who sent Me to accomplish His work.'"* He knew what His assignment in this world was to be. Like Jesus, our work is to do the will of our Heavenly Father each day. When God gives you His work to do in your life, it is up to you to finish the course while He gives you the strength to complete His plan for you. Second Corinthians 8:11 tells us this: *"But now finish doing it also, so that just as there was the readiness to desire it, so there may be also the completion of it by your ability."* We are given the strength and ability to do all the things God calls us to accomplish in our lives.

The journey of our lives continues until God calls us home to be with Him. With each day, there is a plan for us to achieve what He sets before us. To finish the work we have been given, we are called upon to endure the challenges that await us on the path and to persevere to the finish of what we are called to do. James 1:4 teaches us: *"And let endurance have its perfect result, so that you may be perfect and complete, lacking in nothing."* As we endure and persist and deliver the work we are called to do, God supplies our every need and strengthens us to do His will. There is nothing that can stand against us on this as we walk with the God we serve.

At the end of the day, and the work we have been given to do has been done, may we be able to stand before God and know we have completed His plan fully in our lives. John 17:4 says it this way: *"I glorified you on the earth, having accomplished the work You have given Me to do."* These were the words in prayer from Jesus to His Father. May we be able to pray these words as well.

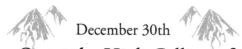

December 30th

Press On to the High Calling of God

As we near the end of another year and move closer to the beginning of a new one, we must consider the direction of our path and make sure we are on the road to the calling God has for us. We are continually examining the purpose we have for the new day as it arrives. God puts us in each day with an action plan for our lives to be worked in a way that is consistent with His will for our lives that day. To be the light shining in the darkness of the world which surrounds us and to be the minister who shares the message of the Good News of Jesus Christ and the path to salvation with others is always the quest that leads us to righteousness. God will strengthen us, and His Holy Spirit will guide us with the words to say when the occasion arises if we in our hearts seek to follow this path of discipleship in our lives.

On this day, may our hearts and souls be ready to embrace the opportunities God makes available to us. Philippians 3:12–16 teaches us this:

> *Not as though I had already attained, either were already perfect: but I follow after, if that I may apprehend that for which I am apprehended of Christ Jesus. Brethren, I count not myself to have apprehended: but this one thing I do, forgetting those things which are behind, and reaching forth to those things which are before, I press toward the mark for the prize of the high calling of God in Jesus. Let us therefore, as many as be perfect, be thus minded: and if in anything ye be otherwise minded, God shall reveal even this unto you. Nevertheless, whereto we have already attained, let us walk by the same rule, let us mind the same thing.*

The aspiration of perfection is something we strive to achieve. The reality is we remain short of perfection in the human form. Yet God will reveal those areas we need to work on each day on our journey with Him. Keep your faith and keep your eyes on the prize of His calling before you.

May you strive to discover the high calling of God for your life today!

December 31st

May the Light of God's Word Shine through Us

The end of the year is upon us, and the eve of the New Year is here. We celebrate the New Year with fireworks and displays of light in the sky as we anticipate a year ahead that will be filled with health and prosperity, which will be greater than the one before. We are filled to overflowing with an abundance of blessings from our Heavenly Father as we reflect on the circumstances of the life He has given us. We measure our life by the course we have taken and whether we are growing closer to the God we serve each day. Ultimately, if we are growing closer to Him, the light of His Spirit is continuing to shine more brightly through our own lives as we grow deeper in our relationship with Him.

Can we say at the completion of this year the words that were written in 2 Timothy 4:7: *"I have fought a good fight, I have finished my course, I have kept the faith."* These words were written by Paul as he faced the end of his life on this earth. We could measure our time each year and determine whether we can say the same thing. Have we done so this year? The disciple of Christ is always being measured against the standard of excellence of being in God's will. The path to God is founded on faith in Jesus Christ and discovering the Love for God and for others in our hearts and minds each day. As we do this, His light and Love will flow through us into the lives of others He gives to us. Isaiah 60:1 says this: *"Arise, shine; for thy light is come, and the glory of the Lord is risen upon thee."* May this Spirit and energy engulf us on this day and always as we rise and know God's glory and His light is shining upon us.

As we celebrate the new year on this night and fireworks fill the air, let us dedicate our lives to becoming the light of the world. Ephesians 5:8 says this: *"For ye were sometimes in darkness, but now ye are light in the Lord: walk as children of light."* May God bless us as we walk in His glorious light today and always! May you light up the world around you with radiance from above!

About the Author

Charles Richardson was born in a Christian family and was raised by parents who were dedicated to the teachings of Christ. He attended the University of Florida and graduated with a degree in journalism in 1973. He spent his career in the real estate business, beginning in San Francisco as a sales associate in 1976. He spent three years there prior to moving to Florida to resume his sales career in 1979. His career in real estate continued with six more years as a salesman, followed by thirteen managing offices throughout Florida for Merrill Lynch Realty which became Prudential Florida Realty, and then Arvida Realty Services. He became a Regional President for Arvida Realty Services prior to the acquisition of the company by Coldwell Banker. Charles served as a Regional Senior Vice President for Coldwell Banker Realty in Southwest Florida, Southeast Florida, and West Central Florida for the balance of his real estate career until his retirement in 2021.

Charles is a family man with a wife, Leilani, and two sons, Chandler and Connor, all of whom he considers to be the greatest gifts he has received from God. The inspiration for this book came to Charles as he ran one day, and God spoke to him to write this book to plant seeds of faith and daily devotions into the hearts of his family and others God chooses to read along the way.

CPSIA information can be obtained
at www.ICGtesting.com
Printed in the USA
BVHW071915130223
658422BV00012B/127

9 798887 382456